Common Tones

Selected interviews with artists and musicians

1995–2020

Alan Licht

Common Tones

Selected interviews with artists and musicians

1995–2020

Blank Forms Editions

Introduction
by Jay Sanders
8

Greg
Tate
15

Michael
Snow
29

Tony
Conrad:
On Angus
MacLise
59

Ira
Kaplan
&
Georgia
Hubley:
On Hoboken,
New Jersey
73

Karl
Precoda
97

Suicide
111

Christian
Marclay
135

Lou
Reed
155

Henry
Flynt
173

Tom
Verlaine:
Recording
and Other
Things
197

Tony
Oursler
221

The Sea
and Cake
249

Matthew
Barney
269

Cory
Arcangel
287

Ken
Jacobs
313

Vito
Acconci
325

Jutta
Koether:
On Sonic
Youth
347

ANOHNI
365

Richard
Foreman
383

Glenn
Branca
399

Rhys
Chatham
421

Phill
Niblock
453

Rudy
Wurlitzer
479

Kelly
Reichardt
509

Alessandra
Novaga
529

Adris
Hoyos
551

Milford
Graves
557

Introduction

by
Jay Sanders

> *Public figures often hate the media because they are being used as material for a writer's work, and they've already used themselves as material for their own work. So the writer's work may be at odds with that. I've been trying to play both sides of the fence by establishing an identity both as a writer and a musician, someone who conducts interviews and is an interviewee, someone who could potentially either play music with someone or interview them.*
>
> —Alan Licht, "A Lecture on Transcription"

Scanning the table of contents for this book—twenty-five years of penetrating and generous explorations of artists' lives—it becomes apparent that one of the many *tones* resonating among a number of Alan Licht's interlocutors is New York City. Here, emergence, infamy, and progress interlace with topography: its venues, its conditions of living and working, social configurations and artistic scenes, allure and myths, and the brutality of its unforgiving forgetfulness and churning development. Whether interviewing ANOHNI or Suicide, in New York or far beyond, Alan is attuned to the hustle of radically self-motivated artists and methodically cross-references their social and cultural environs in service of their fullest reverberation. This unearthing of both personal and intellectual histories—how things happened and how those episodes, overlays, and synchronicities can now be understood more holistically—is a hallmark of each of the conversations here; more than one interviewee demands, "Ooh, ooh, how do you know that?" (Lou Reed in this case).

As I reflect on these important conversations and the theme of "common tones," I realize my own two-decade intimacy with the multiplicity of Alan's work. From the outset, his dual efforts in rock and experimental music as a highly active band member and improviser and, at the same time, as an excavator of their most potent buried histories proposed to me an implicit way of being—of course one should make adventurous work, participate in the scene on its ground level, and fervently articulate its emerging and marginalized histories. As his own first solo guitar albums were being released (*Sink the Aging Process*, 1994; *The Evan Dando of Noise?*, 1997), Alan was indoctrinating the underground with his revelatory minimal "top ten" lists and related profiles in *Forced Exposure*, *Halana*, *Option*, and other pointedly nonmainstream music magazines. His timing was propitious, as the often impossibly obscure albums he championed by a then-lost generation of vanguard composer-performers gained quick CD release via an emerging generation of reissue labels, run by people like Alan's eminent counterpart in Chicago at the time, Jim O'Rourke. These resurrected musicians saw themselves ushered into a newly emerging context of festivals and fandom that reoriented historical antecedents across minimalism, krautrock, and free improv.[1] As Derek Walmsley recounts in a piece about watershed lists in experimental music, Alan's top-ten series "was crucial because it posited minimalism as the hidden wiring of whole swathes of underground music."[2]

That sense of looking forward via the rearview mirror that characterized the 1990s and early 2000s manifests in the intriguing termite tunnels that Alan and others revealed through their own passion, fascination, and occasional disdain. In 1999, Alan began

1 These musicians include Charlemagne Palestine, Terry Riley, Phill Niblock, Henry Flynt, Tony Conrad, Jon Gibson, Alvin Lucier, Folke Rabe, Yoshi Wada, Éliane Radigue, Michael Snow, Anthony Moore, Arnold Dreyblatt, and Elodie Lauten.

2 Derek Walmsley, "Feeling Listless," The Mire (blog), *Wire*, April 26, 2011, https://www.thewire.co.uk/in-writing/themire/20804/feeling-listless/.

contributing to the British experimental music magazine the *Wire* with an extended profile on composer Maryanne Amacher on the occasion of her first-ever CD; a flood of important recuperative articles, often on severely marginalized practitioners with barely any recorded output, soon followed, culminating with this book's not-to-be-missed closing interview with Milford Graves, conducted in January 2018. Some culture writers emerge squarely from the center of a zeitgeist, and their chronicles of a period or scene read like live transcriptions of a fever dream. Alan sparked a different kind of catalysis, counteracting the errant conditions of the music industry by brushing the dust of obscurity from mavericks who had been systematically buried beneath the celebrity avant-garde, and disregarding the arbitrary genre distinctions and high/low art demarcations upheld by both academia and commercial culture. While working on this introduction, I texted Alan about the extreme lack of marketing and promotion for a few of these artists' releases at the time. His reply was: "The impetus for some of these interviews was certainly the thought, 'If I don't do it, nobody else will, and that would be a shame,' or 'If I don't do it, they'll get some hack who will totally fuck it up.'" While it's implicit that many of these interviews were assigned, Alan was clearly pursuing his own larger project as a cultural historian with each conversation, and these full transcripts restore the shape of that directive.

"A continual suggestion of the *possibility* of music," says theater-maker Richard Foreman about actively frustrating the escapism of musical, narrative, and rhythmic resolution in his plays. In this book, *tones* does refer to music, but there's a fervent intertwining of artistic modes throughout, as Alan consistently champions artists who've actively transposed their work across many forms of media. Echoing this is an early statement of purpose about his work: "The point of all this is that it's these far reaching aesthetic ideas I'm interested in more than music or film or whatever as mediums per se. I've been drawn to all this stuff for the last decade plus without really realizing why, and I'm beginning to see that it's all connected in a way I hadn't been aware of before."[3] So, in sweeping interviews, visual and performance artists Vito Acconci, Cory Arcangel, Matthew Barney, Jutta Koether, and Tony Oursler reveal to Alan the enduring tenets of sound, music, composition, and collaboration in their disparate work (I'll let you find out who says, "When I was doing performance I thought I was doing the same kind of stuff that Neil Young was doing, that Van Morrison was doing, a single voice, long songs."). Further, Alan's dizzyingly multitudinous discussions on filmmaking and soundtracking with practitioners as varied as Ken Jacobs, Phill Niblock, Kelly Reichardt, and Rudy Wurlitzer open myriad pathways unlikely to be found anywhere else.

The epigraph above implies a specific equilibrium where consumer, producer, and participant are superimposed—and in Alan's own case, avidly cross-circuited. He's collaborated and performed with a number of the artists here—Christian Marclay, Michael Snow, Tom Verlaine, and Yo La Tengo, to name a few—and additional commonalities in life and work continually appear throughout. Give your full attention to Alan's recent conversation with Greg Tate (whose articulation of "lived criticism" certainly resonates), a formidable writer and musician instructive to Alan's own musical efforts and discursive project. And Rhys Chatham's storied tenure as the Kitchen's first music director finds its equal in

3 Alan Licht, *Evan Dando of Noise?*, Corpus Hermeticum, Hermes022, 1997, CD. Liner notes.

Alan's time as a booker at Tonic three decades later. All to say: Alan's integrity plays solidly throughout.

An obvious lesson I've learned is that turning up, night after night, is the means of invoking a mobile and biomorphic institution, an evident social body (what Wurlitzer here calls the "spontaneity and intercourse of floating relations") that collectively enacts the complexities of cultural history from inside the metropolis ("urban density is the key to cultural progress," says Tony Conrad). In the relatively money-proof and institution-immune worlds of poetry, experimental film and music, dance, and performance, it is the attendees that most often constitute its practitioners, organizers, and historians—often exchanging roles on different nights. And when one of these participants compiles their recollections—here I'm thinking about Jonas Mekas's *Movie Journal*, George E. Lewis's *A Power Stronger Than Itself*, and Tom Johnson's *The Voice of New Music*—all of us who may or may not have been there gain access to some of these extraordinary lived moments as well. In these interviews, I hear Alan's tough-minded on-the-ground enthusiasm and generosity of detail opening what might otherwise be private conversations among practitioners—revealing real contexts, motivations, and affinities directly to his readers.

Greg Tate

I first encountered Greg Tate's writing in the *Village Voice* in the early '80s; the dazzling combination of idiomatic and erudite expression in the pieces he wrote on Cecil Taylor, Afrika Bambaataa, King Sunny Adé, and others was highly impactful on me, and I used to look for his byline back then with as much avid anticipation as I did those of Lester Bangs, Greil Marcus, Nick Tosches, and Richard Meltzer. Tate's marvelously insightful two-part essay on Miles Davis's electric period for *DownBeat* in 1983 (a time when that period of Davis's work was still very underappreciated)—particularly the attention Tate paid to analyzing and contextualizing Pete Cosey's guitar playing—remains to this day one of my favorite pieces of music writing (much of Tate's work from this era can be found in his 1992 essay collection *Flyboy in the Buttermilk*). After reading it, I resolved to find Miles's 1975 live albums. They were totally out of print, but I managed to acquire a used copy of *Pangaea* (CBS Sony, 1975) from Golden Disc on Bleecker Street—the first time I spent big money on a rare record.

I met Greg in the late '90s at a DJ Spooky set in a bar on Bleecker, several blocks east of Golden Disc. A few years later the *Wire* asked me to do an Invisible Jukebox with him, and I was also happy to book his group Burnt Sugar at Tonic. Their genre-dissolving concept was right at home at a venue that was also eager to host Butch Morris, whose "Conduction" system Greg was adapting for his own purposes in the group. In assembling these interviews, I realized I hadn't really talked to anyone about the experience of working as both a musician and a music writer; Greg addresses this "co-profession" briefly in the introduction to the second collection of his writings, *Flyboy 2: The Greg Tate Reader* (2016), but I wanted to probe it further with him. We compared notes over Zoom one afternoon last December.

When did you first start playing guitar, in relation to listening to music and thinking about writing about music? And what came more naturally to you, playing music or writing about music?

I was one of those kids who started reading fairly advanced material pretty early. I remember really being interested in science and science fiction in third grade and getting books on lasers and astronomy, and things like fiction by [Isaac] Asimov, and L. Sprague de Camp, and Samuel Delany, by around fourteen, fifteen years old. I later became voracious in terms of acquisition of vinyl—acquisition across genres, but really centered on the history of jazz. I made a point of going out and getting things from every period, so I had a working knowledge of how the music had evolved.

I dabbled in guitar through high school, because [*laughs*] every other person in my high school played in a band, played bass or guitar, was interested in Hendrix, Led Zeppelin, Santana, Kiss, Bowie, and that kind of thing. But I was still kind of more interested in collecting music, listening to music, reading about music, and thinking about music, all the way through college. And then something spurred me, right before I moved to New York, to buy a Strat, so that would be about '82. I'd been writing for [Robert] Christgau [editor at the *Village Voice*] for about a year and I hooked up with some friends here, started playing in a jam band. And being around Ronny Drayton and Vernon Reid, and [James] "Blood" Ulmer, by osmosis, helped me pull together some technical things that I'd been struggling with. So my playing kind of advanced exponentially just from being in New York and being around all these hotshot New York guitar players.

But it wasn't until '91, when I was about thirty-four, that I really felt serious enough about it that I felt like I had to start a band and start writing songs and playing out, so that was the band Women in Love, and I really grew tremendously doing that. That band was kind of the first experiment, 'cause even more than guitar playing I got really into writing songs, pretty complicated affairs, and trying out all these different ideas and styles and genres in the same band. I was working with people who were definitely genre-mobile, concept-mobile. It came together enough that after three years we did our first album, and our producer was Al Bouchard, of the Blue Öyster Cult, because I knew his wife, Deborah Frost, the writer. And Al liked what he heard enough to bring his acumen into the studio. I'm as proud of that Women in Love album, *The Sound of Falling Bodies at Rest* [Madrina, 1994], as I am of *Flyboy in the Buttermilk*.

So once I committed to it, it became as fluid as writing. But that band dissolved around '95. Kept playing, working with different people, putting together these large ensemble projects, and eventually around '99 it morphed into Burnt Sugar because I was starting to realize I wanted to do something that built on the *Bitches Brew* [Miles Davis; Columbia, 1970] template. Not even so much in terms of the sound but the way Miles had of working with musicians in the studio and with [producer] Teo [Macero]. Realizing that a lot of what Teo, Lee "Scratch" Perry, and George Clinton were doing in the studio with effects were things that modern players had incorporated into their sounds. The people I was working with in that initial version—Vijay Iyer, Morgan Craft, Jared Nickerson, Qasim Naqvi, and various other folks—were the kind of contemporary New York improvisers who've developed this very versatile approach to sound-making on their instruments, had ways of kind of expanding the borders inside of whatever genre they played in. They had absorbed all that music that had come through in the '70s and '80s, so it was just part of their modernist and postmodernist improvisational vocabulary.

I had been following Butch [Morris] since before the first numbered "Conduction" at the Kitchen, which I attended. He stood out as a cornetist and a composer—even with David Murray in the mid-'70s, he was somebody everybody was looking at as a writer as well as an instrumentalist. That first full-on Conduction album he released, *Current Trends in Racism in Modern America* [Sound Aspects Records, 1985], was this great remix of what was going on downtown, with Christian Marclay, Yasunao Tone, John Zorn, and Frank Lowe. It was interesting because it was a much more ethnically integrated group than normally played together at that time. That was what I felt was the inside critique built into the whole thematic about current trends in racism in modern America—you had these postmodernists who lived on the same block, but just because of that kind of tension between Black and white jazz cats, New Music cats, it made for a sometimes racially Balkanized scene. And then Butch began to do all these Conductions with ensembles from different countries, mixing and matching downtown jazz cats with traditional Senegalese, Chinese and Japanese, and Turkish musicians in the '80s and '90s. That had a serious impact. Butch kind of represented the twenty-first-century version of what Miles and [Frank] Zappa and Sun Ra and other people had been doing in terms of really approaching the improvising ensemble as a paintbrush, canvas, and palette—not to mention a repository for ideas you had about the role of society in music and vice versa. If you wanted to do something more than a jam band with this great assemblage of players, that seemed the way you could have the kind of articulation and control over the outcome that I had as a writer.

But to expand on the answer to your initial question [*laughs*], I'd definitely say going through the growing pains of actually playing music in front of an audience softened my critical attack [*laughs*]. You get humbled about anybody's nerve and capacity to put themselves in front of people.

Well, that's why a lot of musicians get down on critics; they feel like a critic's never been in their shoes and critics don't really know what what's involved in doing the work and performing.

If I look at people who didn't play who were writing at the time, it was still important, or it's necessary, because I think music exists in the public sphere in a place that's beyond the practitioner as well. It has a social resonance. And certainly by the time you get to the music that people began making in the '60s and '70s it's about something else, anyway, other than chops or genre. It's meant to connect and conjure up extra-musical forces.

For my part, what I've found is that with writing, I really like going over it over and over and over and getting every single thing right before I send it to an editor, and that I have less patience for doing that with music in a recording studio. And also improvisation is something that I really value and practice in music and that would never occur to me to do with writing. I wouldn't knock out a first draft and just send it off into the world that way.

[*Laughs.*] Yeah, I'm probably the opposite. Particularly writing for the *Voice*, you maybe only have a week to one day [*laughs*] to turn something in.

Right, I haven't really worked with deadline journalism like that so much, just a little bit.

If you've got Christgau as an editor, if you didn't go over every line, he would. And you had to justify your choices. At the *Voice*, too, you were encouraged to take risks with style and content, with statement, with signification. I had experiences with Christgau where I'd turn something in and he'd basically say it was incoherent and unpublishable, but then after about an hour [*laughs*] of going through it together—because you went through everything line by line even before they got a computer system, so you'd be bringing in your manuscript and sit there, at the dean's knee, going through that dread-producing, anxiety-provoking process with him. I became, because of deadlines, a pretty fast writer, but I also became somebody who learned to slow down and move through it line by line, graf by graf, in the second draft process. Everybody's different, though. I remember looking over [*Voice* film critic] Jim Hoberman's shoulder once, looking at his computer screen, and it looked like complete gibberish, and he told me that was his process, which was he would just spew it out and then refine it.

That's kind of what I tend to do, which is to just get the ideas out first and then I have to keep going back to finesse it and stylize it.

I started out, in terms of doing any serious writing, with poetry and then performance poetry, so I know that translated into those first ten years at the *Voice*, thinking about everything as a performance. 'Cause the other thing you definitely had at the *Voice* was a sense of an audience; you knew the whole paper was like a show for people every week, and you knew that from letters to the editor—'cause people were getting bomb threats for what they were writing, and not just the political writers! You also knew that folks were reading it from just being in the greater New York music community. There's two examples: Maybe one of the first times I went to the old Ritz to see a show I pulled out my ID and the guy working the door said, "Are you Iron Man?[1] Yeah, I read you in the *Voice*." And there was another moment: I had to get a lock changed in the apartment where I lived in Sugar Hill, Harlem, and a burly Latinx brother comes over, and when I'm paying him he says, "I read you all the time in the *Voice*." I was like, "Oh man, this thing has got reach." Stanley Crouch was the person who discovered, from the circulation people, that if a Black story was on the cover of the *Voice* it sold maybe a thousand or maybe a couple thousand more issues, so he used that to kind of jack up his rate. Of course we then realized it applied for all of us. As much as anybody performing in theater and music in New York, at the *Voice* you definitely realized you had a performance platform for your writing. And a certain amount of a kind of power and cachet came from that too, for better or worse [*laughs*].

I'm always thinking about Godard, who said something in an interview like, "Whether I write an essay or make a film, it's all the same." To him filmmaking was a direct transference of what he was writing about cinema when he was a critic, just putting it into practice. What you were saying before about Burnt Sugar springing from this kind of continuum of the Miles '70s bands and Funkadelic and Butch et al., it's almost like instead of writing an essay about how all these things are connected, you formed a group to do that. Do you see

1 Tate used the high school nickname in early bylines.

the group as an extension of the sort of through lines you were trying to establish in your writing?

Yeah, certainly. Jon Caramanica actually dubbed Burnt Sugar "living criticism"—he was the first person to wed the two functions. I didn't really think about it in a defined conceptual way. Because even before I started writing there was just a whole set of propositions about Black music and its history and the way it functioned or circulated in the world that was important to me. I came from a very political family. My folks were actively involved in the civil rights and Black Power movements and the African Liberation movement in Dayton, Ohio, where I was born. My mother, Mama Florence Tate, was a press secretary for Marion Barry and Jesse Jackson during their first political runs. I got into studying Black music through [Amiri] Baraka's book *Black Music* [1968]; that's my conversion experience, in terms of becoming obsessive about jazz, and the conversation around jazz, and jazz collecting. Those things really informed the first writing I did. And I recognize that even as early as maybe the first four or five pieces I did for the *Voice*—I'm really interested in this tension between Black subjectivity and Black political collectivity and the working-class Black community in music. Cornerstone of jazz anyway, but when I look at some of the kinds of propositions and conclusions even in reviewing Sun Ra, Bad Brains, Blood Ulmer, this idea kept making its way to the fore.

I also remember you did the foreword to the New Music Distribution Service catalog way back in the mid-'80s, and you're talking in there about how it was a good guide for people who had "extraterrestrial earlobes." NMDS was a real booster for the cross-pollination thing we were talking about with Zorn and Butch, and Hal

Willner fits in there too, but also it's just about being open to all different kinds of music.

And that's the time in funk and R&B where people are kind of expanding the whole notion of what the genre could do. You got Thom Bell and Gamble & Huff and Curtis Mayfield—they're bringing all the serious classical orchestration into the funk and R&B. P-Funk, Funkadelic are all over the map; when you listen to an album like *Maggot Brain* [Westbound, 1971], it's like every cut could have come from a different band. Even in DC, and certainly in New York, you could go out and hear your people play with all of these ideas around sound and genre and style. I came to New York in time to catch the last of the loft scene as well, where you got to hear so many different people's conception of what a jazz band could be. So it would be [Henry] Threadgill one set; he might have Anthony Davis in his band, and then Anthony Davis was the leader the next set. Whatever mythology has kind of survived of what that moment was like creatively, it's all true—people were doing whatever the fuck they wanted to do, on a nightly basis, based on their whole relationship to music, and canon, and genre.

A lot of these musics were still in kind of a developmental phase, so, like any person who's in a developmental phase, they're trying out all this different stuff just to see what they like and don't like, and what works and what doesn't work. And I think it's also a little bit based on the whole idea of appealing to an audience—if they didn't go for this thing, maybe they'll go for that thing. Lou Reed got his start cranking out songs for this low-budget record label; he would write a surf song, a motorcycle song, this and that, with the idea that someone will buy this record for the surf song, someone else will buy it for the motorcycle song.

I just found out that George Clinton, at the beginning of his career, spent a hell of a lot of time in the Brill Building hearing all of those people who were still there—[Burt] Bacharach and Carole King—all of those, as much as Holland-Dozier-Holland or anything coming out of Motown, were major influences. And it explains why he became such a versatile writer as well. As much as people talk about him as a non-musician—to a certain extent that's true, but he's the one who's coming up with all those lyrics and melodies. And he comes out of doo-wop quartets; he's got that notion of harmony, how you stack vocals.

When you listen to Funkadelic or Sun Ra or any of these large ensembles now, sort of post–Burnt Sugar, do you hear it in a new way? Even just after being in the recording studio—if you listen to Bitches Brew *now, do you hear it differently after having had the experience of doing the Burnt Sugar stuff in the studio?*

It's really interesting 'cause I think records that are foundational for you, you never lose your sense of innocence, your sense of surrender to the thing. I mean, *Bitches Brew* became the template for Burnt Sugar because I realized, "Oh wow, that's my favorite recording of all time," but I would never have thought that until I read—you know *Mojo* magazine has that great little column where they ask people what's your favorite Friday night record, favorite Sunday morning record, and favorite record of all time, so one column was Bootsy Collins and another column was Ike Turner and they both said their favorite record of all time was *Rumors* [Warner Bros., 1977] by Fleetwood Mac. So obviously there was a surprise element to that, but it made me ask the question of myself and I tried not to be premeditated, I just said, "Let me see what floats up," and it was *Bitches Brew*. And then I realized, it's not my favorite Miles record, or even my favorite fusion record, but it had a kind of meta quality to it—that it was brought into being by Miles functioning as an auteur, that it extended to his collaboration with Teo, to the Mati [Klarwein] album cover—it just existed as a thing that was kind of wholly musical and then extremely meta-musical beyond that. So when I listen to *Bitches Brew* I'm just listening to *Bitches Brew*, with no relationship to anything that I've done or that I'm doing; it just has a certain kind of a purity in my memory. Any of those things from when we were fourteen or fifteen, listening to music, those things are still visceral.

But a lot of times I can hear things in production that I wouldn't have grasped either because I was only fifteen or sixteen, or because I didn't have any experience with being in a studio; and a lot of guitar sounds were very mysterious to me as a player growing up and now I understand how they did it.

When you're in the studio recording or mixing or mastering you realize you have a pretty evolved sensibility around listening, but when I go back to those older things I don't dissect in that kind of way. They exist in terms of your reference points. There's things that, no matter how many times you listen to them, they never grow old; you've got this emotional and intellectual relationship to them.

Especially with the Miles '70s stuff, you could go through those records and listen only to Michael Henderson, or listen only to Pete [Cosey]; you could pick any one player and it would be interesting. And so much is going on collectively that it takes years to get your head around it.

I did notes for the fortieth anniversary of *Bitches Brew* and I was talking to Bennie Maupin, and he said Miles turned to him and said, "Think of the music as a big cauldron of soup and we're the witches in there stirring." "Witches," not "bitches," cause "bitches" actually came from Betty Davis. Miles was known for calling musicians he liked a "bitch of a player." But it is the ensemble quality of that record that made it so potent, 'cause Miles had that whole thing of the only way you get something new in music is you take the best musicians you can find and you make them play beyond what they know. There's nobody playing any clichés on *Bitches Brew*; they're forced into this environment where they've got to come up with wholly new solutions and responses in the moment, you know? And that's all going on on this ensemble level, which is then collaged into a compositional shape by Teo.

*I did a gig with Henry Kaiser about two years ago—I was touring in California and he's a really old friend and former teacher of mine, and I said, "Let's do a gig together while I'm out there." He's been doing the "*A Love Supreme *Electric" [John] Coltrane project, although it's actually more the drummer's project than his, but he said, "Let's do that and in the second set we'll do some Miles stuff—let's do* Jack Johnson, *and you've got to play all the John McLaughlin parts." Now, I've had* Jack Johnson *[Columbia, 1971] since I was fifteen, but I've never sat down and tried to learn his parts, and nowadays of course there's some guy on YouTube who's breaking down every single lick for you, and it was amazing. When you analyze what McLaughlin's doing, his* *chording falls* right *in between R&B guitar playing and jazz playing, and McLaughlin has a background in both but he's not really synthesizing it that way until Miles gets him to do it.*

And the McLaughlin and the Pete that we know from those records—they're players who emerged from playing with Miles, kind of getting out of their own ways and turning up [their amps]. You hear all the bootlegs of that band, and it's really not until Dominique Gaumont comes into the band [in 1974] that everybody starts turning up. Miles said he brought him in just to fuck with Reggie Lucas, even though Dominique was a very underdeveloped player, 'cause he thought Reggie was kind of lazy. But the consequence of him being in that band is that everything goes up to ten, and then we hear Pete with all the distortion and all the effects; it's all the stuff he was holding back.

*Yeah, in '73 it's so much different than '75. Some of it is, you know, if you get asked to join Miles's band, you might not want to blow him off the stage right away [*laughs*]. I'd imagine there's a certain sense of decorum until he says, "Play some Hendrix! Turn it up or turn it off!" like he told Mike Stern.*

Dominique comes in and all he knows is Jimi; he totally sets the stage for everybody else getting louder and more distorted. At a certain point Miles totally embraced having three loud-ass, funky guitarists in the band.

Michael Snow

In my late teens, I reasoned that because I was interested in experimental music, it would follow that I might also be interested in experimental films, and so I began trying to see as many of them as I could. At college, a class I was ineligible for held weekly open screenings, and it was there that I first saw Michael Snow's structuralist classic *Wavelength* (1967). Perhaps I knew that it was just a continuous zoom in a loft, with a glissando electronic tone as a soundtrack, but I distinctly remember the feeling of realizing, a few minutes in, that "nothing" was going to happen in this nonnarrative movie; that I could just sit back and enjoy watching the details, as foregrounded by Snow, that I might ordinarily miss in a movie. I'm sure I related it to Steve Reich's phase pieces, which were also process-oriented, and to La Monte Young's idea of "getting inside the sound" by stripping everything back to focus on a single component—in this case, what would ordinarily be the backdrop. A few years later, I discovered that Michael was also a musician who had a free improv group called CCMC, a double album under his own name on Philip Glass's Chatham Square label (*Musics for Piano, Whistling, Microphone and Tape Recorder*, 1975), and had directed the film *New York Eye and Ear Control* (1964), for which Albert Ayler had made a soundtrack (released on ESP-Disk). Anthology Film Archives in New York put on a complete Snow retrospective in early 1996 and also helped to organize a CCMC show at the Knitting Factory; I went to see every film and the concert, too. While on tour with Run On in Canada, I also went to Art Metropole in Toronto and bought every Snow book and album I could find there.

Yuzo Sakuramoto and Gary McCraw had done two issues of a magazine called *Music*, and in 1999, when they were starting the third, they approached me about contributing something for it. I thought an interview with

Michael would be appropriate, based on the first two issues, and they agreed to pay for my travel to Toronto to interview him. Michael was extremely hospitable and on November 8, 1998, he took me around the city to see some of his public artworks there, including a notorious sculpture at a sports arena that he claimed the sports fans loved but the art world disparaged. We did the interview at his studio space. Some months later, the late curator Ben Portis invited me to return to the No Music Festival he was organizing in London, Ontario, which was centered around hometown heroes the Nihilist Spasm Band, and asked who I'd like to play with. Having established a rapport with Michael, I suggested him, and we made our debut as a duo there. A little later I brought Aki Onda into the mix to make it a trio, which has one live CD release to date, *Five A's, Two C's, One D, One E, Two H's, Three I's, One K, Three L's, One M, Three N's, Two O's, One S, One T, One W* (Victo, 2008), titled by me—an inventory of the letter counts in our three names—as an homage to Michael's love of anagrams and other lingual deconstructions.

Let's start off by talking about CCMC. You once said CCMC composes "inconceivable" music. I thought you might talk about the idea of the inconceivable as compared with the idea of abstraction. I was also wondering if there could be inconceivable painting or film.

It doesn't really apply to other mediums that I work with, but in music it seems to me that with the best improvising players in a group, you can make something that could not be thought of, because there are certain nuances that will develop in performance that are perhaps not notate-able, that you could not instruct somebody to make. With improvised music, what you do is play music of the moment for the moment in this particular place for the people that are there. It is the idea that the ideal, or the perfection, of what music has to offer is ephemeral. But of course recording changed that.

I'd like to talk about one of the special performances CCMC did: the opening for Sonic Youth.

Opening for Sonic Youth was really a wonderful thing—what those guys did in asking us to do that was great—because there is not that much rock connection in our music. I used to play a Fender Rhodes a lot. For this occasion, I revived the Fender because we seemed to need amplification. We had to pump it up. And it was fun, playing the Fender again, because it is a weird instrument, somewhere between electric and acoustic, with the percussive aspects of real pianos. The sound is interesting and raw. Anyway, the age of the audience ranged from about fifteen to forty, a few thousand people, and they seemed to dig it. I kept glancing at everybody to see what the hell was happening. I felt they were trying to translate the movements that they use in rock into our music. Since the music isn't, strictly speaking, repeated rhythms, you could see that they were grooving on it but puzzled about trying to find the right body reactions to it. They really did seem to like it, which was a surprise [*laughs*].

Did you know Sonic Youth's music at all?

No. I had heard some but never really paid close attention to it. They gave me CDs of recent stuff, and some of it is interesting. The other thing that was terrific and flattering is that they all knew a lot of my work. Lee Ranaldo is a very interesting guy, and so is Thurston Moore. They are very cultured characters and really incredible. They brought some of my books, like *A Survey* [1970] and *Cover to Cover* [1975], for me to sign, and we talked about films.

Has the group done much touring?

Not recently, although we played in France in May or June of '97. In our second or third year—1970-something—we did a European tour. And when the group included Nobuo Kubota, Al Mattes, Casey Sokol, and myself, we did another extensive tour, playing in England, Belgium, Holland, Austria, Germany, and Poland. Once, we played in France at the Centre Pompidou.

And you've played in New York only once? At the Knitting Factory?

Yeah.

Any reason why?

Gee, I don't know. We are kind of ambitionless in a

funny way. With everything else everybody in the group does, it seems as if none of us really pushes to play elsewhere. It's not complacency. It's that there is a level of satisfaction that we are able to do what we do. We want to do another European tour, but there hasn't been any talk about playing New York. It's funny. I have a lot of things happening in France, in Europe, much more than here. CCMC will play sometime during my retrospective at the Palais des Beaux-Arts in Brussels,[1] and then do another tour. It's still a trio.

The trio being you . . .

Paul Dutton and John Oswald.

Can you talk a little about Oswald's relationship to the group? I know he's mentioned as a recording engineer on the Larry Dubin and CCMC triple album, and he's been a member of the group for several years.

When the Music Gallery started in '76, John just became part of it. He used to play with us occasionally, and I always dug his playing. [CCMC] also played with the Four Horsemen a few times here and at the Holland Festival in Amsterdam, and we really liked it a lot. So sometimes the members of the Four Horsemen worked with us. Steven McCaffery, who is really quite wonderful as a vocal improviser, did a lot of things with us, but it got to be more and more Paul Dutton, who is fantastic too. That's how the group developed. John just started playing more and more with us. He is in a couple of the pieces on *Decisive Moments* [Track & Light, 1994], which was recorded mainly in '93.

1 "Michael Snow: Panoramique," July 8–September 5, 1999, at BOZAR Centre for Fine Arts in Brussels.

And you played piano on his Plunderphonics *[Mystery Tape Laboratory, 1988]?*

Yeah, on the Elvis Presley track. John just mixed a lot of layers of stuff in there. I think the piano was slowed down or something.

Was Dutton an influence on The Last LP *[Art Metropole, 1987]? A lot of what's on there could be said to have been sampled.*

Yeah, I do say a thank-you to the Four Horsemen in the notes; but actually, there is this thing on *The Last LP* called "Speech in Klögen," which was recorded in the late '60s, so I had bumped into sampling before it existed. I did the piece for Jonas Mekas's birthday party. I decided to make a tape which would arrive as an anonymous gift that should be played during the party. I can't remember why, but I invented a language called Klögen. It was supposed to be from Finland, and I just started, "*Gashuto bonde glasta bini gusto waila. . . .*" I made up this language. I had never done it before and I have not done it since, although some bits are in *Rameau's Nephew* [*Rameau's Nephew by Diderot (Thanx to Dennis Young) by Wilma Schoen*, 1974].

Was CCMC doing weekly concerts?

At first we did biweekly, believe it or not. And in those days we had so many instruments, because one of the premises of the group's performance was that we should use any sound source. Setting up at the Music Gallery would take hours sometimes, but we were so enthusiastic that we did it. I would think one of the best recorded representations of that time is *Free Soap* [Music Gallery Editions, 1979], because it uses a lot of toy sounds. We played in Amsterdam in the '70s and met Michel Waisvisz. He's this guy who started building electronic instruments quite a long time ago, and he made these synthesizers called Crackleboxes, which were heat and touch sensitive. They were handheld, about three by five inches, and they had feedback devices. They were quite incredible because they were thoroughly unpredictable, depending on the temperature and moisture and all kinds of stuff. We bought a whole bunch of them. And then Nobuo Kubota made a kind of cage within which he played. It had a lot of percussion instruments dangling around and a lot of other toys, but the most fantastic thing he did was rig up two cassette players with volume pedals so that he could play cassettes along with the whole selection of other stuff that he was using—a kind of sampling before sampling. He had such incredible taste. He would use *gagaku*, Japanese court music. When this would appear, it was just phenomenal. We were trying everything you could think of in the beginning, but the selection has pared itself down now. John plays the saxophone and Dutton uses voice and stereo mics, but he doesn't do electronic modification or anything. I continue to play this CAT synthesizer that I bought around 1978. I really love it. It's an interesting instrument. It's hard to know why it was made, because it's definitely not made to imitate other sounds, like trumpets or clarinets. It's for finding new sounds. Since it is all built on rheostats—

—drawbars—

—inherently it is a glissando instrument. You know, you *can't* really stay in tune, so it is great to have it around as a weapon against John and Paul, who are pretty slithery—and of course the piano is not slithery [*laughs*]—so I have a chance to meet them on their own ground. On the other hand, playing piano while they are so all over the place pitch-wise is really wonderful, too.

One of the reasons I brought up the weekly concerts is to draw a parallel with Nihilist Spasm Band. They've been playing weekly for thirty years in London [Ontario]. Did CCMC ever perform with them?

I've played with them a few times, but CCMC, no. We never played as a group. They played at the Music Gallery a couple of times. I always liked what they did. The main spark plug was Greg Curnoe. He was a really great artist and an amazing influence on people in the small town of London. He made a decision to be local, to be regional, to use where he was from. Greg and I used to discuss those issues in the late '50s because he moved to Toronto and was trying to figure out what the hell to do, and so was I. I was interested "internationally" in everything. I was following what was going on in New York, etc. I think the discussions clarified things for both of us, and he moved back to London. He was an inspiration for a lot of other artists in that small town which ought not to have had any art at all. It is amazing what was coming out of there.

Greg Curnoe was also a very strong Canadian nationalist. I mean, he did some paintings where there was a map of just Canada and Mexico!

No, it's a map of North America that takes out the US. It is really terrific. Greg used to tease us for having Americans in the band [*laughs*], but the thing was, he was a jazz nut. I mean, he listened to everything. He loved Albert Ayler—he wouldn't turn it off if he found out it was an American. But I think it's wonderful what they [Nihilist Spasm Band] are. I mean, they are really an original. Their sense of what to do, what kind of sound to make, and the very dense din they make—it's terrific. Now they have had some success and have toured Japan. It's great.

They've even gone to the US, which probably would not have been possible while Greg was alive.

Yeah, maybe Greg would have resisted. Unfortunately, he died in an accident riding his bicycle about four years ago. . . . There was also the Artists' Jazz Band, which is important in this story. They started to play in '62. They were all painters and sculptors. Since I had been playing professionally for a fair amount of time when they started to play, I thought it was really a riot. But I changed my mind. I used to play with a wonderful bass player named Terry Forster, and he started to play with them. Then I moved to New York around 1962, and when I would go back to visit, Terry was still playing with them and the music was developing. It really surprised me because I didn't consider them musicians, but it was one of those miracles. They just got horns, and they never tried to learn about scales or harmony or even tunes. By that time, we were all listening to Ornette [Coleman], but they were real jazz fans and jazz maniacs. They listened to everything, and they sort of represented what they thought the music was like. For example, Bob Markle liked John Coltrane. He made his imitations, but they were based on trying to find out what the changes were for "Giant Steps." It was the quality of, "What is it?" I mean, seeking out sound or something like that. He was an actor in a way. But, given enough dope—everybody took everything in those days—the music was miraculous. These people who could not play anything played wonderful stuff!

It's funny because ESP records had those groups like the Godz and the Fugs that, again, had little or no idea how to play instruments.

Yeah, the Fugs were like that.

When you were talking about pure improvisation, that was one of the things I thought of when I listened to the 2 Radio Solos *tapes [Freedom in a Vacuum, 1988]. You absolutely have to react to what is happening. You can control it to a certain extent, but you don't really have any control over what to input. Was that the only instance of your using radio as an improvising tool?*

No, the first time was in the soundtrack for *Standard Time* in '67, which was completely performed playing the radio.

I guess someone plays a radio in Wavelength.

Well, she turns the radio on, and it is definitely related. Since I was shooting sync sound in that particular part, and in the spirit of what you are talking about, I thought I should accept whatever came on the radio when the two of them walked into the room and turned it on. But what came on was "Little Drummer Boy" by Joan Baez, which was really popular at the time, and I hated it. I just couldn't find a way to rationalize that it would be in the film, which had certain requirements for what it was trying to do, so I substituted [the Beatles'] "Strawberry Fields." That's more appropriate [*laughs*]. In *Rameau's Nephew*, there is some really good use of the radio. It starts out with some people, one of them wearing a great red turban, standing in front of a museum exhibit of Indians. They just move their mouths in basic mouth movements, as if they were making attack sounds or cough sounds, like *muc mmmmm puh puh puh puh*. That is what they were instructed to do—and I put the sound over these moving mouths. In the beginning it is kind of parallel, almost like something is being said by that person, but not quite fitting. It starts with a kind of generalization over the mouths, and then it gets more abstracted. I reshot the original sequence off the screen, and the sound gets more and more broken apart as the image becomes more and more framed, more strobe-y, frame by frame. And there is a long part in the film where I used something that I trapped while playing a shortwave radio. It seems to be a soap opera or something. The voice is all chopped up, but the emotion in the voice still comes through. Speaking of radio, obviously it's John Cage who was the first person to recognize the radio as an instrument. I went to a Cage retrospective at Columbia University around 1972 and heard a radio piece using at least eight radios, maybe more. It was written sometime in the '50s. But you know, there is a line of classicism in Cage's music that has to do with the refinement of the pause. It continues a tradition of elegance in classical music, and it is present in the radio piece, which is conducted with a little pause every once in a while. It was so much that the kind of counting—pause, pause, pause, a sound—even though it was trailblazing, didn't really touch the possibilities of using radios. That is kind of uncharitable, but I just thought, "Shit! So much could be done."

Let's go back a bit and talk about the early '60s in New York, the free jazz scene and ESP records. You had performances at your loft by people like Albert Ayler and Milford Graves.

Yeah. Albert only played once in my loft, and that was to record the soundtrack for my *New York Eye and*

Ear Control, but many other people played there. There was one session rehearsal with the group that Paul Bley had with Giuseppi Logan, and there were some visitors. One of them said, "Can I play?" and that was Milford Graves. As far as I could tell, this was the first time any of the people that were there had heard him, and everybody was, "Wow! Who is this guy?" [*Laughs.*] Phone numbers were exchanged. . . . My wife at the time, Joyce Wieland, and I met Kenny Davern, who is a fine Dixieland clarinetist, and that led to meeting Roswell Rudd. Roswell's background was exactly like mine. He played Dixieland and had played with some greats. Roswell's loft was across the street from mine on Chambers, and I got talked into playing a couple of jobs with Kenny and Ahmed Abdul-Malik on bass. And Roswell sold me his upright piano for a hundred bucks. So I had this piano in my loft where I was painting, and I suppose through Roswell I started to hear what was going on in free jazz. I told the guys I was meeting that I had a piano and they could play anytime they wanted. There really wasn't much public playing because what they were doing was uniformly hated, especially by the jazz people. I heard some incredible things: the Albert Ayler Trio with Gary Peacock and Sunny Murray, the New York Art Quartet with Milford. Word got around to people that it was where they could play, so Archie Shepp, Paul Bley, Mike Mantler, and the Jazz Composer's Orchestra started there. I heard some amazing music, but I didn't play very much, because I was trying to figure out what the hell was going on, and at the same time I was having the internal war, thinking I should stop playing.

You did the cover art for a Paul Bley album on ESP, besides doing the New York Eye and Ear Control *record. How did you get in touch with [ESP founder] Bernard Stollman?*

Well, there were only a few people who were interested in this music. I don't know whether I met him after the Albert Ayler Trio or not, but I'm sure Paul Bley, Paul Haines, or someone else had met him, because Bernard met everybody. I knew him far enough back to remember when he was trying to figure out what to call his record company. I was working on the *Walking Woman* works between '61 and '67 here in Toronto, and he was considering calling his company Walking Woman. I must have met him at some concert or club or something.

A lot of people we've been talking about have records out on ESP, like the New York Art Quartet, Milford Graves, Albert Ayler, Paul Bley, and so on. What was the feeling about these records as they were coming out? Was there any attention paid to them by the press or anything, or were people mostly oblivious?

I think people were mostly oblivious. Of course I was interested, but I don't think there was very wide acceptance. There may have been a few reviews, but it seems to me the general atmosphere was pretty hostile.

Among musicians themselves?

I don't know about the reception of these things except for the little world I was involved in. I was involved in several worlds simultaneously: underground film, painting, and sculpture. Painting and sculpture had the glamour and money and power because it was a very peak period—New York was becoming the art capital—and when you went to openings, it was a mixture of seedy people and wealthy people. But in the free jazz scene and in the experimental film scene, it was basically a small number of seedy people [*laughs*]. At the screenings at the various cinematheques that Jonas

Mekas organized, there would be about ten people, often the same ten people, sometimes other filmmakers. The other thing was that Ornette and Cecil [Taylor]'s widest acceptance in New York was among visual artists. Jazz people in general thought Cecil was insane, and Ornette was easier to take, but there were still jokes about his plastic saxophone and that kind of stuff. But especially with Ornette, painters immediately recognized that he had a kinship with abstract expressionism.

You mentioned somewhere that you were making feedback tapes or loops in '63.

I was really obsessed with tape recorders for a while. Reel-to-reel recorders. I still have about ten of them. I don't think I discovered feedback myself . . . but it reminds me of Max Neuhaus because he did some performances, one of which was a wonderful sound installation in an elevator. He also made a mass-produced edition of a thing called the *Max Feed* [1966], which was a plastic box with machinery inside and a little speaker that you could hold up in front of a speaker, and it would make feedback. That was around '63. He was originally a classical percussionist. I was instrumental in having him come here and play in a series of concerts at the Isaacs Gallery, which was quite advanced for the time. I think they were called Happenings. Also, a university in New Jersey had a summer program and invited Allan Kaprow, Max Neuhaus, and the poet Emmett Williams . . . lots of acid [*laughs*]. But part of what Max did was take everybody on sound mystery tours. We went to a hydroelectric plant, which had incredibly huge dynamos, and the sound was incredible. Max guided us around to various places to listen. He knew the place fairly well, so he put us in one place to hear one thing and then somewhere else to hear another sound.

And the loops, what were the loops of?

Ah, they were sometimes feedback loops of stuff off the radio, and I also started to play with whistling. You know the piece "W in the D" on Chatham Square Records? I worked on that off and on for a couple of years. I have some other versions of it, just pure whistling. This is digressing, but two summers ago Nic Collins, who is a very interesting composer now living in Berlin, organized a whistling festival in Lucerne, Switzerland. I didn't know him, but he said my whistling record was legendary among certain New Music composers and that he would be honored to have an "avant-garde" whistler at Lucerne. It knocked me over. So I went, and it was amazing.

How many people?

Alvin Lucier was there. He did a couple pieces that, strictly speaking, aren't whistling. There was also a group of native people from South America who had never been out of the rain forest. It was a little bit uncomfortable, really. They did a ritual which did not involve whistling but single-note flutes. And there were people from the Pyrenees and Albania, and people who communicate over long distances by whistling. Finally, there was a team of women, one English, the other Swiss or Austrian, who had apparently come out of retirement because it seemed to be an emotional moment for some members of the audience. But it was a fantastic thing. . . . How did we get to whistling?

I guess we were talking about loops.

Well, that reminds me of *Dripping Water* [1969], because that was done around 1970. The faucets in our loft were leaking, and I started listening to them. It was completely arrhythmic. I smoked some dope and listened to it, and then decided to make a tape of it. I made a fairly long tape, and played that with a real drip. But the thing about the tape was that I could play it loud and really hear what the hell was going on in it. It was pretty amazing, and depending on what was in the sink you got different pitches out of the drip hitting whatever it was hitting. A guy named Mike Sahl, who had a program of modern music on WBAI, heard it somewhere, was knocked out by it, and played it on the radio. Twenty minutes or half an hour of dripping water on WBAI! Isn't that great?!

Do you still have the tape?

Yeah. Anyway, Joyce, who was a filmmaker and a wonderful artist—she died recently—suggested making a film of it, so that's how the film came about. Simply put, it's a fixed camera shot of the thing dripping, but the sound is not in sync. I thought it was a good joke because we were shooting the sink . . . and I used sync sound in *Rameau's Nephew*, where I play in the sink.

The whole thing with loops is actually a good segue to talking about your association with Steve Reich and Philip Glass.

I met Steve because he had seen *Wavelength* and liked it a lot and said he wanted to meet whoever made it. At the time, I had never heard his name before, but he wrote something about it—it is published in one of my books, [1995's] *Presence and Absence* [*The Films of Michael Snow, 1956–1991*]. He said he wrote it when he arrived home after seeing the film. So we met and got to know each other because I had a loft on Canal

Street near Broadway—*Wavelength* was shot there—and Steve's loft was on Broadway just a bit above Canal. After the first introduction, I used to just drop in and listen to rehearsals, and I got to hear his music more and more.

Did you have any connection with Terry Riley or La Monte Young?

You could buy hash from [Young]! [*Laughs.*] But I also had the good fortune to hear the group that had Tony Conrad in '62 or '63. La Monte Young had a loft on Church near Canal, and he used to put on concerts there. They were quite phenomenal.

How did the deal with Chatham Square Records come about?

I was with the Bykert Gallery at that time, which was directed by Klaus Kertess, and Klaus was a friend of Phil and he started Chatham Square, funding it from the beginning, I think. So I am not sure how it came about . . .

One thing I've noticed, particularly in the movies but also with some of the recordings, is an idea of all-inclusiveness or an encyclopedic approach to the work, and something like a sense of finality. This is obviously evident in the title The Last LP, *and it's also an issue in the films* La Région Centrale *[1971],* Rameau's Nephew, A Casing Shelved *[1970],* A to Z *[1956],* Wavelength, See You Later/Au Revoir *[1990],* Presents *[1981]. There is always the sense that there is nothing else that can be done with the material in films like* La Région Centrale *or* See You Later *or* A Casing Shelved, *where everything is described down to the last detail. It is a very exhaustive kind of approach. Would you like to comment on that?*

That's an interesting observation, but it's hard to comment on because I think it is just a character trait. At an early age, I noticed I was interested in variations of systems . . . setting up something like *Walking Woman* for six or seven years, a huge variation within and around this contour . . . like playing the blues. It is a bit on the dangerous side because I can be obsessive about doing more than I should with something, because of this apparent need to cover all possible ground. In a lot of cases, that isn't the right thing to do.

It reminds me of a quote from Susan Sontag's On Photography *[1977], where she describes photographs [as] "note-taking on, potentially, everything in the world from every possible angle."*

Well, that's going pretty far [*laughs*].

But the last section of Presents *is . . .*

Yeah, trying to do that! [*Laughs.*]

Even La Région Centrale. *I mean, it is not the world, but it is that one part of land . . .*

Yeah, the last section of *Presents* is interesting because there is a lot of variety and a lot of shots from all over the bloody place. Despite the variety, it indicates how impossible it is to picture the world, and especially because of the system that I used, the handheld, panning glance, the ephemerality is emphasized. You know that everything passes by, and the act of recording it makes it something else. That is a good example, because it was built around all the possible ways of moving the camera: looking up, looking down, looking right, moving right. Even geographically, I made sure that there was something tropical—it happens to be in Italy, and there are palm trees and also the architecture. The idea was sort of the opposite of *Wavelength*. Where *Wavelength* goes down to one image, this was the impossibility of a linear medium, of going further and further away from a sort of home, which was that apartment that is smashed up. It was not exactly encyclopedic, but I did want it to have a breadth of references.

The last section of Presents *has back-and-forth movements punctuated by sounds, almost like a tennis match. Lateral movement is obviously an important element of your art.*

It "presents" movements everywhere. If it was, say, a shot of a landscape in the distance, and the camera movement was horizontal, then the next shot would be something close-up with a move that might be vertical. They define each other so that there isn't any connection from shot to shot. That was the plan.

There is the film <———> [1969], which is also left-right, and the piece "Left Right" on the Musics . . .

Tits and ass on Jackie.

*[*Laughs.*] I guess that answers that question! Manny Farber described it as a pendulum movie. And you performed the Reich piece [*Pendulum Music, *1968]. So this is some kind of interest?*

Well, <———> is sort of encyclopedic because the panning starts with a medium tempo, goes a little slower, and then gradually starts speeding up until it reaches its peak of moving back and forth horizontally. At that horizontal peak it kind of climaxes, to continue the sexual innuendo. Actually *Wavelength* is sexier, I think. <———> goes vertically up and down at high speed, and gradually slows and slows and slows and slows. It shows the movements at all the possible speeds and goes side to side and up and down! [*Laughs.*] What else can you ask for?

<———> *had its premiere at the Whitney [Museum of American Art, New York] series called "Extended Time Pieces."* . . . La Région Centrale *is three hours long, which is an extraordinary length for a movie, and* Rameau's Nephew *is even longer. It's quite extraordinary to sit through.*

I wouldn't put it that way! [*Laughs.*]

How integral was the concept of time to the film's original idea?

La Région Centrale started out as a division of the twenty-four-hour day, with the idea that it could be compressed into twelve or six hours, and it ended up being three. The original idea was to take a bit out of every hour so that it would be a compressed day, but that did not really work. It starts in the morning, goes through a day, sunset, and dawn, and it ends late morning, at ten or eleven. So you do feel as though you have gone through an entire day, but it is not as systematic as I originally thought it might be. *Rameau's Nephew* and *La Région Centrale* are almost complete opposites: one is social—it's all about speech—and the other is completely antisocial.

No people in it.

The length [of *Rameau's Nephew*] was four and a half hours. The premise was that each section would be like a word in a sentence. And like any individual word that you might examine, not only does it have its own function grammatically, but it has its own etymology; there are all kinds of aspects to a single word. What I was thinking of as the language of this film was that each word would be a different sound-image situation, constantly relating to the voice—recorded voice—so that once you were into it, it would build up in a sense that was not really translatable. It was a sense that was particular to the language that was being constructed by the film itself, so in a way it did not represent something. The film had to be long enough so that by the time you came to the end of the sentence, you could only understand the last word because by then you'd learned the language. So you really have to see the entire film, and you know, unfortunately, a lot of people don't [*laughs*]. Actually, I built it with the hardest part at the beginning, so it immediately weeds out the cowards in the audience. Then, after that, those who can dig it have it to themselves . . . usually two people. So the reason for the length was that it had to stretch out over a long period in order to involve memory. *La Région Centrale* is completely modulating from one movement to the next. In *Rameau's Nephew*, these discreet things are very, very different. They are set in this little time and there are space dividers of color compositions. The ideal was to be as nonverbal as possible so that you did not read them. You might look at something and say you read it in your mind, but basically you are just looking at what happens to the colors and what happens optically and so on. Then the sound and image start again.

That film is obviously concerned with disjunction between sound and image.

Well, it is concerned with all the possible relationships between the sound and its source, because sync sound is so dominant in helping to make a seamless realism or naturalism. *Rameau's Nephew* is working with the fact that the sound and image are in fact separate, and they are even separate where they emerge: one comes out of the loudspeaker and the other is projected on a screen. The success of the suspension of disbelief with fiction films is to a large extent predicated on believing that the sound comes out of the moving mouths. I was working with something else, because they really are separate. You know, recorded voice can have the same kind of emotional and intellectual effect on you as a real voice, but it is an abstraction. I wanted *Rameau's Nephew* to be an experience of that abstraction, so that you have both the realism and the fact that there is a transformation in recording. So, yes, disjunction of various kinds was part of it. But there is a lot of sync sound, too, but used in different ways. Like in the fart scene, where the actors learn their lines backward, and then it zooms out and they talk in a strange language, and then the whole thing is flipped and the same shot is shown backward and the sound is playing backward. That is in sync, but it is a special use of it.

Right. There is also the scene with hands arranging something on a table, describing what they are doing, and it goes out of sync.

Yeah, it is a woman's voice and it is my hands moving stuff on the table top. Her voice describes what is going on, but the voice is either way ahead or way behind or simultaneous, which are the three possibilities. It makes for very interesting feelings of both. Especially when it races ahead, when the voice describes something that hasn't happened yet.

Sinoms *[an audio piece from 1989] reminds me a bit of the airplane sequence in* Rameau's Nephew, *like the same way that the voices get shorn off.*

That's surprising. Well, in *Sinoms*, people read a list dispassionately, and in that part of *Rameau's Nephew*, every scene was done using some different method of getting the spoken sound to exist. In that particular case, I read the lines to actors just before the shot—sometimes in single words—so perhaps that is the connection. Because in *Sinoms* there were twenty-five recordings of twenty-five people reading the list, and in both cases the people couldn't have any feeling about it. They could only repeat, so there is a kind of flatness.

You mentioned Presents *being the opposite of* Wavelength *in terms of starting narrow and going wide, and starting wide and going narrow. It is reminiscent of the Chatham Square liner notes, which start off big and get small—*

There, I was thinking of "Falling Starts" [from *Musics for Piano, Whistling, Microphone and Tape Recorder*]—

—which is also similar to the Wavelength *soundtrack, which is a glissando. "Falling Starts" starts off fairly fast and then gets slower and drops in pitch, and* Sinoms *also starts slow and gets fast, although there are more variations.*

Well, there is no change in playback—it's real-time—but it builds up in complexity. It isn't in a shape that is as easy to describe as some other things. It piles up and then goes back to being single words and piles up again, because there is a choir of all the women's voices, and then a choir of all the men's voices, and then they mix.

I wanted to ask you about the electronic soundtracks to Wavelength *and* La Région Centrale. Wavelength *has an electronic glissando and* La Région Centrale *has buzzing and beeps.*

For *Wavelength*, I settled on the idea of it being a slow zoom. Then I thought of what would be the sound equivalent, so I thought about traversing ear space with the glissando so that you pass through everything you could possibly hear—there is that megalomaniac again [*laughs*]. So I thought about trying to make it glissando somehow, with instruments like the trombone or violin, which inherently have the possibility of glissandi. I thought I could record a trombonist, for example, and then I could slow the tracks down and speed them up into a single thing. But someone suggested I do it electronically, and they put me in touch with Ted Wolf from Bell Labs. He explained how he thought it could be done: sine wave with rheostat. You would just have to decide the amount of time and how much you would keep on turning it. That seemed like the best solution. So it was not like "choosing an electronic thing," but rather trying to solve the issue of how to make a long glissando. For the soundtrack of *La Région Centrale*, a guy in Montreal made a little instrument that had beeps at various pitches, and I used that.

You have mentioned simultaneity a couple of times. Even in the Chatham Square liner notes, you encourage people to read them and listen to the record at the same time. Ordinary people probably would not recommend that. Is simultaneity a specific interest?

Yeah, one of the things that attracted me to New Orleans Dixieland jazz is the polyphonic ensembles. When I started to listen to classical music, it was baroque music that I particularly liked. At that time, the early '50s, I discovered [Bach's 1741] *Goldberg Variations*. It is obviously the background for me playing freely, because the whole thing of having simultaneities happen is an inevitable part of it, because if there is no determining prior structure, you don't use the crutch of modes, which I think are basically drones. Of course, there are many different ways to make free unities, which are all clichéd. The most interesting thing is simultaneity because it comes out of the purity of the situation. Things are happening all together.

Another thing you mentioned earlier was recording being separate from the actual thing. The end of La Région Centrale, *with the image of the landscape spinning around so two-dimensionally, calls attention to what it is that the audience has been doing for the last three hours, which is watching a representation of something that is limitless and completely natural.*

Yeah. *La Région Centrale* is a man-made thing that relies on our necessity to frame, because otherwise what you are pointing out is all-inclusive. You can point out with a pointer or with a searchlight, but framing is an architectural thing essential to isolating what we are looking at. One of the things in *La Région Centrale* is that, since the camera is always moving around over this landscape and it is fixed, theoretically you should get a good look at the place the camera was put. But you don't, because it is so limited! [*Laughs.*] Limitation itself is part of the tragedy that is involved. It is just like we don't have eyes in the backs of our heads. The mystery of representation itself is so common that there is hardly any question that you look at something [*points to an advertisement on his desk*], and that is quite a nice ass [*laughs*], but what is it? It is a human hallucination or system of hallucinations that we all share looking at something.

But in a documentary, the news, or fiction films, the success of it is your belief in what you are seeing. And you basically go through the medium toward the subject being represented. You don't consciously recognize the difference when you see "the news," but there is a difference. I think one of the few jobs left for art is to point that out in a way that makes you encounter something that is pretty mysterious and certainly seems to be something that is completely ours. No other creatures seem to do it. At a recent conference, I screened the part of *Rameau's Nephew* showing some people on a bus with a voice-over talking about how there seems to be a human evolutionary desire for a greater and greater verisimilitude and representation. The text was addressing man-machine symbiosis and cloning, and the film shows this guy Stelarc, who is an Australian artist, wiring himself up and using remote controls and robots. . . . If you say that painting represents in a realistic way, and there are many references to surprisingly lifelike paintings in ancient times, you can say that photography answers that same need to have more and more realism, and then film and video even more so because they bring in motion. It seems we want a completely convincing representation. And it also seems to imply that we might prefer a substitute life over life itself, which is a pretty interesting proposition. But it is just like speaking. We have been talking together for hours, and it is an exchange, and presume I'm saying something [*laughs*], but it is a representation, too, isn't it? That is the point I was bringing up in *Rameau's Nephew*.

The other thing I wanted to talk about was hoaxes. You claimed 2 Radio Solos *were recorded in a cabin.*

They were! I have been building a cabin in Newfoundland for the last twenty-seven years. So, yes, it is true.

So what was the idea behind hoaxes?

When I did the Chatham Square thing, I had already realized and was putting into practice the fact that recording was an instrument. And I kept on thinking of ways that I could use the instrument in the same way as I had made things when I was a painter—just going to the studio and doing things. I started thinking of multitracking, trying to do something where all the layers would be made by myself. That desire became *The Last LP*. I think it has a little bit to do with how I improvise music. There are often associations that fly by, and they may not be direct influences. It is just that they touch on things that you've heard before and you say, "God, that sounds like African music," or, "Gee, that's Indian, or Japanese," or any of these things that recording has given us the opportunity to hear that you never could have heard before. It is as if these associations wanted to be fleshed out and become something. So, I set up the Portastudio and had all these reel-to-reel tape recorders and I used everything. It seemed to call for a kind of acting or change of identity from piece to piece. I think I would have been too embarrassed to do it in a studio with an engineer. No one could hear me.

And you used a Whitney Houston song on The Last LP.

Yeah. There are only two things that are based on other things: [Bach's 1721] *Brandenburg Concertos* and the Whitney Houston song. It sort of confuses the issue, because everything else is original—but that returns to wanting to be encyclopedic, I guess [*laughs*]. Well, I was working on a holographic installation piece in Vancouver, and the guys I was working with used to go to a strip club every night, and that was the stripper's favorite song. I just decided to try to make an imitation of it. It was fun because I had to make up a language that would fit and then did all the tracks, boosted with the Portastudio.

There is an interesting change in perception about the record after you read the credits—which have to be read in a mirror. Listening to it, I knew that it was not actual [field] recordings.

Once, I was listening to a so-called ethnic music program, and the host played a Bulgarian women's choir and then the first piece of my LP. It was great to hear it that way. And a friend of mine was having coffee with her friend while listening to my LP, and the friend wanted a copy and asked about where to get it. The next week she called my friend back and said, "Why didn't you tell me it was fake?" Of course my friend was baffled and said, "What, this is not music?" [*Laughs.*] It is so interesting what happens to your mind when you find out that something was not what you thought it was, but still is!

Tony Conrad: On Angus MacLise

While visiting family in Boston in the summer of 1983, I found a copy of the third issue of the Velvet Underground fanzine *What Goes On* in a magazine shop. Inside was an article called "Angus MacLise and the Origin of the Velvet Underground" by Jim Condon, which identified Angus as the band's original drummer, who had also played with La Monte Young alongside the Velvets' John Cale. The article had sidebar interviews with Tony Conrad, Henry Flynt, and Terry Riley. It was likely the first place I encountered any of these names. There were no recordings of Angus available, and I don't think it was until I went to a tape concert in 1987 where La Monte played several of the 1962–63 recordings featuring Angus that I finally heard his hand drumming. I also attended another great tape concert devoted solely to MacLise that La Monte had organized at Dia Art Foundation in 1989, which included a twenty-minute tape of his cimbalom playing (which in turn greatly influenced my use of extended technique on guitar, using a screwdriver on the strings, as heard on *Sink the Aging Process* [Siltbreeze, 1994]), and a remarkable 1963 recording of MacLise with La Monte playing piano, Marian Zazeela on bowed gong, and Conrad on violin, which has never surfaced since.

Afterward, there was a discussion about Angus and his work by a panel of Ira Cohen, Catherine Christer Hennix, Gerard Malanga, Donald Miller, La Monte, and Marian. Gerard related a great anecdote about Angus attending a friend's wedding and then excusing himself to put on Native American warrior face paint midway through. In the program notes for the concert, La Monte wrote that Angus professed to have arrived at his complex, rhythmic conception of drumming after listening to the sound of the rain, following a teacher's advice. As a result, I have always listened to Angus's playing with that in mind, and often think of that story when I hear rain falling on a roof.

Nearly a decade later, I told my friend Tim Barnes about having seen a new MacLise bootleg in a store for $30, but passing on it because I was flat broke. Tim was intrigued and I told him a bit about Angus's background, which inspired him to not only track down the record himself but to begin putting out some of Angus's music on his own label, Quakebasket. About a year later, he issued Angus's soundtrack to Cohen's luminous film *Invasion of the Thunderbolt Pagoda* (1968). I used this as an excuse to pitch a story about Angus to the *Wire*, my second feature for them following a Maryanne Amacher article some months earlier. In October 1999, I interviewed Cohen, Malanga, Loren Standlee, Bill Breeze, and, significantly, Tony Conrad for the piece. Tony and I spoke over the phone, just as we had previously in 1989—practically ten years to the day—for the "Minimalism Update" article in *Option* that I co-authored with Neil Strauss, covering the work of Tony, Charlemagne Palestine, Phill Niblock, and Glenn Branca. Somewhat embarrassingly, my tape recorder malfunctioned, just as it had that first time. So, as with the transcript of that earlier interview, which appeared in the second Blank Forms anthology, *Music From the World Tomorrow* (2018), the source of this text is Tony's tape of the conversation. Luckily, Tony had been in a good mood, and he waxed rhapsodic about Angus, speaking of him in a way that I've never heard him talk about anyone or anything else.

This is October 20, and I'm sittin' here in a kitchen talking to Alan Licht on the phone. And it seems like I'm recording it on this twenty- to thirty-year-old Realistic [*laughs*] cassette player, and that's because his hot-dog new equipment doesn't work, *heh heh*. What is it you've got there? Oh, what I ought to do is put you on the speakerphone—then it would come out and I could send you the tape. I don't know. Then it would get there late, of course. OK, hold on. I'm turning up your volume a little bit. OK, let's go.

Did you meet Angus when he was playing with La Monte? Was that the first time you encountered him?

Oh yeah, yeah, yeah—that was exactly it. There was a fantastic series of concerts that took place in the summer of 1962 at the 10-4 Group Gallery, at the corner of Tenth Street and Fourth Avenue in New York. It was upstairs, and there would be this [*laughs*] beleaguered little band, toodling and whining into the afternoon in the most *remarkable* way, and what fascinated me about the thing that was going on there was that it was really an important confluence of several different sorts of impulses. One was the performative avant-garde impulse, as it was coming into focus through the same kind of energies that are revealed in Fluxus. That idea of things happening, and of things being mobilized and moved through time and space. The second was the Indian influence, which was manifest in a sort of fitful reaching out to work with the drone, and the third was the reversion from a formal kind of high art music to what was clearly an improvisational engagé kind of music—not in the political sense, but in the sense of a politics of music.

And in this band Angus played an important part, along with Billy Linich ["Billy Name"] and Marian

Zazeela. And La Monte of course displayed a peak energy phenomenon, which was truly remarkable. They were all really, completely way out there, and each of the crew seemed to participate in a heterophonic mishmash [*laughs*] that was loosely organized around these three themes, it seemed to me. It was extremely inspiring. The sense of time duration that inhabited these performances was very unusual because the performance seemed to have no particular beginning or end in view, but to be suspended in the middle of the waning afternoon light, and to occupy its own sort of inertia—which was sometimes interrupted when people went in the back to refresh or return to the band—and pursued a course toward some unknown musical goal.

So these were the concerts that really lured me into working in New York and discovering a way to practice music. *Phenomenal*. Great events. You can hear a little of this on the soundtrack to [Jack Smith's 1963 film] *Flaming Creatures*. La Monte and Marian contributed a ten-minute segment from one of these concerts to Jack's effort, and Jack wanted only a small amount of the material actually used in the soundtrack, so there's really only about a minute on the final soundtrack.

When I first met Angus personally, he was living upstairs from Jack in the rear house at 644 East Ninth Street, where Marian was paying the rent, and he invited me and Jack to stay in the course of things during that summer. So I was crashing there from time to time. Angus and [poet and filmmaker] Piero Heliczer lived upstairs, or appeared to, and a month later the place was emptied. Last time I went to look for it, it was a pile of masonry covered with dirt out in the back behind a club on Eighth Street. But Piero and Angus were buddies because they were both poets.

Had they gone to high school together?

Oh, I don't know. Could be. That might be it, I don't know. They were a year or two older than me. Piero had gone to Harvard, where he stole a Picasso statue, I understand, that was at one of the museums there. He didn't cash in on it or fence it or anything—he just took it home! Put it on his mantel because he liked it [*laughs*]. And when he was busted, he was dismissed.

You mentioned Jack Smith. How involved was Angus in the underground film scene at this time?

Oh my God, he was in the thick of it. This was a strange crossover environment. If you could say that there was a Fluxus scene and there was an underground movie scene, and that these things were somehow parallel channels, people who spent time with both and participated in the general demolition of high culture that resulted included myself and John Cale, Angus, Marian Zazeela, the Turtle [Stanley Alboum]—who was the drug dealer for the Factory crowd—Billy, Ondine—that's Bob Olivo—and a whole bunch of others [*laughs*].

But an indication of Angus's interest in the movie scene is this—I'm looking at this scenario for a drug film that Angus thought about doing at one point. This was a part of a scenario that he wrote for a three-part film, as he envisioned it, and what it says is [*reading aloud*]: "Is this too much of symbolic business? Could be altered in places a bit, and so change the whole thread and tone. Stress could be placed to bring out latent violences, slapsticks, different visual accumulations. Turned out by its own working, almost, to be a study in transitions or metamorphoses, begins a somber rite and gradually takes on mood of pagan mystification, then fairy tale, then a kind of high-minded comedy, then grotesque, then pathos, then moral anecdote, then nonsense tale, then tear-jerker. *Then*, knowing tale was done, especially as in last section where changes halt, turn about and go backward, then it gathers itself up for no reason at all and hurls itself into what it first seemed—tragedy, in its gathering storm but then—the grotesque enters again, fleeing king. Then the gruesome rites of the mob, then sinking in intensity to the merely disturbing, figure holding mask, and then plunging with focus change to bewilderment of last image, which offers an ending in sense of explaining and resolving the two segments. End of A, end of C. Enigmatic enough to demand such. But never brings into one focus the demon clearly present in every image, yet the demon is *there.*" And of course, *demon* is spelled "d-a-e-m-o-n."

That's from probably a little later, because Marian had paid the rent at this place at 644 East Ninth Street; the rent ran out after a month, and Piero and Kate [Heliczer] moved to Ludlow Street. I was looking for a place, and Piero alerted me that the place next door to him was available. So I moved next door to Piero and Kate. And then, as I had stayed with Jack, I invited Jack to stay with me, which he did for a considerable time, and so while we were living there, at 56 Ludlow Street, over the course of time [actor] Mario Montez moved into the apartment on the floor below, and Angus found it possible to move into the back apartment on the same floor. The landlord there—who was a rather lowbrow phenomenon, who used to collect the rent with a pistol, which he would pull back his coat to expose—somehow made a deal with Angus that if Angus improved the apartment, his rent would be lowered or compensated for. Angus took this to mean it might be improved by exposing the brick, and he proceeded to expose the brick by knocking the wall down [*laughs*]. In my recollection the electricity there went unpaid because Angus didn't have any money, really. He hardly ever had any money at the time, and he didn't like money. *Really, not interested*—sorry.

But with this density—urban density is the key to cultural progress—with this density, things happened. All kinds of things—dope [*laughs*], strange overtones of sexuality of various kinds. You know, drugs, sex, and rock and roll is sort of the theme, but it didn't really happen that straightforwardly at all. But Jack Smith was a powerful formative influence or element in that mix, and then the friendship between Piero and Angus was powerful, so that when Jack moved out and John Cale moved in it made another kind of mix possible. We used to play music; we used to hang and play music. I have the first tape I made with Angus, which is really beautiful but which was made on a very, very poor machine. The only machine that I had available to record at that time was one that Marian had left in her apartment, and it was a Revere machine, which was a crappy home brand, and it was built so that it would only take the very smallest reels, little five-inch tape reels, and would only operate at 3¾ ips [inches per second]. It also had a wobbly sound, so that the sounds that we made were irregular and weaved around tonally. The fact is, though, that this material continues to interest me, in part because of the way that it was very different from what was going on in the more disciplined context of the Dream Music and in the more rigidly formal framework that was suggested by the Fluxus aesthetic, if you could tweeze out that aspect of it. I'm not trying to say that Fluxus was rigid or formal per se, but there was a kind of bowler-hatted stiff-upper-lip character that went with Fluxus that was diffused to the nth degree in the underground scene, where there was no structure [*laughs*].

So we tended to play different instruments, sometimes instruments that were more sonorous or mellifluous, or with more sensual urgency, and Angus would often play flute—he would often play another instrument than drums. In fact, like a good musician, he could play any instrument. I remember one time Angus asked me, while we were over at the Dream Music space, “Hey Tony, can I try out the violin?” And I thought—this was when I didn’t know Angus that terribly well—I thought, sure, go ahead. “Try the violin, Angus,” I think to myself, thinking about long years of lessons and bitter frustrations and defeats [*laughs*]. Angus picked up the violin and played the shit out of it—immediately. Wham, wham, wham [*laughs*]. It was awesome. I couldn’t believe he could play the violin so beautifully, immediately. And I realized that percussion is a secret.

On May 19, 1963, we performed *Dream* [*The Second Dream of the High-Tension Line Stepdown Transformer*, 1962] by La Monte Young at [George] Segal’s farm [in New Jersey] as a part of the Yam Festival. La Monte, Marian, me, Jack, Joe Byrd and his girl [Dorothy Moskowitz], and Angus, playing lute, guitar, violin, mandola, viola, and mandolin and who knows what else. There was some opium there, and we had a chance to go out and smoke some opium in the back.

What would you say Angus’s influence was on the people he was working with—Jack, La Monte, and yourself?

Well, it’s different. I met La Monte in California, but when he moved to New York and I started to visit with him over on Bank Street, one of the things that would happen was, aside from the fact that there would often be different people hanging out around there—interesting people, by the way [*laughs*]—one of the things that would happen was Gagaku music would be playing, very loud, which was one of the most exquisite things in all of my early experience of New York. Another thing that would happen was that La Monte would bang on the refrigerator, picking out rhythms, like two against three or against four, different exciting rhythmic figures and polyrhythms and so forth. Angus was the only drummer that I've ever known that was so brilliant that he never played a rhythm . . . [*laughs*]. There's never been a drummer like Angus. He never played a rhythm. He could if he wanted to, and he did it as a gag—and if the rock people wanted to do it, OK, fine. But when Angus played, his music never had a rhythm. And the compilation which he gave me later, like ten years later—he came by my loft on Forty-Second Street and gave me a compilation, the definitive tape of Angus. You won't find three drumbeats in a row on there that are evenly measured. It's the most astonishing performance of drumming that I think has ever happened in the novel history of percussion. Things were happening at that time such as *Zyklus* [*für einen Schlagzeuger*, 1959] by Karlheinz Stockhausen, a piece which has very free notational elements and stresses the percussionist's ability to range over a variety of instruments and use a range of techniques, not only in performance but in reading the score [*laughs*]. But Angus achieved the kind of variety represented by this sort of piece using a bongo drum!

There was also an interest among us at that time in tabla playing, and by "us" I mean a whole cadre of people who were alert to the latest recordings. At that time there were really basically two Indian records available on disc in the US. I had some dubs of some 78-rpm records that a professor of musicology at Harvard had imported from India, but there were very few. La Monte had an important collection of several hours of tapes, many of Bismillah Khan and so forth, but we were avidly interested in figuring out what this tradition amounted to, this tradition which had so much structure and so much clarity, even accessible to a casual listener. It emerged that the rhythmic structure was very important, so the tabla was a focus of interest, and there were tabla solos that were interesting to listen to. The tabla was not dissimilar from the bongo, even though the tabla is a more complex tonal instrument than the bongo drums. The kind of things that Angus could do with a bongo drum compared favorably with tabla playing. It was an inspiration—who would believe that this young poet could do what he did with hand drums? I was so astonished by Angus's playing that I asked him how he could possibly have trained to do that. He said that he actually had studied tympani, and that he had performed in a high school orchestra. As I recall he said they played *The Rite of Spring* [1913], and I thought to myself, "Hmm, no small deal to beat your way through a Stravinsky work on percussion." So, he was capable—he could play music, he could play anything, but understood thoroughly that the poetry of expression that poured through his fingertips was the direction of his spirit and discovery.

Which must have been extremely unusual at the time.

I don't think there were that many real poets who were so clearly, as Angus was, inhabited by a mythic poetic sense. I mean, I read to you earlier a little piece from Angus that's about this film script, and I mentioned that he spelled demon "d-a-e-m-o-n" and so forth—Angus lived in this realm. He reported on mythic special places that he discovered, that he went to, where it was obvious that coincidence had driven him there—prior visitations of poets and spirits and people, a conjunction of different influences, some of them visible, some invisible, and where odd visions would occur. He had these experiences all the time. It was a kind of thing that I think was so natural, it had such a natural kinship to drug experiences, that it was small wonder that sometimes he would go off in that direction. I think for Angus, as a truly *possessed* poetic spirit, there was an affirmation that flowed through the drug experience that was extremely important to him. And seductive. I think, in some ways, maybe in later times he may have done too much dope. And I think that didn't help his health.

Did you have much of a sense of how he changed over the years?

None [*laughs*]. I don't think he changed at all. Because his spirit struck me as having such a separateness, of living in a world of poetic truth—a mythic world. He was involved with myth, with legend, in a way that seemed *medieval* and which he brought to the surface of *actuality* in the mid-twentieth century. It was really surprising. It was like you actually met a mystic monk [*laughs*], living in our very midst. Angus had a clear and open smile with a bit of the devil behind it—but a kind of a chuckle—that turned into himself, it turned to him, it turned back toward him, but it was also at the same time very giving, and there was something that wouldn't be negotiated fully with anyone else in his spirit. Now, you may say to yourself, "OK, these are metaphors for Angus being nuts." But that is wrong [*laughs*]—it's nothing of the kind. That's not what's happening here. His brain worked in a slightly different way from others', but not at all in a way that was a problem.

I mean there's more, but this is a good bunch of stuff. I saw Angus suddenly in the park—I was walking somewhere mundane, like LaGuardia Place, and I thought I'd seen the last of Angus. I thought, "God,

I'll never see him again," although he was the kind of person that if you loved him and thought about him, you felt bad that you didn't see him. Sometimes he was too way out, you know, but that's true of everybody. And suddenly there he was, and it was like he had never left. He was smiling, and he was peddling paper, handmade by monks in Tibet and in Nepal, and he was trying to make a living by wholesaling this paper to art stores. He pulls me aside and opens up his thing, and in there he's got original and commissioned artworks that he's imported from Nepal and Tibet, and I couldn't buy 'em. . . . And then he went off into the day, and I don't think I saw him again.

Did you talk to Ira [Cohen]?

I'm supposed to talk to him tomorrow night.

Ira will have a billion things to say. But the main thing that I can offer as far as the music is concerned, because Ira will talk about the poetry: There's what you hear and then there's the emanation that comes from the music, and what that meant. I found the music so surprising and vital and important and different that I've always been stunned that no one has found a way to talk about what Angus contributed. And although La Monte has made a few gestures to celebrate Angus's work, the language isn't there, really, to actually go in between the beats, dish out exactly what's happening. What would you need to do this? I don't know. You'd need a computer to follow the ictus and tease out exactly what the heck is happening syntactically, because the flow of Angus's music is like the flow of speech, and not like the flow of chanting or the artificial beat of feet marching. This is one of the things that I respect about him and his approach to music, is that there is nothing of marching in his music. Everything is inhabited by speech and by the kind of irregular movement—the wonder of that kind of irregular movement that you see in darting schools of fish—and dragonflies. It moves in a way that asks you for a kind of attentiveness, a tracking, a following, which takes a hundred turns a minute. It switches direction at lightning velocity, shoots off in a new direction, switches around, goes off in another direction, in a microsecond. What else can you say about music which sets up its own rhythm but fails to sustain it for more than a second or two?

There's a story about the hypnotist Milton Erickson that he relates in one of his essays, in which he says that he spoke in a way that was irregular in the rhythm of his delivery, and when he happened to be talking with an anthropologist at a university, the anthropologist commented that he had only heard [such] rhythmic pattern of speech among a certain very isolated tribe of South American Indians. In that sense, I think Angus's talking drum is a speech which comes from a tribe that inhabited the legendary space of his poetry.

Ira Kaplan & Georgia Hubley: On Hoboken, New Jersey

As an underground rock–obsessed teen, I felt privileged to grow up in New Jersey. Forget Springsteen and Southside Johnny; it was the state where Patti Smith, the Misfits, and the Feelies were from, and where the Velvet Underground played its first gig (at Summit High School, in the next town over from where I lived). At some point in middle school, I picked up a copy of *New York Rocker* that had a huge article about the burgeoning Hoboken music scene, written in part by Ira Kaplan. I met Ira Kaplan and Georgia Hubley around 1990; I was a Yo La Tengo fan by that time, and they liked my band, Love Child. After college, I moved to Hoboken and got to know them better by spending time at Maxwell's, the much-beloved local club and a mainstay of the indie-rock touring circuit in the '80s and '90s. Our bands played together a few times, and rehearsed in the same space on Grand Street in Hoboken.

My subsequent band, Run On, signed to Matador, the same label as Yo La, and we did European and US tours together. Although they moved around the corner from me, our schedules became more hectic and, ironically, I would bump into them less often. I left Hoboken in 1999, when my building was sold, and moved to Brooklyn. After that, I hardly ever went back to Hoboken, until I began rehearsing with Lee Ranaldo and the Dust there in the early 2010s.

Dike Blair and Bennett Simpson approached me in 2000 about interviewing Ira and Georgia on Maxwell's and Hoboken specifically, for a special section about New Jersey in the French fashion/art magazine *Purple*. I met up with them at Tonic, the Lower East Side music venue where I was working at the time. Tonic had a similarly homey vibe to Maxwell's but catered to both experimental music and indie rock, which in some ways made it a better fit for me. Tonic closed in 2007; Maxwell's closed in 2013, and I played the second-to-last night at the club as a member of the Ranaldo group; Ira and Georgia guested with the Bongos and the Individuals on the final night. They moved to Manhattan soon after.

So, Georgia, were you the first to move to Hoboken?

Georgia Hubley

We actually kind of moved there simultaneously, although not together. I think I was first. I moved there with my sister in 1980. I think he moved there a couple of months after.

Ira Kaplan

Yeah, straight after.

And what was the attraction?

GH Well, to be honest, I kind of moved kicking and screaming. I really didn't want to, but Emily, my sister, and I were sharing an apartment in the Village and she was definitely going to go. So I could either go with her or fend for myself in the Big City, which I grew up in, but . . . the apartment we lived in was pretty small, and getting another roommate just wasn't going to work. So I took the easy way out [*laughs*] and moved to Hoboken, but after a while I got to like it. We moved into this house that was huge.

Had you spent much time there before the move?

GH No, I'd probably only been there at night maybe once or twice—went to Maxwell's. I remember driving around trying to find it and it being really confusing, but I don't remember who I was with or what show I'd gone to see.

Ira, what about you?

IK Naturally [*laughing*] I can remember the first

show I saw at Maxwell's—the Individuals. I wouldn't say I moved there kicking and screaming. I'd been living someplace in Manhattan for free, but I'd definitely overstayed my welcome. I'd seen Georgia's apartment on Bleecker Street, and the East Village and other places that I could afford in New York didn't have much appeal. So there being a place that I liked going to in Hoboken made it more of a logical choice. But I also remember my first time going there, walking down Washington Street—the path to Maxwell's—and just really liking it. It was weird; all the B-level fast food places, it just seemed so . . .

It was so un–New York. And then you got to Maxwell's and it had the cosmopolitan taste but not the same trappings.

IK Yeah, it wasn't like any place or club in New York. It's funny now to look back, but the idea of a place that fed the bands seems so, like, humane.

GH The restaurant gave it a civilized feel. No rock club in New York had anything like that. I think nowadays there's places with more of that. Even Tonic has more of that. . . .

IK It's true. Tonic seems more like Maxwell's than anyplace in New York at the time did.

In New York you had places like the Peppermint Lounge or the Mudd Club there was this fashion and glamour element. Even Max's Kansas City still had some leftover reputation from having been a Warhol hangout in the '60s. No celebrities went to Maxwell's to hang out.

GH Except for Ron Wood, that one time [*laughs*].

And George Wendt[1] *would go, but that was way later. The "no frills" feel was definitely part of the appeal, especially in that era of the '80s when everything was so image-conscious.*

GH Or more underground-y places were more trashy, like A7 or something.

How did you guys get involved in working at Maxwell's?

IK [*Laughs.*] The guy who found the house that Georgia and Emily were living in, that I ultimately moved into—Danny Amis of the Raybeats—had left the Raybeats and was putting together another band, and a friend of his from Minnesota came out and stayed with us for a really long time. And it seemed like he would never leave unless he was told he had to leave—and he wasn't paying rent or anything.

*The man who came to dinner [*laughs*].*

IK At some point it looked like he might be doing sound at Maxwell's, and I remember saying to Steve Fallon,[2] "You can't hire him to do sound, hire me," and that's literally how I got the job. At the time, it was so low-key up there that Guy Ewald used to DJ and do sound, or Steve would do sound. There was no sound man; whoever wasn't busy ran the board.

How many nights a week did they have music?

1 The actor who played Norm on the TV show *Cheers* [1982–93].
2 The owner of Maxwell's.

GH I don't know; I thought in the beginning it was really a weekend-oriented place—

IK —if that; I think there were times where it was just one night a week. This may even be before we were there, but I remember it almost closing, or they weren't going to do it at all, and then they made it once a week. Like a lot of things, the threat of closing kind of rallied interest in it. The period when I was working there, the most common schedule was Thursday, Friday, and Saturday, with very occasional shows on other nights if a big name was there.

But when I started, even when I finished, I knew nothing—I was terrible at that job. To the point that when I started, I didn't even believe that midrange existed. Treble and bass should be plenty, what is this midrange knob in the middle?

*If it's not on a Fender Champ [amplifier], it can't mean anything [*laughs*].*

GH With that PA, it probably didn't make a lot of difference.

IK Georgia worked there too.

GH Right . . . I was DJing for a while. I had a regular night—although I don't remember what night it was [*laughs*]. But it was fun.

Were all the acts local at the time, or were there touring bands?

GH I think there were always touring bands there. The first time I *almost* went out there was when the Soft Boys came, and they only did a couple of shows. But I couldn't figure out, "Where is this place?" and "How am I going to get there?" and I ended up not going.

IK Another show I didn't go to, and you [Georgia] wouldn't have been living there yet, was X; X played there, 'cause Michael Hill talked about giving them a jump start after that show. There was always a big Athens [Georgia] connection there. The Human Switchboard played there a lot—even before they became Hoboken residents. I think there's a misnomer about the "Hoboken Sound"—the bands were united more in what they weren't, you know: New York groovy.

How did the community receive what was going on there?

GH My impression was that Maxwell's always had that not-belonging, outcast quality. Even living there today, I don't really feel any connection to the community, or the town of Hoboken.

I remember not long after I moved there, I was walking down one street wearing a leather jacket and this van slowed down and a guy opened the door and said, "Punk!" closed it, and took off.

IK I've always understood why people would resent us—we were interlopers. But I've never quite understood why Maxwell's was resented—because they weren't interlopers, they were from New Jersey and they started a business. When the *Hoboken Reporter* was running those letters week after week about the Feast of Madonna Dei Martiri, the Catholic festival where fireworks are set off in the summertime, and the new residents would complain about the noise, and the people who had lived in Hoboken for years were writing letters like—

"If you don't like it . . ."

IK Yeah. And the letters were frequently foolishly articulated but I thought they were exactly right.

How did Maxwell's factor into getting Yo La Tengo off the ground?

GH Mostly it was Steve who just made it easy.

IK And I'm sure deceptively easy. Even before the band existed, we had some parties there where we'd play with people we knew, and we'd just say to Steve, "We want to have a party," and he'd say, "OK." Then, when Yo La Tengo started and we asked to play, he said, "Sure." We had an idea to play every Wednesday night and he let us do that, too. It's hard to imagine now an established club anywhere—maybe it happens in other cities—saying to an unestablished band that they could play four times in a month.

*What kind of bands were you playing with? Were there any "big breaks"? [*Laughs.*]*

GH I think maybe the Go-Betweens. It was a big deal when we played with them.

IK Our first show, which was a party, and then the four Wednesdays, which essentially were parties as well, were all with Antietam. Our real shows, the first was with the Turbines, which I don't think was quite such a big break; the bigger break was Green on Red.

GH Oh yeah, yeah.

Steve was also doing Coyote Records in the '80s, which you recorded your first few records for, so it was quite a little empire he had going—

IK And Pier Platters[3] too. He was an owner of Pier Platters and then he got bought out pretty quick, I guess.

That makes a good segue into where I fit into the picture. Growing up in Millburn, New Jersey, Hoboken was just a place to change trains to get into Manhattan—no one seemed to know anything about it other than that, or that On the Waterfront *[1954] was set there, and it being Frank Sinatra's hometown. Then I had a cousin who moved there, who lived on Bloomfield between Sixth and Seventh, the same area that I lived in years later. When I was a kid, my dream had been to move to Greenwich Village, but in high school I started going to Pier Platters and following the music scene in Hoboken. That struck me as a much more reasonable and up-to-date version of the dream. Moving to the Village in 1990 would have been a lot different than moving there in 1960; in 1990, when I moved to Hoboken, my share of the rent was $225 a month. Even for that time, it was dirt cheap; it was like the house that time forgot over there.*

IK We paid very little rent at that time because the landlord had that house as an investment, so he didn't care about raising the rent.

The first show I saw at Maxwell's was the Angry Samoans in 1987.

3 An independent record store in Hoboken.

IK We were there; Metal Mike was staying at our house.

I think I spent an hour trying to find parking.

GH Was Love Child started before you moved to Hoboken?

Yeah, by a couple of years—we were all in college together at Vassar. We played Maxwell's a number of times before I moved there. One of our earliest club gigs was opening for Big Dipper there. Ultimately, we played there more than any other club. And sometimes I'd hang out there even if I didn't care about the bands playing on a given night. For a lot of people in New Jersey who were interested in the music and paranoid about driving into Manhattan, it was easier. . . .

IK It was also cheaper: it was cheaper to get in and the beer was cheaper.

It was just a more inviting atmosphere. I remember numerous hour-long conversations I had there with different people, which maybe could have also happened on the street outside of CBGB, hanging out during the summer, but I can't think of any other club where that would have happened.

IK Well, the layout of the club is so great, where you can be inside but not in the back room.

Todd [Abramson] started booking there in the late '80s?

IK Well, I think Steve started losing interest. . . . For one thing, it got bigger, it took more work, and I think he just didn't have the desire to work as hard as the club started to require. R.E.M. and the Feelies both did a lot to boost it. It was the one place that the Feelies were really comfortable in, so it got to the point that they would only play Maxwell's; it seemed like they almost never played New York during that period, and all the side project bands played there. And then R.E.M.—there may be other bands, but that's the one I can really think of that continued to play there even after their popularity dictated they shouldn't. Just a band that liked being there and continued to play there, which set a tone for others to do that. Once again, I don't have a timeline, but I was aware of Sonic Youth doing warm-up shows there before albums came out.

GH I remember them doing that once.

IK Just once, really?

GH They probably played there more than once, for sure, but . . .

IK But it was still another situation where they were bigger than the club. I booked it for a month 'cause Steve wanted a month off; Michael [Hill] and I had probably been doing the Folk City series either at the same time or right around that time. I think the next year he wanted a month off again and he got Todd to do it, and Todd may have just never stopped after that.

GH I think that was the mid-to-late '80s.[4]

Were you sharing the house with Todd at that point?

4 Abramson took over booking in May 1986.

GH We got married in '87 and he was definitely living there then.

Todd is also from two towns over from where I grew up. . . . I was thinking of the normal institutions that constitute any town with respect to Hoboken—the school system, for example. I heard that the high school was not even accredited by the state of New Jersey. I was on a bus in Hoboken once and someone behind me was talking about all their arrests and upcoming criminal-court appearances; then they paused and said, "If I can just graduate from Hoboken High I think I'll be OK!" [Laughs.]

IK It seems so bizarre that even with the influx of money in Hoboken, the school system—which we know the way you do, only anecdotally—

GH —that nobody can turn Hoboken into a desirable place to—

Right, 'cause they either send their kids to private school or they move out.

IK It just seems like such a wasted opportunity. You look at the difference between Hoboken and Park Slope: Hoboken, in its proximity to New York, could have been, maybe should have been, a community like that. It seems to be a way station; you come there for a couple of years, then you go to Maplewood to have a family and put your kids in school.

I think that's always been the criticism of the gentrification there, that the people who move there don't really put anything back into the community. They take their train to Wall Street and come back.

GH But it's built up that way; they're building housing units for those specific people.

Right, they're like dormitories.

GH Yeah.

IK Yeah. This is speculation, but you would think that some more far-reaching city planning could have done something about that. But it's true, the proximity to Wall Street may have made that impossible, which is something different than Park Slope.

Transportation in general is a real issue there. Especially when I first moved in, the Red Apple and NJ Transit buses would be trying to cut each other off on Washington Street—

GH Oh they still do that, I had that happen to me today.

*Very shortly after I moved there, I was waiting for the bus, and a Red Apple pulled over, and the driver was arrested! [*IK laughs.*] I think he was also the owner of the company, or a dispatcher; I think they would double up and he would sometimes drive a bus.*

GH It's not Red Apple anymore, it's Academy.

I learned that only last week, when I went out to see Will Oldham at Maxwell's.

IK Another thing that made Hoboken attractive to me, or exotic, was the PATH train. New York subway service has improved quite a bit since that time, but you would get on this train that was literally thirty cents at the time, and was always clean and rarely stopped between stations [*laughs*].

And the movie theater.

IK That is right up there with the school system [*AL laughs*]. That's one area where quality of life has really dropped in Hoboken. When we first moved there, we used to go to the movie theater—especially me, but both of us—twice a week. No one would ever go there except on weekends. It was always double features; if they were two movies I hadn't seen, I would go no matter what they were. It was cheap and it had a few quirks—like they'd start the movies before the published time. But you know, you could learn that pretty easily. They closed it for a while to renovate, but it was just as bad when they reopened. For some reason, they can't show movies in focus.

*I've only been to the movie theater once or twice, but I remember they used the wrong lens for the trailers and at least part of the way into the feature, and the image didn't fit on the screen. We went to buy tickets and the booth window had been smashed and taped back together. You couldn't see the person inside—this hand would come out and clutch for your money [*laughs*].*

IK That used to be part of the appeal when the programming was *Psycho From Texas* [1975], but when it became, you know, *Primary Colors* [1998] and *Casino* [1995], you thought maybe this should be shown in focus [*laughs*]. It's frustrating, again, with the number of people in that city, that there is not a movie theater; it's incredible. But two places to paint your pottery.

I've been reminded of Hoboken a few times while touring.

GH Really?

*Maybe it was in Iceland, where the colors of the houses are weird and distinctive—one of the things I liked about Hoboken. Even though the house I lived in was this ugly, aluminum-sided thing that was just thrown up in what looked like a day and a half, a lot of the houses there are very pretty, especially on Garden Street. And there was one time I was somewhere in South Dakota on tour, and we were "doing" Main Street and I thought, "I'm glad I don't live here," and then when I got back to Hoboken I thought, "You know what?" [*Laughs.*] "Washington Street is kind of reminding me of Main Street that afternoon in South Dakota."*

GH It used to remind me more of Baltimore, where I lived for a while, just 'cause all the houses were the same height, three stories; in Baltimore a lot of the houses are like that.

That's a real complaint with the new high-rises: before, you could look out your window and see the New York skyline, no matter how far back you lived.

IK I guess that's why it doesn't really remind me of anywhere else, because it does seem like such a wasted opportunity, what's happened there; nobody thinks three steps ahead for anything. A city with forty-five realtors, no movie theater, and one supermarket—one *bad* supermarket.

GH Plenty of pottery opportunities [*laughs*].

That's one of the things that disturbed me, because I grew up in a town where they had three gourmet ice cream stores but no bookstore. So when this stream of boutiques started opening, like Please Kiln Me—

IK [*Laughs.*] Was that really a place in Hoboken?

Oh no wait, that was a joke someone made.

IK There was A Time to Kiln, that's definitely there.

When was the last time you went to Maxwell's?

GH We actually just went there two Saturdays ago—pretty recently—although we hadn't been there before in a really long time.

I went last week and that was the first time I'd been there, or in Hoboken at all, since I moved out a year and a half ago. It seemed almost exactly the same as when I left, which was certainly not the same as when I first started going there.

GH Actually the night we went—I'm sure it was totally packed for Will Oldham—but we went to see Amy Rigby, and it was really reminding me of the old days. Maybe not the highlight of the Maxwell's era [*laughs*], but there were not that many people there, and you looked around at some of the people who were there and they seemed to be completely oblivious to the fact that they paid money to come and see this music. A couple of them were kind of rowdy in that New Jersey way; it was a throwback. I'm sure that was an isolated incident but it was really bizarre.

IK Yeah, we don't go there that often anymore.

GH Of course, we don't really go anywhere that often anymore.

IK Our friends don't play there very much—Antietam, Sleepyhead, or Rick Brown and Sue Garner, they play New York when they do shows. Maxwell's has changed in that regard, it's more of a stop on people's tours than it was.

It's true, looking back, most of the people we played with when we didn't even have a full-length album out, just a single . . . I'm trying to remember if our album was out when we played with Pavement; we played this show with them there, and Soul Asylum had done an early acoustic set, and they just split right afterward, and Todd hadn't paid them. So at the end of the night when he was paying us and Pavement, it was the money from our show plus . . . I think they were just kind of doing it to do it, they had a big show, or maybe more than one big show, in New York, and maybe like you were saying with R.E.M., they wanted to touch base with Maxwell's while they were in town; that's probably why they did it acoustic, not as a serious show. But as far as I know they just blew the money off.

GH [*Laughs.*] They might come looking for it now.

*I lived for a month on what I made that night [*laughs*]. But to play there was kind of a big deal at that point: it was still a center point for the scene; Pier Platters was still open and it was still the place where everyone went to buy records, whatever new single was coming out. Within a few years, that all dissipated and the scene changed to where it wasn't about the new cool seven-inch but what band that just played Maxwell's had signed to a major label. It became a different set of priorities.*

GH I think we missed that era of Maxwell's [*laughs*].

When I first moved there, the rehearsal space was three blocks from my house, the record store was seven blocks from my house, the club was seven blocks from my house—that's what my life was at that point.

We could talk about that rehearsal space: you guys rehearsed there, Love Child rehearsed there, Sonic Youth rehearsed there, Das Damen . . . that was another focal point.

IK Tiny Lights, the Raunch Hands.

GH They were, really?

IK That was the room we shared with them, the first room we were in.

*No stairs [*laughs*]—that was probably the prime selling point. Other than that, it was pretty rough.*

IK It was pretty shocking when we went to our current space to find that it could be warm during the winter and cool during the summer.

*The changing seasons [*laughs*].*

IK It's interesting. That space, when we were able to start practicing during the day, it made a difference—we could play quieter, more often, certain songs you couldn't rehearse if there was another band playing in the building. That was just not something that we had to worry about as often in that place.

It's now a parking lot, is that right?

IK No, it's now the Millenium Condominium building, that's *Millenium* with one *n*. They were in such a hurry to get that building put up, they didn't have enough time to consult the dictionary [*laughs*].

GH They got that thing down and up so fast. . . .

What used to be Pier Platters is still a real estate agency?

IK Of course now Hoboken is like Forty-Eighth Street.

Well, Guitar Bar, is there another music store?

IK There's another store two doors down—another vintage guitar store.

GH That's bizarre.

IK Sort of exemplifying the best of Hoboken—I've never been in a music store that I find as comfortable as Guitar Bar, in the way Maxwell's felt years ago.

So how do you feel about Frank Sinatra after twenty years of living in Hoboken?

GH Probably the same as I felt before [*laughs*].

IK I like that aspect of it, actually, the identification and the pride. It also seemed pretty appropriate to my feelings about Hoboken that Sinatra himself did not share those feelings [*laughs*]. That just seemed to capture the spirit of the city, that he was born there and couldn't wait to get out and never came back again, except that one time with Reagan. That was an amazing day. You weren't living in Hoboken then, were you?

No.

IK In a city of that size, when the Secret Service gets to town, you *know* it. I can remember walking from Foodtown and back to our house, which may have been the route that they were going to be on, but I definitely felt the presence of people on rooftops, helicopters going overhead.

I kind of liked the fact that whenever you walked by Piccolo's, the cheesesteak place, they were always playing Sinatra out of a loudspeaker.

IK We've always [enjoyed] cheesesteak as travelers; a cheesesteak for us is something we do when we're in Philadelphia; we rarely indulge when we're at home. I don't know if you've seen the library's CD collection, but it's kind of half Sinatra and half everything else [*Georgia laughs*].

If someone offered you a huge apartment in Manhattan for very little money, would you take it?

GH I would take it [*laughs*]. At least you think you would, because it's not going to happen [*Ira laughs*].

I mean, anybody would. Or an equivalent to what you have now, in Manhattan.

GH I'm sure I would; I'd rather live in Manhattan, if I could have this, this, and this. . . .

IK But I'm sure we'd miss things that we take for granted now.

GH Yeah, I think so.

There's something to be said for the isolation.

GH I like that about it, it's true.

You're five minutes away from Manhattan, yet you're—

GH Worlds away.

Yeah, worlds away. Even for being in a band, it was easier to focus on doing band stuff in comparative isolation than if you were practicing in the Music Building[5] *or in some basement on Ludlow Street.*

GH Right, I'm sure that part of it I would not enjoy.

Because you can't get into the fantasy of it there; you're too reminded of reality at every turn. In the Music Building you look out the window and you see Midtown, the Port Authority. Everything that Love Child did post-Vassar was either in our parents' houses further out in New Jersey or in that space in Hoboken; in both situations, you were really removed. That sense of being the only band in the world in that one space, at that one moment, fuels the fun of it, and energizes it.

IK It *is* special, it certainly makes a difference. I've always thought that if we were under other

5 A long-running rehearsal space on Eighth Avenue and Thirty-Ninth Street.

circumstances, which I'd hope would be no worse, it would certainly be different, that feeling.

GH If you are in a band and you're renting out hourly places, a lot of people have to do that, and they're coming from work, so then it's like, "We've got two hours here, and then I've got to go do this and that." I'm sure it would be a different way of thinking, very schedule-oriented. . . . It's nice to have it be pretty open.

When I was getting ready to go on tour with Papa M, we would just rehearse in Dave [Pajo's] basement in Louisville. He lives in a neighborhood that's very suburban, and he records his records in his basement, too. And you can kind of hear that in the stuff that he does; it's not part of the rat race or a big-city music scene; it's taking place in this one little house in the suburbs. A lot of the whole punk thing is pretty suburban anyway, like the Modern Lovers or the Stooges.

IK Where we are, it's more than physical—

GH It's mental.

IK We have the feeling that there are few places in the world we can go where we are more unknown than Hoboken. When we went to Chapel Hill last week, the first place we went to was a coffee shop; you're in a city with so many bands and so many college kids, it's likely people are going to know who we are. The first place we went, somebody asked what we're doing there, but in Hoboken, unless somebody knows us personally, nobody has a clue our band exists, and it's a really cool feeling.

GH There was that one day I went to the supermarket

and there was this guy with our T-shirt on, which was so bizarre. I was like, "This is so wrong." [*Laughs.*]

Karl Precoda

Karl Precoda was not only the most exciting guitarist to come out of the so-called Paisley Underground of Los Angeles in the early '80s but was also, arguably, the most exciting one in the entire genre of "college rock"—as that music was known in the period before "alternative" and "indie" came into parlance. On the Dream Syndicate's classic debut album, *The Days of Wine and Roses* (Ruby Records/Slash, 1982) he splays out caustic solos rippling with feedback, deftly navigating the space between the Velvets' "I Heard Her Call My Name" and Mountain's "Mississippi Queen." He left the band after their second album, *Medicine Show* (A&M Records, 1984); played in the Droogs during the late '80s; and then pursued a career in academia. In the late '90s he formed an improvising rock band, the Last Days of May, who recorded four albums.

I saw the Last Days open for Will Oldham at Tokyo Rose in Charlottesville, Virginia, circa 2000, and I met Karl after the show. Precoda's work in the Dream Syndicate had been a key influence for me as a player, and in those years I was still weighing working with structured songs in rock bands versus performing in more ad hoc settings with improvisers. So I wanted to talk with him further, especially about his current thoughts on improvised music. I was also curious as to whether he and his Dream Syndicate bandmate Dennis Duck, who had been involved with the Los Angeles Free Music Society since the '70s (and, incidentally, was the one who had owned a copy of the Tony Conrad album from which the band took its name), had discussed improvisation much back then. (Precoda didn't want to talk about the band, but he did say he had no idea that Dennis was making any other music during the time they played together.) We had this discussion by phone shortly after that night, with the idea that I might try to place it somewhere as a Q and A. At one point, Yuzo

Sakuramoto had intended to start a new magazine, post-*Music*, and we had discussed the possibility of running this interview there. The magazine never came to pass, and this interview remained unpublished until now.

I suppose the basic premise of talking about improvisation—where it comes from, or why—is that it represents a kind of leading-edge expression, more interesting or sophisticated than the three-minute pop song.

It's actually a more basic way of making music, one that had gotten lost because of Western classical traditions.

Which are continuous with the eight-hundred-year progress of modernization. You have the progress of modernity, and we've reached a point now where we want to call it postmodernity, but in fact it's still modernity, the phenomena that you're describing: technological progress, advancement, and all that stuff. Everything comes out of the Enlightenment, which was all about precision, specialization, and compartmentalization. You've got thousands of people writing songs or compositions attempting to create a dream reality, an Apollonian dream of reality, like pop songs—an Apollonian dream of perfection.

Right, I said in my CD Evan Dando of Noise *[Corpus Hermeticum, 1997] that songs are dreams and improvisations are your subconscious.*

To be perfectly Nietzschean: songs want to be Apollonian, whereas improvisation tends toward the Dionysian. Except if you look at the reception of songs that have connected with mass audiences gathered in masses.

There were all those bands in the late '60s who were walking a line between the two, whether Quicksilver Messenger Service, the Dead, Pink Floyd, or the Velvet Underground. These bands would take a song and then, in the middle, there would be this kind of free-for-all, and then work their way back into the song.

Right, that Nietzschean balance. From my own perspective, I'm not sure I have a lot of Apollonian elements, because I didn't discard traditional elements at a higher rate than I acquired them. Many of us have no conception of all the forces that conspired to convince [us] that the three-minute pop song is the apex of Western culture—ironically or not, irony being a defense against the weight of history. "How can what I do be actually meaningful now that such-and-such commercial sellout does it?" Well, I'll do it anyway because I don't know what else to do, or I'm still chasing that romantic dream. But I wonder if improvisers are similarly confused, in the sense that they don't necessarily recognize the weight of history that is behind them. I wonder if improvisers are any more clued in to history than the pop songsters that they propose to replace or supplement.

Especially in European improvisation, there's this whole political motivation behind some of it. With a group like AMM there's an idea of working together to produce something apart from the commercial world, which they relate to communism.

Look at, say, Freud, how Freud describes civilization as this increasingly impassive bureaucratic monolith. The monument of modernity is this institution, of which the three-minute pop song is a perfect commodity, dispensed from a vending machine. Latent in Freud is the idea that through some sort of polymorphous activity one might be able to defeat this enormous machine. If you somehow give free play to Eros—that's the only thing to counterbalance the death drive of Thanatos, represented by the forces of modernization. And the great critique of the Frankfurt School shows you how the concentration camps are the absolutely logical outcome of these forces. When you've got that enormous technological capacity, how are you going to keep people from exterminating every one of us? That's what Freud asked. So improvisation, according to that, has this incredibly optimistic view that by dispensing with structures we can express our innate goodness. This probably goes hand in hand with what you said about socialism or communism—these are deeply romantic people who think that improvisation shows whatever is good about the human spirit.

Does improvisation try to discard language and get back to a direct kind of communication?

A lot of times improvising people are using instruments to create a syntax beyond the accepted one. Keith Rowe just has a guitar lying on a table, doesn't tune it, uses different implements on it; he's not playing it in the accepted fashion. Derek Bailey's another one, playing clusters and odd harmonics.

And he was really good at it.

He was already a good guitar player. But both in music and in film, if something isn't essentially narrative, it's dismissed as not being valid. Poetry, though, is acceptable as nonnarrative. No one really says that a poet can't write the same way that someone could listen to Keith Rowe or Derek Bailey and say, "Oh, he can't play."

Well, generally poetry is taken to be a challenge to the "prison house of language," or the prison house of narrative. The idea that narrative is a logical system implies a logical order to the world. Poetry implies an order but it's not logical—*onto*logical. And I think in its modern existence poetry has been swatted off as a kind of alternative realm that we need as a sort of curative. The whole academic reception of poetry in this country anyway was all about resisting the tyranny of science, the idea that you could have higher education reduced to a practical engineering sciences curriculum; you needed to have poetry occupy a legitimate sphere of higher education precisely to challenge ideas of progress for its own sake. We have to progress, right? The economy has to grow, we have to discover more stuff, we have to make life easier, more efficient, better [*laughs*]—that's just what we have to do, use these techniques to manipulate reality. And of course poetry questions that in a pretty severe way most of the time. Poetry is about challenging how you use your time. If you use your time to get from A to B to execute a plan, or if you use your time to live in the world, to live ontologically, to find a way of being. Curiously, poetry has a closer relationship to reality than does narrative. Isn't that strange? [*Laughs.*] Poetry is very specifically about the mapping of specific amounts of time: How do you transcribe this period of time? Whereas narrative is about imposing order. Poetry is so anti-modern, so non-useful; it's returning to that primitive mode in which ritual would be about transcribing reality. That's probably what's going on in the cave paintings—somebody is trying to transcribe reality in a way that we don't recognize now. Today, if you want to transcribe reality, sit and listen to it, whether you're in New York City or out on the frontier.

There's a lot to listen to. What you said about trying to get from A to B more efficiently—I think this is really at the core of why human beings have evolved into human beings, and why they've dominated the world, and why our brains have developed to the extent they have. Originally, we were more on an even keel with the rest of the species, and because man proved to be a better toolmaker—

Language maker—

The fact that we had thumbs. That gave us the edge over the rest—

I think opossums have thumbs.

OK, but human beings became the one species that wanted to take over the world. That's an inherent feature of human identity.

To take it back to Nietzsche: If you get a pack of dogs together, you get a more Dionysian expression of "dog" than you do with just one dog, but toolmaking, symbol making: we're talking about the Apollonian side of human beings. That one pole, or capacity, is greatly exaggerated above other animals. The human being, unlike virtually any other creature, is able to imagine or to dream perfection, and that leads to progress, civilization, material comforts.

And problems.

And extermination camps. The Nuremberg rallies were purportedly a very Dionysian situation, wrapping thousands of people into a single organism, but I'd suppose that some of their sensations weren't totally unrelated to those of the crowds seeing the Beatles at the Cow Palace or Shea Stadium a generation later. Right-wing cultural critics in the 1960s always seized on that comparison.

I was watching Gimme Shelter *[1970] again recently. When you look at the audience screaming in the midst of the violence it's not that different from the girls screaming at the Beatles in Shea Stadium.*

And that's the substance, historically speaking, of right-wing critiques of rock and roll: that it unleashes a Dionysian frenzy in which human reason is lost—remember, right-wing critics used to be overwhelmingly Apollonian in their outlook; they could all see the ideal world if everybody would just wear a tie and stand up straight. . . . Put these dirty beatniks in their place.[1] So this helps counteract the incipient tragedy of Apollonianism and yet has the potential to unleash even more devastating problems. Not that Altamont was really comparable to Nuremberg, much less to the concentration camps, but improvised music, by virtue of being so obscure . . . no one ever got stabbed at an improv show.

Speaking of stabbing, a cliché of American literary modernism lives in Hemingway's description of great matadors, the greatest physical improvisers. It's the purity of their gestures, their absolute grace, avoiding total destruction by inches, then standing their ground as the bull charges, and from a foot away putting the sword in perfectly, dropping the bull on the spot.

Is bullfighting an example of—this is probably true of sports or any creative function—is improvising a way of stripping your needs down to thinking about one thing and one thing only?

You want to locate that essential need. There's

1 Certainly, the symbolic expression of "right wing" has changed substantially since this interview was conducted.—KP

a real question of whether or not there is an essential human character or essential human spirit. All those words sound like fictitious terms. If you spend your time with poststructuralist philosophers, you find that human beings are constructed at the intersections of existing structures, and that there is virtually no space on the grid where human beings are essentially themselves, as opposed to a composite of predetermined possibilities. Foucault was criticized for this, and called pessimistic. He didn't seem to allow any space for human agency; everything seemed to be totally determined, so in that sense he was more of a structuralist, a structuralist attempting to put some kind of value, abstractly assigned value, to every single deterministic moment or every single decision. So what is actually human doesn't even exist. We don't have a preference, we just have culturally instilled preferences. A human being does not have a necessity to create art—it has a culturally instilled ethic [*laughs*] from the Romantics, which says, "If you're really an artist you have to do it spontaneously, you have to feel you're compelled to do it, and you have to constantly reiterate this claim." The post-Romantic, modernist quest is to find the one essential, pure gesture, which is simultaneously revealed to be a "necessary fiction," to quote Wallace Stevens. Confronting this idea of fiction, the postmodern notion that there is no essential human identity naturally follows.

But the fact that you have to create an identity as an individual is unique to human beings.

Foucault, late in his life, says something like, "Well, actually, in the intersections where these various structures meet there's a little bit of play, a little bit of slippage, and in those cracks between the various discourses that outline the world I can do other things."

I guess you could either be a positive postmodernist or a negative one, the negative one simply saying, "We're caught in the structure of late capitalism and everything you do is determined, including your record collection," and the positive one saying, "Well, if I assemble things the right way, if my record collection is broad enough, if I can have Fela records over here and Leslie West records over here, somehow, in this, I can actually determine who I am, and I can express that to other people. My juxtaposition of the brands, as opposed to the brands themselves."

Is it plausible to imagine being satisfied with your own work? Is there a lag time? Like the poet Alexander Pope, supposedly, whenever he wrote something he put it on the shelf for two years. If he came back to it and still liked it, then he'd put it out.

It's a good idea. It's really true of songs. If you're going to put a song out, it's like a romantic relationship; you might not want to get involved if you're going to be bored with it in two months. The best songs are the ones that are built to last.

But you can't tell if they're built to last until they do last. With recorded improvisation it seems you just put it right out [*laughs*]. "I just did it, here it is." But maybe that's the place for Apollonian judgment.

That brings up the whole question of how appropriate releasing recordings of free improvisation is. Someone like Derek Bailey, despite the fact that he owns and operates his own record label, is not a fan at all of recordings of improvised music. After the time and place of the original event, it's time to move on to something else.

But the problem is that the time and the place often doesn't include—

*—most of the human race [*laughs*].*

Right, the best music you've ever played, or at least a fair amount of it, there was no one around to hear it.

But is that why it was the best music you ever played?

No, I don't think so. But this question of improvisation—does it become simply another method of being cooler? Me being an improviser, am I cooler than somebody who's just in a jam band, who by themselves are cooler than somebody who's just a folk singer? I wouldn't claim any of those things.

Maybe some people are doing it now because it's better publicized or disseminated than it was thirty years ago, but you have to arrive at it through an understanding of your own motivations. In coming around to improvisation as a pursuit, my realization was partially from asking myself, what did I like about [the Doors'] "Light My Fire"—was it really the verse or the chorus, or was it that whole section in the middle where they're improvising over this two-chord vamp? And then when I heard John Coltrane I realized it was the same thing. In fact they quote "Afro Blue" in "Universal Mind," which is on the Doors' Absolutely Live *[Elektra, 1970]. Or "European Son" by the Velvet Underground—the song part is OK, but I really like the next five minutes or so where they just go crazy. And that was how I learned guitar, playing along with these records. I would not copy the solos but would play my own solos along with "Light*

My Fire," and once the middle section was over, I'd just go back and do it again.

See, I never did that. I understand exactly what you mean, about which part of a song did I like, except I don't think I did that. I think I was too lazy to make that leap right there. I'm not altogether lazy in every area, but musically I've always felt that way.

What if I were to say that I improvise because I'm lazy? Would that appear higher or lower?

To a certain extent, I'm an improviser because I like the fact that mistakes are part of the game. I don't want to get up there and think, "If I make a mistake it's gonna blow the whole thing." In improvisation, if you make a mistake, that becomes another way to go.

That's decisively anti-Apollonian, to embrace the mistake. If you want to look for an essential human quality, it's probably making errors.

This is a whole genre of leaving mistakes in, whether it's Ed Wood, or this movie Truck Turner *[1974], a blaxploitation film with Isaac Hayes. There's one scene where Hayes and this other guy are talking. One line is really stupid and they both start laughing. It's obvious that the two actors are laughing at the line, and they just left it in there. Harmony Korine calls himself a "mistakist filmmaker" 'cause he leaves all the mistakes in.*

But does that count? Can you actually be a mistakist or have you just commodified an aesthetic?

People are still resistant to mistakes.

But, I mean, I try not to make mistakes, at whatever

I do. But if I make 'em, it doesn't preoccupy me. I don't spend time trying to pretend they don't exist.

But do you find something interesting in them?

I find it interesting that it's the essence of human behavior. And when you talk about the urge to dominate—human history, the progression to modernization—obviously it's founded on nothing but mistakes. It's the High Middle Ages and we're trying to build a Gothic cathedral, we're trying to cover Europe with Gothic cathedrals—think how many times you drop six tons of stone on the heads of the village workmen. Think of the generational carnage just in building one cathedral. "This wall just can't hold this arch, let's move it by a couple of degrees. Oops, did it again. Let's put a flying buttress here."

Suicide 111

Suicide was formed in New York at the dawn of the '70s by light sculptor and vocalist Alan Vega and keyboardist Martin Rev, proving to be one of the most unnerving, farsighted, and controversial bands in the annals of rock history. Stripping the music down to the bare essentials of voice, a drum machine, and a keyboard, adopting a fearsome leather-and-chains image well before it was fashionable, they presaged the shock tactics of punk and No Wave in their infamous, polarizing performances that antagonized concertgoers and sometimes maddened even their most devoted followers. But they also anticipated the post-guitar electronic mindset of Depeche Mode and others, and their influence continues—every few years, there seems to be a new microtrend that can be traced back to the Rev-Vega duo in some way. Suicide occupied a paradoxical position as a band that represented to its high-profile fans such Bruce Springsteen and Ric Ocasek the ultimate in a kind of deviant rock-and-roll purism but one that was also guaranteed to alienate 98 percent of rock's mass audience. It's hard to think of a more perfectly realized debut than their 1977 self-titled album; on the strength of that material, they maintained a career, albeit sporadically, for the next four decades, until Vega's death in 2018.

Suicide was never exactly prolific; several years passed between all but one of their albums, but fortuitously *American Supreme* (Mute) came along in 2002, when I was doing features for the *Wire*. The magazine contacted me, typically, at the last minute—I did the interview on a Thursday afternoon and handed in a five-thousand-word cover story the following Monday. We met in a hotel room at the Roxy in TriBeCa that Mute Records had rented for them to do press in. Rev and Vega were a great tag team and a great interview—for every question I rattled off, they would wax on for ten minutes. The only time they got wiggy was when it came time to do the photo shoot with Chris Buck (a great guy who also photographed Lou Reed when I did the *Wire* feature on him that December). The chosen tiki bar–style backdrop was not to their liking—“What is this, tropical Suicide?” an irked Vega snorted—but that was ironed out and everyone went home happy. To this day, Martin Rev tells me the *Wire* piece stands out in his mind as the best article ever done about the band.

The things that people are going to comment on the most about American Supreme *are the hip-hop element and the post–9/11 things about it. Let's talk about the hip-hop first—that's a new area for you guys to work in.*

Martin Rev

That's the direction we were in that just came out of us. It's not quite hip-hop; it's groove-oriented.

There's scratching and stuff like that.

MR Yeah, but it doesn't seem to be scratching in the same way; it's used in another context. On a Suicide record, it sounds different than if it's being scratched on a hip-hop record.

Alan Vega

Somebody asked me to describe this album; they hadn't heard it. I said, "It sounds like the Supremes, Thelonious Monk, and everything in between," because there's a lot of those different kinds of influences. That's why I like the title, *American Supreme*: it takes the best of all of these mostly American musics and puts them into this mélange, but it's still Suicide. There's conscious things happening, and I'm sure there's a lot of unconscious things happening. Marty's always had that thing—there's always been a Latin thing in his music. He gave me about twenty or twenty-five songs to listen to, and do vocals with, a lot of Latin things. Some of them were so obviously Latin that I almost couldn't deal with it, I couldn't even sing to it. But you can hear it in other songs, there's subtle hints of that, hip-hop, blues . . . a lot of stuff in there. I'm still listening to [*American Supreme*], and every time I put it on I hear so many things I never heard before. It's still very fresh to us; we finished in December. It's a real curve ball for me.

We did this record in a way we never did a record before. This was the first one we had a shot at producing on our own. We had been doing a lot of gigs, doing a lot of new songs for the shows, and I'd been used to singing a certain way. He gave me all these new things; it was totally unexpected, it was coming from a whole other place.

At first I didn't know what to think of it, and I was having a hard time singing to the things; I knew it was going to be a different kind of phrasing than other Suicide records or shows. It took about a month, and then I started to get into it. I already had some lyrics, and then 9/11 hit. And my life changed, of course, as a result of all that. I went back in, maybe three or four weeks later, and I had whole new sets of lyrics. I kept some of the older ones, but I just couldn't sing these same songs the same way anymore. Everything was upside down. Doing this stuff, one song after another, it was rough, it was tough, but it was good; at first I went, "Oh fuck, man, this is gonna be a bitch," but the more I got into it I was really happy, because I love the challenges. I always used to do that with my solo records: I would do kinds of songs that I knew I couldn't sing to, and I would be challenged, push myself to other places. So I really wanted that to happen to Suicide. I knew we needed a new thing, another thing. It was time. It's also ten years in the making: this is an album that we've talked about over the last ten years, "Let's make a record, let's make a record." Suicide's a funny thing, man, it's an entity all on its own. It's been telling us what to do, so we needed the ten years—otherwise we wouldn't have made a record like this; we wouldn't have made a record like this last year, or the year before.

MR That's probably where the hip-hop thing comes in: it's so [much a] part of the times at this point. Now we're in what, the second generation of hip-hop? It's part of our culture.

AV You can't ignore it—it's all around you, everywhere you turn. Walking down the street, cars are going by, blasting hip-hop. . . . When I first heard that James Brown thing ["Televised Executions," a track on *American Supreme*], Marty wasn't there, but I said, "What the fuck is this?"

MR My wife said, "You're not gonna use that, are you?" But there was something there. It's what happens when you combine the vocal with the track and then the sequence of the tracks. "Televised Executions" wasn't really working where it was [in the sequence]; putting it first, it opens up the whole record to a whole other attitude of the world of the record. Sometimes when you open up a play, or any kind of work, you don't come out with your strongest thing right away. Like the old Shakespearean things, there's always a kind of prologue, the so-called Fool came out and introduced the scenario to everybody, with no backgrounds, no other actors.

AV Yeah, [the track] was third from last, I think. I said, "Let me come up with something so far on the other side of this thing, with a really crazy lyric"—especially now, it was a month after 9/11 so my head was in that place—my head is always in that place anyway, I tend to be more crazoid. . . .

You were saying that you rewrote a lot of the lyrics on American Supreme.

AV I think so, I really can't remember offhand. Maybe even all of them. "Child, It's a New World"—that started out as a romantic love song: Oh, it's three in the morning, I'm lonely, blah blah blah. I had a hard time with that because I thought it might be a commercial hit song. I said to Marty, "Let's get a professional singer in here, somebody who knows how to sing this damn thing, and we'll sell it" [*laughs*]. But after 9/11 it became about a child who's in the world.

"I Don't Know" was the song that to me really captured the feeling of those first few weeks after 9/11.

AV That actually helped me break through the whole album. I was having a hard time, I really was; I couldn't find a groove. For years I'd stand up and sing, and for years after that I'd been singing sitting down, trying to get a different thing. So I'd been sitting down, trying to do this thing, and one day I just got up, I just flew off the top of my head. I didn't have any lyrics written down, I don't know what am I going to do, where am I going to go, blah blah blah, it was like a rap song almost—sang it continuously right off the top of my head, didn't stop, and then after I finished that thing I said, "Wow, now I know how to do this album." That was the breakthrough for me. I loosened up, I stood up, then I got into this groove. I went on to every song after that one. I nailed it after that. That was the key: that song, I expressed what I was feeling. It was a one-timer—that's how I do my best things, one time, live.

MR The first [Suicide album (1977)], we came closest to producing ourselves, because Craig Leon had to leave the production. He set up everything, he did a lot of stuff, it was great, and then he left it to Marty Thau, and we stayed in the studio for weeks after that. Marty, this was his first production; we all sat there at the board with the engineer, and as Marty would figure things out he would look at us after every pass. It was really a joint thing. So that's why the first album has the thing it does.

AV I remember I walked out and I saw three doorknobs—that's how intense it was. Marty never could be satisfied with anything, so he'd go home and listen to the shit all night long and come back the next day saying, "No, let's do this again."

MR He'd isolate each track saying, "How is this?" Always turning his head. A *Way of Life* [Chapter 22, 1988] we did even before Ric [Ocasek] got to the studio. Ric usually comes in for a twelve o'clock session, like, at two. He just takes his time because he knows the engineer has to set up. They had a real big studio performance room at Electric Lady. We had to write a few things; we knew exactly what to do, and so we were rehearsing, and they were recording, and some of it sounds so good they said, "We're laying it down." So before you know it, we had nine or ten tracks. Ric comes in, his usual two o'clock thing, he says to the engineers, "OK, where are we at, when do we start?" They said, "They did ten songs already, they have the album done." The first album we actually cut in one day; we cut it in three hours because we'd been doing that stuff for years.

AV [The studio where the first album was recorded was] in upstate New York, and the board was the board Bruce Springsteen recorded his first album on. The engineer, Larry Alexander, hated the music, hated Marty. Craig Leon, I think, left out of desperation or something. Then we got signed to ZE Records, and we were going to do the second Suicide record. We were recording at the Power Station, and right next door to us was Bruce Springsteen doing *The River*—it turned out to be the same engineer, Larry Alexander. [Alexander] heard we were coming in and said, "I quit, I'm not going to be able to deal with it." He calmed down when he heard Ric Ocasek was producing; he was able to do it.

How did you meet up with Ric Ocasek?

AV He came to a show at this place in Boston called the Rat in '75, '76.

MR It was before the first record came out, like '76. We played the Rat, and they had the Cars, but they hadn't recorded yet. And they came to the dressing room, and they told us how much they dug us.

AV There were always these groups going back and forth between New York and Boston: come to Max's then go to the Rat. We heard about this band called the Cars, a pop kind of band. Then we heard they were going to come to our show and we're like, "What for, they're a pop band?" Turns out they were cool.

MR I saw them at CBGB on a Monday or Tuesday night just before the first record came out. There was nobody in the audience—the record hadn't come out yet. Then the record came out and it was a huge hit, and as soon as they started doing interviews, Ric was saying how much he dug Suicide. He was really touting us, and early on he was saying he'd like to produce us. So we were on ZE, for the second album—actually before that, Marty Thau arranged for Ric to produce "Dream Baby Dream," that single, on Red Star. We opened for the Cars in Providence [and] Boston. And then we did the [television show] *Midnight Special* with Ric. And the third and fourth record—Ric just wanted to do another record with us.

Let's get back to your roots. I know you were doing electronic stuff in the '60s.

AV I did toy things, toy sounds, tape recorders, static from the radio. I was into Terry Riley and La Monte Young in those days, and the German bands—Can. I was just fooling around, no idea I was going to be a musician. The last thing on my mind was that I was going to be a singer onstage somewhere—that was the bottom of the list for me. I was too shy. I was coming out of school as a visual artist—painter, sculptor—but I always loved music. I listened to Bartók, Stravinsky . . . I'd take a Bartók record and scratch it up to hear it more crazy; I'd have staticky shit along with Bartók on a two-track tape recorder. A toy band, a little monkey banging drums in the background. So that was my early shit.

Did you see La Monte or Terry Riley perform back then?

AV I saw La Monte; Terry was in California. La Monte was my favorite of all of them. I loved the drone. He has a place now, a house where he performs [the Dream House].

It's right across the street from here. I saw a flyer for one of your early shows and it said "Dream Music by Suicide," and La Monte used "Dream Music" to describe his stuff, too.

AV I don't remember that.

MR We used to say "Punk Music," too.

AV We should have written "Nightmare Music" [*laughs*]. I'm sure it had nothing to do with La Monte.

MR I hadn't heard any of those guys. I knew they were around. It was two different worlds, I always felt. I was developing from where I had been, so I was following my own path. You knew there was a crisis in European classical music. Jazz was starting to end. So you had people coming out of conservatories, like Philip Glass—they still wanted to write classical music, but they also were from a generation brought up on rock and roll. You couldn't avoid it. And classical music after Schoenberg, Stravinsky, and Copland: it was really gone. [Composers like Glass] wanted to write classical music, but they had to deal with rock. They got into repetitive things, and that's really rhythm and blues. If you're a kid now and you want to be a composer, what are you going to do, write a symphony? You can't re-create that. There was something unavoidable about rock and roll. I grew up during that whole time, late '50s, early '60s. They took classical to that one extra level, that minimal thing. It's really very rococo; it's more like Mozart. We're more electronic, more expressionistic. More like the later Germans—Mahler and Wagner. Phil is more like Mozart and Haydn.

Were you guys aware of the Silver Apples?

AV Oh, I was.

MR Alan was, and told me about them. I didn't hear them.

AV This friend of mine said, "You have to listen to this shit." That's when I was into electronics. I tried to tell Debbie Harry—the few interviews I did in the early '70s, I was like, "Silver Apples." I just met them a couple of years ago; it was great to meet the guy, Simeon Coxe, after all those years.

Did you guys ever listen to Moondog?

MR I used to see Moondog on the street—on Fifty-Third Street—this guy selling his music.

His music reminds me of Suicide, sometimes. And free jazz was an influence on you guys . . . ?

MR At the time that we met, that's where I was coming from.

AV Marty had a band called Reverend B, the greatest jazz band I've ever seen. He was the first guy using an electric piano, before Miles [Davis] and all those other guys.

Sun Ra?

MR Sun Ra was the only one, but I was using an organ. . . . Sun Ra was so underexposed, and I hadn't really listened to him at that point. But in retrospect, he was the only one.

AV They had three trumpet players, a sax, two drummers—amazing. I was doing a light show for a concert of electronic composers and went to see Reverend B after this boring thing. I couldn't believe it. Amazing sound—I never heard anything like it. I picked up a tambourine, something to play along, and Marty turned around and said, "You and I are going to be doing something together someday." We had already known each for months—we used to hang out in the same place together. That was it, man, the official word came down.

We were both ending things in our lives. I was into my art thing that I knew had to be going somewhere else, and Marty was in the music thing that was ending a cycle, too. We needed Suicide, in a way, to take us to that next place. There were nights we'd rehearse, and we'd tape the stuff and listen back to it and we loved it so much, but sometimes we'd look at each other and say, "Are we losing our minds?" It was so fuckin' out there. Sometimes I'd be blowing trumpet—this guy [Rev], by the way, is the fastest drummer alive. The first Suicide show we did, he actually played drums. It was all basically free jazz–electronic; we had no songs at all. It was like the Big Bang. It was nothing but a big gas cloud, that's what Suicide was, and slowly but surely we pulled things into stars, because we let Suicide be that way. We just let it happen. One night "Cheree" came out, then one night another thing, then another thing, all on its own without us imposing a will on it. We let Suicide tell us what to do, in a way.

It always takes two to form a great band, Mick Jagger and Keith Richards. . . . We always knew in our hearts that guitar and drums—we started with a guitar player, another visual artist, who couldn't really play guitar, but it was crazy enough, so we got him to play crazy. But he left after three gigs. He said he'd be committing suicide by staying with the band and then went off and got married and moved to Brooklyn. We thought about bringing in the drummer from Reverend B.

MR Marev played [drums] with us.

AV That's right, [Rev's] wife.

MR She started rehearsing and it was great having her there, but there was so much drum music [already]. It had reached its peak in the late '60s, early '70s, and if you don't need them . . . We could do without that because we also had the real survival necessities of where are we going to rehearse, how are we going to keep this band together, with all these instruments? As soon as you have more than two people there's always going to be problems, so that's what formed us a lot, too. And it is a lot of what made hip-hop and rap: the necessity of having to do something with less, so you scratch records, get a turntable; you make music out of that. 'Cause you *have* to make music, that's the bottom line. If you don't have anything to make it with, you take the door off of that closet over there [*laughs*]—you start cutting it up and making a xylophone, or whatever.

AV We were living on the streets ourselves. The rehearsal studio was where we would sleep. But one day [Rev] walked in with this strange brown box: you couldn't imagine what it was, and you couldn't open it; it was totally sealed. And it was a drum machine, which he didn't buy in a music store or anything. He bought it in a furniture store.

MR No, I'll tell you what it was. I went to the "Buy-Lines" to get something used, 'cause we couldn't afford anything in those days, and someone was selling a drum machine for thirty dollars, which in those days was a good amount of money for me, but it was something that I could just about do. So I took a trip out to this place in Queens, to this family who had a drum machine—nicest people in the world, and their daughter had just committed suicide, they told me that, and she was a poet, young, probably a teenager, but for some reason she had the drum machine. It was made by Seagrams, not the liquor one, but a company that made pinsetters for bowling alleys.[1] I took it home and we started rehearsing with it right away.

How far into the history of the band was this?

MR '75.

AV No! We started in '71.

MR Yeah, but the drum machine wasn't until '75, the beginning of '75, March or April.

AV Really?

MR Yeah, 'cause before that, when we were playing the Mercer Arts Center, I was playing a snare drum and a cymbal in the middle of two keyboards on an angle, facing like a *V*. I would play keyboard with one hand and keep a beat on a drum in the middle. It was fun, it was great, and we played a lot of gigs like that. We played the Village Gate one time; I hit the ride cymbal and it spun out into the audience. Luckily there were only three people in the audience [*laughs*], 'cause that thing'll go right through you.

Were you playing songs when you were playing Mercer Arts Center?

MR Mercer Arts Center [sets were] starting to be—we had like four ideas, but to everybody else it sounded like

1 Martin Rev's first drum machine was the Rhythm Prince, produced by home organ manufacturer Gulbransen and jukebox maker Seeburg. For more information on this instrument and how Rev came to acquire it, see chapter eleven of the group's authorized biography by Kris Needs, *Dream Baby Dream: Suicide—A New York Story* (Omnibus Press, 2017).

one long thing. We had early songs like "Methedrine Mary," "Junkie Jesus"—that was the only song that was kind of different because it was a slower ballad, "Creature Feature." They were all so incredibly intense that, for us, they would be singles of a different song, and Alan would do different lyrics, but basically it was like a wall of sound. "Junkie Jesus"—we've got to do that again sometime. That was like a pre-runner to "Cheree." We wouldn't wait in between: we'd do four songs, we'd run one song into another.

Were they riff-dominated?

MR They'd be more wall-of-sound kind of things—

AV But you could hear the riff—

MR The riff was there. You were starting to hear the riff, but there was so much feedback.

AV We would we hear the riff, the implied melody, but people out there, as Marty was saying, people hearing it for the first time would be saying, "What the fuck is this?" At that time we were probably the loudest band in the world.

And you were using props, too—chains. . . .

AV Chains, knives, myself, which is a prop in itself [*laughs*]. One night at Mercer Arts Center, we came out—how much did that room in the back hold, about a hundred, couple hundred?

MR Maybe two at the most.

AV Yeah, there was a stage and a big space between

the stage. They had these seats. We start to get into our shit and then, ten minutes into the show, people start to get up and leave. I jumped off the stage and just stood by the door and everybody went back to their seats; it scared the crap out of them, 'cause I was a lunatic onstage. People thought, "What the fuck is this guy going to do to us?" 'Cause I'd be cutting myself—I was impervious to pain.

You had a wig, too?

AV A blond wig sometimes . . . really fuckin' crazy. When I see pictures from those days I think, "Ah, what a way to make a buck." Of course, we weren't making a buck.

Then, later, were the CBGB and Max's scenes.

AV Yeah, we were more of a Max's band, ultimately. We were banned from CBGB. It's a long story—there used to be a pool table in the back. Remember the time we got eighty-sixed. . . .

MR We were one of the first groups to play there.

AV But then, one night we were standing back there—

MR It was late afternoon or evening; there was nothing happening then.

AV Marty doesn't drink but I'd be drinking, and so Merv, the bouncer—nice guy—of all people came over and said, "You have to buy a drink." Marty said, "I don't drink." "I want you out of here." So I said, "Merv, cool it, I'll buy Marty's drink." "No, I want you out of here," blah blah blah—he threw us out. And we couldn't get in to play there for a year or two after that. It was Marty Thau who talked to Hilly [Kristal]—let us do a gig, got us a Monday gig, Tuesday gig. When you got to the weekend you made money, for the first time in our lives. Three grand or four grand, I'd never seen that much money in my life. I remember on a Thursday night I had pneumonia, a 106 fever, but I had to do the gig 'cause it would have put us back to Mondays if I didn't do the gig. 'Cause we built up an audience. That's what Hilly did, he built you up an audience.

MR Max's had a jukebox of singles. I went up to Tommy Dean: "What do you think, if we make a single?" He said, "Sure, we'll put it on there." So I went up to one of those guys you'll never find again on Forty-Eighth Street who'll cut a 45 for you. We only had two copies, brought it down, and there it was in the jukebox. That's where Marty Thau first heard us. Max's was more urban, Italian, New York, Jewish, Jersey—somehow the owners and everybody could get behind us. As funky as it was, CB's was maybe a little more highbrow.

AV After Patti Smith, the artistic community suddenly decided to visit CBGB, and they were always our worst audience, even when I was showing at OK Harris and Ivan Karp let us play there. Those were the worst audiences—they really fuckin' hated us. You'd think they'd be the most open-minded; they turned out to be the most closed-minded.

We got a review, "Suicide is meaningless," [which] turned out to be the biggest boost for us 'cause people wanted to know, "Why are they meaningless?" So we packed out Max's the next night. It turned out to be a really helpful review for me. Sometimes you find out more important things from bad reviews; this guy ripped the shit out of me, but he made some good points—about my performance being so fast that it went by in the blink of an eye, you can't really grasp it, and I thought maybe that's true, 'cause it was speedy. So I started to slow my thing down after that.

Did you have more of a rapport with some of the No Wave bands than the earlier punk bands?

AV Yeah, in a way, 'cause we were the daddies already. I met James Chance on his first night after he moved to New York at CB's. He said, "I know who you are, can you tell me anything?"

MR Lydia [Lunch] was seventeen when she came to New York, a poetess. She showed me some of her stuff; it was so good, I knew she had something. She wasn't even doing music then, she was just hanging out at Max's and writing poetry. The poetry was so sharp. She had a great personality.

AV Oh yeah, she was like the Mae West from Rochester.

I used to play with [No Wave guitarist] Rudolph Grey.

AV Oh, no shit, Rudolph and I were such great friends. I love him. We did a show one night, Arto [Lindsay], Rudolph, and myself. We all decided to switch identities. I played drums. We rehearsed for a week; it was the hardest thing I ever had to do in my life. I discovered bones in my body I didn't even know existed, especially around the neck area, and my hands were like chopped meat. I was trying to keep a beat for the guys, and people said, "Your eyes were rolling into the top of your head." It was so painful [*laughs*]. Rudy was singing. I said, "I'm never going to do this again"—it took me weeks to get over it. I had a new respect for drummers. I got [Grey's No Wave band] Red Transistor signed to Red Star; when they played at Max's, no one would sit in the front part of Max's, always in the back part, and I would sit in the front row of Max's while they were playing, even though guitars were splintering all over me. I purposely sat there 'cause I wanted other people to come in and not be afraid of it.

This is around the same time as the legendary tours you did with Elvis Costello and the Attractions, and the Clash. They were both fans of Suicide?

AV Yeah, Elvis was a fan, and the Clash were fans. Elvis asked me for a riot one night. They had been on tour for nine months, the last leg of the tour, and they were *cray-zee*—the roadies were in even worse shape. There was the night in Brussels, and we caused that big riot. So the next day we went to the Hague, and during the afternoon I was at a pay phone out in the street; all of a sudden I saw Elvis coming out of the hotel carrying a laundry bag. Elvis, the big star, he's still got to do his own laundry, which is cool—that was Elvis, man. He comes over to me and says, "Hey Al, you think you can give us another riot?" Because [that night] in Brussels [the Attractions] never got onstage, so it gave him the night off. They probably got paid as well. I said, "Sure, Elvis." The Hague was beautiful, a symphony concert hall, beautiful leather seats. We caused a riot; the next day you see in the newspapers, "Suicide causes $100,000 worth of damages." [The audience] knifed the seats, all the leather shit was in shreds, that was what he wanted. They never got on that night either.

I thought the Clash tour was going to be cool because it's more like our thing, punks and shit. And then I realized, it was from the frying pan right into the fire. The skinheads, and the National Front, guys walking around with swastikas, heavily politicized times in 1978. But then we got our own Suicide tour, and we made such an impact on that tour: Leeds, Liverpool, the dressing rooms were packed every night. They had me cornered sometimes, I'm sure those guys were Soft Cell, Haircut One Hundred—all those guys, all kids, we influenced them. One night—this is after getting every kind of shit thrown at us, riots, my nose broken—I got trapped in a dressing room with all these guys with Nazi armbands—I thought they were going to kill me. I was the only one in the dressing room; finally everybody came rushing backstage and got those guys out of there. I thought I was going to die on that one. . . . The first night was Edinburgh, about a thousand people, a low stage. About ten to fifteen minutes in, I see people milling around and say, "Marty, watch out. The riot's going to start." We're playing and all of a sudden, out of nowhere, it's bright because they had a disco crystal ball in the ceiling, and lights are bouncing off the thing. I look out and people are fucking dancing to Suicide! I said, "Marty, I think we're out of work," 'cause we wanted the riots, we tried to inspire the riots. On the Clash tour, the skins pushed everybody else to the back, so we didn't know who was liking us. On our own tour suddenly it was a Suicide crowd, and much more than I expected—and dancing!

What is the audience reaction these days? Somewhere between dancing and a riot?

MR Some places there's an edge, but it's not a riot edge.

AV Every night we play now it's packed houses, and

it's an audience of kids who weren't even born when Suicide started and they know every one of our fuckin' songs. They ask for the songs, sing along to the songs. We have to play two-hour shows sometimes 'cause they won't let us off, and it's blowing my mind. Austin was two hours and ten minutes—we had to play every song that we had.

MR In those days, we were opening for other bands and they didn't know what to expect. We were hitting them with a whole attitude, with a whole instrumentation, a whole theater, a whole music.

AV And there isn't anything you can do onstage to shock people anymore, either. What's on TV, what's in the newspaper, what's on the streets—we used to give them the street back in their face. They came in to get entertained.

MR That was our reality.

AV Right, we were just giving them the truth. Now you give them the street, it doesn't matter; the street is everywhere you go now, in reality. I couldn't think of anything to do. If I killed somebody onstage—"Ah, what's that?" I was just reading today that Cheney said we decided to kill Saddam. What is this, a mafia now?

MR Yeah, they used to have a lot more tact, even Reagan. These heads of state had a kind of protocol; now it's so transparent. They wouldn't say it before, they would do it.

AV They complain about violence in movies and TV and now they say kill? Are kids supposed to look up to these assholes? No wonder they look up to athletes and rappers.

MR It's not a brightly lit time right now—the bulb is getting dimmer and dimmer.

You guys stopped performing after the second record.

MR [Alan] was doing solo stuff.

AV Yeah, I had a hit with "Jukebox Baby," out of nowhere. That led to me getting signed to Elektra. We never quit or anything; we did gigs here and there.

MR After 1980, '81, there were fewer and fewer gigs for Suicide. Then a few years later people were saying, "You've got to go to Europe, all these groups are talking about Suicide," the next generation, Sigue Sigue Sputnik, Billy Idol. "If you guys go back, there's an audience for you there." Sigue Sigue Sputnik were cool—they gave their producer a copy of our first record and told him, "This is what we want to do."

Springsteen was a fan, too.

AV Bruce is a great guy. He is who he is—what you see onstage is who he is. He's a sweetheart, he loves Suicide. He's so supportive. He talks to this day about how "Frankie Teardrop" is one of the greatest, craziest rock-and-roll songs of all time. Ric [Ocasek] told me he was in a clothing store in Hollywood, all of a sudden he hears, "Psst, hey Ric!" He turns around, he sees it's Bruce. "Hey man, how's Vega?" Ric said, "Fuck, he doesn't even ask about how I am, he just asks about you" [*laughs*].

Have you heard some of these New York bands that are referencing Suicide now?

AV Here we are in the year 2000—we influenced bands in the '70s, '80s, the '90s. I'm going to say it unashamedly—fuck it. Marty and I have always had this humble approach to things, that's why I said it's got to be *American Supreme*, because Suicide is one of the supreme bands in the world—fuck it, we happen to be American, that's another thing. It's time for us to fuckin' say, "Yes, we did. Yes, we have." I'm tired of being humble. I'm proud of what we've done. We're a great band and we've proved it once again with this record, and we're going to continue to do that. At shows people have been telling me the shows get better and better all the time.

MR The bottom line will be twenty, thirty, forty years. You can influence a pile of mud or a shit pile, too, you know what I mean? You don't know what the real influence is until way later. Turns out, it's already been thirty years since the first album, twenty-five years—so that's a good sign. But who knows, maybe everything we're influencing, and us, might be not worth a nickel anyway in fifty years. I'm going to be the humble guy now. Then again, within fifty or sixty years [Suicide] will probably have its place within its world.

Christian Marclay

Somewhere in upstate New York in the late '80s, a college radio music director tuned into her station while driving back to campus. In a panic, after hearing what seemed to be silence, she hit the accelerator, fearing dead air. Soon enough the DJ broke in, announcing, "That was Christian Marclay's *Record Without a Cover* from 1985." If you haven't guessed, I was the DJ, and had been looping the first two minutes of the one-sided LP, which is entirely composed of pops and clicks recorded from other vinyls. It's an ingenious conceptual art piece: the recording, which documents Marclay's performance style, in which he makes sound collages using only other records on multiple turntables, is on one side of the LP, and the album information is engraved on the flip, without any protective packaging (believe it or not, you used to be able to find a stack of them at Tower Records in the East Village with the price sticker affixed directly on the vinyl). I found Christian to be the most interesting musician to come out of the downtown New York improvisation scene in the '80s. His visual art practice, for which he's now best known, eventually claimed the majority of his time and focus, but sound remains a primary subject of his artwork.

I got to know Christian personally while working at Tonic, and I later played with him in Text of Light —a group (including the two of us, Lee Ranaldo, Ulrich Krieger, DJ Olive, William Hooker, and Tim Barnes) formed in 1999 to improvise music for the films of Stan Brakhage and other American avant-garde filmmakers of the mid-century. When curator Russell Ferguson was looking to commission an essay about Christian's musical work for the catalog of an exhibition he was organizing at the Hammer Museum in Los Angeles, Christian recommended me, in part because he had enjoyed an article I had recently written about experimental musician Yasunao Tone for the *Wire*. Though I was already collegial with Christian, we hadn't discussed his work in depth, and this was an exciting prospect for me; I interviewed him at his loft on Fulton Street in 2003, just after New Year's Day.

In that interview with Lee [Ranaldo, in BB Gun *#6], you were talking about punk rock being a real motivating force in the late '70s, when you were still in art school, and that performance was important to you because it allowed the audience to see what you were doing, as opposed to the mystery of a recording—which is like punk, happening right in front of you in a small club.*

Punk rock was physically aggressive in the same way that Vito Acconci's works of the time were. Vito was a punk before punk in some ways. He was always very interested in rock and roll, even though it may not be obvious. I think that aesthetic attracted him, and I remember seeing him a few times in clubs, hanging out. In some cases, punk performances were virtually interchangeable with the body art of the era.

What did I like about punk? My background was not in music, and I didn't know much about music, and when I first started going to these clubs in New York, hearing DNA and Mars, these minimalist noise bands, I was really attracted to it and I was interested in the presentation. It was so anti–show business in a way, but there was also a theatrical quality to it. I didn't grow up listening to a lot of recordings, almost none, and I never went to any live shows, so it was kind of a brand-new discovery. And the music could be so physical and aggressive and loud, I used to love the loudness, and feeling the music through my body. The performances at CBGB, where the sound system was so great: I still remember DNA, when Tim [Wright] would play his bass, the whole place would be vibrating, just shaking. And there he was barefoot, tiptoeing across the stage—it was quite something. I remember a DNA performance where they had invited Nam June Paik to do something; he smashed a violin, that performance he does—moving in slow motion and suddenly smashing it. And it was just perfect in that club context. And I remember seeing a Dan Graham performance at the Mudd Club where he was just talking to the audience about relaxing [*laughs*]. It just felt like a normal context for these performances. Or seeing Sid Vicious at Max's Kansas City; it was almost like an Actionist performance, the guy was just such a wreck, bruised and cut—it was almost a kind of public sacrifice, with him hurting himself onstage.

I went back to Boston in 1979 to finish my BA [at Massachusetts Collage of Art] and curated a festival there [Eventworks, 1980]. I invited performance artists, dancers, musicians; I brought DNA, I brought Rhys Chatham, Karole Armitage—she was doing this kind of ballet-punk thing—a bunch of people from the West Coast, Johanna Went, Z'EV . . .

Boyd Rice?

Boyd Rice; RoseLee Goldberg came to speak; there was a series of lectures and one of them was supposed to be a Vito Acconci lecture, but sadly he canceled at the last minute. Some local bands from Boston, this all-girl band called Bound & Gagged . . .

Mission of Burma?

Yeah, yeah, they played. There were films, art performances. Pat Hearn, who was a student then, did a performance.

Jack Smith?

Jack Smith, yeah, that was interesting [*laughs*]. He came up and showed excerpts from *Flaming Creatures* [1962–63] and played Hawaiian records in the background as a live soundtrack. Dan Graham came—he brought this band [Introjection, aka CKM] that had Kim Gordon in it, and Miranda Stanton and Christine Hahn. It was this performance where Dan was speaking while they were playing, talking over the music about the relationship we were having with the performers, the identification and exchange that was going on between the band and the audience. Similar to the pieces he did with mirrors, and the audience facing their reflection. So the festival was fairly varied; it wasn't just bands, but it was about the punk-rock aesthetic that was influencing many other art forms. I had spent a year in New York, where I used to go to clubs a lot and see amazing things. I wanted to show that energy and cross-pollination. It felt really strong at the time: punk, No Wave, performance art. A lot of what was going on in the galleries was still Minimal and conceptual art, and I felt the real energy was in the music clubs.

It seems like punk inspired a lot of people like you who had no background in music to then start creating music—

Yeah, it was part of this do-it-yourself aesthetic. You sensed that it was very amateurish, so, you know, why not? You don't have to study in the conservatory for ten years before you can play—[*laughs*]. When I was a kid, I wanted to play the piano. I was about fourteen, but it was a little too late, and I had a bad teacher and gave up. But I felt the energy in New York was very liberating and when I went back to Boston I got involved in making music. Started my first band: the Bachelors, Even. It was very performance-oriented—we had slides, films, props.

Recently I've been using video to show the turntables—like with my djTRIO, we just did this gig in

Detroit: we had three cameras showing each DJ's setup. In those earlier days, if [you were] on a proscenium stage, nobody could see what the hell was going on; people would say, "You should put some kind of mirror behind your turntables." I thought that would be too gimmicky. I always tried to play in small clubs where the audience was close enough to see what I was doing. I thought it was important to show how the records were treated and the manipulations involved—how music was made out of simple devices. In this case I didn't have to learn how to play the guitar or the drums or whatever; I just used this very familiar stuff. There was no mystery to it; everybody knew what records were all about and how to play them. That was the medium of choice then, how people listened to music. The turntable has become this marginal tool, but then it was still very mainstream.

Records used to be this thing that people would treat very carefully, and then to go to a club and see this guy . . .

Yeah, I think it had more of an impact then because people really felt, "Oh my God, I can't believe he's breaking those records." Now it's a little different.

It was like Hendrix or Pete Townshend smashing their guitars.

Right. I was ready to give up the turntables in the early '90s because I felt vinyl was over—it's this obsolete medium. It didn't have the same meaning, you know: Why keep doing this? But then this whole movement of alternative DJs blossomed—it became an alternative medium, a different way to listen to and make music. It became relevant again. I had people to play with, there was a DJ scene open to improvisation and experiments, so it still made sense to do it. That's when I started djTRIO. I think if that hadn't happened I would have just gone to something else. Otherwise I felt like I was playing with these antique objects—LPs didn't have the same meaning anymore. It was amazing how it picked up so quickly; it was a time when record companies were going out of business, they were selling their pressing plants, majors were not pressing records anymore. So the alternative scene, hip-hop mainly, and dance music in general, reinjected energy into it and people started making records again. I kind of like the status it has now—it's mainstream but still has a kind of marginal, homemade, indie quality. When you're breaking records today it's not like you're symbolically smashing the big record industry.

It kind of has that relation to musique concrète. It's almost a punk take on it . . . musique concrète was something you associate with someone working in a studio for hours and hours cutting up tape, whereas the turntable stuff is right there in front of you, and very immediate. And it's not something that uses a lot of high-tech equipment either, especially in your case—the Califone turntables and these records that come out of thrift stores.

With early musique concrète it was very different: it was before tape players, so recordings were cut directly on lacquers; it was how you recorded then. It wasn't associated with the idea of found records, the multiple, mass-produced pop object that DJs use now.

You were also influenced by Fluxus music performanooo.

When I was still in Geneva there was this little group of artists—they were older than me but they had organized a few Fluxus performances. The group was called Ecart, which means "off to the side" in French, and backward it spells "trace." John Armleder was the artist behind this group. He had a little space, kind of an alternative gallery/bookstore—he would sell a lot of artists' books, small magazines. I would go there, look at the books and magazines, and then I went to performances. What I remember is they were almost spoofs of classical music performance—they would be dressed up in tuxedos or take a music instrument and do something like polishing it instead of playing it. I was interested in that kind of parody presentation and humor. That's how I became aware of Fluxus; that was in the mid-'70s, 'cause I came to the US in '77—so Fluxus was still fairly contemporary. I was aware of this kind of performance in art; it wasn't just about making objects but about doing very ephemeral performances. I was interested in that. When I was in art school I was interested in things that weren't objects that would last, more site-specific installations that would only last a few days. So music made sense.

And in the early '80s, after I got out of art school, the music just became more important in the sense that I was just busy with it. I performed with [John] Zorn and then started touring. In art school I had a band called Mon Ton Son; we played a few times here [in New York City]. Then I was starting to develop a big band project to tour in Europe, and my projects with David Moss. I was struggling with the visual art. I just thought, "Oh well, maybe this is it, I'm enjoying what I'm doing." I wasn't really eager to make things and show them in galleries. At the time, the only objects I was making were these homemade records, "Recycled Records" [1980–86], that I used in performances or displayed on turntables so people could listen to them. I liked the idea of making a record that was unique; it plays differently every time you play it—the needle jumps around. The more I was working with records, I realized the potential of all the sounds I could generate just with a simple turntable and LPs. I was starting to appreciate all the unwanted sounds that traditionally were rejected, like skipping loops, and the clicks and pops of scratches, all this stuff that people didn't want. But that was so much a part of the experience of listening to records, and the whole ritual of putting a record on a turntable—that whole experience to me was really interesting. So I started using some of these sounds just for their musical quality: performances with skipping records and transforming the surface, doing all kinds of aggressive, destructive stuff to the records for the purpose of creating new music.

*Were you aware of the Cage pieces for turntables, like the one for twelve turntables where people would come in at random and put records on [*33 1/3, *1969]?*

I knew about his use of records in *Imaginary Landscape No. 1* [1939]; I hadn't known about that work [*33 1/3*], I saw that in 1989. It was in a show I was in called "Broken Music." No, I wasn't aware of that piece, but I was aware of musique concrète, and I had found out by reading books about early electronic music that actually records had been in used in early twentieth-century pieces, like with Respighi—music that required a recording, like of birds singing. Or László Moholy-Nagy, who did these experiments at the Bauhaus—he came up with this idea that I thought was really revolutionary: instead of thinking of the record as a way to document music, to actually create music from it. So he would hand-engrave grooves that would create a sound that doesn't really exist in nature. There's a whole list of early experiments with records because before the cut-up of tape, that was how you could record sound. And Cage definitely saw the potential in this. And it's funny, Edison early on never really saw the potential for creating music with his invention. He thought it was just a way to record speech. The myth goes that for his first recording experiment, he sang "Mary Had a Little Lamb." That was a song, but he thought it would be a great way to record speeches, not music.

So, I was aware of these things but I wasn't really trying to make New Music, I was trying to make . . . performance music, performing in clubs, it was such a different environment than serious musique concrète or even John Cage; they were always associated with serious contemporary music. At that time, I never even thought of what I did as music. Why would I call myself a musician? I never studied music. Afterward, playing with musicians like Zorn, who always had a roster of these totally talented musicians, I always felt like the outsider—not knowing that much about music. But it was a hugely influential experience, to be around these people who could really play, but at the same time were just having fun. These crazy performances, those game pieces—it was fun, they were like games. The process is partly revealed to the audience, but to really enjoy it you have to be an insider. You have to be doing it, that's the fun part.

How did you first start playing with John [Zorn], how did you meet him?

He heard about me through someone, and he called me up to do this *Track and Field* [1982] performance—asked if I would be interested. I didn't know who he was; it was the early '80s. I had never gone to Morton Street, which was sort of the beginning of that scene, so I didn't know much about this. . . . I knew Fred

Frith, I had seen Fred Frith at the Squat Theatre. That was in the late '70s when I was still in Boston. I came down for the exchange program with Cooper Union, '77, '78, and then I went back to Boston in '79. I saw Fred Frith do his tabletop guitar performance and was very impressed. But I didn't know Zorn. He called me up and I played, and he liked what I did, and then we did something else at Danceteria [*Rugby,* February 1983, with Arto Lindsay, Ikue Mori, and Tom Cora], and then I did a lot of duets with David Moss. Then he [Moss] formed Dense Band, and then he and Zorn had a falling-out. I met many musicians through Zorn—Wayne Horvitz, Zeena Parkins, Butch Morris, all these people, from playing in all his game pieces. He really enjoyed my stuff 'cause I could throw the band into a totally different direction. At the time, I was using a lot of what I'd call quotation-type things—little jazzy, little classical, rhythmic stuff, disco, polka [*laughs*]. My eclectic taste was perfect with John's idea of collage and jump cuts. I think it became really important to his aesthetic, so he liked having me in his groups.

I learned a lot from that experience—I learned how to improvise. Unlike a DJ who would smoothly segue one record into another, in those game pieces I had to be fast and quick, and in some cases rely on chance. I learned how to accept and believe in improv. It took me a while, because when I did my solo performances I was totally into rehearsing and organizing my records, which were numbered. And when I did a performance I had a beginning, an ending; I had everything worked out. Then I realized that I would spend a lot of time rehearsing and in the process damage the fragile records—some loops would disintegrate after a while. I realized I was spending too much time trying to achieve what I had in my head instead of listening to what was happening during the performance. I started trusting my ears more and more and performing with no preparation. It took me many years before I could show up at a gig with just a bunch of records, not really knowing what I was going to do. It happened through this first-hand experience with these talented musicians. I always felt like an outsider, like, "What am I doing?" [*Laughs.*] These guys, they know what they're doing. But then it was very encouraging to hear them say, "Don't even try to learn" [*laughs*], you know, because they were envious, in a way, of my very naive approach. They enjoyed it because it didn't come out of the training they were sometimes totally enslaved by. If they played a bad note, it totally upset them, like a child who had played a bad note [*laughs*]—I didn't have that problem.

Arto Lindsay and Ikue Mori also played quite a bit with Zorn back then—they were also untrained.

Arto was always someone I admired because he invented his own unique way to play the guitar, and all that really came out of this punk aesthetic. That's what they were doing, inventing.

Did you ever draw comparisons to or think about assemblage artists either in the context of Zorn's pieces or in relation to your solo constructions with multiple turntables?

A lot of my work uses collage as a process, my visual work as well as my music. I've always liked using found things and doing something new with them. I just thought it was a normal way of making things—I don't know that I thought about it that much. I was aware of Burroughs's ideas. It was always part of my aesthetic interest: collage, putting things together. In the early '80s there was a lot of appropriation art, from hip-hop to Richard Prince. Sherrie Levine would rephotograph Walker Evans. Why create something new and unique when there's so much around to deal with? The idea of sampling things, collaging them, transforming them, was a natural way of making art for my generation.

You wanted to make a record about records—to call attention to its identity as a record, which you certainly did with Record Without a Cover *[Recycled Records, 1985]; did* More Encores *[No Man's Land, 1989] fall into that also?*

Less, in a way—it was more about the identity of the performer. Each cut is titled after the person I took records from: Jimi Hendrix, Maria Callas, or Louis Armstrong. I used only the records of a specific performer or composer to create each piece. Even though the end result might not always sound like the sampled artist, it's a way of saying it all originates from their sounds, but then it's transformed. It's more about homage, less about the medium itself, such as *Record Without a Cover* or *Footsteps* [RecRec Music, 1989], which were underlining the fragility and the pitfalls of the vinyl medium: when it fails to preserve forever. Instead of lamenting over these failings, I used them creatively. This awareness of the medium comes out of an art training rather than music. I think of film, for instance, like with Michael Snow. If you're using a medium that creates an illusion, you don't want to pretend that it's only an illusion. Michael Snow always made you aware of the medium: he changed the aperture, changed the focus, used filters; something else happened, subtle changes that revealed the mechanical process.

Some of the disjunction between sound and image, also.

Right. All these experiments were definitely influential, not just Michael Snow but different art practices. Understanding that photography is going to be manipulated, it's not truth, you can make it say something else. I wanted people to listen to *Record Without a Cover* with this kind of push-and-pull of the attention, never able to forget the record spinning on the turntable, thinking twice about what they were hearing, instead of a smooth playback where you just sit back and listen to the recording and ideally forget that it's a recording. The musicians are not around; it's this disembodied experience. By making the record play at the wrong speed, slowing it down or speeding it up, making it skip—these were different ways to keep the vinyl present, play with moments of doubt. Even at the end [of *Record Without a Cover*]—is it finished? [*Laughs.*] Lasting a little longer than usual, and then the locked groove skipping. All these little things that make you aware of the medium and force you not to forget about it.

I was never very interested in putting out records to document live performances, to freeze the spontaneity. I liked that they were ephemeral performances. It happened at a certain time; whoever was there experienced it and then it was over—it only lives in their memory. I never really liked live recordings; I would record my performances with a cassette player and then listen back to them for myself, as a critical tool, see what I could improve. And I always hated those recordings [*laughs*], because I always felt like something was missing. And the understanding of time is so different when you are in it, as a performer or listener. It's harder for me to listen to a recording, because I have a memory of what happened. I can't listen with a fresh ear, because I'm still remembering the experience instead of listening to the actual recording. Now it's so easy to pull out a portable DAT player or minidisc and record off the board. So, there's too many bad documents of my performances. I was really against documenting performances for a while. But I think it is important sometimes to document things for people who couldn't be there. I'd rather rework a recording and make it work as a recording rather than being just a document of a performance. Ultimately, what's important is the experience of listening to a fulfilling recording.

Did you ever videotape performances?

Again, it was always hard because no one had access to this kind of equipment then. But there are a few things around. The Kitchen did some documentation. The whole process for me was so important, and a sound recording could not show that, but with video I could show some of it. There are few things: my Phonoguitar—there's a couple documents of that, but there're very few. Some of the performances I did with Zorn were documented.

Can you talk about the One Hundred Turntables *[1991] piece you did in Tokyo?*

I made a record specifically to use in this performance—it was an extravagant thing, but it was Japan in the early '90s, the economy was doing really well, and they had tons of money. So I came up with this crazy idea, thinking they were going to say no [*laughs*]. One other thing that I really admired in hip-hop—besides the whole text-based music that became this Black militant voice, and the whole poetry of it—for me, the most inventive thing was their use of the records. It generated these EPs that were not conceived so much as normal records, as documents of songs. With hip-hop, the record was made as a tool for DJs, and it offered a variety of mixes of the same song on one EP—you had bonus beats, a cappella parts. I thought that was great: with two copies of these EPs you could make a song last for a whole evening if you wanted to. *One Hundred Turntables* was a way of making a record to be used in a performance. So I pressed two hundred copies and we had two performances. For each evening we used one hundred copies of the same record. It had two sides, one with shakuhachi flute loops; the other side had harmonica and accordion loops. It had locked grooves and a whole section of samples, kind of premixed stuff, and it had two holes, centered and off-center. All one hundred turntables were set in a spiral configuration, and I had three other DJs assisting me; we were each responsible for twenty-five turntables. We were running around, changing the speeds, changing the loops—it was very drony, loopy stuff. It was important to create a record that had no other function than being a tool to compose music with. Because the records I usually used were found. We also played one other piece using found vocal records, all spoken-word records. I brought to Japan one hundred records I had collected, and that were prepared with stickers, to create loops.

There's some video recording of the performances. It was in the Panasonic National Hall, a showroom for Panasonic—it was huge. It was this temporary structure in the middle of Tokyo; there were different showrooms for everything they made, from vacuum cleaners to electronics and home appliances. Panasonic also made the ultimate turntable at the time, the Technics MK2. There was this large performance space where they had developed a new speaker system—shallow flat speakers covering the walls, like wallpaper. They had the whole space covered with them and synchronized by a computer. You could program the setup, so we made the sound spin around. All these sound loops spinning. Perry Hoberman installed video projections that were spinning, and there were people with cameras going around, filming close-ups of the action, which was spinning around us, and all kinds of weird images of domestic objects, also spinning.

Video Quartet *[2002], seemed liked the next step from the music you've been doing combining different instruments, like that first track on* Records *[Atavistic, 1997] where you're sampling one instrument at a time. Was that something you were conscious of when you were making* Video Quartet*?*

Video Quartet was an idea I had more than ten years ago, and it's only recently I was able to realize it. Actually *Video Quartet* had another piece at its origin, a piece I did for Naut Humon, for Asphodel Records. He curates at Ars Electronica Festival, and he commissioned me to do a seven-minute piece. And I remembered years before applying for a grant with Carole Ann Klonarides—she had MICA-TV and she was producing videos for artists. I wanted to create a circle of ten monitors and each one would have a close-up of my turntable. I would be playing with myself multiplied by ten. But back then it was impossible to synchronize the videos; we didn't have DVDs, it was tape or videodisc, everything was so expensive. We applied to get money but didn't get it and it fell through. I put that idea aside, and when Naut approached me, I said I'd like to do a quartet of four turntables, playing with myself. I did this piece and it was shown I think in '99. It showed close-ups of my hands, just one turntable per screen, bird's-eye view, just doing simple actions with each record, each one a different manipulation, but there were still problems with synchronization. Anyway, it worked more or less and they showed it at Ars Electronica, but I couldn't go for the show so I never even saw it. I saw it at the Compound, at Naut's place in San Francisco, and later Otomo [Yoshihide] did a performance playing along with it, because I couldn't be there, so it was like a quintet [*laughs*]. Later that experiment became *Gestures* [1999], a four-screen video.

That was the beginning of seeing the potential of using video to create music. But with *Video Quartet*, instead of filming myself, I wanted to use found film excerpts. I had done *Telephones* in 1995—that was also a sketch leading to *Video Quartet*, but it was a single-channel piece. I started thinking of four screens side by side as a way to compose visually and sonically, like for a quartet. Then the technology became available to synchronize, so I could do it at home on my computer. I learned how to use Final Cut Pro and worked for almost a year on it. To me it was no different than working with Pro Tools. Even in Pro Tools you're always looking at some visual representation of the sounds. I wanted to compose like that, using found little fragments. I could do it live on four turntables, which was a number I liked for a long time, but then I became lazy carrying four turntables [*laughs*]. So I replaced the extra turntables with effects and electronics. Now with two turntables I can do a lot, using other sampling and looping devices, such as the Boomerang, to sample on the fly. It's the same kind of approach, using little snippets of sound and mixing them together to create a new, unified composition. With the video it's different, the visual adds another dimension. It goes back to this idea of live performance versus recording. The film footage is charged with an emotional content you can't dissociate from the sound. If someone is smashing a glass it's not the same emotionally as someone hitting a cymbal; it has a totally different meaning. That's why I like working with images. I edited the video with sound and image as one, the image is always a part of the sound. It was about selecting the right sound image; if there was a perfect sound for a certain sound combination but the image was wrong, I couldn't use it. I still wanted the whole thing to have a kind of narrative or structure, an emotional continuity. We tend to think of music as this sightless experience because recordings have distorted our understanding of music. We think it's this totally abstract thing that comes from nowhere and just exists as a recording, a disembodied, invisible performance. Going to a club and experiencing music being made on the spot is totally different. That's why I don't like "live" recordings—they never give you the full picture.

Lou Reed

The *Wire* asked if I'd be interested in doing a cover story on Lou Reed for the impending release of *The Raven* (Sire/Reprise, 2003), a sprawling two-CD labor of love for which Lou Reed and Hal Willner alternated Edgar Allan Poe works with Poe-inspired songs by Reed; the project was based on a previous Poe-based collaboration with Robert Wilson, the opera *POEtry* (2000). It was good timing, as it was certainly one of his more intriguing solo efforts; I hadn't really sat through a Reed album from beginning to end since 1983's *Legendary Hearts* on RCA. With its dramatic contrasts (the child-like melody of "Balloons," sung by the sisters Kate and Anna McGarrigle, and the sonic holocaust of "Fire Music," for instance), *The Raven* epitomized the artistic extremes characteristic of Reed's oeuvre, as first outlined in the now-classic deviant rock radicalism and '60s pop readymades found on *The Velvet Underground and Nico* (Verve, 1967) and continuing through the Velvets' second and third albums—the fantastically assaultive *White Light/White Heat* (Verve, 1968) and the intimate, quintessentially subdued *The Velvet Underground* (MGM, 1969). Because it was the *Wire*, there was latitude to ask about *Metal Machine Music* (RCA, 1975) and drones, besides querying him on the latest release. Ornette Coleman played on *The Raven*, which prompted me to ask about both that and Don Cherry's previous work with Reed. Part of Reed's appeal for me, I've come to realize, is that he was maybe the first rock performer I felt I would have something in common with, based mostly on the worldview of his lyrics and his love of noise; but as it turned out, we both had grown up in the New York suburbs, in Jewish families whose patriarchs were accountants by trade. More pertinently, as fellow musicians, we had one collaborator in common—saxophonist Ulrich Krieger, who played with me in Text of Light and with Reed in Metal Machine Trio.

Reed was inarguably the most famous person I had interviewed at that time, and he had a reputation as an occasionally hostile interviewee, so I was nervous, but I had thoroughly reviewed the various Reed/ Velvet Underground histories at my disposal and was well prepared. I sought counsel from a journalist who had interviewed him several times, and when I asked about the best way to approach Reed, he said, “It’s no problem—just tell him he’s the greatest artist of the twentieth century.” When I arrived at Pastis brasserie near Fourteenth Street for the interview, on December 9, 2002, Reed was winding up a morning of press and rather grumpily autographing CDs for the interviewer who preceded me. (When I saw the resulting article by that writer, I could see why Lou was annoyed: the questions mostly tried to confirm his sexual preferences and the current status of his drug use.) I was supposed to have an hour to talk to him, but when I arrived the publicist told me the interview would only be thirty or forty minutes; she also advised me to start off with questions about *The Raven* and then, time permitting, to ask about whatever else. I sat down and Lou was standing a few feet away telling the publicist, “No, no, no, no, no, no, no,” rejecting a suggestion about where to do the photo shoot. Lou joined me at a table, looked at my old-school handheld cassette recorder and said, “I see you’re really keeping up with modern technology,” to which I replied, “If it ain’t broke, don’t fix it.”

You can't get much more experimental than this one.

That's true. And it's incredibly wide-ranging, too.

Thank you for noticing. Do you know what it's taken to do that? Even a few months ago, there were still some little teeny decisions for Willner and I to make, putting a track code next to a speech, separating it from a song so you could isolate it, little things like that, going over it yet again for the two billionth time. And Willner's a lot better at that than I am 'cause he remembers and I don't, and we were saying, "My God, how did this even get done, look at all of this," because Willner had to put together the credits. It did take a seriously long time . . . so many different areas. At the time it didn't seem like that, because it seemed logical: *x* happens so you do *y*, but that gets blocked so you go over here, something lucky happens and this opens up, you say "ah!" OK, you're in there, but later on, if you look at the whole thing—you know what I'm saying? Holy shit. Wow.

Now this is really funny. We needed a copy of the script. That would seem simple enough, right, but it had been rewritten and rewritten and rewritten for the CD, specifically to be heard—not to be seen, to be heard. Things were then moved around with Logic, so now the script isn't the same anymore; that's gotta be moved too. But we weren't worrying about that, who cared about that? Because it had been done, they said it, it's on tape. Now here's the final version, where's the script? It's in the box over there with the cues, they saved it. Is it in order? No, it's not in order, so what do you do? Willner tried to put it in some kind of an order. At some point, if there really is a need to see that text, someone's going to have to transcribe the whole thing and go over it again.

It's funny to think about because there was no person in charge of that; we were in charge of that.

How did you think about incorporating the songs with Poe's poetry? You've got "Fire Music" on one hand, then you've got "Balloon" or "Broadway Song," or "Vanishing Act" . . .

Yeah, you put 'em next to each other, it's like, "Whoa, who did that?"

And the new versions of "The Bed" and "Perfect Day."

Antony [ANOHNI], our big discovery. When we heard that voice, we had to use him as much as possible; his voice, his instrument is so extraordinary. "The Bed" had kind of this perfect lead-in with "House of Usher," with houses and flames and all this. . . . The balloon song always ended act one. Why? I don't know. I mean, I can't give you a logical reason for it, it's just—it did, and it always did, it was always supposed to be there, it was always that way, and that was that. Having the McGarrigles do it, that's a Willner idea—those amazing harmonies they did, those kind of things, that's where they all come from. Instinct. Or 'cause I like it that way. I mean, I could think of reasons, I used to in interviews, but it's all after-the-fact, make-believe reasons—"Oh yeah, we did that because actually there is a balloon mentioned in 'The Cask of Amontillado,' we're referring back to it"—no, there isn't [*laughs*]. It was because of rhythm, really; it was time to have a little relief from some of the other things that had preceded it. The way things were divided up—act one, act two; CD one, CD two—it broke down the same way, [*knocks table*] thank *God*. And we kept it that way, although things were rewritten to be an audio experience. In the original play, you'd see something happening; it didn't have to be explained or have someone comment on it, it was right there in front of you. Here that's not true; you hear things happen, which in a way is really more fun, 'cause your imagination comes up with some amazing things. Willner has a huge collection of sound effects from old radio shows, not to mention all the sound effects libraries they have now, CD-ROMs and CDs, plus what we made ourselves, electronically and combining things or using some of my favorite machines linked together. We wanted, really, our own effects, including door knocks, thunder, whirlwind effects. Willner actually had a whirlwind effect: "Get away from the window, there's a whirlwind" [*laughs*]. I love this kind of stuff. It's not like an old radio show; this is way more 3D. The imaging, where things are placed—that is a lot of fun. Things sneaking up behind you; someone's going to appear here, *what is it?* Or a sound that's suggestive of an emotion more than anything—then *boom*, it's gone, there's another one, and it's *moving*.

The thing's not compressed like regular records are compressed. Right now we have people downloading things by the track. Most records only have one good song, so they download it and move on. With this thing, first of all, no one can download two hours, you'd have to be out of your mind. Two, *if* you do that, we did not compress this, so the record has a lot of volume differences. And if you bother to listen on any kind of a system, it'll move forward; "Fire Music" in particular is a real example of that. That was a real thrill, no kidding around, and it kills me that you can put something like that on a little CD, something that has that kind of potency, but it's *there*. But if you compress it, you will *absolutely* defeat it, completely and totally. You'll squash it and you won't hear it.

Can you talk a little bit about the construction of "Fire Music"?

Ah! Well, I did a thing called *Metal Machine Music* that was taken off the market in three weeks. It existed underground for a while. Twenty years later, in 2000, they repackaged it, put it out. I did the mastering with Bob Ludwig. A year or two after that, zeitkratzer, an orchestral avant-garde group in Germany, asked, "Can we transcribe this and perform it?" I said, "It can't be done." They said, "Let us try, we'll send you a sample," and they did and it was fantastic. And accurate. I know that record, I know people think I don't but I do, I know every little dot in there. So I appeared with them in the fourth section of it; I came out with a guitar and these guys had actually transcribed all these harmonics, I don't know how they did it. It was astonishing to hear an hour's worth of that live.

"Fire Music" was always supposed to be there, all the way back to the original play [*POEtry*], but it was different. I still had to do a "Fire Music" that had the power of fire music, and this is two days after 9/11, which I was here to witness; I watched it from my building. I'd been fooling around with these programs, Logic, a whole bunch of machines, and I composed "Fire Music." It's in real time and there's no overdubs. I had wanted to pick up where *Metal Machine* left off, but more. I had a lot of techs over to go over certain things I wanted programs to do, that I could do on guitar. With tape recorders, we had different speeds. You're recording over here, you can't record at *x* speed and then play it at *y* speed, it doesn't even exist anymore; you'd have to go back to old machines or go frame by frame. I said, "No, no, no." Then it changes—how can I do it? I don't want the key to change. So I hooked up a bunch of guitar effects. I've been using guitar effects with keyboards, being able to set them a certain way and then record it with Logic and have a bunch of things going on at once, in real time. That's what "Fire Music" is.

I actually know Ulrich Krieger from zeitkratzer. He and I play together.

Really? What did you play?

Guitar.

Really? No shit! Ulrich did the transcription [of *Metal Machine Music*]. I don't know how he did it, to this day. Did you ever see them do it live? It's really fantastic; he's a very talented puppy. I asked Ulrich for a copy of it, not that anyone else could use it. Where am I going to go with it, the Philharmonic? It was just a wonderful thing to have. Very hard to get it booked, to this day. It played in Venice and Berlin. . . . It's part of these subscription series of avant-garde whatever. There's a chance it'll go to Royal Festival Hall in London; right now they want, as a prerequisite, that I'm there for a half hour of it. But it can't be a prerequisite; what I do is I play on the last part of it. There's no way I could do a half hour of that—how could I? I did three or four minutes, maybe, where my guitar just completely replaces them, and it's really awesome. No, seriously, it's awesome—one guitar replaces the whole thing.

There's this English genius, Pete Cornish, who builds a lot of machines for me, who built some things for me where I could do some of that live in real time. I really can, no bullshit; this can be proved, it's documented. Not that anyone cares, but I'm just telling you that one of my goals as a guitar player was to able to do that without having to go in and layer three more. Which gets to "Fire Music": I didn't want to have to go in and layer it, I wanted it played in real time. Real time is real time. It's not a loop—it is, but it isn't. It's real time, and it lasts as long as I can do it [*laughs*]; where it ran out, I couldn't keep it up anymore, and that was enough for that. Pete built pedals for me where I could do these things. The orchestra disappears, so the sound had better be big and really be something else. And it is. And then I stop and they replace me. It's so cool. It'd be really cooler if it was appearing places, but it's still . . . at least now when people hear it it's not far out to them . . . not the way it was.

When I put [*Metal Machine Music*] out, they took it off the market; every record store in America said [*laughs*], "We'll never carry a Lou Reed record again, this is the most returns. . . . We don't want another record from him, *ever*." And then there was the *Metal Machine* clause [in recording contracts], "You will not record anything like Lou Reed's *Metal Machine Music*." People think I didn't really like it, that I did it to get out of a contract—*Jesus*. People really can't figure out how you could like that. Or how you could like that and do "I'll Be Your Mirror," or "Perfect Day," or "Satellite of Love," or "[Walk on the] Wild Side" . . . why not? *The Raven* is one huge why not, it's like the why not of all why nots, 'cause like you said, it's got "Balloons" and "Fire Music" and there they are.

The original tape of Metal Machine *went back to the time around [the Velvet Underground's]* Loaded *[Cotillion, 1970]?*

I recorded that in a loft on a three-speed Uher, and then I brought it to Bob Ludwig, all those years ago, and we played around with it. And we even made a quad version, which is the ultimate.

Which I have.

You have it? Are you serious?

Yeah—unfortunately I don't have a quad system.

Well, yeah . . . that's before 5.1, right? What I had hoped to do [when the album was reissued], and I asked the record company but they wouldn't do it: "Can we make this now for surround sound?" "No." But at least it's there, twenty years after the fact.

The quad version was the tape played both forward and backward?

Yeah. We flipped the tapes over. I probably shouldn't tell you this, but Bob had said we had got to get over to Columbia, where they have a quad system. I said, "But all we have is stereo." He said, "Don't let that hold you back, we'll hear what it sounds like when we flip a tape and listen to it." It was just—more. I said, "Wow, OK, great. Just don't tell anybody." We did it four times.

Was zeitkratzer able to replicate the weird, imbalanced stereo effects of the record?

On *The Raven*, there's a track called "A Thousand Departed Friends"—a perfect example of my idea of mixing, which is imbalanced stereo. It's all over the place. I can't *believe* people want to just balance things, it's so insane. This record, all through it, if you pay attention, if that interests you, there's imbalance—not only imbalance but zooming in to hear one instrument all of a sudden. Why? Why not? [*Laughs.*] It's like a movie and you're directing: "I want you to hear this. Here, got it? OK, now we'll go over here." That's why.

Can zeitkratzer replicate that? That's more of a mix thing than their thing. It's astonishing to hear it live. That kind of imbalance doesn't occur. But *The Raven*—I really wanted to get into that with songs, too, not balanced. Not compressed and not balanced. There's so much fun to be had the other way. It's like uncharted territory or something. That's why people sometimes really like bootleg tapes—they're unbalanced, they're not compressed, of course you like it. Then they put it on a CD and they compress it. You just undid what you liked about it. Put it out as it was, this *is* the way it was.

I was interested to see that Ornette Coleman was on The Raven, *which also makes a connection to* The Bells *[Arista, 1979], which Don Cherry was on, and which was partially inspired by Poe—at least the title track. Can you talk a bit about working with those guys?*

What a character Don was, what a musician. Once you get into that, you can't just play with anybody, not when you hear that. Granted, very few people are that good, and I accept that. Anytime I run across somebody like that, I try to get as much of that as I can. Don could do more with three notes than most people can do with a thousand. He knew the sax player with these guys I was working with; they knew him, they backed him up sometimes. He came to Germany, where I was doing *The Bells*. He says, "Hey Lou, we all come from the pussy." I said, "Thanks for sharing that, Don, that's great. . . . OK." But we had a lot of fun from there, once we got over this . . . *hello*. He played the Bottom Line with us, played out in LA with us; there's recordings around somewhere of him doing "Wild Side" with us. You can hear it in your head the minute I say it, you ought to be able to hear the kind of trumpet Don would play on it . . . just such an amazing player. God, makes it look so easy—it's just a few notes. But it's that instrument, the sound will break your heart. Antony has that sound in his voice.

Ornette . . . Ornette did seven versions [of "Guilty"]. I used to follow Ornette around in the '60s. I couldn't afford to get into the clubs he played but I would listen through the grating to him when he was with Billy Higgins, Charlie Haden, and Don. And then I wanted to play guitar like him after I heard *Free Jazz* [Atlantic, 1961]—oh ho ho, wow. If you asked me my favorite song, I'd have to say "Lonely Woman," because probably not a day goes by I don't hear that in my head. So finally working with Ornette was a big deal. I'd love to put out an album of the seven versions he did. "This one's with the drums, this one's with the guitar, this is with your voice, this is with the bass, this is with the other guitar, this is with everybody." And we put a total take down, because his thoughts are really long. You can't say, "Well I like that thing he did, drop this and we'll put it in," y'know, and edit it, no, you can't do that with him. Take him for what he is, take the idea for what it is, it's one long idea, you can't interfere with it. Which actually sits very well with me, 'cause I have a long idea too. It was *easy* for him to do it. Easy. We had other people come in—"No, no, nope, nope. Oh well." And then he came in, did seven in a row. I was in tears. The version we picked was a more accessible version. It was neck and neck with another version that Willner called the "clear the room" version; only true believers will stay for this. People were saying it's a bitch of a key for a sax player—not for Ornette it wasn't. For him it was nothing—as in zero, nothing. It's like saying it's a bad key for [Andrés] Segovia or something—I don't think so. Reassess what you're saying. We just wanted to be sure we recorded him with the right microphone, got out of his way.

Can you talk a bit about the track "The Bells"?

One of my favorite, favorite tracks. Every time they put out a compilation where I get a chance to say something, BMG's going to do one that'll be out in April, "The Bells" will be on there. We edited it down—they don't have the tapes anymore, they lost the tapes.

Really?

Of course they lost the original tapes. Bob Ludwig and I bought *The Bells*, the album, for fifty bucks, put it through Sonic Solutions, really worked on it, and then edited it down. On CD there's the nine-minute version, and there's also, on this compilation out of Canada, a six-minute, thirty-one-second version, and that's the one that will be on this BMG compilation; that's the one that's seriously remastered. I really went in there to try to dig those tones out. A lot of these other CDs they make, I'm not involved—whap! Over and out. Tone, what tone? And because mastering has gotten more sophisticated, they got a lot more going on now to preserve some of those tones. People say that vinyl sounds better, well, *yeah*, of course it sounds better; these guys didn't even make any effort to make the sound any good. It's not like a CD can't sound good, but you have to put some time and energy into it. That translates into money, money, money. How much are you talking about? Big deal. Thousand bucks? Two thousand? What's the big deal? To make it sound good? These guys say, "Exactly like the album." Well, not quite, Jack. And they know that. If you see on the back, I write something or my name's there, that means I went in with Ludwig and supervised. That means it will sound good with whatever the equipment available then was. And if we get a chance to go back in and do it again, we do.

I love that track, I just love it. That was done live too, and it's a spontaneous lyric, which I used to do a lot in the studio. There's something so emotional about that track, there's Don's plaintive trumpet. . . . God. Amazing.

The ending is fantastic on that too, where it builds up to—

—this huge crescendo. That was recorded in Delta Studios in Wilster [West Germany], where they were affiliated with a local university and had done research into binaural sound, 360-degree sound. It didn't quite translate; nonetheless, if you listen to that thing through some speakers with any kind of volume, it's this *mass*. I was listening to it the other day because I needed to compare it to something; I put it on and . . . [*gasps*]. No one even knows. For them to know, they would have to sit in front of two good speakers, turn the volume up, just sit in the right place. We did a thing once—I was up with Bob when we were trying to do "The Bells." I've got these same headphones he's got, naturally, because if Bob has it, I go and get it. But his was a really expensive model with a phase switch on it. I was sitting there, listening, and I threw the phase button and the thing suddenly went into binaural, for real. I said, "Bob, they had the phase wrong! That's why!" He said, "Oh, please Lou, not now. You can't redo it." Anyway, I got killed with that album before it even came out. The head of the company was down on it, gave me a three-page written critique of it, "Doesn't sound finished," it's this, it's that. All of a sudden he's a record critic: "What the fuck is this shit? What?" I was dead in the water. It was the equivalent of him saying, "Go back in," and me saying "No." "*No?* We will release exactly *three* copies, hello goodbye." There you go.

I also wanted to touch on the drone. There are a lot

of backgrounds on The Raven *that are drones, and that's always been a big part of your work:* Metal Machine *but also "Like a Possum" and going back to the Velvet Underground. . . .*

"Like a Possum," one of the great—see, that's using that thing Pete Cornish built for me, that's called a Death Pedal. The amount of harmonics you get out of that, the thickness of the note—*man*, there's the drug of choice. I don't know if people can hear that, but *I* can; it's certainly there for me. That drone can cover a lot of territory when you have a machine—a musical instrument extender, I guess, because if you're dealing with electric, you start out with a Fender Blackface overloaded, then you move on to the Jim Kelley with power amp distortion, then you move on from there, keeping those sounds in mind, because how can you replicate that? That's how I end up with Pete Cornish, where I am now, that sound. *That* sound, cubed. So that "drone," where you can spread those harmonics all around, this huge wave, there's a lot of places it can go, and you can also just break it. You can break it in a way that's OK, like a normal right-hand turn, or you can break it where it's jolting, like the bottom fell out of an elevator or something. It's fun. Fun with sound.

That was also there in the Velvets, in things like "Melody Laughter."

Ooh, ooh, how do you know that? "Melody Laughter," that's one of my favorites. Where did you even hear that? [*Sings.*] "Melody Laughter went through for me / In the privy sea, by the privy sea." See, I remember it. I love that, I love those things—but with the right musicians. That's the kind of thing that gave me an interest—since you brought it up—in wider, longer experience. I mean, you just start out with that, and then you can go from there. That's why *The Raven* starts out the way it does, and the way "The Bells" starts—actually I hadn't even thought of that, "The Bells" starts out *bom, bom, BOM*. There it is. It's the same ethos behind it. And the overture in *The Raven*. That's many layered things in there. The horns and the guitar in there—Jesus Christ, it's really something.

There's certain kinds of Lee Allen sax solos that I'm enamored of and Doug Wieselman did one on my *Ecstasy* record [Reprise, 2000]; he almost died doing it, he kind of fell over by the time . . . but he's blowing his ass off on that overture, that really funky high note playing, screaming—that's Doug. He's a phenomenal player. He doesn't look like who you would think it would be. We had a number of guys go out and try to blow the roof off, but it was Doug. What was the director's direction? "Go out there and blow the roof off, do whatever you want, go for it," and he did. And he could.

On Metal Machine, *you mention La Monte Young. Did you listen to any other examples of drone music?*

There were things from Billy Linich [Billy Name]; [John] Cale introduced me to that stuff. There are still people around now who apparently were doing that then that I haven't heard. Once I got into feedback and having a sustained note, started playing around with that . . . and again, different kinds of machines can really open all those harmonics. Out of an electric guitar, you can really get some things going, tune all the strings to the same note—

—which you did for Metal Machine Music.

Yeah, and also for "All Tomorrow's Parties," the

guitar solo's taken that way—but also on *Ecstasy* and, actually, on *The Raven*, on "Guardian Angel," I have this seven-string guitar built by this guy in Brooklyn, Carl Thompson. We open with it and close with it. It's the hugest guitar I've ever heard in my life; we gave it the full center stage. The bottom note on that guitar is piano length, so it's like, "Whoa, listen to that drone chord."

The end. All right? Thank you. [*Speaking to publicist who has walked over to the table.*] This guy is very, very, very knowledgeable, more knowledgeable than almost any one of those guys, by light-years. . . . I can't think of many people who'd even know what he's talking about.

Publicist

That's good to know.

It *is* good to know. Keep in mind. This is the kind of person, you could ask him a question—no, because we get asked things all the time, and there are people who know more about it than I do. "Melody Laughter," that's . . . I very much appreciate that you even bothered. That's a lot different than the guy who shows up, "Well, tell me about your album." I really appreciate that. Those are interesting questions too, I hadn't even thought of—once you said that, the relationship between the way the records start, the songs start, and then you get to *The Raven*, and then it's like, well of course it starts that way. Of course it does, it would have to, there's that same idea carried to its conclusion. Interesting for me.

Henry Flynt

Until 1988, I was only aware of Henry Flynt as a figure involved with "concept art" and Fluxus. Then, Donald Miller played me a cassette that Henry had gifted to him as a wedding present, *You Are My Everlovin / Celestial Power* [Edition Hundermarkt, 1986], which pits Flynt's "avant-garde hillbilly" violin against a forceful backing tape of a tanpura drone by Catherine Christer Hennix—a stunning piece then and now. I included this cassette in my first "Minimal Top Ten" article for *Halana* magazine in 1996, and Henry wrote a letter to thank me—as this was the first critical notice the tape had received in the decade since its release—as well as to note the exact dates when he had filled in for John Cale in the Velvet Underground.

The *Wire* contacted me in spring 2004 about doing an article on Henry; I was surprised, as it seemed like they had run a piece on him somewhat recently, but there had been a slew of archival releases in the interim and they wanted a longer profile. Indeed, following the 2001 CD reissue of *You Are My Everlovin* (previously his only release), there were suddenly seven albums of Flynt material in circulation. When we met up at a SoHo café to talk, I had only seen him perform once, at the Emily Harvey Gallery in 2001, and instead of performing music, Flynt demonstrated some of the idiosyncratic dances he had devised to accompany his compositions, which played on tape. Many years after this interview, I was able to attend a private concert, again at Harvey, where he played guitar alongside a loop that was sampled from a thrash metal song (when asked, his technical assistant was evasive about the source of it), which seemed like a worthy successor to "Everlovin."

You've said you're classically trained, but you've also described yourself as a "folk creature." I'm wondering how you reconcile the classical training with your long investigation into Delta blues and country forms?

Yeah, although I am from North Carolina, I just completely ignored what was going on around me when I was young. I suppose I just decided, apropos of nothing, that I ought to be academic; I don't remember how or why, but I just gravitated immediately to classical music. I wanted my mother to buy me a clarinet and she came home with a violin, and it didn't occur to me to do anything with the violin other than learn how to play European music, as I would now call it. I guess that I'm a self-chosen intellectual, very much so. When I was in high school, I was trying to acquaint myself with everything that was considered to be the latest thing—nuclear particles or whatever it happened to be. By the time I was in twelfth grade, I had gotten ahold of some Bartók and was enthusiastically reading that. I mean, I didn't actually find out about what is called International Style until I got to college. I did not know that there was a sort of late-serial, post-post-Schoenberg serialism; I did not know that that existed. But I also remember very well buying the score of the Schoenberg violin concerto when I was in high school, so I just completely cut myself off from what was going on around me. And I guess I assumed that it was a loser's game or something like that [*laughs*]. So I get to college [Harvard University], and I find out that whereas I thought Bartók was the latest thing, there was a whole generation that had come along, people who are ten years older than I am, who had this enormous publicity machine going and had effectively displaced the classical moderns. I fell in with that crowd. Christian Wolff, actually, at that point was the dean of the so-called New Music; I mean "dean" in the generic sense, I don't mean in the academic sense. Of course David Behrman was there, Tony Conrad was there, and he was actually a little more aggressive than I was in finding out what was going on. There were a lot of people that I heard about for the first time from him. So I played that game; I was uncomfortable with it, but I made myself do it.

Because of a classmate who was interested in jazz, I finally came to the point where I decided that I should listen to jazz just to verify that it was as bad as I thought it was [*laughs*]. By that point I was taking Cage as the standard for composition. Any kind of music, when you improvise, you're dealing with what you can process in your own consciousness in real time, whereas Cage had completely disconnected music from that—completely! So I started listening to jazz and I thought, "You know, maybe there's something here, maybe it's not all bad," and then I came across [Samuel] Charters's book *The Country Blues* [1959], and I sent away for this privately manufactured record that he was putting out of 1930s blues records, and when I got that I guess that is what turned me around. I mean, I just underwent a total conversion as a result of hearing that. And I immediately decided that the best musicians in the United States were at the bottom of the social ladder. The rest of the time that I gave to music, I've been kind of working out the implications of that. I come to American ethnic music really as an assumed identity; I did not know anybody socially who played *anything* like jazz or pop, anything like that at all. I don't think I was ever in the same room as a pedal steel player until 1974, which is like, fourteen years after I changed sides. I didn't really have proper instruction; if I was really wealthy now and could afford to do anything I wanted to do, I might start taking music lessons.

Had you taken violin lessons?

In classical, yes. They were mediocre lessons, they were North Carolina–level lessons; they would not have prepared me to play as a professional soloist. Although there was a schoolmate of mine named Julia Adams who went on to become a viola player—she has premiered viola concertos and so on and so forth—and she had essentially the same training, the same start that I did. But I look back on it now, and I'm pretty annoyed, actually, at how limited my violin teacher was. I think Julia Adams, before she went off to Oberlin, she may have found somebody to teach her who was a little more professional than the guys that I had. If you know the classical repertoire, I don't know if you do, but something like [Pablo de] Sarasate's "Zigeunerweisen" [1878], I didn't learn how to play that because my teacher wasn't qualified to teach it. It's a standard piece, very, very standard. The [Max] Bruch violin concerto, that's one of the first that you learn when you're learning how to be a soloist, and my teacher probably couldn't have played it. Looking back on it, I'm mad, I think I was screwed, you know [*laughs*]. But it's a problem for me, if you want to do long runs, to use the entire range of the instrument—that's a whole separate technique which I never really got into adequately; that would have helped me as an improviser, to be able to do that. I mean, you can actually hear me struggling with it on *You Are My Everlovin / Celestial Power*, you can hear me struggling with those long lines that start at the bottom and go all the way up the E string. I'm having a really hard time with it [*laughs*]; one is supposed to just rip right through those. I'm one more composer that can't play his own pieces [*laughs*], but there's a lot of honorable composers who can't play their own pieces.

When you mentioned "going over to the other side," it reminded me of the story you told of Cage being at one of your concerts at Yoko Ono's loft, and when you told him about Chuck Berry and Bo Diddley, he said, "Well if that's what you're interested in, what are you doing here?" It wasn't until the mid-'70s when Peter Gordon or Jill Kroesen or Ned Sublette were playing the Kitchen but playing cowboy songs, in Ned Sublette's case, and Kroesen and Gordon playing pop songs; it seems like you were probably the first person to explore doing that kind of thing in a theoretical, avant-garde art context. And then I noticed that Peter Gordon had played with you.

In '75, and then he did studio work for me in '77; he's the saxophone player on the red record [*Graduation and Other New Country and Blues Music* (Ampersand, 2001)].

So did you feel a connection when you saw this sort of thing happening later on?

Not really, because we're more or less in the neighborhood where, I guess, New Wave happened. I really was coming to this as a folk creature and it wasn't a preassembled audience for me; in other words, it wasn't an art band as such; I wasn't thinking in those terms. I mean, I would have loved to have had a country rock band that played big auditoriums, it just didn't work out that way at all. Not at all. [Nova'Billy] was the central rock repertoire—that's what I thought I could have actually worked with, played out. People always mention the Grateful Dead to me when they hear it. It was different, though, because I am a composer and I do things that only a composer would do. I was really just transferring the techniques that I picked up in the whole modern music thing; I was just transferring them into rock. The people who have written about me, I don't get any real sense that they're aware of that. I guess what I'm doing is like an acoustical trompe l'oeil; I'm fooling them into thinking that they're hearing something much more conventional than it actually is. That's the whole point of giving you a score, although that piece "Hoedown" [1968] is not rock—but still, I wonder if the people who hear that have any idea at all what the nuts and bolts are, what they're actually hearing.

No, I was not actually thinking of myself as being a part of New Wave—in fact, it was a problem for me, because punk hit like a ton of bricks in 1975. It came back from England, even though it started in the United States; they'd been playing it I guess at CBGB, but it really hit in 1975. The sidemen that I'd been working with, they abandoned me for punk—I was like a fish completely out of water. My attempts to have a financially self-sustaining rock band—they just crashed immediately. We did three concerts, and that was the end of it. It only lasted six months. And I had a concert at OK Harris—I mean, already that's bad, if you're playing in an art gallery something is already wrong, you know [*laughs*], but I was just glad to get that. But the other guys quit—I had to call Ivan [Karp, of OK Harris] up and tell him that my band had quit, that was the end of that. I never played rock again except in studio situations.

There was that quote from a friend of yours in college: "I was afraid this would happen when jazz musicians discovered John Cage."

That's about La Monte [Young], and La Monte's earliest pieces were just outrageously theatrical, and he used the instruments just as noisemakers, and that's what the guy was talking about.

But a lot of your audience now is basically what happens when underground rock fans discover Cage, or the equivalent of that—it's sort of a self-fulfilling prophecy.

The people that I would have liked to have played with would be Waylon Jennings or somebody like that. The problem is there's already a considerable distance between him and me, even though I have tremendous respect for what he did. But there's so much distance, we could not possibly have played at the same gig; I don't know. But I did not want this to be only country. The Nova'Billy tapes, maybe the most interesting song—what do you call it, a soul mash, that's what it is. I wanted to play jazz rock, rhythm and blues, and just move back and forth across the whole range. That's another thing that would have shut me out of the country circuit, aside from the fact that the music would just be too weird for them. I mean, something like "Lonesome Train Dreams" [1975, from *Graduation*]—I played it for one guy who was in country, and he was really annoyed with me, because I guess they really have a tremendous investment in the chord changes, and to have something that's just tonic pedal point . . . it's like driving on a highway with no stoplights, that's the way that I experience it, and I guess that a normal country guy doesn't like that, is very uncomfortable with it. Whereas I'm the opposite—I find chord changes to basically be very confining. Although there's something to be said for them, you know [*laughs*].

You talked about how La Monte's style of playing blues, where he lingered for a long time on each chord change in a traditional twelve-bar structure, was a jumping-off point for you.

Our unreleased duet from 1962—that's unfortunate, but I guess La Monte owns the material. It just hasn't occurred to me to make an issue out of that, but I'm afraid he's not going to release it in his lifetime. And that's bad for me because you can hear where I'm coming from; it explains a lot of what happened later.

Another song you mentioned in relation to [Flynt's band] the Insurrections was Bob Dylan's "Subterranean Homesick Blues."

We have a take of that which they told us not to release.

Both that and "Maggie's Farm," he's staying on the one chord, maybe on "Maggie's Farm" he goes to the five chord after a while. But it's very similar to what La Monte is doing at the same time. And in your piece "Blue Sky Highway and Tyme" [1969, on Back Porch Hillbilly Blues, *vol. 1 (Locust Music, 2002)], you go to the four chord twelve minutes in, and it's roughly the same time period . . . so was there something in the air?*

I was trying to translate La Monte's aesthetic principles into basic country. It was conscious. I did a private concert in his loft in 1969, and a tape of that was played at the private concert. Some of these pieces were self-conscious country music tributes to La Monte. I guess from the outside that's a very odd agenda to have; I hope I made it work so that one doesn't have to apologize for it [*laughs*].

In your essay "The Meaning of My Avant-Garde Hillbilly and Blues Music" [1980/2002], you talk about the Beatles—

They're a cop-out if you're interested in the fierce authenticity of it—they're a cop-out. Of course, it was unbelievably commercially successful; that doesn't even have to be said.

But the Rolling Stones, did you see them as—

Well, there were other British bands of that period that sought to have more edge than the Beatles did. The Animals, the Rolling Stones . . . the Nashville Teens, I liked the Nashville Teens. I thought their rock version of "Tobacco Road" was great, actually.

From my point of view, rock started getting old at some point in the '60s. . . . By the time you get to Kiss and so on and so forth, I'm not interested anymore. I mean, New Wave, to me, is post-post-all of that. I would have wanted people to feel that they were hearing something that was as fresh from the source as Waylon Jennings, but my premises are very different from his.

Country music also became much more commercialized, to some extent in the '70s but more so in the '80s and '90s.

There were two different things that were happening: one was that they simply modernized the instrumentation and the recording techniques. And I think that that was actually good; as a matter of fact I have a piece where my niece [Libby Flynt] plays lead guitar, which I hope someday to release, because it was done in 1980, and this is where rockabilly is in 1980 as opposed to 1955—that's why I want to release it. It shows that rockabilly did not stop with Carl Perkins; they kept finding new things to do. What I would call the fierce authenticity, the ferocity of it, is still there. For obvious commercial reasons it was very advantageous to have some kind of middle ground between country music and pop. I don't even know—well, I would recognize the names if you said them to me, I've forgotten who they are, but just awful, horrible stuff.

Garth Brooks?

Yes, yes.

You were talking about the spirit versus the body in music.

I've spent a lot of time trying to think about what in the university would be called aesthetic theory. It's the same reason I deal with written music and with scores: once I like something, I want to know where it came from, how it works. You can also ask that question about musical style, about sensibility, about inspiration, the source of inspiration. Those same questions: what is it, where does it live, where does it work . . .

La Monte really had this idea that man has an animal nature, and that's rhythm, and that man has a spirit nature, which is pitch and vibration, and the whole idea . . . I really dislike that. I guess the reason that I admire African tribal music so much is that they do not have that, they don't carve it up like that at all, as far as I can see. They have a tremendous cultural superiority for that reason. I think we are impaired by having been indoctrinated in that way. In Indian music, it's always a problem of how it should be handled, but Indian music certainly has the rhythmic side, although La Monte just happened to take as his master the man who placed the least emphasis on that of any of them ever, probably [Pandit Pran Nath]. La Monte also had the idea that low notes should be loud and high notes should be soft, or something like that.

It reminded me of this essay by Michael Ventura where he's talking about how the roots of the blues in Africa eliminates the mind/body split that post-Christian Western people have made. And dancing is a big part of that elimination, where you're not supposed to just sit there and listen to music; your body is supposed to react to it while you're listening to it.

Yeah, and I must say that's why I'm really committed to—to use another pretentious word—choreographing all of my music.

Which I was going to bring up—I saw you demonstrate some of the "club dances" you've made up for your music at the Emily Harvey Gallery in 2000, and it seems like the stuff on Graduation *is meant to be dance music, and some of the earlier pieces too.*

Yeah, you're supposed to be able to dance to them. As a matter of fact, this soul mash—the piece is called "I Was a Creep" [1975]—my engineer [Tim Barnes] told me it was a soul mash, and he knew how to do the dance and he started showing it to me. At some point I actually need to start taking lessons from him; we need to maybe even videotape him to show the steps and everything like that. This is the first time I've gotten involved with something where I have to painfully learn it, step by step. I guess it's James Brown, it already exists; I have to try to learn how to do it. It's an important discovery about that piece, "I Was a Creep," these particular movements. The one thing that I remember is that the feet go in one direction and the body goes in the other—that's why it's a mash; the feet are sort of on the floor, like that [*demonstrates*].

What do you think of disco? To me, disco can be very trance-oriented, but it's also dance music.

It probably influenced me in the sense of just wanting to do club dances. . . . Most of the stuff I do doesn't involve these really tight moves; I have a problem with that, although some of that stuff is great, but it's difficult for me. [Catherine] Christer [Hennix] and I went to a bar where they were playing that kind of music, and we just turned around and walked right back out. For us that is like psychic brutalization . . . and terms used like *airhead* . . . unfortunately that's the other side of this. I think that it's a deeply escapist practice for people who hate their lives, as far as I can make out. Almost a way of making them feel they are doing something worthwhile, but it's meant to pound their mind to a pulp.

In the WFMU interview, you had said how in the blues they reinvented European instruments. And again, in this essay by Ventura, he's talking about Black churches—

What's the name of the essay?

It's called "Hear That Long Snake Moan," in a collection of his writing called Shadow Dancing in the USA *[1985], and he quotes James Baldwin: "Blacks did not so much use Christian symbols as recognize them—recognize them for what they were before Christians came along—and thus reinvest these symbols with their original energy." Is there a similar thing with what they did with Western instruments?*

Well, I've always accepted it as just some incredible communal creativity that Southern Black music came about. I don't have any description of it programmatically or anything like that. Memphis Slim, the boogie pianist, he's someone that I really recommend, if I'm thinking of the right person—the boogie performances on his first Folkways record . . . The piano, as long as it is a piano and you haven't done something to gimmick it up or something like that, is the most confining instrument, as confining as an instrument could possibly be. It just puts you in these little boxes and that's all you can do. Finger pressure is basically the only thing you have to work with. Memphis Slim, if you do listen to that—he is taking that instrument somewhere else; that's the most incredible example. In the guitar you have more to work with: you can deflect the strings laterally—in a piano you have nothing to work with. He is in a completely different language from European piano music, as different as Chinese is from English. And to me that is just phenomenal. I mean, I can't really begin to tell you why somebody felt compelled to do that [*laughs*]. When somebody does something good, that's the hardest thing to explain [*laughs*].

Marcus Boon wrote that You Are My Everlovin *is kind of a version of* Raga Tilang. *Is that accurate?*

There's a period of alap that I'm playing at the beginning, which is close to *Raga Tilang*—or that's sort of the closest equivalent. That's what La Monte and Marian [Zazeela] told me.

Raga Tilang *was supposed to be on this record that La Monte was planning on doing called* The Blues According to La Monte Young, Pandit Pran Nath, and Terry Riley. *I've heard the recording of it that he was going to use, and Pran Nath is almost yodeling at a certain point. Was that a connection you ever made from listening to him?*

No, as a matter of fact I just decided that this is what I ought to be doing and I had to be told after the fact that it sounded like *Raga Tilang*, because the ragas that I actually know are not blues-like. The term that they use is *ta*, *ta* is the scale of the raga, and *Tilang* is the nearest that *ta* comes to blues.

And it seems like "Jive Deceleration" [1978] is also incorporated in there.

I think it's just me. It's not drawn directly from any particular source.

And "Celestial Power" [1979] is sort of an evolution of pieces like "Jumping" [1976].

Actually, "Celestial Power"—I think two different versions have been released now, the four-guitar version on the red record, and then the [1980] performance with the violin solo. The one on the red record—hopefully one day that will come out as a double CD, so you can use two CD players and have the four guitars coming from four different speakers. The violin solo probably heavily depends on *Raga Todi*. *Raga Todi* tonicizes the major third. It makes a kind of conventional scale that starts on C, and then it treats E as the tonic. And what I'm doing is keeping that scale but going back and treating C as the tonic.

That was the "psychedelic version."

Yes, I'd been told that I'd taken artificial mescaline, or synthetic mescaline, or something like that. I must say, it made a big difference, because I have a performance where I did it without the benefit of the drug, and it's just not the same thing. In the one without the drug, I'm sort of walking steadily toward a destination; it doesn't have the lazy sort of—

Is that what expanded the length of it as well?

No, they're both forty-five-minute performances, it's just more like a walk from A to B without the drug [*laughs*], not the kind of floating that I achieved.

The four-channel version was originally a sound environment?

At the Kitchen in 1979, yeah.

Are there other sound environment pieces?

I have a sound environment called *Glissando* [1979], which hopefully someday will be published, and Christer's *The Electric Harpsichord* [1976], which has been published only in a boutique edition—I think it's four hundred dollars for half an hour [*laughs*].[1]

*Pretty steep [*laughs*]. What was the Dharma Warriors?*

That was a jazz rock band from 1983; we did one concert at Phill Niblock's space. There were three or four compositions that I wrote—as a matter of fact, in 1978 I started playing rhythm guitar, with Christer on jazz drums. And then somehow or other we brought Arthur Russell into it—I forget which instrument; it might have been keyboard. There was also a bass player whose name you would recognize but I can't recall

1 *Glissando* [1979] was released on CD by Recorded Records in 2001 as *Glissando No. 1.*

it right offhand, but he was around on the New York scene for several years after that. We made some tapes in 1978 in a rehearsal studio on Charles Lane, way over in the West Village. I would like for that material to be released. And then we came back to it when Christer was living in Woodstock in 1983. We came to New York, we hired Marc Johnson to play acoustic bass, we did a studio recording and then the concert at Phill Niblock's. I guess for the choice of the title [Dharma Warriors] to make sense you would have to hear the music. Christer's main influence as a drummer was Elvin Jones; we have a really great recording where Marc Johnson sounds like a rudra veena, which is a plucked North Indian instrument that has a very low register—beautiful instrument. And then eventually I would have added violin solos, but it never got to that point.

How did the cassette release of You Are My Everlovin *come about?*

I knew [gallerist Armin] Hundertmark at that time, and he just announced that he was willing to publish. The red record was supposed to be published by Cramps Records in Italy around 1980. When I went to Italy around 1989, I was told that the masters had been lost, gone. And then it resurfaced, and they got in touch with Dawson Prater [of Ampersand Records] and he got in touch with me; that's how I met him. That would have been my first record. Hundertmark and I talked to each other, and he wanted to do something; he was in New York and picked up a copy from me here. There was some confusion having to do with Dolby, it was Dolby A on these old tapes, and as a result I think side B of that cassette, *Celestial Power*, was published in such a way that there was no treble on it—all the treble had been killed. It was awful, it was a travesty. But that was all I had out for fifteen years or something.

It didn't seem like you made too many changes to it when you transferred it to CD.

We made no changes to it. The treble was not even a change, we just made it right.

How did you record all this stuff that's come out? Did you have your own tape recorder?

Some of it is studio, some of it is just done at home. Or in various amateur situations.

I also wanted to ask about Angus MacLise—how you got involved with the Brain Damage in Oklahoma City *performance [1967–70]. I guess you knew Angus through La Monte?*

Yeah—am I on that thing on the song flute? You barely hear it, just snatches of it. . . . As I remember it we did it at Anthology Film Archives on Wooster Street, isn't that right? I mean, I was just hanging out; for me that was just free-form. I had no aesthetic agenda to speak of when I did that. But yes, Angus and I obviously met through La Monte. The one time that we tried to play together, it didn't work for two reasons: One is that his drumming was very complicated and it was actually so complicated that I needed for it to be greatly simplified just so you could tell what was going on, to react to it. It was just like he was machine-gunning you with his drumming. He was not necessarily comfortable with simplifying what he was doing. The other one was that I decided that the piece that I should rehearse with him would be "Spindizzy," the one that has been published on the second *New American Ethnic Music* [Recorded, 2003], and the problem with that piece, which I was not even thinking about, is that the violin is playing the riffs and the measures start with a slide, and that means that they don't have a legitimate accent. There's not a clear downbeat—I mean, there's literally a clear downbeat, but what you actually hear is the violin sliding in; it's actually unaccented. It's only when it slides and hits the note where it's going that [it] creates a kind of accent. I was trying to put that together with Angus and I just couldn't do it, and I realized after the rehearsal had aborted that I was not working with a legitimate downbeat. That's why I couldn't align it with him. That was the last time we ever tried to play together.

You played with Walter De Maria in the Insurrections. Was he also someone you had known through La Monte?

Yes, yes. Let's see, it's hard for me to remember the first time I may have ever met him, but he and I were at the AG Gallery in the summer of 1961; we [performed on] consecutive evenings at the AG Gallery. Some time went on, and he was the one who let me give the anti-art lecture. It was touch and go because his wife actually had a problem with that. He had OK'd it, and I came to New York and when I called him up it turned out that his wife was really having a problem—she didn't even know that her house was going to be invaded by all of these people that evening, but he let me do it. And that photograph of me, which has been published dozens and dozens of times—he enabled that to happen. I think that he was the one who said we could play together: "You can come over to my place." He had a tape recorder. He found an apartment on the Upper East Side, somebody had an apartment up there, which we kind of treated as a recording studio, and I did book a studio for the third session we did.

I liked Walter; I enjoyed hanging out with him. I'm different now; in the '60s I was extremely self-centered because I felt I had something that I had to do and I wanted to get on with it, and I probably struck people as being overly self-preoccupied at that point. But I liked Walter and as far as I know he is now a recluse. And that is unfortunate. I feel that if we met again I would have something to say to him, but I probably never will. I don't know anyone who has seen him in decades [*laughs*] or whatever it may be. I don't know what his thing is now.

Regarding the Insurrections, you said you didn't like protest music of that time—was the Insurrections a reaction to that?

Oh, it's actually much more elaborate than that. I was moving left and moving toward Marxism at the same time that I was finding out that the country blues existed. By '63 I'd moved to New York and actually was in a sectarian Marxist organization. It was intuitively reasonable to me that the music of the people should express the people's real interests, which I would have thought had something to do with Marxism at that point. It seemed to make sense that since the people had in fact created a musical language—and I'm now speaking specifically about Black people in the United States—that the content should not be all, "My man done me wrong," or something like that. It should be socially conscious. In the Communist Party of the USA, with a lot of help from the Soviet Union, they had adopted the Woody Guthrie aesthetic as their official position. The Soviet Union was extremely happy with Paul Robeson and his so-called singing of Russian folk songs. And I thought that was an unmitigated disaster. I was horrified. They were not even drawing musically on the originality, the creativity, of the people that they claimed to be speaking for. It seemed more ironic because Woody Guthrie, apparently, did a hillbilly radio program in LA—that was one of his jobs. I find that very curious because the man didn't have a hillbilly note in his repertoire. Has nothing to do with it. I don't even know how to describe it, they're European nursery songs, that's his aesthetic. The Soviet Union had a problem with Black music; they were seizing on certain aspects of the jazz lifestyle, or something like that, and calling it "American Decadence"—these are complicated things, these are things that one could say a great deal about. Also, the whole crossover phenomenon between actual jazz on the one hand and the bobby-soxers and Frank Sinatra and Glenn Miller, and all that sort of thing . . . in the final analysis it is the public that has the power to make something important. And the public may vastly prefer the Beatles to Robert Johnson and Buddy Guy, and in fact it does vastly prefer them [*laughs*], and so the Beatles, in a certain sociological sense, become far more important. That's just the way it is, you have to figure out how you want to live your own life in relation to that reality.

I did the Insurrections material almost as if it was heuristic, telling these people, "You shouldn't be going with this Woody Guthrie stuff." It was supposed to say, "This is what you should be doing, please do it better than I did" [*laughs*]. So it was done in that spirit, but at the same time I found rock content to be unacceptable. A lot of times it was humorous, and in some cases it was interesting in a personally subjective way—I liked the "Surfin' Bird" [by the Trashmen], yes, I *loved* "Surfin' Bird" and "Sally Go 'Round the Roses" [by the Jaynetts] and so forth and so on; I think those are masterpieces.

But there was far too much of that "my man done me wrong" stuff. I wanted to really crank it up politically.

Was this before or after your substitution for John Cale in the Velvet Underground?

It was before.

Had you heard the Velvet Underground?

I had not heard them, but first it was my guitar lessons with Lou Reed; then the Insurrections, where I applied the guitar lessons with Lou Reed; and then, after the Insurrections was over and done with, I played with the Velvet Underground.

You said that Lou showed you the Bo Diddley guitar technique.

He showed me everything that I was taught about rock guitar. Mark Saffron was my first guitar teacher and he fingerpicked the blues, and it was great but it was too complicated for me. The thing that was so great about Lou Reed was, it's like the difference between an IBM and a Macintosh, he just showed you what you needed to walk right out onstage and start playing. Really great.

The last thing I wanted to ask you about was the "Central Park Transverse Vocals" [1963], and also "Free Alto" [1964], the very free-form style, which I guess was inspired by Ornette Coleman—or other things?

Well, Ornette probably had more influence on other things that I did. There was a lot of Ornette influence in Nova'Billy. You know, I've really got to get those records out, because they're central to my project and people haven't heard them. Coming out of modern music, it was another influence of La Monte's—that you improvise music that has no references to any traditional musical language. You're making noise, it's sort of controlled noise, and then you're presenting it, you're framing it as music. So I developed my own theory, which I called "audart." It's the idea of trying to treat something as music, and to get some kind of response from something, that has no musical language at all. The "Central Park" vocals, I was living on West Eighty-Fourth Street at Central Park and I would just go out at midnight and practice torturing my voice in these ways, and they became these little set pieces that have been recorded. "Free Alto" was done in a very similar way. "Raga Electric" [1966], I would put that in a separate category; at that time I thought that I was pushing sitar music, making it completely over the top, screaming, which I guess I did. I now listen to that and my first reaction is, "This is flamenco" [*laughs*]. I didn't really have any bona fide raga down at all; that scale is a flamenco scale, it's what I think is called in theory the Neapolitan sixth. It's kind of embarrassingly flamenco to me today, to think that I thought that sounded Indian. . . .

The reason that I liked it enough to release it—George Maciunas was living with his mother, who was a devout Catholic, and I came over to his place on a Sunday morning just to play this tape. We put it on and his mother started shouting, "Turn this off, it's the devil's music," or something like that. So I decided if it's getting that kind of reaction, it probably should be out [*laughs*].

Tom Verlaine: Recording and Other Things

A guitar hero for people who are embarrassed to have guitar heroes, Tom Verlaine came to prominence in the '70s CBGB punk scene with his band Television, yet his work seems almost diametrically opposed to the stereotypes associated with that era and subsequent punk. Under Verlaine's stewardship, Television was notable for exquisite guitar interplay (between Verlaine and Richard Lloyd) and longer group improvisations, more so than virtually any other band of the era, save the Patti Smith Group. In this way, they really effected "alternative" rock in the purest sense—music with a different set of values than contemporary arena rock. Television carried over some of the same qualities of the '60s music once heard on both AM and underground FM radio, but built on them in a different way—more esoteric, and introspective—than did prog, glam, and heavy metal. I tend to the think of Television as somehow analogous to cult film director Terrence Malick: both made two rapturous, visionary classics in the '70s (the two albums on Elektra, *Marquee Moon* [1977] and *Adventure* [1978], and the films *Badlands* [1973] and *Days of Heaven* [1978], respectively), disappeared from sight in the '80s, then reappeared in the '90s with comeback efforts (the former with the 1990 LP *Television* [Capitol] and the latter with *The Thin Red Line* [1998]).

Verlaine launched a solo career in 1979, and after a few albums of rock songs he made an influential instrumental record, *Warm and Cool* (Rykodisc, 1992). By the late '90s he was doing live instrumental music for silent films; I previewed one of those shows, at St. Ann's Church in Brooklyn, for *Time Out New York*, writing that "the author of such Television classics as 'Marquee Moon' and 'Foxhole' doesn't seem to have much interest in writing songs these days, and who can blame him?" I heard through the grapevine that someone had shown Tom the preview and that he liked it. After 9/11, Tom and

Sonic Youth joined forces to do a benefit at the Bowery Ballroom in Manhattan, and he needed a second guitarist; Thurston Moore recommended me, so Tom called me up and I played the show, with Television's Billy Ficca on drums. A couple of years later, Tom tapped me to do liner notes for the remastered reissues of the first two Television albums, and in 2006 I wrote a cover story for the *Wire* timed to two simultaneously released Verlaine solo albums on Thrill Jockey, *Songs and Other Things* and *Around.* Thrill Jockey wanted Tom to tape an interview for European radio in advance of his tour behind the records, and he chose me to do it. Sue Garner, my old Run On bandmate and a Thrill Jockey recording artist herself, recorded the interview at her studio space in Greenpoint, Brooklyn.

The one thing that I haven't seen anybody else ask about these two new albums is where their titles, Songs and Other Things *and* Around, *came from.*

The title for the vocal record [*Songs*] came from not wanting a concept laid over it all—in other words, not wanting an idea or a story line to it. So that became *Songs*. And then I thought, "Since there are instrumentals on it, too, I have to say something else," because then people start saying, "Well, it's not songs, there's instrumentals"—so I added *Other Things*. The title for the other record came from looking at the picture [on the album's cover], which has a semicircular train track, and the idea of the jeep going around something, and also the idea of a pun on the word *squares*—the old beatnik term *squares*. The term in the beatnik era was, "Oh, that's so square," but they never used the word *round*. It goes back to this book *Flatland* [1884, by Edwin Abbott Abbott]. This was this odd book of ideas, where the whole idea of squares as unhip people came from. People that were round were whole and energetic and positive, and things that were square were not. *Flatland*, as I remember—I read this as a teenager—was a crazy combination of theory and almost poetry. . . . But the idea of "rounds" never showed up in the society of the 1950s—

*[*Laughs.*] Or since.*

—just the idea of squares [*laughs*].

Although, the roundheads—that was Cromwell-era England.

Also the idea that a round house was the ideal architecture—the Indians with the teepees, that things should be in the round.

Crop circles—there's a whole mysticism around the idea of circles. Circle dancing, too, like the Shakers.

Oh yeah. Shaker circle dancing. I've never seen anybody do this—actually, I'd love to see that. There must be a film of it somewhere.

I only know the engravings of it.

The engravings are great—they're really, really cool. Some of the songs are really beautiful too. But I wonder what the dance was. I mean, the people were falling out in that dance—it was an ecstatic thing, it wasn't just a social thing. I think the last Shaker woman was in Maine. I read an interview with her in the '80s—she was like ninety-six years old. I went up to see the community. There's just a few buildings in the valley; there's a shop there selling some things. Maybe there are some Shakers alive, I don't know.

There must be some descendants, some renegade Shakers—

Renegade Shakers who propagated and left the cult, as it were. The music is very good.

It's cool that the Songs *album starts and ends with instrumentals, because it makes a transition between the two albums where you can listen to them in either order if you have both of them, making a bridge between the two. Was that something you had thought about it, making the two albums a pair that way?*

It was something I thought about when I went to do a vocal on the first track, and didn't really get anywhere with it, didn't like it. I took what I had done off of it and just realized the song doesn't really want a vocal—it sounds kind of nice the way it is. I think there's a little bit of a history of people doing these instrumentals first [on an album]. There might even be a Beatles record, but even that might have some *la-la*'s on it. What's the first cut on the *Magical Mystery Tour* [Capitol, 1967] record?

I think it's "Magical Mystery Tour," although there is an instrumental on that record ["Flying"]. The first Neil Young record starts with an instrumental; actually both sides of that record start with an instrumental.

Ah. That record, I still don't think I know it. . . . The instrumental last track on the vocal record ["Peace Piece"] was this thing I had done in somebody's apartment where he had a lot of nice, really big tube limiters and interesting '50s gear, and actually nice microphones as well. I've always liked recording in apartments, so I thought I'd make something in there. I totally forgot [the track] existed, and then when I went to master the record I thought, "Oh, there's that thing," and then I mixed that in five minutes and put it on the end. I've since been told there's another recording called "Peace Piece," which I guess is a Bill Evans solo piano composition. Curiously, a day after a journalist from Sweden told me about this, I was in Starbucks and heard this really great piano piece, and I asked them what it was, and they said it was called "Peace Piece." Very spacious, very nice piece. So now I have to try to change my title [*laughs*].

*"Peace Piece 2," "Peace Piece Jr." [*laughs*]. Where did you find the guys who are playing on the record, besides the guys you've used before?*

Well, Jay Dee [Daugherty] was in my touring

group after Patti Smith took a break in the '80s. The drummer, Lou Appel, came from the recommendation of a studio engineer as a guy who was extremely fast in learning things but who was also kind of sick of doing rock stuff. I think he was doing Southside Johnny or something and he wanted to do something different. The other drummer, Graham Hawthorne, came from a guy who had worked on David Lynch soundtracks. He'd done a lot of really oddball stuff, but had actually grown up in Chicago playing really hard-core funk music, and he's really adept at playing oddball beats. That song "The Day on You" was a jam session in which I said, "Do you remember this sort of early-'60s New Orleans thing? Let's try that faster." And he would just start playing these things that were really, for me, great, because there's not a lot of drummers who can play that style of stuff and play it really enthusiastically. So that was about a ten-minute jam session that I just edited and put the vocal on. It's kind of unusual, because it's almost like a folk-strummy rhythm guitar against a very weird beat.

And Billy Ficca is playing on these records—you've been playing with him since high school, right?

Playing with him since '66, probably, in garages in Delaware. The great thing about Billy is he doesn't care if you rehearse or not—you just sort of throw an idea at him, like, "This is sort of up-tempo, and let's not use the hi-hat," or, "This is kind of tom-tom thumpy Haitian music" [*laughs*]. And he immediately plays something that's suitable. And he plays it well. And he plays it in one take. He's actually much better at that than he is at learning a song [*laughs*].

Did you guys have similar influences growing up?

We both liked jazz. When I first saw him play, he was playing with some guy from Chicago who was a lot like Charlie Musselwhite—this hard-drinkin' white guy playing blues harp who was absolutely amazing. I never heard his name again and can't remember his name. He was just passing through and they were playing a church basement concert [*laughs*]. There were about eighty people there to see this blues thing—totally traditional, Muddy Waters electric blues stuff. Billy was playing drums, and I thought, "Gosh, this guy plays great." He has a liking for any sort of music, and he gets the spirit of it right away, I think. And if you want something played really lightly, he'll do it and not screw it up. He'll play light and won't suddenly hit something so loud that it breaks your mic—he'll play the whole thing light.

Have you been a big Middle Eastern music listener, or Indian music listener? Because there is stuff on these albums that point in those directions.

I wouldn't say I'm a big listener of that. I kind of get the idea of it and I don't even have a lot of records of that stuff. I know one really great record of an oud—I don't remember the player's name. I think he was from Iran, and it's probably an early '70s record. I think the thing about playing music that, for better or worse, has that flavor—it just comes from picking a scale. If you're tired of the Western scales then you pick a scale with different intervals and improvise on it. For me it's a challenge because I'm not really fluent in that, so it slows me down, but it also immediately lends a different mood to things, I think. The other way to do it is just to change the bass note and play a regular Western scale [*laughs*]. Have your bass play a C but start the song with the guitar on a B and you get very odd things going.

Was [John] Coltrane stuff like "India" something you were listening to back when it came out?

I can't remember that record. I'm sure I had it at one time. Coltrane in general—of that period, Coltrane, [Albert] Ayler, [Eric] Dolphy, and Ornette Coleman, I probably liked Ayler the most, who is probably the least modal of those, strangely enough. And also Dolphy, as a soloist, I probably liked a lot more than Coltrane or Coleman even. The thing I really liked about the Coleman records, when I remember them now, is the Scott LaFaro bass stuff and the Eddie Blackwell drumming. I've been trying to find Eddie Blackwell's drum kit. In the '70s someone said he had made his own drums—he was fed up with drums you could buy. For years I thought I should look him up and go in and play with him for a while. I never got around to it. I don't know where his drums are now, because he's passed away. . . . I wonder if that was a true story, that he had made his own drums. But his drums definitely have a certain sound on those Coleman records, the way they're tuned.

I saw him play with somebody and it didn't look like it was a customized kit—

Probably something they had rented for the gig . . . Another New Orleans drummer, actually.

Is that where he grew up?

Yeah. Knew all the parade rhythms and all that stuff.

And you're really into Chris Kenner and [New Orleans] stuff like that.

I really like Chris Kenner's stuff—I mean, there's not much of it. That goes back thirty years. When I first was in New York, I was at a flea market and this guy had a box of 45s for five dollars, and it was all New Orleans stuff that I hadn't really known. Lee Dorsey, things like "Working in the Coal Mine," those kinds of hits, but there were also these twenty-five other singles that I'd never heard or seen since, which had much more quirky rhythms and oddball guitar things. I've since read that Allen Toussaint wrote out every note for the bass players and drummers. You had to be classically trained, and the guys he used over and over on all those sessions were sitting there reading music. And the guitar player was a seventeen-year-old kid who'd be going *chink, chink-chink* through the whole thing [*laughs*]. That the rhythms, especially the bass stuff, were charted is really surprising—that it was approached as this written-in-stone music. You know, play it until it's right, play it with no mistakes. There it is in front of you; that's what you play. It wasn't like, "Let's get a groove going, guys," or something.

There's some stuff from New Orleans which is super sloppy like Huey "Piano" Smith—

Mm, yeah.

—but the stuff on the Chris Kenner album—

That's all Allen Toussaint stuff.

—there's almost like a trance element to it, which, like [Steve] Reich or [Philip] Glass, is very precisely played.

But unlike Glass and Reich it's not just streams of

eighth notes flowing by. It's very, very—it's absurdly syncopated, actually. A lot of it is things that no drummer would ever think of to play when sitting down to play dance music. It doesn't really, to my ears, make people want to dance, but when it's all together it somehow creates some kind of weird, itchy thing that, I think, only in New Orleans people used to dance to this stuff. If you listen to the so-called club music, or funk music from the '60s, it's not quite like that. Some of James Brown gets into that stuff, too, but . . .

Have you been to New Orleans much?

I was only there once, for one day, in '85 or something. It had an interesting atmosphere—you really kind of had to watch yourself. This local guy took me around to all the after-hours clubs, and they were really cinematic scenes. You would go into a club with a couple of purple bulbs, and it would be twelve barstools and two small tables and it would be packed, and some half-naked girl would slink next to you and rub on you next to the bar. The guy who was with me was nudging me, saying, "Don't get close to that—her boyfriend's in the corner." And you look in the corner and it's this murderous face, with scars [*laughs*]. You don't know *what's* going on there—it's really strange and slightly sinister. Unthinkable stuff like you've seen in some crap movie would be completely true to life there.

I remember when I checked into the hotel, I went into my room and there was a bone on the pillow. This strange bone [*laughs*]. I said, "What is this, some strange voodoo trick from the maid or something? Why is there a bone on my pillow?" So I went down to the desk and I said, "Is the maid around?" They said, "Do you need something?" "Nah," I said, "there's a bone on my pillow." It became this big discussion. They said,

"Oh, just a minute." I didn't hear anything that went down. And then it was like, "Do you have the bone?" And I said, "No, I threw it in the river," and they said, "That's a good place for it" [*laughs*]. I thought, "This is so bizarre, there's a bone on my pillow."

*[*Laughs.*] Not a mint, but a bone.*

[*Laughs.*] Yeah, exactly. I asked everybody else on the tour, "Did you have a bone on your pillow"? They said, "What are you talking about?" [*Laughs.*] So who knows what that was about.

Do you read much hard-boiled fiction or see film noirs? Sometimes people compare your music to that sort of thing.

I read that stuff in the late '60s. I read probably all of Raymond Chandler—but that's like real poetry, those books. They were unique in my experience. [Mickey] Spillane was actually pretty interesting. Spillane I know for a fact was a huge influence on Patti Smith's writing—this extremely staccato, short stuff. But Spillane's books tend to be all alike, more than Chandler's. That whole era, in my childhood, of black-and-white films with lots of shadow, tough-talking guys, all that kind of atmosphere, probably had some effect. I couldn't specifically say what [*laughs*]. Even more so than that, I remember being terrified by really trashy science-fiction films in the '50s. They didn't show a lot of those on TV, but occasionally one would come on. There was one called *When Worlds Collide* [1951], which is actually, I think, in color, and it was about this planet moving closer and closer to the earth, and it was going to burn the earth up, but only one hundred people could leave in these spaceships. It must have been before the age of seven; child specialists say that before the age of seven kids can't tell the difference between language and deed, so if a mother says, "I'm going to kill you," it's like the worst thing a mother can say to a kid because it's like the kid experiences being killed, and he doesn't know what that means, really, either [*laughs*], except that it's terrible. But for months after this movie I thought the sun was getting closer to the earth. I would go outside in the day, and you can't really look at the sun, but you think, "God, it's getting hotter" [*laughs*].

*[*Laughs.*] Here it comes!*

I would look out at the moon at night, and the moon was getting more and more full, and I thought, "Oh gosh," and I would ask my father about the spaceship—"Is the spaceship gonna take us?" And he'd go, "No" [*laughs*], "what are you talking about?" For weeks I was really scared, and then I think my father realized I had seen some movie or something and told me, "Don't worry about it" [*laughs*].

Have you ever met any of these directors? Did you ever meet Nicholas Ray?

I met Nick Ray because the kind-of-patron of Television in the '70s, Terry Ork, was a film expert and had some connection with Nick Ray. So he said, "Well, I'll bring Nick to the rehearsal," so he came down to this rehearsal. He was a giant guy, like six foot six with a patch over his eye. I think he was drunk even when he got there. He had his girlfriend, this very devoted younger woman who helped him out on many things. I think he gave us a quote we could throw on our poster; I don't know what the quote was, but it was kind of meaningless, because nobody knew who Nick Ray was. It wasn't like getting a quote from Bob Dylan or—

I think I remember that—it was something like "These guys are tough as nails, they make me cry."[1] *At that point I don't know if he was living in New York or still teaching at Harpur College [at SUNY Binghamton], but he was spending a lot of time in Times Square.*

Really?

*Yeah. There's this great collection of his writing [*I Was Interrupted *(1995)] and transcriptions of some of the classes he taught upstate, and his wife [Susan Ray], who you're talking about, did this long introduction where she talks about what his life was like in the '70s.*

I think he was ill for a very long time.

He was. That movie, Lightning Over Water *[1980], that Wim Wenders made, documents him in the last couple of years of his life.*

I finally met Wenders last year after some show. I wish he wouldn't use pop people in his movies, though.

Like Nick Cave?

Yeah, I don't think these people are so wonderful in movies, really. That's just my opinion. Real actors are people that are somehow inspired or passionate that seem to be much better than some rock singer just waltzing through. I like the way Alan Rudolph would use Neil Young as a gas station attendant for a minute,

1 The quote reads, "Four cats with a passion."

or Tom Petty as a parking lot attendant—that kind of thing makes more sense to me.

Bowie in The Man Who Fell to Earth *[1976] . . .*

Yeah, I mean what is that? That's just a context, isn't it? If you say somebody's an alien, you're going to think they're an alien through the whole film no matter how they act [*laughs*]. The context becomes the act and you become a successful actor, in a way. It's like *The Elephant Man* [1980], the same thing. The appearance does the whole thing, so you could say your lines as a joke and it would still have a pathos to it. I should get some roles like that. I could play a vampire. I wouldn't have to do anything—the role would be so consuming [*laughs*] that it would be believable.

So how many sessions did it take to record these records?

[The] instrumentals was two nights of recording, and a third night of editing, and erasing mistakes, and then the fourth night was overdubbing background things, maybe some organs . . . I don't think there's any feedback drones. Adding some guitar parts here and there. Maybe there was a fifth night, mixing and remixing some things. And, actually, when it got to be mastered I ended up doing even more editing—a lot of the cuts were a lot longer. On the instrumental record as well, I wound up shortening them. They just seemed to sound better being more succinct. The vocal record was a couple of years of recording but only a day or two every third month [*laughs*], so it would be calling up the drummer who was in town that week and saying, "Are you available Thursday and Friday?" And that would be it for January; in March or April, doing the same thing again. And often those sessions would produce maybe three usable tunes, of which I would pick two or maybe even one. When I had a collection of eighteen things or more together, I decided to use maybe fifteen or fourteen and then started editing those and overdubbed on them. So the maximum amount of days—I don't know, maybe it got up to forty days to record and mix that whole record. I'd still be mixing it if I had my way—it seems to take forever to mix things. I always hear, when a record's out, how much better a mix could be, and you wonder why you didn't hear that at the time you were mixing, that kind of detail. But it seems to have everything to do with the vocal. Once the vocal's out of the picture it seems to be really simple to balance instrumental music—but with the voice, for me it gets a lot more complicated.

In trying to see where it's going to sit.

Right. Most people seem to like loud vocals. I hear pop records that I like, and I realize when I'm hearing them that the vocal is twice as loud as everything else, but if it sounds good . . . But I tend not to do that myself. I tend to pull the vocal back.

If you go back and listen to the Rolling Stones' records of the '60s, and other people too, the vocal is nowhere near as far out front as it is on a lot of stuff today.

And it could be that those were the first vocal records I heard, so that's what's in my sound-picture of a way something should sound. I do like the way those records sound. People sang farther from the microphone back then, too—no one would be up on the mic. Julie London would be up on the mic—in those early days, I think she was the first singer who was told to sing within an inch of the microphone to get that kind of intimate thing going.

Was this done in studios, or home recording?

Ninety percent of it was done in studios. Fred Smith, the bass player—we did some guitar stuff in his house, and some editing and a little bit of vocals, and the last piece on it was done in an apartment. I like the apartment recording situation. The more I do it, the more I like that. I can't find an apartment for drums yet, though.

*[*Laughs.*] That might take a while.*

When I lived on East Eleventh Street we decided, "We'll rehearse in the apartment" [*laughs*], and it was less than twenty minutes—there were cops at the door. And that was the end of drums in an apartment.

Have you ever had a four-track cassette recorder or something like that?

No, the most I've ever had is literally a twelve-dollar Radio Shack cassette thing, which is like a note-book. I get an idea, sing it in there, talk it, or play it in there. I very rarely listen to them again. When I had broken my arm in the mid-'90s I remember listening to dozens of cassettes, most of the time thinking, "Why did I record that little thing? It wasn't very good" [*laughs*]. There are a few things on there, a few minutes of this and that, that wound up being made into songs, but not as much as I thought there would be.

Do you write down chord changes when you're working on stuff before you go into the studio?

Yeah. Well, the easiest way for me to record is one guitar, bass, and drums, and so I go through it real quickly with the bass player and drummer while someone's setting up the mics, and throw a chord chart on the floor for the guys and then experiment a little bit. Like, maybe the A chord on the guitar doesn't want an A on the bass, maybe it wants something else, that kind of idea. Or in the instrumental record it would be picking a scale; each scale or mode has a name, but I've never been able to memorize them, so I'll just say, "This is the scale, but let's use that note for the bass and move it around here or there," that kind of thing. Or hum a bass line.

You produced all your own records, right?

Yeah—I mean, in the early days, on *Marquee Moon*, I didn't even know what a producer did. I started listening to records and I didn't know what an engineer did as opposed to this or that, and Fred Smith again played me some Rolling Stones and Led Zeppelin—there was this key pile of records that all seemed to be done by Andy Johns. I thought, "Well, we don't sound like any of these people, but I guess these are good-sounding records" [*laughs*], "so let's get that guy." We somehow found him in his apartment, he was living in LA, and he was a real riot—"How the hell did you find *me*? What do you want *me* to do?" [*Laughs.*] He said, "Well, OK, I'm not doing anything around Christmas—I'll come to New York." He had no clue what we were doing. He also had an enormous appetite for alcohol; the first night it was two large bottles of wine and a case of beer. He came in with this under his arm, a shopping bag with wine and a huge case of beer [*laughs*]. We were playing within two hours—he was really fast. And he would pull me out in the hall: "What kind of music is this? Is this a Velvet

Underground trip? What is this, is this New York subway music?" So that went on for about ten days, and then he said, "Well, I guess you don't really need me, I'm going back to LA tomorrow." So we did the overdubs with the tape-op guy, who was actually a decent engineer, and then we had to beg him to come back to mix it. He came back right around New Year's to mix it, and suddenly, I guess, he heard what we were doing or he had an ear for it, and he said, "Ah, I see what this is, I see what this is." He became really enthusiastic in mixing it. It turned out well. It was probably one of the five oldest studios still working in New York at the time. It had a board with tubes, with the valves, which gave it a kind of sound. And there was no equalization on the board, and there were no compressors, so it was this very basic kind of thing, which he was really mad about when he saw it—he thought, "What are you working on here, a World War II recording desk?" [*Laughs.*] "This is crazy." It was at A & R, a room that Phil Ramone had built for himself, so they didn't rent it out much. I think Dionne Warwick records were made there. It wasn't a giant, spacious place but it did have a nice sound. The reason I liked it was that it looked like our rehearsal loft—it was a bit sloppy and not gigantic, but easy to work in.

*Have you ever gone back since, now that you know what a producer and an engineer are [*laughs*] and gotten interested in specific producers and engineers from records?*

There were records where the sonic quality really hit me. I remember late '70s, early '80s, hearing a Cars record. I actually heard it in England—someone from our record company was driving me somewhere and this thing came on, and I thought, "Jesus, this thing sounds amazing"—the song didn't do anything for me, but just the sonic quality of it was really amazing. And she said that [it] was produced by this English guy who had done these Queen records, and Queen were probably in my top three most despised groups of all time. I thought that this opera showbiz, and the fact that people liked it, was a real bad sign for guitar music, and the vocals as well. Anyway, so I thought, "Well, that's interesting that the guy who did that could also do this little, dinky Cars sound but make it so explosive sounding." So I started to have an ear more for engineers and what things do, and the different types of gear.

That was Roy Thomas Baker who did the Cars and Queen; Jim O'Rourke is super into him.

Yeah. There's one great Roy Thomas Baker record—I don't know if I talked to O'Rourke about it—I found this thing in a thrift shop. I don't know if he produced it. I think it was one of the records he engineered before he decided to become a producer. It was some English singer, very pop, but again an explosive sound. I sort of learned everything that that guy did through grapevines of things and other engineers in the early '80s, and I decided my Roy Thomas Baker record was going to be *Words From the Front* [Warner Bros., 1982]. That was actually all Roy Thomas Baker techniques, but of course not those guitar sounds, and not giant rooms for explosive drums, but very much an overload sound of pushing not the board amplifiers but the tape compression. Then I went to mix it and totally hated the way it sounded [*laughs*], so we would try to find little tracks that had gotten recorded by accident. We found a drum track where there was a mic on that was very low level on tape—in other words, not compressed and not distorted—and we would use that for the main drum mic because it sounded normal. We had to try to undo all this crazy tape compression stuff. I think it's very good for distorted guitar, if you're pushing the limits of tape; on things that are already somewhat distorted it's good, but for other things it's not really so good. I've gone back to liking Rudy Van Gelder sounds—not so squashed, put a microphone in front of it and leave it alone kind of sound.

Have you gone in to do other records with specific ideas like that, about a certain way to produce them? I remember reading somewhere that for Dreamtime *[Warner Bros., 1981] you put tape on the VU meters so no one could see what the levels were [*laughs*].*

Yeah, that was a thing in the early '80s. I remember the engineer was recording the first day, and I said, "Look, don't look at the meters." He said, "You're crazy." I said, "Let's just not look at the meters." So we would do this, and I would say, "Don't look at the tape machine meters," and just record it and play it back. And we did this, and the meters—you don't know where they were, because they were so far into the red. They could have been not just plus ten, they could have been plus forty. You don't know where they were, but the distortion didn't sound bad, so we just let the thing go like that. On that record it seemed to work better than on *Words From the Front*. But the guitars are a little more distorted on that, too—things are pushing more in a different way. That record was also one microphone for everything—we had one old German microphone, I think a [Telefunken] 251. I don't know why we loved this—we used it every time we dubbed a guitar or vocal or anything. I don't know how wise that is, in retrospect—I mean, that record sounds very loud. I play it every couple of years just to see how good or bad it is.

It's very low-mixed vocals with very loudly recorded instruments—it has a certain thing to it.

Was there a production idea you came in with for these two new records?

Yeah, the new stuff was much more back to the old school. By 2003 or 2004 I had found the microphones I liked, basically these ribbon mics that are, again, I think, German: a Beyer ribbon mic and a mic from Denmark, a B&K. Just really high-quality mics and minimal processing, dumping it onto tape. So there's not a lot of complicated engineering or concepts of recording going on—it's the right microphone and the simplest way to do it.

Although there's one track where there's some kind of processing on the drums.

There's really heavy processing on the track called "Documentary," because it was recorded in a really bad studio on a really bad desk. . . . I dumped that one into a computer right away, so it has a lot of digital-type recording on it, as opposed to the old tape thing on it. I think that's the only one on the record that's like that. There's a little bit of that on "Day on You," too, I think—those drums needed some real help. Because, again, it was very quickly recorded in a room that I only recorded one day in. I wasn't quite sure what it was going to sound like. But the drummer played well. So . . . you work with it.

There's also things about record pressing and mastering, too.

Yeah, that's true. That's a whole science that's probably dying out because there's so few mastering people that know how to do vinyl now. It's disappearing.

There was a guy in Nashville who's been mastering vinyl since the '50s, and he says now he had to get computers because all the rap guys who want the vinyl send him a file, so he had to learn computers. And everything has to be loud—the digital file of the music is insanely loud, squashed, and then they want the vinyl to sound even louder. And vinyl has real limits with volume, especially in the bass. When I went to master a record in '81, I went to the guy and he's rolling off loads of low-end, 40Hz deep bottom, and I said, "What is this?" And he said, "Yeah, this is what the disco music does." I go, "What are you talking about?" He says, "You go to a club and you think you're hearing all that big bass, but it's the sound system. If I had tried to cut these records with the bass that people wanted it would just rumble the whole club." So the bass, where you think it's that deep thing of 50Hz or something, is really like an octave higher, like 100 or 200.

Somebody once played me a Beatles record which was a safety copy of *Abbey Road*, and the bass was like—I guess McCartney was the one who was always around during the mixes and saying make the bass louder, but the bass is so loud on the original Beatles tapes, it's insane. It's like reggae music, it's so loud, and the joke was that when the Beatles handed things in to master, all the cutting guys immediately plugged in this thing called a low-pass filter and had to dump tons of low end, because if you tried to cut your vinyl with that kind of low end you wouldn't hear anything but bass, and you'd have to bring the level down so low. You never think of Beatles records as bass, although they have great bass playing. The tape I heard was just insane—it was like an insane person mixed it, put the bass on ten and then everything else on four. It was very funny.

Tony Oursler

When I set up this interview with video artist Tony Oursler for *BOMB* magazine in 2006, he was on a streak, with several recent New York exhibitions combining video, sound, music, and poetry in multimedia environments: “Thought Forms” at Metro Pictures and “Sound Digressions in Seven Colors” at Nyehaus, both in spring 2006, and “Studio: Seven Months of My Aesthetic Education and Then Some (NYC Version)” at the Metropolitan Museum of Art in April 2005. Oursler had been in a band, the Poetics, with Mike Kelley when both were in school at CalArts, and this collaborative practice was highlighted in the Met show in particular—inspired by Courbet’s painting *The Artist’s Studio: A Real Allegory in a Seven-Year Phase in My Artistic and Moral Life*, 1855—through the inclusion of works and videos by many of Oursler’s artist friends. Shortly before our meeting, I had also gone to see yet another of his projects at the Whitney Museum of American Art, *DTAOT: Combine (Don’t Trust Anyone Over Thirty, All Over Again)*, 2005—made in collaboration with Dan Graham, Rodney Graham, Laurent P. Berger, Bruce Odland, and the band Japanther—a video installation and puppet show which took inspiration from the 1968 hippie fantasy B movie *Wild in the Streets*. When he arrived at the door of his home/studio building to greet me, the most surprising thing was that I didn’t recognize him. We had never previously met, but because we had so many friends in common, I figured I would have known his face from a Sonic Youth or Tony Conrad aftershow.

Since I just saw the Don't Trust Anyone Over Thirty *thing at the Whitney Biennial the other night, I thought we'd start with that. Attaching "Combine" to the title for the video was certainly pretty timely, considering the Robert Rauschenberg exhibition ["Combines"] at the Met.*

Yeah, which I didn't really know—or maybe I subconsciously knew—but I think it was a kind of mistake. I would have changed my title had I known, because that was a total, like, blip. I was just coming up with titles—I like to use dictionaries and software to look up words, and that just came up and it was such a beautiful word.

So it wasn't a reference to the Rauschenberg show?

No. [*Laughs.*] Not even close. And the day the exhibition announcement went to press, or whatever, I realized of course . . . because Rauschenberg is kind of a hero of mine. There might have been a subliminal thing in there, something I read somewhere, because I had shown at the Met recently. Probably [curator] Gary Tinterow told me he was going to be showing the Combines there, so it was probably a word that was just in my head. But the thing was that we had to distinguish that installation from the live performance, because it was a nomenclature; it was a problem with the whole thing, like how to tag it. It was a sprawling collaboration with all these millions of people.

But the main thing about that piece is that we wanted to take elements of the project that could never make it into the live show and make something out of it that was ambient and contemplative in some way. And then it developed into this double-layering projection idea that came out of work I did with Kim [Gordon] and Phil Morrison [*Perfect Partner*, 2005]. Because there's two high-definition projections that overlap. So the idea of making a double exposure, sort of, live with your brain somehow—that you're actually doing it with your eyes—that's fascinating to me. There's a bit of an optical thing happening. I don't think anyone notices, probably just looks crystal clear. That's the thing about it, if you do a double exposure in a machine, it sort of halves everything. But doing it live, it has a kind of crystalline effect to it. And then the two channels combine randomly, which I'm really interested in. The whole thing has this cascading . . . Things are getting brighter and darker all the time. And that causes this shifting of power from one projection to the other. It was a really fun process.

You also get this feeling of ebb and flow while you're watching it, or the idea is sort of washing over you.

Exactly, and I think that's partially because of the music, because we used a 5.1 Surround, which I'm really interested in, too.

Yeah, to me the flow of images fits in with the whole Biennial thing, and also kind of relates back to Rauschenberg—Rauschenberg's famous quote about operating in the gap between art and life. That seems to me to be more prevalent now than ever. Just walking around the Biennial is like walking around New York on the average afternoon. There's a little window shopping, you see a little graffiti, and then maybe you stop in to see a movie, or go to a couple of galleries. . . . There's a lot of music around. There's the ringtones from cell phones—it's all sort of been incorporated into what's permissible in a gallery or a museum environment now. And so what I'm wondering is, if the art world now is like reality TV, how wide or small is the gap between art and life?

That's a really good question, because there was always an issue in the '70s—the whole thing was crossover, everyone's fantasy was crossover. And having done a little crossover myself, as soon as you do it, with people like David Bowie or something like that, the art world's not interested at all. That's somehow too far, which I always thought was amusing—it just, like, cancels out. It's just been embedded in my generation to get out of the art world to make better art because you reach people on this class structure system that is implied by this museum system or whatever. People have been chipping away at that in every different direction, but maybe they've chipped so much that there is no real definition, and that everything is possible. I'll go with that. I like your take on it, because the old-school thing—it was more showbizzy in a way, various artists making movies with crossover, or the David Byrne paradigm, making popular music. Of course, that was a lot harder than people thought, all these ignorant artists thinking it's much easier to make TV shows, or records, or movies, and they find out it's a much more disgusting environment than the art world, or that it's much more difficult than the art world. But that's an older notion of crossover. What you're talking about is much more interesting, that it's like life now, and it's not about the artist propped up on a stage in some way. It's more slipping into life, which I'm really interested in, in terms of public art, getting stuff out in public places, where it just flows in with the architecture. It becomes a piece of somebody's commute or what have you. Maybe that's what's happening at the Biennial, more of that.

But part of what's happening, I think, is that reality is the new fantasy. Reality is escapism now, partially because of the political climate, where all these actions have been taken based on what turns out to be fiction, whether it's weapons of mass destruction or whatever, and there's also these two memoirs that have come out recently, which have proved to be falsified—this guy [James Frey] Oprah was so upset with, who had fabricated large portions of his story, if not the entire thing. I think people are looking toward reality TV as an escape from a reality which is now based on lies or fantasy.

I like that theory, because all that kind of Baudrillard stuff has come true, every bit of it, and Philip K. Dick's world—he was only twenty to twenty-five years off in a way. If you can get away from levitating vehicles, a lot of his predictions—life is really stranger than fiction in a lot of ways. Sometimes it makes me not want to read the newspaper—it's voided out before I even look at it, it repeats itself, and it's really just about certain people making money, the spectacle. . . . But the reality TV show thing—you're saying that reality is a fantasy, and that's now—

Reality's something they're not getting from reality—it's something they're looking to to entertain them. It's like there's been this reversal, where the powers that be have funneled reality into the entertainment sphere, and entertainment has been funneled into the sphere of policy making or whatever.

Yeah, that's good. I'll go with that. I always looked toward pop culture to decipher things as a mirror of the world, and now I don't at all, because I know who the creators are, and I can kind of see through what they're trying to do, and so it's null and void for me. It doesn't work on me at all. I wish it did—in a weird way, I miss it. There was a time when I used to look at pop culture and take it apart piece by piece, to figure out how this engine worked. I was very paranoid and full of conspiracy theories. But now I don't. I just look at it as a bunch of morons who are barely getting by; they can barely figure out how to push the buttons on this machine that's rolling forward. Just the most boring stuff. I don't get, you know, people who are fascinated by Paris Hilton, phenomenons like that. I don't find that fascinating anymore, like someone who does nothing and becomes like a celebrity.

You know, it's funny, because I never actually watched that show The Simple Life, *but I was in a hotel a couple weeks ago and I was flipping channels, and they had a behind-the-scenes of that show on the E! channel, so I was watching it for a little while, and as I was looking at it, I realized they may as well call it* Bush and Cheney. *Because they had this one episode where Paris Hilton and her friend [Nicole Richie] go undercover as maids in this hotel, and they're supposed to be cleaning up this room, this one room that's really disgusting. And they're like, "Forget this, let's just call down and have someone clean the room." They get out of their maid costumes, and they call downstairs, and say, "This room's a mess, can you send someone down here immediately?" So another maid shows up and cleans up the room, and they're sitting there ordering a pizza; then they get back in the maid costumes and the boss comes in to check in on them. And he's like, "Good job girls, this is nice going."* [TO laughs.] *So it's the same thing—these two rich kids who are faced with this mess they have to clean up. They say, "We can't be bothered with this"; then they call the hired help, who are actually their coworkers, except they still have this thing where they think the maid will take care of it. Bush and Cheney don't realize, like, "No, you* are *the maid, you're the servant, you're supposed to be the public servant." They still don't consider themselves that way at all.*

Yeah, you're absolutely right, those guys don't think at all in terms of that. Let's go back to Katrina. My wife, Jacqueline Humphries, who's an abstract painter, comes from New Orleans, so we spend a lot of time down there. We love it. We're trying to partially locate ourselves down there part of the year, because it's so close and it's such an amazing place. But we were there around Christmastime [in 2005]—I just couldn't believe how badly it got hit. The strange thing is, it doesn't come across on TV. There's this new kind of way that disasters are shown, and this happened around 9/11. They show the disaster, and they focus it down to a few-second clip that's a symbol of the disaster. That's an acceptable thing—it doesn't really move you in any way. But it becomes a signifier. And that's what they show, and they don't really show anything again, to actually transmit to you—did something really bad happen there? It's some kind of Band-Aid way that they work in the media, and it's very strange. Because you could easily go down there and shoot. We did. We shot tons of video of Fats Domino's house, with all of the shit thrown out on the street—his recording studio's there. Here's this guy who's arguably one of the inventors of rock and roll, some say *the* inventor. And this guy's house might be plowed under. It's incredible. I just couldn't believe the level of devastation. There's a human element to that city that was really special, and I hope comes back. Maybe through music, I don't know.

But the way Bush dealt with that? Let's get this straight. He's got all these troops over in Iraq, and he waits like three weeks before he gets amphibious vehicles to rescue people in one of our own cities? That's totally insane.

The other thing about the coverage that you hit on is where they're presenting all these short clips, and the thing about this whole 24/7 news coverage is that they keep presenting all these really short things over and over again. So you're not really left with any concrete image of what's going on there—it all becomes a blur. And the other thing about that is that there's no fact-checking—they're reporting all these rumors that are floating around as fact. So you're left completely confused.

Exactly. They'll say stuff that may or may not be true.

Yeah, because there's simply no time to confirm—they have to get something on the air instantaneously. And it leaves you in the dark about what is actually going on in any situation.

Back to Katrina, they reported all this violence that happened there, and it turned out to be all bullshit. There was very little violence, and I would venture to say the violence was on par with the violence on a normal day in a city—might have been even less because people were scared. All this looting that was supposedly going on, I didn't see much evidence of that.

The other thing about Don't Trust Anyone Over Thirty *that I think is extremely relevant to things today, and also sort of relates to the whole political climate, is this idea of overlapping generations, and the emphasis on youth, especially in that original film,* Wild in the Streets *[1968], where of course the voting age is lowered to what, fourteen, and the twenty-year-old rock star becomes president, and the old people are all crammed up and sent to, like, concentration camps. I think part of Bush's appeal is that people see him as a child—they see him as the child of the other president, President Bush. I think that's the ultimate result of this emphasis on youth since the '60s, which really started with* Rebel Without a Cause *[1955] in the '50s, which is one of the first films to portray teenagers as the ones who are with-it and wise as opposed to the parents, who are out of touch. This has more and more become an accepted thing.*

Yeah, that's the ticket. To me there is very little adult entertainment. It is all marketed to the kids, and the kids don't make any money, but they spend the parents' money, so I guess that's the strategy: to think about how to get the money through the kids. But then again, there is this thing, especially with the computer, with the dot-com thing—I really like that—where everybody looked to the twenty-year-old for wisdom because they could run the computer, and the computer was seen as the new messiah.

My gut intuition is that we're at a turning point, where we're either going to completely accept this and become a completely brainwashed country, or things are going to go a different way. The only saving grace is that, as these body bags come back, that's real—that's one thing that's real in all these false reality TV shows. When someone dies who's like twenty-four, because Bush and his fraternity boys are having their romp . . . But I felt like we were at a turning point somehow, the country—I don't know if you feel that at all—because things could go one way or the other, because things could get more and more conservative, and then it's going to be a place I won't want to live, and probably a lot of people won't want to live—well, maybe New York. I tried with the pieces in "Thought Forms" at Metro Pictures to work with these elemental subjects, like dust, mercury, and water, because all three of them felt like they had these very temporal moments where they could go one way or another—a dust storm could either dissipate or turn into a further storm—and each piece had this kind of feeling to it. The pieces are pretty dark, because I think it's become a very dark time really quickly—because I think, just before Bush got elected, it was a very optimistic time. The internet was sprouting, and that's my real hope for a kind of answer to all the questions of '60s and '70s utopia. You can produce music and distribute it, or video or movies, or interactive art—there's so many opportunities. But they haven't figured out a way to filter it yet, which I think is great, but I'm worried that these guys are figuring out a way. I know that they're listening to everything that goes through it, but that's a given. I think everything is listened to now pretty much—you assume that what you say on the cell phone or telephone, or what you write, that everything is watched. Would you agree?

I think it's pretty likely, but what are they going to do with all that information? It's a lot of conversations.

I think they're scared shitless that there's going to be another attack here, and because that will certainly ruin this administration. But let me ask you this. Why is it that the previous Democratic administration, every little thing that they did got hyped up by Rush Limbaugh and all these guys, whether it was Whitewater or anything. But everything Bush does, he gets a pass—letting the bodies float in New Orleans for three weeks without bothering to send the amphibious vehicles or anything. He just gets a pass. People from New Orleans are pissed at him—I guess the sex thing Clinton had almost got him knocked out of office. It's not on par.

The thing you said about it being a turning point right now is definitely true, but the last two decades have been this long, drawn-out turning point, and it touches on something else I wanted to bring up that sort of relates to Don't Trust Anyone Over Thirty. *It's about computer technology and religion and the hippie movement of the '60s. The thing about computer technology is that it's a binary system, like yes and no—that's what it's all based on. I think that relates to this Christian thing of good and evil, especially the way these fundamentalists see everything as either one thing or another, good or bad. I think with the rise of computer technology, people are kind of transferring what they used to depend on—a binary system—a religious framework to a technological framework, and I think what some people are afraid of is that religion is going to be replaced with a technology. So a lot of what's going on is, if you think about where the moral majority got firmly embedded in the Republican Party around 1980, which is also when home computers really got started coming around, I don't think it's a coincidence. I think the organized religions in this country have really been worried, since then, that religion's going to go out the window, and that people are going to rely on technology for what's good and what's evil.*

And the other thing with the '60s is, I was reading this interview with Arthur Clarke about 2001 *[1968] in the book* Expanded Cinema, *by Gene Youngblood. Part of* 2001 *was that Clarke was envisioning a future where there was total unemployment and then people would just play—well, obviously people had to run computers, so it would never be total unemployment, but I think to some extent the hippie movement was a very futuristic one, where they were kind of saying, computers are here, now we can play instead of having to worry about these responsibilities that our parents were so weighed down with. And I think that's why the film* 2001 *resonated—the whole thing of having to go through the Stargate Corridor, and then when it ultimately arrives at the Star Child. I think that's sort of where it's at: technological progress is going to take us to the point where the species is somehow reborn.*

I like the feeling; I wish it would be true. I hope so, with my son. He has the chance. The thing with good and evil, positive and negative—when I wrote my timeline on virtual media around 2000 or so, I realized that as a video artist, there was never any art history written for me, because all this stuff that plugged in, all the stuff that moved, anything that had to do with light, was very finicky, and so curators, if a bulb broke or something, they just put [the work] in a box in the basement. It was much easier for them to put paintings on the walls, and photographs. So we were left with no history of virtual image production, and it goes all the way back to the camera obscura in the year 1000 or whatever in China, mentioned in a poem—I think that's the first known record of a reference to the virtual image—and right there, it was associated with evil, because the image was upside down until they found lenses to correct it. Anytime there was a new kind of technology, there was this association with evil connected to it, so I think your theory is correct. The computer will definitely spook out people who will believe in that. In every human invention, every one—rock and roll, it's the devil's music; photography, there was spirit photography; the radio, it was Konstantin Raudive who did that kind of tuning-into-the-dead radio; and television, there were lots of different examples, but there were people who believed they could communicate with the spirit world through feedback. I trace it right up to the computer, and with the computer, though I never found any large organizations being fearful of the computer—there's a lot of possessed computers and things like that. So it doesn't surprise me at all that there would be a widespread fear of the computer, and also, it opens up the playtime you're talking about. It is a play machine, especially with the internet.

It's a time-saver, too—you can do so many more things in a shorter amount of time, which leaves more leisure time.

Yeah, but it in itself is play. It's an identity-dissolver, number one—you can be whoever you want to be. But eventually every computer will have a camera attached to it. I think that will change things, because they'll be able to see you. But at this point, you can be whoever you want, whatever you want on there, and that's a special moment.

Related to what you were saying about the optimism of the internet in the '90s . . . I think it kind of cuts across all these race or class barriers; having an email address rather than a nationality or a gender or this or that—it levels the playing field.

Yeah, it certainly does, if you can get ahold of it. Apparently it's pretty difficult for a lot of people to get ahold of.

*It's true. In fact, I was on tour maybe three years ago, and we were in a hotel in Little Rock, Arkansas, and I asked the guy in the lobby if there was a computer I could check email on, and the guy looked at me like, "Email?" [*Laughs.*]*

Yeah, that's the devil's machine. But then it kind of goes back to the politics of what you were saying earlier, about what we were both talking about. If all this information is available, why are we living in the null and void moment of complacency, when everyone has the information? They know how many body bags are coming back, they know the lies they're being told, because they get unearthed every day. But it's still a complacent time.

Because the convenience makes people complacent. And that was the thing about ancient Rome—the reason it was sacked by the barbarians was that people stopped leaving the house. They had all the, what we now consider modern conveniences, and it just kind of—

They stopped leaving the house. It's such a random fucking thing.

I think that's what was going on. I mean, that's the thing I always found eerie about 9/11 is that only a few months—no, a few years before—you could just order your groceries online. You don't have to go to the grocery store. It's like people are coming up with more and more ways that you would never have to leave the house. And I knew that about ancient Rome—that was sort of their undoing. They had become so self-sufficient, they had stopped paying attention to what was going on outside their borders, and that was ultimately their undoing.

I want to talk about the Nyehaus installation also, which I liked. It seemed to me that it was almost like a dinner party—it was kind of like boy-girl, boy-girl . . .

You should have been in it.

*[*Laughs.*] I can be in the sequel. But I was wondering if that was something you thought about, because the social thing was such a big part of the artist-studio installation, too, and to what extent were you thinking*

about the people's personalities when you were making the selection of who to be in it?

That's a question I had to work my way through, because some of the people, I didn't know them at all—but some I knew really well, some for about twenty-five years, such as Tony Conrad or Kim Gordon. Stephen Vitiello played electronic effects, Lee Ranaldo played a very distorted guitar. And then Ikue Mori, who did drums, I knew for a few months, and then Zeena Parkins I didn't know at all, but I wanted a harp—but little did I know that the electric harp she played didn't sound very much like a harp, and Jim Thirlwell . . . I've known him for a year or so. So there was a range of people, and I liked that about it. When I was thinking about the group, I thought it's really good to have some people that I don't know at all, because that expands the project into a random or new exciting field of discovery. The people that I knew could actually be more problematic, because they might have preconceptions or something. So it wasn't necessarily that it was more positive to work with someone I knew for a long period.

Tony Conrad, who I've known probably the longest out of that group—I had no idea, I thought he was going to play violin, because that's what he usually plays, but I really didn't want him to play violin. It just so happened that he started to get obsessed with these bells, and that worked much better, because it's a percussive instrument. Had there been much more drone stuff in the mix of "Seven" I think it would have really brought the piece down instead of up; it was a serendipity that he had come up with this bell thing. Because it was very much a piece that was about chance, rolling the dice at the moment. But I wanted to have male-female breakdown in the music, because it's often like a male-bonding deal—music fantasy band or whatever.

*Boy band [*laughs*].*

Boy band—it happens to be still the thing—so I wanted to mix it up at least in that way, to have somewhat of a balance, of male and female energies, I guess, a new age term. But the pairing of people there . . . I guess a lot of them have collaborated.

I was wondering when you heard Tony Conrad's music for the first time, because I'm assuming the first time you met him, you met him as a video maker.

I actually had heard his album with Faust before I met him, because I had the good fortune of being Jim Shaw's roommate for a couple years, and Jim had such a big record collection—he was scared the fumes from it would give him cancer or some shit [*laughs*].

So Jim really gave me an education, a musical education. Because he had the most incredible amount of stuff. I don't know if you know Jim, but Jim makes music too. He used to make really incredible improvisational guitar stuff back in the '70s. It's just unbelievable when he played guitar with, like, an electric knife and stuff. But he's not much of a self-promoter, so he didn't save any of his tapes, destroyed them. But he was lightyears ahead of all of us. It was too bad, a real shame that that stuff was all lost. Because he was so far advanced.

Is he doing some of that on the Destroy All Monsters stuff?

I think so. But his solo stuff was really the coolest. Because he used to play a lot of solo stuff, just go in the garage and play. He sings, and I was like, "Oh my God, this guy is like Hendrix or something." It was just incredible, because he had collected all these toy synthesizers and shit—what everybody does now, finds gizmos, but back then it was not so easy to find things that made different noises. He was playing toy things and a really ancient Echoplex and stuff that used real tape. He had all this stuff around. And that's how I made my soundtracks for all my early videos. I grabbed all that stuff and just started playing with it and made the soundtracks.

Conrad, I didn't know much about him when I met him. I think I may have also known his flicker films. I think they were already being shown in art school. But his films were so extreme, black-and-white, light flickering, I don't know if I saw them or not. Then when I met him, I was very impressed with the fact that his music history was incredible, the fact that he knew John Cale and did all this stuff with John—I didn't know anything about La Monte Young at that time, but I did know the Velvet Underground, and then after that the drone stuff like Terry Riley, and I had Steve Reich and early Philip Glass and stuff. I knew all of that, basically through Jim, and also Phil Glass played at CalArts, and John Cage was in residency there, giving talks and hanging out with students and stuff. To me, it was somewhat normalized, even though I was just a kid. I didn't really understand that some of these people are very important historically, like Cage. Phil Glass played *North Star* [1977], where he was trying to kind of cross over. He had this amazing setup with these big amps, like four feet high, and they all sort of matched, and it was like a wall on either side, and the musicians perform somehow. They were obviously custom-made, and they were bizarre looking. The group played this really loud, very, very fast stuff. It was really impressive. I was blown away by it. But [Glass] was really into amplification at that time. Now his records are so thin-sounding.

But Tony, I met him first when he was doing an army movie called something like *Hail the Victoria* [*Beholden to Victory*, 1980, and *Hail the Fallen*, 1981]. It was a sad sack–type thing, where it was improvisational and there were certain things you could do or couldn't do because of your rank. You had these systems that were his way of directing. It was very funny because he would talk for an hour and half about what you could and couldn't do, and what would be right for this person, what would be wrong and why. That was the way he would prepare you for the role, and then you just go into the role. It was very curious, a passive-aggressive way of directing, because he obviously wanted something very specific—there's always that dilemma in improv. People say with John Cage, if it was truly improv, then how come everybody sounds the same? [*Laughs.*] From certain periods. Glenn Branca said that. It's kind of true. [Cage] sort of cheated in his improv. They do sound the same, and if you look at the [Conrad] movie, it's kind of amazing that he gets similar performances from everybody.

But when I first met him he wasn't interested in music very much at all. He also rejected his structuralist film. So he shed a lot of skins, that guy. That's what I love about him, how he's pushing the envelope in such a fantastic way, that he's really a guy who, in my mind, is always adding things to the world rather than remaining in stasis so that he could *take* from the world. A lot of his generation, they were all about staking out territory and capitalizing on it, and he was more about getting to that point, making that certain distinctive body of work, and then moving on to the next one. That's a very unusual artist, and I think he paid a lot of dues for that. It takes a long time—people can't follow someone who goes from one thing to the next. I can. I think artists can very easily. I think you can see all the connections through that stuff, but the curators can't and the art administrators can't. That's what's weird to me, that it stops with other artists. Even the more radical curators have a hard time. But I think his moment is coming.

I think even in the last couple of years, he's had a much higher profile. That sort of drone music that people used to associate La Monte with much more, I think now Tony successfully lobbied to be recognized as someone who helped pioneer that, just because Tony is out there performing much more than La Monte is. People are kind of recognizing that.

Speaking of youth overlapping, generations overlapping, he's really a good example of an artist who's done that more than anybody than I can think of from that generation, except for maybe Lawrence Weiner or maybe [John] Baldessari; Laurie Anderson a little bit, but she's a little younger.

There was the whole period in the '80s where people were unaware that he did anything beyond the video stuff. That record with Faust was virtually impossible to find. I read about it in an article in Creem *magazine, about the band Dream Syndicate, that said that was where their name came from, and I was a fan of that band, so I wanted to hear that record, but you never saw it mentioned anywhere else, and you never saw it in a record store or anything. And I remember [Conrad] telling me that he had staged some concert in New York sometime in the mid-'80s, because he had sublet a loft for a winter just to be back in New York for a spell. And I think he staged a concert in the loft—he said absolutely no one came to his concert. I don't know how he promoted it. He said he was very discouraged by that.*

Yeah, he had very discouraging things happen that I thought he took more with a grain of salt, but I think he worked really hard on it. He showed that film, that army movie, and I was there at the premiere—me and Mike Kelley and Jim Shaw all went over there, and there was the weirdest mix of people. This was like 1978, '79, maybe '80 at the latest, when I was still living in Los Angeles. And he had people who knew him from Harvard. Then there were people who knew him from the video-art community, and they were all there. He had a serious contingent of people who would follow him who had these connections with him. Anyway, it was interesting to see.

In a way, it's taken so long for people to just connect the dots between the stuff that he was involved in in the '60s and '70s with both experimental film and experimental music, and the whole rock thing with the Velvet Underground, and all these worlds were sort of touching on each other, but since there's so little graspable evidence of it, it remained kind of unavailable to the public until the CD era. I think it's much easier now for people to connect everything up. This sort of brings us back to the Biennial in a way, where you have people like Ira Cohen and Tony and Michael Smith, and the same thing in music, with Daniel Johnston or more recent people like Jim O'Rourke.

[Biennial curator] Chrissie Iles is really interested in that—I mean, in music. She's from my generation, we're around the same age, so you know that whole question of whether music is art or art is music—it's something I've always, since "The Poetics Project,"[1]

1 "The Poetics Project: 1977–1997," an installation and research project by Tony Oursler and Mike Kelley, inspired by their late-'70s band the Poetics, at Metro Pictures, New York, May 28–September 12, 1998.

been interested in, and then that series of interviews I did that spun out of that called *Synesthesia* [1997–2001].

We were trying to dig into where the visuals and sound meet, as much as I possibly could. In a way it's impossible, because they're two different holes in your head.

But a lot of times they're not as unrelated as you might think—this is something, especially with the whole Text of Light project,[2] *we've caught a lot of flack from some quarters, and admiration from others. The story I was going to tell in relation to that, when I was in college—they were showing* Intolerance *[1916], the D. W. Griffith film, and for whatever reason the print didn't have a soundtrack on it at all. It's a silent film, but usually they have some sort of music. People were a little restless, and there was some random classical music cassette lying around the projection booth, and we just put it on. And it was uncanny how often things completely synced up with the visuals when it was just a random thing. Of course, there's all sorts of rhythms being suggested by the editing and also the story line, but that's the thing about working with the [Stan] Brakhage films, because even though they do have their own rhythm, which is created by the images and its editing, if you put any kind of music with it, there's going to be certain synchronizations and certain kinds of polyrhythms that develop just by that juxtaposition.*

This record I did with the band Run On, which was one of my bands in the '90s—there's one track where I remember I hung the microphone outside the window of the studio, because we were actually recording this one track live. It was like seven or eight minutes, and I wanted to record everything that was happening outside in the

2 See p. 136.

same seven or eight minutes to see if anything interesting would happen. Well, sure enough it was a thunderstorm. And right at this climactic part of the song, you hear this big thunderclap, which we mixed into the track. So the idea was, these sounds are going on simultaneously, and you actually keep track of them, superimpose them or put them together—you'd be surprised how often they really come into sync.

That's funny, because Kim called me up right before Sonic Youth did this recent set of tours recently, like three or four months ago, and said, "Would you be interested in doing projections for the show?" And I was like, "Yeah, that would be great." And I said, "Well, how long?" She said, "About two hours." I said, "When do you need it," and she's like, "The end of the week." [*Laughs.*] I happen to have this ongoing series that I call my ambient series that I sometimes show when I find the right moment, where I just set up cameras, kind of like what you did, where I feel like something good is happening, and I just let it go. And there's sometimes camera movement, sometimes not, mostly not. It might be a theme park, and I just find a frame where there's people, or fluorescent inner tubes going off in this space, and shoot that for twenty minutes. I've been doing this since the late '80s, since Hi8, when you could really do that. So I took a lot of these things and edited them together and gave them to Sonic Youth for their tour, and I went to see it, at Northsix. And I was totally moved by the experience—it blew me away. They would pretty much turn off the lights, maybe just have side lights, and the lighting people are hip enough now to know about projection stuff, to figure out how to let it be. It was totally insane. And because it was projected right over the band, with the light wall behind it, certain things would happen with birds flying, or certain things appearing on people's faces, liquid, different edits. I just couldn't believe the complexity of the relationship between these randomly put-together clips and the band. And it totally worked, because they still use it—I think they're still using it. We had no idea what their playlist was, and it probably would have ruined it had we known what it was, because as soon as you start to illustrate any kind of music it's horrible.

Yeah, I had the same realization at one of the early Text of Light gigs in Philadelphia. We had done it a couple times before, and up to that point I thought it fell into the category of a normal improv gig, with a bunch of name players coming together to see what happens. But when we show the films, none of the players really looks at them so much—we kind of look up once in a while and see what's going on. We just kind of play and let the film ooze into the music by osmosis. But when I sort of looked up at the screen I was also looking at the drummer, William Hooker, who was in front of the screen, of course not looking at what's behind him. And something he was doing with his hand on the drum was corresponding exactly with what was happening in the films.

Huh, fantastic.

That's when I realized this is a lot bigger than just a normal improv show, that we were really onto a whole new chapter in terms of the way we look at these films.

So the question then is: What is the new thing? You have this whole history of strategies to get to where we are today, when anything is possible. But what seems most interesting is to get to the impossible, which is to do it through some random processes, which fills in some magic-moment thing. What do you think about that?

I think it's probably more just like synchronicity. I don't know if people realize it or not, but it's something they're much more attuned to. And since things are not as discrete now in the society, everything's just sort of blending together, like what I was talking about earlier with the Biennial, just walking around New York—I think that's accelerated things so that an even greater degree of synchronicity is happening. Maybe random isn't as random as it used to be. Whatever's random is not quite as random, because everything's much closer together than it used to be twenty years ago. Even in different art worlds or art circles, it's not as unusual for someone in a rock band like Sonic Youth to be kind of working closely with different artists, with video and different kinds of media.

To tweak the experience, take it one way or another. I first came across it—the idea—with the man himself, that's the weird thing. John Cage was like a teacher in a way, and that's pretty funny in itself. But then all my installations, every one of them that had more than one channel going, they were always random. What made that decision, even though it was almost impossible to synchronize decks—I think that the three-quarter-inch video players, where you're going to play back video at that time, and then as VHS became more popular . . . But there was no way to synchronize them unless you had a lot of money. But the whole budget of an installation is like twelve hundred bucks or something—what it would cost to synchronize a couple of decks would be the entire budget of the *whole* installation. Plus, I felt it deadened the experience, so I was always doing that in my installations, and it operated on the soundtrack as well as the visuals. So it's something I've been doing since the early '80s with my installations. And I would love it because the soundtracks, just being a hyperactive person, I liked that the soundtrack would always be different. I'd walk into the space and be surprised by my own work, and be like, "Oh, that's interesting what you're coming up with today." It had a life of its own—I plugged it in, which was really cool, because I always made ridiculously long tracks, so the combinations would be many and varied; they would be long loops.

I think it has to do with the internet, too, to get back to the computer. Because I do a lot of research for my work, and it's part of my process that I really love. With the Metro Pictures show, it's like dust, mercury, water, so I'll immerse myself in those three subjects and just read books on them until I'm filled, then I'll write, and then I slice and dice that, and get performers, and work with that, and then cut it up again, and that's how it sort of ends up being a text. And then, now there's this great 5.1 stuff; I think it's the best for installation because it's allowed you to put sculpture back into sound—literally, we're at the beginning of a new phase of sculpting sound in space. To go back to the internet, all this information, everyone has the same information now. It used to be that if you were a scholar or an artist you might have access to certain information, just because you were doggedly researching it—you'd find things other people wouldn't find. But, you know, that's all out the window, because all you have to do is google, this beautiful search engine.

That's what I was saying before about connecting the dots between stuff. Now if you google Tony Conrad, you come up with all these things that would have taken someone years to trip across on their own and then relay it back.

Yeah, exactly. It spooked the hell of me at the

beginning. I was like, "This is really a profound change in the way information is going to be dispersed." I remember this very specifically happened because I was curating a show called "Guys & Dolls," kind of a silly title, but it had to do with people who work with dolls and video and simulacra and things like that. I found this one video clip about a guy who had attacked a Barbie doll in Sandusky, Ohio, and molested it, its genitalia, in the store; cut it up and stuff. Must have done it to a couple of them. Somehow it got on the news, somehow I recorded it, so I was really happy that I had this recording that I could put in this curation. I was like, "This is the most weird, obscure thing ever." And then as soon as the internet got going, I realized you just type "Barbie" and that incident comes up just like that. Previous to that, I thought I had this thing I had dipped into a stream [to get] that was like going off a waterfall into infinity, into the garbage heap. But now, information stays, everything stays, and everyone can get it. So it's no longer like, I have this clip and it's incredible, no one will have ever known about this. . . . That's not the case.

That's the whole thing with the information superhighway, where everything is an exit on the highway. It's one highway that's all over the entire planet. To go physically from New York to London, you have to go on a plane or boat, but if you go on the web to go to the Tate Modern website it takes two seconds.

Yeah, and then Conrad, being the malcontent he is, last time he was here—he stays here generally when he's in New York, he just left a couple days ago—he was bemoaning that there's not enough stuff on the internet [*laughs*]. It's so Tony. He goes, "Yeah, it's not on there, man."

The Sea and Cake

In the fall of 1995, my band Run On did a mini-tour with Tortoise and the Sea and Cake. I already knew the members of the former, but had yet to meet the latter. When we arrived at Princeton University for the first show, guitarist Sam Prekop was sitting backstage, grousing about a Grachan Moncur III album that he had noticed hanging on the wall at Princeton Record Exchange, from which he'd just returned, being priced well beyond his means. I had never before (or since) heard anyone mention Moncur, a relatively obscure trombonist even by free jazz standards, at an indie rock show, and was immediately impressed.

A dozen years later, Bettina Richards of Thrill Jockey prevailed upon me to write something for the *Wire* about the Sea and Cake for their new album, *Everybody* (2007). I had just finished writing the book *Sound Art: Beyond Music, Between Categories* and, knowing that Prekop, guitarist Archer Prewitt, and bassist Eric Claridge were all visual artists, I was interested in approaching them from the angle of artists' music—to consider the Sea and Cake as an art band in the way that Half Japanese, for instance, could be viewed as one. I flew to Chicago in March and we did the interview over lunch at a brightly lit faux-'50s diner before making a trip over to Corbett vs. Dempsey gallery, where gallerist John Corbett, who is well versed in the city's music and art scenes, showed us some work to contextualize Sam and Archer within Chicago's lineage of painters. The *Wire* story ran with some of the parenthetical notations of laughter edited out, which muted any sense of Sam's dry wit and the general affability of the conversation; they have been restored here.

I wanted to focus on the fact that all three of you guys are involved in the visual arts; maybe you could take turns, to start off with, describing what you see as the relationship between the time you spend working on that and the time you spend working on music, either individually or together as a unit, and to what extent you feel there's a relationship between the visual art practice and the music practice. I would assume that you've been painting or drawing longer than you've been playing music—is that true of all of you guys? Or that's not true of Eric?

Sam Prekop

That's true for me, yeah. I went to art school to make art, not rock. I ended up making rock and stopping art. My activities have all become project-oriented, so when I'm doing a record I'm not making paintings. I'm often asked to find the connection between the two, to no avail. It's all cut from the same cloth. I'm trying to be as accurate as possible with each of those disciplines—an honest, basic, *base* expression of what I'm ultimately interested in. There's no practical usefulness to doing both, except that they each keep me away from the other, which is handy, ultimately. There's always a way out, from one or the other. This could be a cop-out, but perhaps there's always a link to being more fulfilled with the other discipline when you're failing with the one that you're working on now. I ultimately feel not entirely satisfied with any of them, but I look forward to getting on to the next one, and that will probably help me to move on. It's almost habitual, the way I move off from one and start another.

Do you feel like you hit a wall with one and then that almost serves as a cue to go to the other?

SP I think so, but it's a little bit different with music because it's involved with other people and it's always got an external timeline. That differentiates it from the art in a handy way. Other people are depending on me being creative at a certain point. And before I had to meet deadlines for painting shows it was more difficult to get it going. Now it's more like working toward a record. Lately I've decided not to agree to do any exhibitions, because I'm afraid that I'm getting too programmed to work in that way. I'm recognizing certain things I do all the time just to get it done, so I'm trying to cut that out. Therefore I've not painted in quite a while [*laughs*].

Does that happen with songwriting also? Have you noticed similarities in songs when you're trying to come up with a new group of songs for a record?

SP I'll say that the best way to get some unexpected results is to begin that way; I don't think you can pretend to eradicate all your habits. I was working on this music for a commercial a couple of years ago. They wanted me to do what I know how to do—"We want it to sound like what you would do"—well, that poses a few problems because I know that ultimately they need a very specific kind of thing . . . but through that, I felt really let off the hook, in a great way, and it was a really interesting, new thing to do. So whereas I consciously dipped into my own repertoire, I didn't feel bad about it at all. "I've done this kind of thing a billion times, I know how to do this." But in the end, even thinking that way, it didn't sound like anything I had ever done before [*laughs*], so it's this weird catch-22.

I've noticed I'll be working on something and I'll throw things away that I think are too much like other works I've done, but then sometimes when I keep something, much later, when I go back and listen to it I'll realize that it's actually just like a work I've done that I hadn't remembered before. Everybody makes certain choices about things they've heard and want to repeat in their own way, so if you sit down and analyze it, you can factor out where you got certain ideas from.

SP I've always felt limited in what I can actually do, musically. I feel like we've had to invent this very specific way for us to make sound and songs. I don't feel versatile within musical language.

[Addressing Prewitt and Claridge.] *Is that how you guys view it also?*

Archer Prewitt

I always just see it as an extension of your personality and how you choose to refine things or come up with something you feel is finished. One kind of art I do is comics. It starts with one panel that leads to the next—in the same way that one chord leads to the next—and eventually a story comes out of that. I tear apart the lyrics over and over again until I get something I'm comfortable with. But I think that's the only similarity in terms of stringing together ideas. I don't craft a story and then illustrate it with drawings. But I've also been doing more abstract, minimal stuff for a long time in my own personal world; it isn't seen that much. I don't know how that would relate to music, other than that I sometimes like to play drones without particularly wanting to present them for anyone else to hear, just for my own pleasure in making sound.

Did you, like Sam, feel more limited in terms of musical expression?

AP Yeah, I'm self-taught; I haven't unlocked the secrets of the guitar neck or anything. When I go to play a solo on the fly, I'm going to hit bad note after bad note.

It's frustrating but it's really not my inclination to play solos per se; it's more sliding into something that sounds right against Sam's chords and Eric's bass lines. We've always talked about it in terms of a sonic fabric, where nothing's really poking out necessarily. But if a melody comes out of it, it sort of sounds like a guitar lead.

Do some of the comics or the artwork start that way too, kind of "sliding into it"?

AP Definitely. I was talking to Chris Ware about this, and he does comics the same way, which I found shocking, because his comics, more than anyone else's, seem so premeditated and thought-out in terms of how all these things interlock. I couldn't believe it, but he just starts drawing on the page and then it falls into order. That's what I do too, but to a much lower degree of complexity.

SP The process is related on that level, in terms of the chance elements, but within your own language that you collect over time. When I start a painting, I sort of know what's likely to happen; you give yourself enough guidelines to get started. And it's similar with a tune, in that we've chosen guitars to start with.

AP With your paintings, and with Eric's paintings too, you'll have information on a canvas and then there'll be a choice to go in a different direction or to blot out something completely, and I see that restlessness in the creation of the music as well.

SP I think of each as an accurate document of thousands of decisions, and which are collected and then presented.

A commercial illustrator is going to work from a

very set idea, whereas an artist is more likely to follow that process to create the work. It's the same as a session musician who's being hired to play on a specific song and is looking at the chart, as opposed to someone who's composing by fooling around on their instrument and coming up with something that they then start working on. Is that the way the songwriting happens?

SP Basically. We fool around a lot. I think we always start with a strategy where we're not quite sure what's going to happen, exactly. We definitely try not to premeditate a record; they gain steam as they develop and we work on them. I usually start all the songs with little kernels of ideas, and it's a process of elaborating those very innate impulses to begin with; we make decisions to push it one way or another. Lately, most of our work is toward finishing a record—it's usually pointed at one project, which is how we've worked on the past four or five records. It's been a long time since we just wrote songs for the fun of it [*laughs*], for good times, that's *way* over now [*laughs*].

Eric, I think I heard that you actually started painting as a result of seeing some of Sam's paintings.

Eric Claridge

Yeah, it's all his fault [*laughs*]. My art is actually much closer to the music in terms of an ongoing process of discovery for me. I've never had an art class—I fuckin' hate art [*laughs*]. I did, I was not a fan, but now I like it all right.

SP We started as destitute roommates with a *lot* of time and not really anything else to do. We also worked for the same woman, painting houses. The work had dried up; that's when we started again. It was really weird, I hadn't painted for a long time out of art school. That's about when you started as well.

EC Yeah. I started selling my work, mostly to Archer.

SP Yeah, Archer kept us afloat for several years, buying our paintings [*laughs*]. Was this before the Sea and Cake started?

AP I remember you guys asked me to come over and—

SP —join the band, *and* buy some art [*laughs*].

[Laughs.] *In order to join the band, you had to buy some art.*

AP You did mention to bring my checkbook [*laughs*].

SP Archer basically paid his way into the group [*laughs*], like a session dude. . . .

Do you have much of an art collection, Archer?

AP Oh yeah. I have stacks of Eric's early washes, a whole bunch of Sam's paintings. My wife and I have a weakness for art. You get inspired and maybe you can't afford it but somehow you find a way. I bought one of Sam's paintings from a gallery before we were in the Sea and Cake.

You've mentioned in interviews that the Velvet Underground, especially their third record, was something you listened to, which made you think maybe you could be a musician, too.

SP A little bit. I don't know that I felt it was something

I could actually play; I think maybe I was interested in their legacy, coming out of Warhol and the art scene. At that time period, the late '80s, there seemed to be a resurgence, in art schools, of interest in the Velvet Underground, so basically that's what everyone else was listening to at that time. I mean, it certainly did make a big impact on me. But those Tom Waits records, *Rain Dogs* [Island, 1985] and *Swordfishtrombones* [Island, 1983], were also influential to [my previous band] Shrimp Boat in terms of breaking the mold of the kind of music rock bands made—the expansive attitude toward instrumentation.

The Velvet Underground is a bit more primitive than most of the stuff I've heard you do.

SP Have you heard some of the Shrimp Boat stuff? We really started at zero in terms of musical capability. We were fostered within that art-school party circuit, where you could get away with murder. We didn't actually have to face the public till many years later. There's this box set on AUM Fidelity that's an immense document of really difficult listening [*laughs*] over four CDs. It's pretty wild to hear in context of the Sea and Cake stuff, which does come off as pseudo-sophisticated music. We've been accused of being music students, Berklee [College of Music] students—that's always hilarious, because I can hardly name a chord, really.

Is Afrobeat something you guys are into?

AP I listened to a lot of Zulu pop stuff in college. I was obsessed with these Zulu songs, and the way the guitar was, and it was probably the only optimistic music I had in my whole collection at the time. In the summer, I would listen to it all the time. It definitely formed a way that I like to play against Sam's summery, optimistic chords. He sets up repetitive loop chords without even thinking about it or making a decision to play in that vein; that's the kind of guitar stuff that comes out every now and then.

SP A lot of our stuff is pattern-based, short figures repeated over and over again. It's one way to expand on not knowing what you're doing, in an interesting way. I've always appreciated Afropop music; technically, I would not claim to know how it's played at all.

AP When we get together to work out the music, in order to work out a part that everybody's satisfied with, it involves going over a part obsessively. And invariably we say, "We should play it that long, that feels good to stick on that one chord and just hold it." I think to some degree that makes the first record unlistenable . . . but I think now we have an editorial process that's a little more refined.

The new record is the first one in three or four years—early on, you released two records in a year, or a year and a half. It seems like there have been wider gaps between releases since then. Is that an attribute of your schedules?

AP Primarily. When there's gaps in the schedules, they widen because of other releases and touring, which goes hand in hand with that. Where one initial gap created the opportunity to make something else . . . we've already started work toward another Sea and Cake record, to not wait as long.

Do you think the longevity of the band has something to do with taking your time from record to record, as opposed to being on the usual schedule of album-tour-album-tour every year or every other year?

AP I wouldn't say that we're necessarily the kind of people who can be road warriors that commit to just one band as the only outlet. With every album, there's a lot of touring.

EC With John [McEntire, the Sea and Cake's drummer], earlier, when we were touring a lot more with Tortoise, he was pulling double duty, which sucked for him.

AP It would've sucked worse, though, if he'd tried to do two independent tours.

EC That was also before Soma.[1]

Do you guys do much touring if you don't have a record out? You don't do a tour just to do it.

SP No, not really. Or local shows.

No local shows?

AP I can't remember the last local show we played.

SP With the various solo projects, we end up playing pretty often. I don't feel like I've stopped touring, really. At least of couple months of the year we're on tour somewhere.

AP I do feel it helps us to step away from it and not

1 Soma Electronic Music Studio in Chicago, founded by John McEntire in 1993.

just be on this cycle, but I do think the widening gaps are detrimental.

SP Yeah, I do think if we waited four years again, forget it. Although you never know. . . . I'm certain it would make it a different record if we waited four years.

You have a relaxed attitude; it doesn't seem like being a rock star is a stated goal for any of you, or that the band is a brand name you're trying to push in people's faces.

AP Right.

SP We've lucked out. It would be more difficult to make another record four years later if we really felt that no one would pay attention at all. I suppose we still would. . . . Most of the people who pay attention to us have been really long-term fans who pay attention to our career as a whole, to our output in general.

Do you have much of a sense of who your audience is? Is there a Sea and Cake fan type?

SP I talked to this guy who writes for a skateboard magazine and he asked if I had any idea how popular the Sea and Cake is within the skateboarding realm. I had no idea, I can honestly say—but I've talked to several skateboarding magazines for this record. Which is baffling. 'Cause the kid was like, "I'm guessing you assume, like everyone else does, that skateboarding kids are just into hardcore."

Traditionally, yeah . . . I remember when Run On played with you guys at the Magic Stick in Detroit *and during your set, it was this mass make-out session [*laughs*]. Is that something you're aware of?*

EC That goes on.

*You're like four Barry Whites [*laughs*].*

SP We're not playing any traditionally love-oriented tunes, really.

EC I've had a lot of contact with people in the last couple of years through selling my work online, and a lot of them found me through Thrill Jockey or the Sea and Cake website, and I get that all the time, like, "Me and my wife love you," or, "The only thing my baby will go to sleep to is the Sea and Cake." Very homey music, I guess.

It's funny how people latch onto certain things—it's not marketed that way, but people find it somehow.

AP When we would tour with Tortoise, when [David] Pajo was in the band, he would say to us, "Man, thank God you guys are touring with us. . . . That's when the ladies come out" [*laughs*].

SP Yeah, the crowd would shift quite radically between bands: the spectacled dudes recede, the ladies move up [*laughs*].

The new record is more of a live-in-the-studio kind of thing . . . ? It's being touted as less electronics, less overdubs—was that by design?

SP We usually respond to our last record—whatever we did on the last one, *don't do that again*.

Because you didn't like it, or you just want a change?

SP Oh, it's usually just a matter of changing it up. I guess we feel like the last one wasn't one of our favorites and it seemed like nobody else liked it that much either [*laughs*]. The record before *One Bedroom* [Thrill Jockey, 2003] was *Oui* [Thrill Jockey, 2000], and the recording process there was similar to what we did this time. The tunes were pretty well finished before we started, whereas with *One Bedroom*, they were not finished, with the intention that we would see what happened to them in the studio, use the studio as the extra facet. It could have been a time thing too—unusually, we weren't sure we were going to do a record until the last minute, so it had to happen really quickly, which sort of facilitated this documentary-style record. And we also knew that we wanted to make a different record than *One Bedroom*, which was a much more labored and drawn-out process.

AP One thing I remember about *One Bedroom* that was frustrating, at least for me, was the decision to work with John from the outset. We normally get together and get the music down and then present it to John, and he takes it even one step further, and that's when it becomes the band sound. When you can't really hear what your ideas are and the drummer gets tired playing the song twice . . . like I said before, we loop a part and we flesh it out; at least you can kind of hear what you're doing. It didn't really happen like that for *One Bedroom*. And then we went back to our way of us forming the melodies and everything. I prefer that.

SP One thing John and I noticed on *One Bedroom* is that Archer had, like, no parts [*laughs*].

AP Well, with drums slamming, I just got more and more minimal. I did a lot of atmospherics, which is a result of us four in the room. 'Cause rhythmically, when you're coming up with parts in a three-piece without drums, you put more information in there, more rhythmic parts.

SP I'm not dissing you, that's what happened.

Was this the first time you've used an outside producer besides John? Or any producer?

SP Depending on your definition of "producer." I don't think we've used them as much as we could have in the traditional sense of a producer. Ultimately, we're always pretty much self-produced. However, I felt like we were pretty hungry for outside input. The dynamic of how the band was working shifted a bit, and that was his most important contribution; rather than him imposing anything on us, it was more us being open.

AP But also knowing his history and the kind of music he's done, I think it was exciting to think about someone like Brian [Paulson] bringing a more straight-ahead approach to how things were going to be recorded. We talked about doing an album that's more like a band playing in a room. When we do it ourselves, John sets his drums up next to the mixing board, and he's pressing play, and there's a whole other thing of, "We'll fix it in the mix." This was more like, "Well, let's get the song down, let's go to this little town in Michigan with no distractions, eat, sleep, make music. . . ." I think it sounds like that. It sounds like a concerted effort by four people in a room.

Do you ever think about records by other people in terms of sequencing or production values? Would Brian say, "This reminds me of such and such, let's try this"?

SP I kept saying, "Phil Spector, Phil Spector" [*laughs*]. "Ronettes, come on" [*laughs*]. That's what I was thinking about.

AP You were playing some stuff that sounds like Spector when we were first getting together and talking about all the musicians coming together to make one glorious sound that was kind of minimal and to the point. . . . I think it was good to underline that going into it, 'cause we've always thought of it as kind of a weave of our sounds.

SP We're always hoping the material tells us what to do at the right time in terms of when it becomes a record. We recorded fifteen songs—

AP We talked about how you listen back to these songs after you come from a tour and they all sound sluggish and slow. Every song, we'd say, "This is the tempo we feel comfortable with, what do you think Brian?" and he'd say "Let's bump it up six bpm."

SP "Let's bump it up fifty bpm" [*laughs*].

AP And in the end I think it's right, because even now it sounds kind of sluggish [*laughs*].

I always had the opposite problem: when Run On was recording Start Packing *[Matador, 1996], we recorded all these versions of the songs and came in a few days later and they were all—*

SP Double time?

Yeah, literally double time.

AP We always had the opposite.

So we had to work to slow things down. Even if I listen back to certain shows I've done solo, sometimes I'll think, "Where's the fire?"

AP Oh yeah, live we often play too fast.

*In the press release for the record you mention the Kinks, which I didn't hear at all [*laughs*].*

SP See, someone put that in there, 'cause I didn't even bring it up. I'm like, "Where did that come from?"

EC That didn't sound like you.

SP I've never even heard the Kinks [*laughs*].

AP Maybe I said it, but I don't recall.

SP All those Éthiopiques records have been my latest inspiration. Some of the recording quality of that stuff, the compressed, sort of gnarly textures.

AP He bought all these fancy pedals to make his amp—

SP —sound like shit, a fuzzy ball of crap—

AP —which was hilarious. We spent the whole first day getting drum tones; we had never really spent that long getting drum tones . . . and that was, in the end, a good thing.

SP We still made this record in a really short period of time. And I can't even imagine working much longer than that [*laughs*]. I mean, after we did all the basic tracks, then I had to write all the lyrics for a month, so in the end it does take a long time. I think a record's more effective if it represents a somewhat compact amount of time; it becomes more elusively interesting if it is this document of a very specific moment rather than a drawn-out, piecemeal thing.

The CD booklet has some of the lyrics, but in notebook form—I thought it was interesting because the notebooks are on grid paper, and it's sort of a fluke but I often think of writing lyrics as similar to working on a crossword puzzle. Has that ever occurred to you?

SP I like that idea and I plan to take it up. The lyrics are often a visual stimulant before they're sound. But often the way I start is just singing whatever, improvising, and then stuff will stick out from that. Oftentimes those notebook things are just words that I would love to get in there somehow, but they don't necessarily make it in; usually like 25 percent of my "wish words" get in there and, in a crossword-puzzle kind of way, I strategize a way to link the good ones with the less interesting ones. The organization of them is definitely not linear or literal.

Any kind of writing is different on the page than when you hear it spoken, especially lyrics, where they're going to be sung. When you're reading silently, you're really hearing it read in your own voice, so what makes people popular writers, in a way, is that their "voice" is adaptable to a wide variety of people—on some level people will read something and feel like it's something they could have thought of, but they didn't, whereas if it's too dense or convoluted they just think, "What is this?"

What about the three photo postcards that you chose to include with the record?

SP I wish there was more of a reason [*laughs*].

AP They feel related in terms of a vista, open space.

SP Within themselves, on a wall, it made sense to see them together, visually. Why they're in the record is the question [*laughs*] that I haven't resolved. I think it was just trying to be friendly, to give people a bonus gift for buying the record—

Instead of downloading it?

SP Kind of. Bettina was quite adamant that we make the package as attractive as possible. The covers have no direct correlation to the music except that we chose them to be there, so the photos are an extension of those ideas.

Thrill Jockey's done a couple of projects where there's kind of an art package, with a book, and there was that Eno record, Before and After Science *[Polydor/Island, 1977], which came with a set of prints. From the mid-'60s to the late '70s at least, there was a lot of thought put into album packaging.*

AP Coming from that period [of LP packages], we struggle to try to make the small format into something that's still exciting. The most outrageous thing I've seen recently is Tool's last record [*10,000 Days* (Tool Dissectional/Volcano/Zomba, 2006)].

SP Tool?

AP Tool. You can look at individual pages of the artwork through this pop-up stereopticon, and it's in 3D. I mean, it's all this ridiculous goth imagery, but you've got to hand it to them, they really gave the fans something to look at—it's completely over the top [*laughs*].

Matthew Barney

It's not often that an editor at one publication contacts me about writing for somewhere else, but that's what happened in August 2007, when I received an email from Chris Bohn at the *Wire*, who wanted to gauge my interest in doing a short piece on the artist/filmmaker Matthew Barney. His friend at *Sight & Sound*, a British film magazine, had asked him to recommend someone for the job. Barney's latest film, *Drawing Restraint 9* (2005), had been made in collaboration with his then partner, the singer Björk, and *Sight & Sound* was looking for a music writer to handle the piece. I was familiar with Barney, but not overly so; the Pop surrealism of the "Cremaster" cycle, 1994–2002, his best-known foray into filmmaking, was not my cup of tea. Still, I went to a screening of *Drawing Restraint 9* with a reasonably open mind. Barney and Björk star in the film as "Occidental guests" on a Japanese whaling ship. They undergo a matrimonial tea ceremony as well as bizarre biological rituals that involve cutting away at their own bodies before making a final transformation into sea creatures. Meanwhile, the ship's real-life crew is struggling to fill a giant casting of Barney's "field" emblem (an oval bisected by a bar) with petroleum jelly (a favored Barneyan substance). I found much to explore in both the film and its accompanying exhibitions of associated drawings and sculptures in relation to Barney's overall aesthetic—one rooted firmly in first-generation performance art, body art, video art, and Earthworks.

Barney and I met up at the New York offices of Gladstone Gallery, which represents him. I wasn't sure what to expect but found him to be extraordinarily articulate about his own work; I often like to point out things in the work that an artist may have done unconsciously, but it seemed like Barney accounted for every detail I brought up as being the result of a very conscious decision, which struck me as rather remarkable and admirable.

How important is it to you for the audience is conversant with certain things that they're seeing—for instance, in your film Drawing Restraint 9, *that it's you and Björk playing the characters, and that you're a couple in real life?*

To be honest with you, I don't think very much about the way somebody comes to the film for the first time, sits down, and watches it. I tend to think of it more in terms of the experience one could have with the piece once they've seen the film, the sculpture, the books, some of the drawings. . . . I'm more preoccupied with the relationship between all of those things, and less on how the film functions autonomously. That said, there are some fairly esoteric things that are explored in the narrative that I wouldn't expect anybody to know anything about, but I need to construct this narrative somehow; I made a structure, and this is how I do it. Find these paths that can connect to other paths that might be more legible, and those paths are layered, and hopefully there's a way of leaping from one to the next.

You've talked in some interviews about opera; is that something you see as a template for constructing a film? With opera, often viewers may not understand what's going on, especially if it's sung in a foreign language, but they're adjusted to that idea going in, which moviegoers tend not to be—they want everything laid out for them very quickly.

Yeah, that's right. I would say on that level, yeah, opera is interesting for me. The reality of sitting in a theater and watching an opera isn't satisfying for me, on the other hand. The two-dimensionality of it bothers me. My idea of opera is much more about how the spaces—the auditorium, the house, the stage, and the pit—can all be understood as one space that contains the narrative. That excites me very much. The architecture of opera excites me very much; the reality of opera doesn't.

The books, and the exhibitions that surround these projects—does that relate to the Wagnerian idea of the total artwork, but spread out rather than appearing on one stage?

Well, that's something that the visual art form makes available. The small audience of people who are interested in this stuff do tend to read the supporting material around what an artist has done. I don't think it's particularly a stretch to assume that that could happen, and that could cross-fertilize all of these parts. To be on one side of town and see a film, and go to another side of town and see an exhibition, and draw those relationships. I feel like it's something that's already available to me in the structure of the art world, less so than thinking about it in Wagnerian terms. Although the Noh singing [in "Holographic Entrypoint," from the *Drawing Restraint 9* soundtrack] is an interesting example, because there is a text I wrote that was translated into the Noh form by a translator who had done the same for *Hamlet*. Björk and I became acquainted with this guy and it was a really interesting process to have this text, which was written more like verse, to be sung in English translated into the Noh form; and then to consider the question of whether this text, which does attempt to distill the entire story, would be subtitled or not in the film. Where there is dialogue [that has been translated into the Noh form], I elected to not subtitle it. And I did think about opera, about how annoying it is for me, actually, to have supertitles at operas, and to have to read what I'm seeing—I'm not interested in that. On the other hand, the attempt at making an accurate text is interesting to me, embedded within the narrative, no matter how abstract it is.

In Drawing Restraint 9, *would you say that the soundtrack of the film takes the place of what would ordinarily be dialogue? The kind of environment that the soundtrack helps create is interesting to me, especially when it breaks from the electronics to the acoustic instruments in one sequence; was that something that you and Björk discussed?*

We talked a lot about it, but that was one of the scenes that was probably approached in a more traditional way. It was more about the way the ships feel, the propulsion of one of these hunting vessels and the masculinity of the brass instruments, the rhythm and the propulsion of the engine. The scene was discussed in those terms, the color and emotion of it, whereas there were other scenes where there were more clear music or sound cues.

Ritual seems to be the basis of the film, even to the extent that the way the man and the woman are being prepared for the ceremony parallels the preparation of the food, and the idea of the transformations that happen within these food chains. Do you see ritual as a kind of external restraint, as opposed to self-imposed restraints found in the earlier "Drawing Restraint" series [1987–]?

No, I guess I don't feel that way. You mean as an outsider to that culture? Are you suggesting that the ritual in this case is a barrier of some sort?

No, just the marriage ceremony itself, as a ritual and a process that you need to go through to achieve a goal. It's another form of restraint, but not the exaggerated kind that you put on yourself in certain performances and in other films, and I'm wondering if that's something you were conscious of in developing the story.

The content of the film ended up being the issue of making a piece in Japan—how I could do that honestly, for myself. Being somebody who works in a site-specific way, and having worked for a number of years on a project which had a viral relationship—with the "Cremaster" cycle films, my relationship to the location, to the environment, was somewhat viral, and that was really the goal, to try to get my language to be a part of the environment, seamlessly. When I realized that couldn't happen in Japan, it became the subject of the piece, in a certain way. I think the whole endeavor was a restraint.

*I thought of the jelly on the boat as being like [Robert] Smithson's Earthworks translocations, in taking material from one place and imposing it on another pre-existing setting. There's one shot of a crane pulling a large sheet of metal onto the ship, and I thought of this film I'd seen of a Richard Serra show being installed [*Seeing the Landscape *(2003), directed by Alberta Chu] earlier in the summer, and in some cases Serra has the metal shipped by boat, from Germany.*

I never asked him this, but did a piece of his fall off of a container ship and it's actually now at the bottom of the ocean?

*I do know about that, because I actually saw the piece [*Te Tuhirangi Contour, *1999–2001] in New Zealand. It belongs to this millionaire named Alan Gibbs, and the father of a friend of mine worked for him.*

I was in New Zealand playing concerts, and we went out to the Gibbs Farm sculpture park.

The piece looks amazing—

*It's incredible; it's the largest single piece of his, I think. And the story was that they were transporting all the metal, and they told the ship's captain, "Whatever you do, don't pile the pieces on top of each other," and he went ahead and did it anyway [*laughs*], and it went right through the bottom of the ship, to the bottom of the ocean, and they had to start from square one.*

Wow.

Eventually they got it over there. Serra was moved to tears, apparently, when he saw it.

And it's too deep to be a dive site?

I don't know how far down it is.

But it would be good to visit it.

Well, that sort of brings me to my next question—

A James Cameron question? [*Laughs.*]

Not quite. The question was about evolution, and the transformation at the end, of the man and woman into whales, which goes along with the belief, from Japanese mythology, that whales are our ancestors—is this meant to represent a way of coming full circle, in the story?

I was interested in there being a development that

would start with this land-mammal state and would somehow emphasize the departure from land, and then to think about the function of a processing ship as a place where something is transformed from one thing to another. Like the evolution of the whale, the guests would start off as land mammals, go off to sea and transform into sea mammals. This was one of the first structural notions of the piece.

At the end of Cremaster 3 *[2002], there's something similar, when you put your mouth on Aimee Mullins's neck and she transforms into a leopard lady. Is transformation something you're interested in on a deeper level—do you see the human species going in a particular direction?*

It's more about trying to make a decentralized work. One that avoids binary relationships, one that's multiple. There's a way in which the early "Cremaster" pieces, and *Drawing Restraint 7* [1993], some of the pieces that I was making ten years ago, were a little more fixated on this desire to erode the differences between gender, and now I think it's become more general than that, to try to create a system where the differences between all of its parts are eroded. The scenes of transformation have something to do with that goal, where two things can become one thing, momentarily, and they can become independent again. Those notions of relationship continue to be interesting and important for me, whether they're pantomiming more fixed ideas of relationships or trying to describe other, less understood notions of relationships. The piece in Japan ended up being quite interesting, for me, the way that this notion of relationship is so central to Shinto, and the way that the universe is described by a multitude of relationships.

So many of your pieces have involved climbing, whether it's climbing a gallery wall, or scaling the ramps of the [Solomon R.] Guggenheim [Museum, New York]. I'm wondering if climbing in the evolution of our species, or other species, is something that you thought about also?

Only to the extent that the climbing is often a way of trying to effect a scale change, to resist a situation where you have the scale of a figure constrained by the set of a film, [and] to propose [instead] a cellular or atomic scale, where you have particles that are in relationship with one another. The climbing, in the way that the climbing is often photographed in long shot where the scale and the figure become very small, and the architecture becomes more of a body, or a cell, I think the intention is often to do with that—to take what is insistently narrative and make it biological.

There's an obvious evolution in your work in the way it grows out of some of the early video art pieces, particularly the ones that document performances. Like some of the stuff Bruce Nauman did in his studio, where it was one person in a room and not witnessed by an audience but documented by himself—your films have multiplied that, where you'll have a large cast of characters and more scenery. And if you go back to the development of motion pictures, the very early films just showed someone doing an activity and then later it became a narrative and a spectacle, too—did you think about any of that when you started making films coming out of your study of video and performance from the '70s?

Yeah, and it's one of the things that's compelling about doing this "Drawing Restraint" exhibition. . . . The show in London [at the Serpentine Gallery,

2007] is sort of a distillation of the bigger survey show that had happened in these other places.[1] It's an opportunity to contextualize these more cinematic works with the early *Drawing Restraint* pieces, which are very indebted to that period and that tradition of performance-based sculpture. And I do feel very close to it, particularly to the more narrative artists, like [Joseph] Beuys, like Marina Abramović, to some extent Vito Acconci and Chris Burden. You mentioned Smithson and I think something that was very clear to me when the "Cremaster" cycle was being developed was that it was in the tradition of Earthworks. It hadn't occurred to me that the "Cremaster" videos would be shown in cinemas; when I started making the project, it was very much about imposing this narrative onto the landscape, and bringing back narrative sculpture. It's very much a notion that belongs to Smithson.

Even having [hardcore punk band] Murphy's Law in the Guggenheim in Cremaster 3 *is almost a non-site [*laughs*]. I also wanted to ask, since you're interested in Harry Houdini—both Georges Méliès and Orson Welles were magicians, and there's the whole idea of the filmmaker as being a type of magician; have you ever thought about your filmmaking in that way?*

Yes, I have. My understanding of Houdini has always been complicated by what are probably myths about him, about how on the foundation there's this very physical practice, a disciplined, learned physicality, and then there's this way in which he wanted, at a certain

1 "Matthew Barney: DRAWING RESTRAINT" was shown at the 21st Century Museum of Contemporary Art, Kanazawa, Japan, 2005; Kunsthalle Vienna, Austria, 2008; Leeum, Samsung Museum of Art, Seoul, South Korea, 2005–2006; and San Francisco Museum of Modern Art, 2006.

point, to demystify what he was doing—he published his methods. Then there are other tricks that were never revealed, and I always have wanted to believe there were things he did that couldn't be explained, that did transcend physicality. I think there's something about working at this scale where the will and the craft and the endurance and everything else stop being accountable for something that can happen. There's a synergy that occurs between all of the people working on the project. Very magical things happen, and I don't think they could happen if my practice was more individual, I just don't think they could. And those two things relate, somehow.

In Visions of Light *[1992, directed by Arnold Glassman, Todd McCarthy, and Stuart Samuels], a documentary about cinematography, the interviewees talk about one scene in* In Cold Blood *[1967, directed by Richard Brooks], where Robert Blake is delivering a monologue, and it looks like tears are streaming down his face, but it's an accidental trick of the light reflecting on the window, where it was raining—the raindrop shadows were reflected onto his face. That's an example of what you're talking about.*

Yeah, there are a lot of serendipitous things that happen, for sure.

Was there anything like that in Drawing Restraint 9*?*

We did a lot of setups that were weather-sensitive, on location in Japan, and had incredibly good luck with weather. It's quite banal, but with some of those scenes, we felt kind of blessed in that way. This is slightly different, because this is more to do with will, but here's another layer to *Drawing Restraint 9* that's nearly as important as the one we spoke about already, which is the relationship I have to the boat, and what it took to get on that boat, the [whaling ship] *Nisshin Maru*—how significant the trust was that we developed with the people who were in charge of that ship. In the way we've talked about Smithson, and art languages, I think the readymade is probably significant in terms of *Drawing Restraint 9*. The *Nisshin Maru* really felt like that to me; it had such a heavy aura to it, had such a clear metaphorical resonance, one which clearly defined my position in relationship to the piece. The ship metaphorically represents the island of Japan in regard to this international debate on whaling.

At a certain point, it became clear to me that the piece had to be made on that ship, and I went to Japan over and over again and met with these people, and was turned away, turned away, and turned away—which made complete sense to me, if I put myself in their position. Why should they let me on the ship, given everything they go through with activists, when really anybody from the West who asks questions about that boat is bad news for them? Just the persistence of coming back again and again and developing a relationship between the story and the historian of the Japan Whaling Association became very interesting, this letter writing that was happening—eventually the trust that he had in the story.

Did the moment during the tea ceremony where the guy elliptically explains the history of the ship reflect your experience in trying to get permission to use the ship?

It was important to acknowledge the conflict, and it is very elliptically expressed [*laughs*], but there's also the way that the vessel, the tea bowl, is discussed among the guests and hosts during tea ceremony. The tea bowl is turned to present what's called "the face," or what is agreed to be the front of the bowl, back to the person you're passing it to, and it's often a flaw in the ceramic, or a scar of some sort, that gives it its identity. So this idea that the Greenpeace ship had rammed the side of the *Nisshin Maru* and left a scar on it became interesting to me, although you can't actually see it, and that there are certain things in tea ceremony that need to be said, where dialogue happens.

I felt like we needed to follow the rules of the tea ceremony, and talk about these things, and that is the moment in a tea ceremony where something like this would be described by the host. There's this opportunity at the end where the guests can ask more questions, either about the tea ware or about the garden, the teahouse, or anything else.

In one interview you said that you would feel uncomfortable directing actors. To the extent that you direct what's going on in a film, do you relate that at all to when you were a model, and the photographer was directing you?

No, although that experience was important for me in other ways, but for me it's more to do with wanting the piece to remain in the language of sculpture, and for the characters to have behavior, but not to have the kind of dramatic projection that, in my opinion, wipes out the nuanced behavior of an object or a person.

Do you direct in terms of body language?

I try. . . . I think what I'm quite good at is setting up a situation, a situation that will affect the behavior of a person. I think I'm fairly good at choreography, but directing people is harder for me, and it's less interesting.

Are you comfortable coordinating the larger production numbers of the film with all the dancers?

Yeah, the coordination is quite natural, and I think it's a holdover from team sports; I am comfortable with that.

People sometimes mention directors like Ken Russell or David Lynch when writing about your films, and I thought of Alejandro Jodorowsky or even Harmony Korine, or Peter Greenaway, Derek Jarman—are any of these people whose films you've looked at seriously? The way Harmony Korine cast Werner Herzog in Julien Donkey-Boy *[1999] made me think of you casting Richard Serra in* Cremaster 3*; there's a certain loosely patriarchal relationship there. Harmony takes a grungier way of presenting images, but some are perhaps not far off from the "Cremaster" cycle. What is your status as a moviegoer—is it something you do frequently?*

I go through phases. Up to the point where I started studying art I was a horror film fan, and I still am, I would say. I think those films were very influential on what I eventually did on video. Also in terms of the way that I think about installation, and the environment that holds the object somehow, the behavior of objects—I think that horror has influenced me that way.

I'm more responsible in the way that I follow art; I'm quite irresponsible in terms of the way that I follow film or directors. I definitely feel an affinity with everybody you mentioned. Of those who are still working I certainly would go see everything that they do, but at the same time, especially now that I've decided to take a break from making films for a while, I feel a lot less committed to doing that. Lynch, for sure, particularly his use of sound, I feel very committed to.

I wanted ask about the Bahian Carnival collaboration with Arto Lindsay and how that in some ways paved the way for Drawing Restraint 9*; and there's a film [*De Lama Lâmina *(From Mud, a Blade), 2007] that came out of that, too.*

That's right. It's to do with this transition between the "Cremaster" language, really wanting to step away from that project and realign myself. We had always talked about project in Bahia as a performance: we were going to go to Carnival, to make a float and create a *trio elétrico*; we were going to perform in Carnival . . . and at a certain point it may be that I lost my courage a little bit. I started developing a script for a film that would be shot during that performance. So it ended up straddling the fence between these two ways of working, which was very hard for me. Both things suffered, the live performance and the execution of the film. But I learned that there is something very compelling for me about being in a situation like this, a live situation that's not something I've constructed, and I'm stepping into that situation and trying to tell a story. Which is the case with the whaling ship, too. That is the relationship between the two projects: having gone through that more gestalt experience in Brazil, with all of its shortcomings as a piece, I learned something, and I was able to approach *Drawing Restraint 9* in a more learned way.

In terms of experiencing another culture's customs—was that something that also led into Drawing Restraint 9*, or was it already in your mind?*

I think they're also similar in a way; they're very non-Western environments, whereas, again, the "Cremaster" cycle is very Western in its narrative and locations. But what I was speaking about more was the restraint, the simple proposal that we would tell the story on the mothership of the Japanese whaling fleet, and the majority of the characters would be the crew, from the ship, and that kind of intervention would take place. It felt quite new. Even though there are scenes in the “Cremaster” cycle where a very real situation was constructed and professionals from that world were used to enact a scene, this was different. It was more like trespassing, or asking permission to temporarily occupy a situation.

Cory Arcangel

In August 2008, I attended a performance by media artist Cory Arcangel at Light Industry in Brooklyn. He was playing all the glockenspiel parts from Bruce Springsteen's *Born to Run* [Columbia, 1975] on a toy xylophone. I immediately felt an affinity with him, as my own work shares his penchant for initiating postconceptual art ideas around classic rock and pop music, with tongue at least partially in cheek. Nearly a year later, I saw Cory's new work *Drei Klavierstücke op. 11*, 2009, at Team Gallery in Lower Manhattan, for which he had culled videos of cats walking on pianos from YouTube, and carefully arranged it into a rendition of a Schoenberg piece. I came away impressed, and figured Cory would be an interesting person to get to know better, so I pitched a profile of him to *ArtReview*, and they accepted.

I took the subway over to his Brooklyn apartment on October 29, 2009, and unusually, this interview sparked from the moment I walked in the door. Six months later, I was in Chelsea at Greene Naftali Gallery for a concert by XXX Macarena (Tony Conrad, Jutta Koether, and John Miller), where I noticed Cory talking to a mutual friend, curator Howie Chen, and I went over to join them. Our conversation turned to the ubiquity of bands, and, with the *Seinfeld* notion of a show-about-nothing somewhere in the back of my mind, I blurted out, "We could just go onstage and talk about music, and that could be a band." The two laughed, but Cory quickly said, "You know what? That's a great idea. I'm going to write that down. I'll look at it again in a couple of days and if I still think it's a good idea, I'll let you guys know, and we should actually do it." That was the beginning of Title TK, the world's first and only "talk rock" band. A collection of transcriptions of our performances/conversations was published by Primary Information in 2015.

When I was looking at the videos Drei Klavierstücke op. 11 *at Team Gallery, at first I thought I should really be watching this on YouTube, not on a projector. But then I thought maybe it got something from that. So I was wondering, in terms of presenting work like this, moving between doing something on the internet to showing it in a gallery space—how you approach scale?*

I guess the first thing I would say is that it would be hard for me to give a solid answer for every case, obviously. Trying to figure that stuff out for the last couple of years I find that those questions become really difficult. For this video I had to justify to myself why I would put it in a gallery, because in a way it's most comfortable on YouTube; because it's YouTube footage, and it's dealing with what happens when the bar for publishing gets so low, do you know what I mean? [*Laughs.*] It makes the image way worse, it amplifies how degraded it is, and I think that is one thing that was a plus for the piece. And it's a plus in reference to the type of videos that more often than not you would see in a gallery. But I was also thinking about the audience who steps into a gallery, because they are going to engage the work on a different level than viewers on YouTube. This video was conceived for a "multi-tiered rollout" [*laughs*], meaning I knew that it was going to be a piece that I would show in a gallery and online. That was part of the conception. As the histories of these kinds of gestures shoot off from the present to the future, where is the place for the fringe of composition, or the fringe of art, or the fringe of video? This video is about that, so it can move around between different places, and I feel confident—at least now; if you talk to me in a couple of years I might not feel so confident—that it's fortified in every context it appears in because it knows that it's going to be appearing. And so Cute Overload—the site is normally bunnies and kittens.

Just to get a site like that to even mention Schoenberg I felt was a positive contribution to the trash—and I say this because I love it all—that circulates on the internet. It feels like anything that technology can amplify is kind of interesting, whether it's bad or good.

The other thing you notice in that video is that the recording quality really varies, but you get used to it and that becomes another element. It reminded me of the John Oswald piece Grayfolded *[1994–95], where he takes all these different live recordings of "Dark Star" by the Grateful Dead over a twenty-five-year period and puts together different sections.*

I've never seen that. Is it linear, or a mix?

Well, it's both. A lot of it is different recordings of the same section playing at the same time; the 1968 Grateful Dead will be playing at the same time as the 1985 Grateful Dead.

I was thinking of similar things, like Christian Marclay's *Telephones* [1995], or his records, or a lot of the stuff that goes around the internet now, like "Ultimate Canon Rock"—it's "Pachelbel's Canon," some dude in Taiwan made a wicked shred transcription of it, put it up online, and then guitar players all around the world started playing his transcription, and somebody put them all together. I have a list, on the web page for the project, of all the things I was looking at: like *The Sopranos*, where someone edited together every profanity; *The Big Lebowski*, where it's edited to every single "Fucking Dude." Or there's a great artist from Berlin named Oliver Laric who cut together fifty 50 Cent videos.

I had done an earlier one with Glenn Gould and

[Bach's] *Goldberg Variations*, and I put a few cats in there, and I had seen people react so much to just the little cats, and so the idea was—it was a test of a hypothesis, were the cats alluring enough to pull Schoenberg through the door? Or the needle. Are people attracted to cats on video enough that they would not only tolerate, but celebrate, a hard, atonal music? It's kind of a tough swallow for a lot of people.

*When atonal music first appeared, it sounded like a cat walking on a piano keyboard [*laughs*].*

Which a lot of people say when they record their cats on the piano—they don't say it sounds like atonal music, they say it sounds like jazz, or free jazz.

So it ties in with the original controversy over atonal music.

I like that it gets posted on sites where people are not aware of the controversy, or they're baffled by it, and that's one of the other things that the internet is good at, it's always these portals into these worlds that you're not necessarily involved in—which is unhealthy, but interesting [*laughs*].

When you studied at Oberlin with Pauline Oliveros, was that where you learned about Schoenberg, Steve Reich, and Alvin Lucier, some of the people you've referenced in your work?

Referenced, that's a nice way of putting it [*laughs*]. Part of my education at the Oberlin Conservatory was a "1900–Present" music history you just had to learn regardless of anything. That was kind of standard, and then Pauline was way off the map; she came in and was like, "Let's collaborate over cyberspace, let's meditate, let's learn how to listen to music," which nobody ever really taught. You kind of learned stuff without knowing you were doing anything. But that's where I got a foothold on that stuff. Certainly the Reich, I remember walking into school one morning and kids were swinging microphones over speakers, that was the kind of environment, they were reenacting [Reich's *Pendulum Music*, 1968], and John Cage was in every discussion. I'm always referring to it because I felt very comfortable learning about that stuff and I enjoy it.

Where did the art world enter, in terms of your development; when did you decide to start presenting things—

—in the more classical art context? Well, I had always made videos, including in school. I was lucky enough that I could do that, and it was through the video work and coming to the New York Underground Film Festival, also through media festivals . . . through a weird combination of being involved with media art and underground film I then learned that the art world existed. And of course once I saw what galleries were up to, I was like, "Oh yeah, this seems like it would be cool" [*laughs*]. It was more like, "Why don't they show one of my videos?" It was pretty simple and not premeditated. I had grown up with video, being from Buffalo. Video was such a big thing there.

Were you aware of Tony Conrad, and the Vasulkas?

When I was in high school I was aware of them in the way that you're aware of a lot of things in high school—I had seen their work but I had no idea who they are. It wasn't until I moved out of Buffalo that I had learned all those people's names, and why they were important. But I had certainly seen bits and pieces of their work, because it was on cable access, or I had seen it in a video-art class that I had in high school, which is kind of random. I remember watching a Bill Viola video and just hating it, in that kind of high school way where you just kind of hate it and don't care about it, but it's the one time in your life where your receptors are totally open. But it obviously sunk in; if you look at a lot of my videos, in terms of duration, obviously I picked up a lot of stuff from it.

The parallel there is that Bill Viola, and a lot of the other first-generation video artists, had a background in music. With experimental filmmakers, also, the question was always whether the work should be screened in a movie theater, or belonged in a gallery or a museum—

—or a club. And that's a difficult question, going back to the beginning: Should it be on YouTube or should it not be on YouTube? But learning about John Cage, and learning about the minimalists, and the San Francisco scene, if one has an education—in that they really have an education in all the practices that fuel a typical art practice today, maybe space and volume not so much, but all the concepts behind the stuff that a lot of those people were doing—the concepts could be transposed pretty easily to sculpture or painting. . . . People are and were dealing with the same kind of ideas. It's just a different way to learn about the same stuff.

I was interested in the comparisons to [Lucier's] I Am Sitting in a Room *[1969]. There's a piece by Louis Andriessen called* Il Duce *[1973], where he takes this speech by Mussolini and he rerecords it over and over again so the tape hiss keeps building up and it turns into a noise piece.*

I've never heard that. I know the artist Jonathan Horowitz, who did a video with the Maxell logo. Lucier's piece is about physical space, and his voice, and resonance. . . . I've done it with compression. Eventually I got into compression. My last compression thing was an essay on why JPEGs look the way they do; I ended up forgoing the product and process and just trying to understand the structure. It was called "On C," funnily enough "on compression." That title was an idea by Dexter Sinister that they suggested when I first published the essay in a book that we had done together [*A Couple Thousand Short Films about Glenn Gould*, 2008].

Part of the reason I brought up I Am Sitting in a Room *is I wanted to talk about virtual space versus physical space. Something I thought about while looking at the things you've made accessible online is the Smithson quote, "The world is a museum"—is that how you see the internet, as a museum to explore?*

Yeah—that's a great question, you know, this is what I think about all day long. I have a lot of thoughts about the internet, and I haven't organized them, but I'll try to give you a rundown. Putting artwork on the internet, we're gonna start there—what is that good for? You could have artwork that references the internet, like searching Twitter for "my cat died yesterday." That could be like the world as a museum, and now we're just pointing at one particular part of this world that we think has relevance in the way that art, hopefully, could have. The compression essay, which appears in different ways and gets passed around the internet in the same exact way that a JPEG might get passed around, that's another site-specific . . . you can't really call it an intervention, 'cause that would give it too much credit, and also you can't really intervene in the internet, 'cause it's too big, it's like intervening in the ocean. You can just place these things around. Like the Springsteen thing, which floats around kind of unknowingly as Bruce Springsteen MP3s, so there's some Bruce Springsteen files out there that have a little more glockenspiel, that's another way.[1]

What I would stress is that I don't really know what I'm doing, and each product is trying to feel out a slightly different territory; I certainly don't have any answers. I don't know why I'm drawn to the internet; I like the idea that some random kid, just somebody random will stumble across the work, either on my website or embedded in some context that has nothing to do with it. And often, if my game is really on, the artwork will reference the possibility of that situation without diminishing it, but that's often difficult. You put it out there and you just have to let it go, and that's the weird meditative thing, right? When you put something in a gallery, people are like, "Oh I saw your show, I really loved it," blah blah blah, but when you put something on the net, aside from maybe one or two blog posts right when you post it, it's done, usually. It's gone, usually two people a day are looking, and you have to be Zen about it.

1 Arcangel's *The Bruce Springsteen "Born to Run" Glockenspiel Addendum*, 2006, is a work with three components: a performance where Arcangel accompanies Springsteen's *Born to Run* on glockenspiel, a twelve-inch vinyl record containing only the added glockenspiel track and silence, and CDs of Springsteen's original audio mixed with Arcangel's glockenspiel, which were given away for free as "takeaway" sculptures with the intention and hope that they might eventually show up on file-sharing networks.

It's tempting to look at it as a non-site, but it's not completely, because someone in a gallery is probably surfing the net all day.

It'll get everybody, that's the thing about it. You will eventually get one of everybody, and that's the difficult part about conceiving of what the internet is and basing it off all the ways that we've distributed artwork previously. For example, what is the idea of a portfolio website? Do you just put the projects you like, or do you put even the shitty projects, because everybody is eventually going to come to your site—there's going to be someone who's going to like that project. The spirit of the internet is to bare it all, and it runs counter to the idea of manicure. You can't erase a film from your filmography if you're really doing what the internet dictates.

When you did the Team Gallery show "Welcome 2 My Homepage Artshow!!!!!!!!!" [2005], that encapsulates your transition—a homepage is like "Welcome to my room," and an art show is more of a temporary thing, or, "Here's what I've been up to."

Or, "Here's some extremely well-thought out ideas placed in a context in which they are appropriate, presented in a way which deals with the history of the space." I have been trying to understand those conflicts, I'm just trying to figure it out. The internet is the place where I do actually feel comfortable, I kind of understand it, in a weird way, and a gallery I'm still a little bit . . . even narrative cinema space I feel comfortable in, even concert time I feel comfortable in . . . but because the gallery can be anything now, you can put a film in a gallery, you can play music in a gallery. It's a kind of "everything," and the question of where in that everything you want to make your work is difficult.

When you mentioned "well-thought out ideas," I thought of your artist lecture Continuous Partial Awareness *[2008–2009], which I was interested by because usually when artists give talks it's sort of like their greatest hits. I was participating in this symposium about Vito Acconci in Philadelphia, and he did a lecture the night before the symposium. When we were coming out of it, I overheard these two women behind me saying, "I was really disappointed he didn't talk about the bicycle piece." And it hit me, "Wow, if he doesn't talk about* Seedbed *[1972], it's like the Rolling Stones not playing 'Satisfaction.'"*

Exactly.

And what I thought was cool about what you did was rather than a greatest hits, it was unfinished ideas, or as if a stand-up comedian got onstage and said, "I've been thinking about telling a joke about this or this" . . . but my guess is that people still found it entertaining.

Yeah, when I do those I like them to be entertaining. How many ideas I picked, the order I presented them in . . . I had, in the last couple of years, done a bunch of artist lectures, just 'cause people would ask and I'd say yes, and then I found out all these weird dynamics during the lectures. I found I could go to a place and give a lecture that makes my work seem like it's institutional critique, and then I could do another lecture and make it seem like it's just a bunch of jokes. I found how easy it was to construct these narratives, 'cause when I started doing it of course, I did what everyone does, you construct the narrative of this is who I am, this is what I'm proud of . . . but it seemed kind of boring, it was more interesting to let people in on the process, a little bit, of what it means to be an artist and to filter through all this trash. And at that time I was having trouble censoring myself, and I'm still having trouble censoring myself, which gets us back to the internet, you know, 'cause in the internet you don't need to censor, and the art world is *all about* censoring. Music too, what songs you put on your record, do you put these eight, or do you want to put on that single, or the B side.

That was something that I found attractive about the whole free improvisation scene: you're really watching the process unfold in real time, and if someone makes a record out of it you can go back and edit it. If you make a recording of something composed ahead of time, like a song, and it becomes the definitive version, then how do you reconcile playing it over and over again after that?

Bob Dylan in an interview said, "Elton John and all those guys, they made perfect records, and they now have to play the songs perfectly, and luckily I never made the perfect record, so I could play my songs different every night." Which I thought was pretty smart, right?

And now I'm thinking it could be good for other things too. 'Cause I have four unfinished ideas for albums and I figured, "Well, why don't I just throw them all together?" Maybe that whole process, if you put four maybe not-so-good ideas together maybe it makes one pretty good idea.

People are so afraid of records leaking now on the internet, but wouldn't it be interesting if someone started putting rough mixes up on the internet?

You know who I heard did that was Kanye [West]. A friend told me that the first release off of *808s & Heartbreak* [Roc-A-Fella, 2008] he put on his website and then felt it out, and then posted another version a couple of days later after he had kind of felt it out publicly.

Did he ask people to comment on it?

Yeah. And you know who else did something like this? Lil Wayne. I've never heard it, but he's someone to read about, because he's really on top of all this stuff. He's someone who apparently always seeds stuff on the internet randomly. He had something called "10,000 Bars." He took all his notebooks, and in one recording session he just rapped it all, completely got rid of any idea he had had. And then it was a clean slate from that time forward.

And then he released it?

Yeah. But he releases stuff all the time, you just YouTube him and there's all these weird songs that have never been on a record. He's working on a rock record right now. I heard one song and it sounds so bad—it's kind of emo-ish? But I read an interview with him and he said his thing is, "I'm gonna be the rapper that works the hardest, and releases the most stuff, and people will have to respect me." Apparently he gets offstage and he has a recording studio in his bus, and he just goes right in and records. You never know how much of it is the legend, but in a way it doesn't matter, 'cause he's a rock star.

I've heard that Adam Sandler is the hardest-working comedian, that if you go to a set of any film that he's doing, he's in his trailer writing his next movie with two other guys during breaks.

Really? Ten hours a day of work, you either get a Lil Wayne single like "Lollipop" or *Happy Gilmore* [1996].

You're really into autotuning and preverb. How did you become aware of these sorts of things?

I had a couple years of my life that I lost to Pro Tools, where I was a Pro Tools engineer. I did audio books, which was fun. The one thing that I remember most fondly was I had to remove a little bit of silence in between every word on a whole side of a tape, because the audio books were on tape then. You get to be hyperconscious. But preverb, I remember being a kid and seeing a Def Leppard video, back then it was the one moment of, "I don't know how that sound can exist," but now when I think back, of course, the whole record couldn't exist, 'cause it was all [producer] Mutt Lange stuff. So preverb has been an interest of mine since then. And just reversing drums in general: sometimes you'll hear in Detroit techno where it's totally straight out of the box, a drum machine and a synth, and there'll be two bars that are reversed—I don't understand why people think, "Oh it's fake," but that's acceptable.

It's like some of the stuff you have in Super Mario Clouds *[2002], or the* F1 Racer Mod (Japanese Driving Game) *[2004] where background is also foreground; like how some of these effects that are made to enhance the song become the focal point in some of your pieces. You have the fake structural film [*Personal Film, *2008]—*

Yeah, and of course it's a structural film, because you can't have a fake structural film [*laughs*]. It's just that you notice things, and some of them end up being so consuming of an interest that I'll try to turn them around somehow, and of course the turning around is the difficult part. How do you re-present it in a way where people can get the same kind of feeling. [With] preverb I never quite figured out how. One possible way would be to go and do a real documentary on it, interview Mutt Lange, and interview all those hair-metal bands, and interview people who are still doing it. You hear it every once in a while in metal. It's just cultural commentary, I guess.

Sans Simon [2004] is a good example of both—it's subtraction but it's also heavy commentary about Simon & Garfunkel, but not really—it's about what the two people represent.

Why did you want to block out [Paul] Simon and not [Art] Garfunkel?

Every decision was made to enhance the final part of the piece, which is this kind of mirror effect where people read into that thing—whatever weird stuff they've got going on they read into it, which is a goal sometimes when I make something. The particular way I arrived at it was, well—the classic story is they don't like each other, Garfunkel started going on talk shows, getting all the attention, Simon wrote all the songs, and if you notice in that *Monterey Pop* [1968] film, the cameraman is transfixed by Garfunkel, the cameraman is just like, "Forget about the other guy." The way they cut and the way it's edited, that footage itself sort of told the whole story about them breaking up.

Something I thought about with the cat video, and some of the other things you do, is that making them is extremely laborious, an incredible amount of work, and so many of the materials you work with were originally leisure-time things, like video games or pop music videos. How do you feel about the amount of work applied to these things that are meant to be part of playtime?

It's something that I have to think about a lot, because if I'm going to spend the next four months on a project I have to make sure it's worth it. Meaning, not only do I have to enjoy doing it, which sometimes I don't, but it has to conceptually be . . . with the cat thing I knew that the only way it was really going to fly on the internet in a "this is something that someone created" kind of way—it would have to be an overwhelming amount of work. One, on the internet, because that is a lot of stuff that you see on the internet, like some guy who made something out of a million pennies, but large amounts of labor often have a deadening effect on the humor of a piece, where it then throws into question the intent, which then, sometimes, has a benefit. So people are like, "Oh this is kind of funny," but then they're like, "It's sixteen minutes, and it obviously took months," so then people start questioning like, "What exactly is going on here?" which I think is a plus.

If someone was playing the Super Mario Bros. *game they wouldn't think about how much work goes into it.*

Well video games—labor is a big part of beating the game, you have to spend a year . . . and when people upload speed runs, playing the game as fast as possible, that is all about labor.

But people don't ordinarily think about how much work went into the programming.

Oh yeah, that's a good point.

There was one show where you posted the code that you had used to program a work, so it's something you're interested in.

Yeah, I do that with most pieces, I posted code for the Schoenberg piece, and that is a way for the piece to live on. It disrupts the way that pieces are supposed to work in a gallery, and again, 'cause things don't really have to be "done." Music doesn't have to be as done as it used to be, 'cause you can just keep throwing up MP3s online, albums don't exist so much—

Remixes too.

Yeah, of course. Have you heard the Lady Gaga where she references all of her own recent hit songs?

She samples them, or lyrically references them?

Lyrics and melody.

The Beatles started to do that after a while, especially on the "White Album."

Metallica—their last album was them referencing their earlier albums; I guess it happens a lot but I had never heard it so quickly in succession, like one a month, one hit to the next.

*That's pretty rapid [*laughs*]. I was reading this article about Urs Fischer, this exhibition he has coming up at the New Museum, and he had changed one piece 'cause he thought it was too funny, he thought it was too much of a joke. Humor is such a part of a lot of the things you do; are there things that you toss out because you think it's too much of a joke?*

I toss out a lot of ideas because they're too funny. It depends what show it is, and the tone of the show. I did rename a piece once: it was a collaboration with a guy named Ben Jones. *Untitled Translation Exercise* [2006] was its official title, and it was the movie *Dazed and Confused* [1993], where all the voices were re-dubbed in English by an outsourced firm in Bangalore, India, so you would watch the movie normally but all the accents were Indian English, and was originally called *Lost in Translation*, and I vetoed that title because it was too funny. That was a piece that I didn't want to appear funny, and that isn't funny. For example, I've shown it in cinemas, and to sit through an hour and a half of that is really painful, and that's what the intent of the piece was, and the title *Lost in Translation* interfered with that. So yeah, I'm conscious of it, but the art world is so tough with humor that it's always a pain in my ass and I hate it. Humor is always a wrench in the gears of art, if it's laugh-out-loud humor. I'm always bumping up against that and trying to not give in. . . . I like things to be funny.

Richard Prince and Bruce Nauman have things that are almost like one-liners.

There's a certain "art humor" which is different from real humor, 'cause you're not laughing out loud in front of a Bruce Nauman . . . not literally. Or Richard Prince's joke paintings, which are very good, because they do play on this exact thing, humor, and what does it mean to make a masterpiece, and what does it mean to be a master painter? Those paintings are very clever.

Do you know any comedians?

I have some comedian friends, yeah. Hanging out

with comedians is amazing. Artists are kind of moody and self-centered, right? But comedians are just pure moody—hanging out with artists is relatively tame, hanging out with comedians is like—those people are living on the edge. I think it's because every night they go onstage it's like jumping into a cold pool. Everyone in entertainment or the arts needs to respect comedians more.

*It's the ultimate job insecurity—all of us basically realize we shouldn't be making a living doing what we're doing [*laughs*], but it's even more so for comedians. You're getting paid for being the wise guy in class. And there's no comedian school you can go to for professional credentials.*

You can't—you have to grind it out, you have to embarrass yourself night after night to get good at being a comedian, so any good comedian has been through what would be a normal person's worst nightmare.

I have comedy friends and every once in a while they invite me to do their stand-up nights. The last time I was redoing *Seinfeld* routines, and that was like a nightmare of what it would be like to be really terrible. I've been scared to go back. But I've done the Bruce Springsteen thing in comedy clubs, and that works. It comes off as very Andy Kaufman–esque, because the piece does reference Andy Kaufman.

Did you read the Steve Martin book Born Standing Up *[2007]? I was amazed by the part where he described his eureka moment: "What if there were no punch lines?" Which is almost like an art concept, like James Turrell looking at the beam of light from the slide projector in art history class and having an epiphany about making light art from that.*

Yeah, totally. Recently I saw Zach Galifianakis, do you know this comedian? I saw him do stand-up, and I had an art epiphany. I was thinking, "I don't think I've ever seen anything this smart in my life." All the twists and turns he was doing were one or two steps beyond what you could conceive in the start–finish–end narrative environment. I was on a night with him, and usually when I do these things there's like four people there. There was a line around the block and I had never heard of him and thought that people were lining up for the club next door. It turned out that they were all there for him.

Over the summer I went to [Walter De Maria's 1977 Land art piece] The Lightning Field—

Oh wow. Not funny!

[Laughs.] *Not funny, but I was looking in the guest book and it said, "Steve Martin, Beverly Hills California." I figured, "Wow, must be him, 'cause he's an art collector." We asked the caretaker if it was him, and he said, "Yeah, he's been twice and he just wrote a letter saying he was going to come back again next summer."*

When I read Steve Martin's book I liked when he talked about his performance being really ramshackle. For *Continuous Partial Awareness* that was part of the encouragement; it was around the same time as I read that book. I was like, "Oh it's OK to just throw everything together"—at the end I even brought a pet onstage—"it's OK to just let it flow." I was encouraged by his book.

It's also interesting that he quit doing stand-up at the height of his popularity too. He's never gone back to it, either. That's pretty rare.

Jerry Seinfeld went back to it. Jay Leno has done it the whole time.

Yeah, Leno would always be saying [on The Tonight Show*], I'll be performing in Las Vegas on such and such a date. Steve Martin was wildly popular and arenas he was playing were so huge he felt like he was losing—*

Right, it's the Beatles problem, or whatever.

His records were top ten.

And that's when top ten records—

*—really meant something [*laughs*].*

Right, now it's whenever anyone with slight name recognition releases a record that week.

It doesn't take as many copies sold, like if you sold forty thousand records last week. When Michael Jackson died they said Thriller *sold a hundred million albums over the last twenty-five years, and sold twenty million in the US the first year or two after it came out. And I remember when his last record came out it only sold five million, and Sony was really disappointed, and I thought, "Are they crazy, five million albums?" But when you do the math, if one of your records has sold a hundred million copies and then the next one only sold five million, that's one-twentieth. So it would be like if I sold a thousand copies of one of my records and then I did* *the next one for the same company and I only sold fifty copies [*laughs*]. Proportionally, you would be absolutely shocked.*

That's a very good point. And he was the last mega-guy.

Yeah, in the discussions after he died people were saying there will never be anyone else that big.

There can't be. The mechanism of culture can never go back to that. Which is probably good, 'cause it just distorts people.

I think it's worse to be a celebrity now.

Oh really?

Yeah. I heard that Mariah Carey went to get her hair cut, took out her Blackberry when it was over and she had 250 messages, just in the hour and a half it took to get her hair done, can you imagine?

That would drive me crazy.

I also wanted to talk about the do-it-yourself thing in a lot of your work, where it's performative but it seems like a break from the idea of an artist doing an instruction piece—

"Walk around in a circle and draw a line."

Yeah, something like that. Does the DIY thing partially come from music, punk and things like that?

Like me playing the glockenspiel?

Just something that you feel like you have to undertake yourself, not hiring someone to play the glockenspiel.

It doesn't come from punk. I might even say it would be the opposite of punk. I'm pretty psycho about playing it right; I get nervous. That's an unwanted relic of my conservatory education. When I picked the glockenspiel I knew it was an instrument I could handle, that I could play at the level that would be on the record, and when I do it live, of course I screw up, but I really practice, and the John Denver thing as well.[2] I'm an artist actually doing something, which is kind of a twirl on what people would expect. 'Cause artists aren't expected to appear at all anymore, and the same thing with those lectures, that's what they're playing on. People don't expect artists to be honest, or to say anything that isn't highly constructed. So to play it myself, it's like, "Oh look, it's the artist, he hasn't hired somebody to do it."

Even artists who hire people to actually make the work, whether it was Warhol—

Which I will do in my other work, but for some reason music, I think I can't get over all the other things that were put into my brain. Not the progressive side of my education, but the classical side. So I want to make a folk record, and I'm like, "Oh, I gotta learn all the songs." I'm burdening myself with these things I don't necessarily need to do, but there's nothing I can do about it. I'm happy with it, I guess.

I'm doing a performance at the University of Michigan—they have a kind of technology music school there, so I told the students just make whatever

2 At Kunsthaus Graz, Austria, in 2009, Arcangel performed John Denver's "Last Night I Had the Strangest Dream" on acoustic guitar while auto-tuning his vocals.

instruments and interfaces you want, and on the night of the performance they'll be onstage and I'll try to figure them out, put them on and try to do a show. Like the idea of the nightmare that you have, that all of a sudden you're supposed to give a lecture, it's like the technology performance equivalent of that. That would be pretty fun, I think. And I don't have to do anything for it.

That's another example of a do-it-yourself thing, but also that kind of vulnerability we were talking about with comedians.

And I'll be straight with the audience as well, it won't be a big put-on—like, "Look, here's the situation, let's try to get through this together" [*laughs*].

Jerry Garcia said that one of the things that audiences liked about the Grateful Dead was watching them struggle onstage sometimes, or mess up.

That's nice. Was that a part of punk too? Was there a difference?

Part of punk was people thinking, "That could be me up there," and then the next week it would be. It was being on equal footing; the performer wasn't towering above them onstage. And some of the audience response, especially in England with spitting on the bands—it became this kind of battle, the aggression of the music was being met with this equal aggression from the audience. It wasn't someone showing off and then feeling the love from the audience, there was more give and take.

And with the Grateful Dead, they're up onstage but people are relating to them, because they're struggling, there's a little bit of everyman in that.

I think it's more a mini-community, and they're working together, and if something goes wrong you're seeing people working together trying to get back on track. Like Hurricane Katrina or something, part of the drama becomes people coming together to try to work on a problem.

I saw the Grateful Dead. I remember two drummers; that was my first two-drummer experience and I've never been the same since. Did you know that their bass player used to room with Steve Reich?

Yeah. In fact I just saw him on the street, a week or two ago, in SoHo. That's the fun thing about New York, you never know who you might see on the street. I went to see Maryanne Amacher at Roulette and I was walking in as Kramer, Michael Richards, was walking out—

—of Roulette?! That is crazy.

And he said, "Hello!" and just kept walking; he was with somebody. . . . And I was like, "What is the story?" I don't know. He didn't come back for the concert.

Ken Jacobs

Ken Jacobs's *Tom, Tom, the Piper's Son* (1969–71), which takes an old silent short and then rephotographs it in detail for close to two hours, is one of my favorite experimental films. It's a big influence on my version of the Minutemen's "Polarity" (on *Sink the Aging Process* [Siltbreeze, 1994]), which takes the last few seconds of the original song and loops the final chord, putting it through a process that accentuates different overtones over twenty minutes. Later, Ken extended five minutes of footage of his friends and cinematic cohorts Jack Smith and Bob Fleischer into his ninety-minute feature *Two Wrenching Departures* (2006), this time via a digital version of the 3D film projection technique he calls the "Nervous System," which made use of a spinning propellor that functioned as a shutter to alternate between images on two film projectors set side by side. Ken had also been Lee Ranaldo's film instructor at Harpur College in Binghamton, New York, and he was someone Lee and I often discussed when we began our group Text of Light.

In 2008, when Ken was touring his collaboration with field recordist Éric La Casa around the UK, I petitioned the *Wire* to let me do a piece on him—partly on the grounds of the rarity of these live appearances, and partly because John Zorn's Tzadik label had recently released two DVDs of his work, *Celestial Subway Lines/Salvaging Noise* (2005) and *New York Ghetto Fishmarket 1903* (2007). I went to Electronic Arts Intermix and watched as much of his work as I could in preparation for querying him about his extensive and unusual use of music and sound. I met up with Ken at a Le Pain Quotidien near his TriBeCa loft; this turned out to be a poor choice for recording our conversation, as it was quite noisy and the acoustics were dreadful. It was also the morning after the Republican National Convention where Sarah Palin had been announced as John McCain's running mate. Ken, who is politically engaged, to say the least, was livid, spending the first five minutes at the table expressing his state of shock. His magnum opus, *Star Spangled to Death* (2004), gives free rein to his personal politics, appropriating TV coverage of protests, the 9/11 hearings, and a horrifying '60s documentary about lab experiments on animals. Aki Onda and I performed a score Aki made for Ken's 3D film *A Primer in Sky Socialism* at Brooklyn's ISSUE Project Room in 2018, which I was proud to participate in, having so thoroughly studied the use of sound in Ken's work for this article ten years earlier.

I wanted to ask you about using found sounds. There's a lot of simultaneity between image and sound in your work. And you use black screens a lot. Is that to draw more attention to the sound?

Every so often, the image and the sound lift their hats and greet each other in passing [*laughs*]. I think that we are weighted toward the image. The black screen allows us to refocus our sound; especially if it's not a fixated sound, but an ambient sound, you want to be in that for a while, and let those things happen, and then come back to the image refreshed.

But sometimes it's someone speaking, like in the films Blonde Cobra *[1963] and* Krypton Is Doomed *[2005].*

Blonde Cobra is a special case. I felt at the time that [the narrator] Jack [Smith]'s fantasies were so full of images that any added image would be a counterimage, but I also felt, psychologically, that it would be very correct for his voice to be heard in blackness—he was in a deep depression back then.

Was part of the idea to disrupt a narrative form by doing it that way? I think it's interesting how you punctuate Krypton Is Doomed *using silences that were not in the original radio broadcast.*

The narrative is a very straightforward story. I think I used all the sounds from the original broadcast. I'm using only one picture—

One comic-strip frame.

You wouldn't believe it, that thing is about *this*

big, the whole picture is maybe three inches by three inches. I'm making minute shifts with enormous effect on-screen. It's an old hand-painted magic lantern slide. There is the consistency of a single picture, although you travel through it piece by piece, and the consistency of the narrative development. And I think that helps hold together the spatial craziness, and the oblique reference that's happening in the story. The images refer to the story mostly only in one's mind; one adapts the pictures to the narrative. There's a few moments of blackness, but they're punctuations. I always loved blackness in film, just like silences that happen in music. They're measured, they're part of the whole thing. A lot of music builds in volume, louder and louder, very often the end is a huge smashing of sound. But that really is building against silence, nothingness. And only occasionally will artists play on this black, silent bottom, or let that silence come through.

I really like the Rick Reed soundtracks. Were those made specifically for—

Absolutely. He's amazing. He really watches the rhythms.

The one for Capitalism: Child Labor *[2006] really reminded me of a piece of mine, "Polarity," which in turn was partially inspired by* Tom, Tom, the Piper's Son.

Really? Could I hear it?

Sure, I'll give you a copy. Do you have a record player? It's only on record.

Yes, I have a record player, and I have 78s, 45s, and 33s.

Sounds like you have an extensive record collection.

It's either that or the shrink [*laughs*]. This way I still have records [*laughs*].

You've said that documentaries, with their controlling background music, try to assure us we're still at the movies. And you use live radio during screenings of Blonde Cobra—*do you want to remind people that there's a real world outside?*

Yeah, there's two parts in *Blonde Cobra*, in the beginning and near the end. The radio comes in, and the instructions are to tune it, as much as possible, to local talk. The first time you're going to fish for the station, with the audience listening in. And the second time it comes in, just play the local talk. The theme being that it's enriching—we were fucked, we will stay fucked, and no matter where we go with this show, we will be fucked. And that's been the case. And the radio is, with the exception of WBAI, with its problems, a controlling agent. At the beginning of *Star Spangled to Death*, I suggest to people to go through the dial, stop at any station, and listen for a full minute, and see.

Is the disjunctive sound another way of undermining the background music of regular films?

Yes, *disjunctive* is the right word. I'm lonely, really, and I want other individuals in the world to be with. I really address myself to other living, thinking individuals, and I'm the last person that wants to conduct them someplace, and my problem with most, not all, documentaries is this fucking movie music that's going to compel toward a certain verdict on what you're seeing. People go through hell to get these images, and then they come back and this gravy is poured over them.

How do you decide which of your pieces get sound, and which remain silent?

I think it's taste, a sense of aesthetic balances, what things can support, what interferes. I try some things and they don't work, and I try other things that should work and they do. To make art is to feel out some pattern that is sanity.

Is it trial and error? Is that how you came to use the Carl Orff music in Two Wrenching Departures *[2006], or the Harrison Birtwistle thing in* Chronometer *[2006]?*

Wow, you're very good. Well, I hate Carl Orff, he's a fucking Nazi. At the end of *Two Wrenching Departures* I use music from another Nazi [Florent Schmitt], but it's one of these fabled *Arabian Nights* [1942] compositions, and it's sympathetic to Jack—that is, Jack in his 1940s Hollywood idea, when he was a little kid in the sticks, who saw this as beauty. So I'm sympathetic to him, and he's the subject. At the same time . . . I'm sort of vestigially Jewish; I'm not simply not religious, I hate religion and I consider most people who are religious [to be] zombies, but I'm sensitive to Jewish history as a cult that's out of step with the major cult, and got punished for it. Jack had some weird stuff, he was attracted to Italians and Jews, but had some very weird, basic, conditioned ideas from where he came from. Soon after I met him he told me about a problem he had had, a Jewish landlord who owned the paint store beneath him on Twenty-Sixth Street. When he was forced to leave, because he had built a lagoon in his loft and the lagoon was leaking, he painted swastikas on the guy's window.

I think that World War II was more of a fantasy for Jack than Maria Montez [star of *Arabian Nights*] was; the movies were real, the war was interesting, but not *that* good. He was out of it. I could see Jack in a certain way, and this glamorous, over-the-top Nazi music was appropriate. Jack was six foot two or three and blond, or so he said, and so he did his best to be blond. Look at Buster Keaton; he's little, he's this and he's that—people have a physical presentation, we try and figure out who they are from that, so it matters. I don't think Jack believed that much in physical presentation, but he saw that the world around him did. He fell into line.

It is caricature—look at what he's doing as this heroic Carl Orff march music is taking place, it's so nutty. But what he's doing really is heroic. What a creation, you know? Or this tragic dance at the end on the little traffic island, it's observed, but those are heroic gestures, not the expected ones.

I was interested by how you put the Margaret [Shelton] Meier piece "The Dawning," [1994] at the very end of Insistent Clamor *[2005].*

Yes, right—oh wow, man, you're really knocking me out, that's pretty good! I didn't think anybody ever noticed that. I liked this CD [*Music from Six Continents: 1996 Series* (Vienna Modern Masters, 1996)], that piece, which proceeds in silence, expresses this immense sense of the tragic just at the very end, I think. . . . We are living in such a fucked-up time.

What made you decide to put it in only at the very end?

You're an artist, man! [*Laughs.*] You get taken with something, and you obey! I have a subconscious, I do everything it says [*laughs*]. I listen to it, I say, "OK boss, you want a little sound at the end, you got it." And then I feel, "Was I right?"

In Star Spangled to Death *there's an intertitle about old records as a Josephine Baker song plays; it says, "Old songs seem life-sized."*

You can sense somebody's standing there, and all that's between you and them is a microphone, but they're not hyped up, they're not an electronic voice. They're really coming through the fidelity of a person, of a certain height and weight, standing in front of a mic and singing the song. I wish people were recorded more in their habitats rather than in a studio. The sound studio is a terrible idea. Only a few guys go on the road, take a microphone with them, and even they rarely know to get the ambience. If you listen to old jazz, recorded in the clubs, in their natural habitat, man, it's a whole other thing. Even the length of songs—the two-and-a-half- and three-minute sides from studios are a caricature. The background noise, that's life.

Is that something you also like about the vintage films that you use?

The ones I use are pretty straightforward; the camera just records. What you bring up is interesting; I certainly have not been interested in being someone like [Josef] von Sternberg, who really shapes his shots. I guess what interests me is life on the fly—just record it. Mistakes are interesting, noises are interesting to me, the living ambience of something—very, very interesting. *Tom, Tom the Piper's Son* [1905] is a stage work that someone documented on film, and it just keeps revealing layer upon layer of penetration for myself to realize what's there; I'm very moved by it. I'm probably as married to *Tom, Tom the Piper's Son* as I am to Flo [Jacobs].

Do you see there being room for revision and retouching in all your works, or only specific ones? Star Spangled to Death *obviously has gone through a number of different iterations.*

Oh, but that's it—it was cursed. I wasn't allowed to finish it, I didn't have the money. So I would show it occasionally as concert performances, but it was provisional; I never intended that. At the same time, I was very bothered by the thing just being wasted, [I] couldn't get the money up to finish the damn thing. Finally video allowed me to do it. And then Nisi, our daughter, she was deep into video, she got me thinking about, "Well, what about doing it as video?" Digital video, being another world from analog video, was wonderful.

Do you have similar feelings about digital versus analog audio, as opposed to video?

I can tell the difference, yeah. Analog's better. Analog recording, going back to the '20s, unbelievable. You really hear a voice. You hear their inner organs.

Does digital video account for the amount of work you've been doing recently?

Yeah, also I don't have to work a job. Do you know about these jobs? [*Laughs.*]

*I've had jobs [*laughs*]. You've made a lot of recordings at home—I went to the "Audio Vérite" program at*

Anthology Film Archives, where you were playing some of those tapes of the water faucet, the railroad sounds—

Wow, you knock me out, really. I should be supporting you, I believe you [*laughs*].

You've used a lot of train sounds, and even in a statement you made about Tom, Tom, the Piper's Son, *you referred to a "train of images."*

The train and the projector have been a big working tool for me. Not just for showing the final result, but the projector itself has been a formative element. The projector and the engine are cousins, you know, and when one is working two of these projectors, as I do in a lot of my work, there's a sense of *Ben-Hur* [1959]. You're riding these two horses in front of you, but here it's iron horses, these chugging things under my hands, controlling them, controlling with them. So there's a lot of technological connection between them.

Even if you're looking out the window during a train ride—

Yes! Yes! That's a movie!

And the sound is a disjunctive sound, it's not the sound of what you're seeing out the window, it's the ambient sounds in the train itself.

That's absolutely true. That's something I hadn't thought about, that's very good. So it's making the world out there a silent screen movie and meanwhile you're hearing either the engine or your own music coming in on radio—

People talking . . .

That's very interesting. In the nineteenth and twentieth centuries, the composers and performers were traveling by train very often. The composers were writing on the trains—how was the beat of the train not going to enter into their music? Prokofiev must have been in the train a lot of the time. And I think that jazz permeated the train, and not just the harmonic innovations—going from place to place, day after day, to make a living.

Since you've described your work as being hard on audiences—

Not that I want it to be—

I wondered how you felt about film installation as opposed to a regular screening presentation.

People wandering through museums, wandering through galleries, getting the idea of something by a glance, is not my idea of immersing yourself, taking chances, risking some time, seeing what you get from something, so the traditional way of seeing a film is more to my liking. Peter Kubelka and his *Invisible Cinema* [1970], you saw that thing? He built this theater where everyone is in this little monastery, cubicle. . . . I was very much against that. I think that sort of isolation takes place when someone simply locks in on the film. I don't think I've ever been part of a crowd—maybe when I was a kid, ten years old, but since my teenage years, I don't think I've ever been part of a crowd while looking at a film. The communion is between me and the filmmaker. Where my mind is—I'm not with the audience around me, I'm with the filmmaker.

Vito Acconci

I came across Vito Acconci's work while learning about '60s and '70s performance/body art; though for whatever reason I was more interested in Chris Burden and the Vienna Actionists. Later, when Ugly Duckling Presse published *0 to 9: The Complete Magazine*, a 2006 collection of Vito and Rosemary Mayer's jointly edited poetry magazine from the late '60s, I began reinvestigating his practice and realized I had overlooked a fairly amazing artist. I also went to see Vito and Rosemary do a book talk in conjunction with the release, and while I often dislike poetry readings (I prefer to read things at my own pace), Vito's distinctively deep voice and his recollections about the era made for a compelling evening.

James Hoff of Primary Information had been working with Vito to release his extensive audio works and sought me out for advice. A symposium on Vito's work was happening at the Slought Foundation in Philadelphia, and James offered to recommend me to them to deliver a paper on the role of music and sound in Vito's video and audio work. This was an untapped area in the scholarship around his output, and I found the proposition extremely interesting, so I did some research and James connected me to Vito for an interview. Vito graciously met me at the F train stop in DUMBO, Brooklyn, and we walked down the block to his studio space. Vito was a big music fan, and I think he really enjoyed speaking about music, maybe even more than he liked discussing his own work. I used some quotes from the interview in my lecture, but it has remained unpublished until now (and the lecture itself remains so).

In pieces like Other Voices for a Second Sight *[1974],* Ten Packed Minutes *[1977],* The American Gift *[1976], and* Airtime *[1973], there's so much simulation of radio. What significance did radio have to you in the '60s and '70s?*

I really grew up on radio, not on television. I don't think my family had television until I was in high school. When I looked at television when I was a child, I did it at other people's houses. What kind of radio? On the one hand there were half-hour and hour-long narratives, a plain sound kind of thing, I can't remember titles . . . and on the other hand there was music stuff, especially a program called *Make Believe Ballroom*—every Saturday, the top twenty-five songs, counting down. By the time I was grown up, after graduate school, and I was back to New York in the '60s, that was a time when you assumed you could get music you liked from the radio [*laughs*]; it's very different from now. I certainly had radio on all the time in the '60s—I certainly don't now; we play music in the studio all the time. I used to listen to Jonathan Schwartz a lot; at that time he was still doing pop and rock stuff. His father wrote music for movies, I think.

But radio is important in a way. . . . I remember in the '60s there was this incredible commercial for Dr Pepper. The commercial had these people kind of chanting, but the chanting itself was preceded by a voice saying: "The following commercial is being performed in the nude" [*laughs*]. I was struck by that—orally presented words, as a kind of quick hypnosis, aurally heard words as rhetoric. That was kind of important to me; is all language rhetoric? When you say something, whether you're saying it to try to persuade somebody [or not], you want them to listen to you, and not to somebody else.

In moving from Running Tape *[1969], an audiotape*

work, to video and then to the installation pieces where you were back to just using audiotape, did you reach a point where you thought the disembodied voice was more powerful?

One side of me thought the sound, the voice, was always a part of an installation. . . . There were very few pieces I did that were just for a record.

The first tapes I did, *Running Tape* and another one with breathing—taking a breath, holding it as long as I could, releasing it—I don't know if I even concentrated on the notion that this was an audiotape. It was approximately 1969, and they were the first pieces I did after I thought of myself as a writer. These were all attempts to get up from my writer's desk and out into the world, thinking I could use photographs, I could use audio; I was trying to connect myself with the world around me, so I would run in Central Park, take photographs in Central Park, take photographs on the Lower West Side. . . . I was obviously interested in activity, but I didn't want to take a photo *of* an activity, I wanted to hold a camera while going through an activity, snapping a photograph, almost photographing *through* an activity rather than [taking a photograph] *of* an activity. It was probably kind of like that the first times I used tape. By the time I used voice in installations, after I had done performance stuff for a while, I had connected my performances with a particular time: with the end of the '60s, with the early '70s, a time that had language like "finding oneself." When I was doing performance, I thought I was doing the same kind of stuff that Neil Young was doing, that Van Morrison was doing, a single voice, long songs. But it was starting not to be the '60s anymore [*laughs*], and I started to think, "Is work of mine stuck in the '60s? Is work of mine stuck in notions of finding oneself?" People were having different notions by 1973, '74, '75. Self wasn't this thing you could isolate, self wasn't something you could contemplate, self was only part of a social system, a cultural system, a political system. I wanted work of mine to be part of that system, so I felt like there shouldn't be this focus on me anymore. Also, it started to bother me, while I was doing live stuff, that everybody who knew a piece of mine knew what I looked like, so . . . Is this doing work, is this doing art, or is it developing a kind of personality cult? I wanted to withdraw from myself. But I didn't know how to do that totally. I could withdraw from the presence of my body, but the way I started using audio in the installations—I didn't know how to completely let myself go. So voice was a kind of vestige of myself. It might have begun that way; what I started to really be attracted to about voice, and about voice without the body there, was that . . . I started to be aware of things, like the fact that you can close your eyes but you can't close your ears, that sound seemed to be this pervasive thing. In Western culture, we talk about a mystic 'seeing things,' but an insane person 'hears things,' common expressions like a song you 'can't get out of your head.' It seemed like Western culture attaches sound to some kind of pressure, possibly oppression.

Well, it is a physical thing, the vibrations—

Yeah, well this is a side thought—especially recently I've felt that I grew up learning all the wrong things, I never paid attention to science, and now I feel like this is what I crave. Sound, it seems like as soon as it's there, it's inside you, you just can't keep it out. Sight seems different, even touching seems different.

Did it ever occur to you that you might be, in some way, kind of a DJ; that you were recording these events and then, in a gallery situation playing back the recordings of what were first performance events, and then—

I don't know how conscious I was of that, except that, like you pointed out, I did this thing called *Other Voices for a Second Sight*, which was like an all-night radio show, this guy playing songs. . . . I got that from the Bob Rafelson movie *The King of Marvin Gardens* [1972] [*laughs*]. The beginning of that was the most astonishing thing I'd ever come upon, this face with this blinking red light. I saw that movie in '72, which was kind of coincidental with the first installations I was doing.

Theme Song *[1973] is also like a DJ where you're playing song after song, but what's interesting there is you're building off the lyrics of each song, and it seems like you're recognizing the subtext of all these pop songs, which is basically a come-on. You're taking it literally, as if the viewer is someone you're trying to pick up, but in a way, that's what every pop song is about, whether it's a love song or not—it's trying to lure you in, to buy the song. It's all kind of a con game [*laughs*].*

Yeah, yeah.

It also brings up the question of the singer's voice, and how authentic that is. It's the singer trying to get people to believe in the voice singing the song; but do people assume that it's the real person, or is it a persona? Is that something you thought about when you were doing the voice tapes in installations?

Yeah, I could play with my voice. I probably wasn't at the very beginning, but gradually I realized that if I did a recording and I [used] this coffeepot that I could get an echoey voice. I started to use a TEAC four-track where I realized if I put it out of phase I could be a version of Les Paul and Mary Ford—so I could play with it. . . . I didn't need to have a cast, I could *be* the cast: I could be a number of voices, for a number of roles, at the same time. I could throw my voice.

Were there certain instances where you wanted people to think that it was you, and not a role that you were taking on? In the video Face-Off *[1973], you're playing an audiotape where you're revealing secrets about yourself, and then you're shouting at it to drown it out; did that represent a conflict you were having about how you would be perceived?*

Ah. . . . This may be something that started to take me away from performance. When I was doing live stuff, maybe I wanted that, but realized that I obviously didn't want that, I'm playing roles. . . . In the last performances I did, in 1973, I was doing performances as if I was making an approach to you, the viewer. I did a piece called *Ballroom* [1973], in a gallery in Florence. There were three spotlights in the middle of the space; I'm also in the middle of the space. Surrounding us are circular tables and chairs, in the background is a tape of me humming Al Jolson's "Anniversary Song," that's on one track, and the other track has my voice addressing a person in my life—"I'm dancing with you, Nancy"—then addressing a person I used to be with: "Now I'm dancing with you, Kathy." Then every once in a while breaking away from the circle, going to one of the tables and saying, "Neither Kathy or Nancy really understands me, maybe you can understand me," or, "I really want you, so I'm throwing myself to you." And while doing that piece I realized I'm going for this guise as if I want to start a relationship—was this really true? [*Laughs.*] Do I really want to start a relationship in a gallery? No, it seems like it's all a fake. I want to make an approach, an invitation to a relation, but I certainly don't want this relation to happen, and that became significant to me, because at one point a person got up and started hugging me, and I realized I didn't have any idea what to do. I wanted it just to reach the invitation stage, but I certainly didn't want to carry it through. So the performance becomes this simulation, this kind of fake. . . . Significantly, that was the last performance that I did, because I had proven to myself, I'm faking [*laughs*].

I—and a lot of people of my generation, I think—was desperate to separate the idea of performance from theater, but I'm not sure if it really was that different. I tried to make it different by saying I would never really repeat performances, because I thought performance wasn't about rehearsal. Performance was about stage fright, you know. . . . What I loved about the word *performance* was "perform" in the sense of perform a contract—you said you were going to do something and you do it, but if you do it again, then the first time was just a rehearsal, so it doesn't count. . . . Yeah, you could do it for a number of days over a one-week period, two-week period, but to do it later was like going through the motions.

When you're using audiotape, the tape can do the repetition for you. You're transferring it onto a mechanism, instead of making yourself the mechanism.

Yeah, yeah. [*Pauses.*] The use of sound in installations changed a lot according to the way the music I was listening to changed. When I first started doing installations at the end of '72, beginning of '73, I didn't know what to do with installations. When I was doing performances I wanted so much a kind of “I” and “you, the viewer” space. Maybe I didn’t know what the time of an installation work was. I was so used to a piece being me being there, that once I wasn’t going to be present I probably didn’t understand what was going to happen over the next three weeks—“I’m leaving this thing?” So the first installations always tried to be something else. As you pointed out, *Other Voices for a Second Sight* was installation as a radio show, installation as chapters of a novel, installation as a movie. . . . I don’t think it was until ’76 or so when the music was significantly different, it started to be the Sex Pistols and the Ramones, etc. . . . Even the New York Dolls, I don’t think I took them seriously until after the Ramones. When I first heard the New York Dolls, I thought this was kind of make-believe Rolling Stones; I didn’t get it. The Velvet Underground certainly meant something to me, meant a lot to me, but I also didn’t know what to do with it at first, because it was too much the world I was in. Before the Velvet Underground, all music seemed to be country music; suddenly with the Velvet Underground, it was the city. Suddenly you were in this pressure and density of the city. And it was startling. But I think only in 1976, when the Sex Pistols and the Ramones were second nature to me, did I realize that my installations were about the viewers: the viewers could be in this place and it was as if they were in a kind of community meeting place, and I can be addressing them. It took me a long time to realize that [*laughs*].

Since CBGB was a place where people in the audience could very well be onstage the next week, it became this almost town square.

Yes, yes . . .

People remembering that time period who were art students then, like Christian Marclay or Kim Gordon, say they weren't really interested in what was going on in galleries at the time, that clubs were more exciting than the galleries. But there was also this element where these nights at CBGB must have seemed like a kind of very short-term, time-based installation.

I think that was true, yeah. And for me, once I started thinking of installation as a kind of community meeting place, and it took me a long time, I started to realize I didn't want to do things in galleries. I don't think my stuff has anything to do with art, I'm treating a gallery as if it were a plaza or a town square. But I'm kidding myself—a gallery or a museum is never going to be a plaza or a town square [*laughs*]. If I really think my work needs that, or I want that, I better find a way to get there.

There was a quote where you said that public works are a place "where my voice might bring 'you' together, a place where my voice might speak to 'them.'" Do you see music as a thing that brings people together? The Ballroom *piece you were talking about, and the video* Walk-Over *[1973], where you're also talking about dancing with a couple of different people—*

—done exactly at the same time.

Part of music is that it's a really social thing. I was wondering how literally you meant "my voice" in that quote.

Maybe this comes from my writer's background, but I always think, "How am I thinking of people?" Am I thinking of people as "you," or am I thinking of them as "we"? Am I thinking of them as "they" or "he" or "she"?—seems like a really significant thing. Now I'm not always sure [*laughs*]. I hate the fact that when we're designing a place for people, we have nothing to do with these people. These people *are* "them"; are we making a kind of trap; is doing architecture necessarily a totalitarian activity? If you're designing a space you're designing what people do, which is the last thing I want to design, but at the same time, we do it all the time [*laughs*]. I'm not sure you can have a "we" except in some kinds of performance situations, except there's one person here and the rest of the people here. But I don't know how much of a "we" that is, either [*laughs*].

*There's that video that Dan Graham shot of Minor Threat playing at CBGB [*Minor Threat, *1983]—this is at the height of the hardcore movement and the audience, the slam dancers, are just swarming the stage, it's like there's no difference—I mean, the band are playing their instruments, obviously, but it's not like a stage and an audience. And Dan Graham was very interested in architecture also. You've said you listen to music while you're designing architecture; are there other parallels in your mind between music and architecture?*

I've probably said this in interviews. . . . Architecture seems to me to have nothing to do with sculpture and everything to do with music, in the sense that both architecture and music are making a surrounding, they're making a context, they're making a kind of ambience. This probably doesn't apply to live music—it probably applies much more to listening to [recorded] music. Live music maybe requires too much attention, whereas music we listen to is almost like a version of [Erik] Satie's wallpaper music: it's a surrounding, you don't necessarily have to pay attention. In fact just recently I was saying to someone that suddenly I'm not sure if I'm as interested in noise music as I thought I was; it's taking too much attention, now I prefer more electronic stuff. I can listen to Vladislav Delay more easily now than I can listen to Merzbow or Keiji Haino, I want music to be more surrounding. . . . But strangely after I said that I realized I was totally wrong [*laughs*].

But the other thing that connects music and architecture for me is that—I don't know if I can say that you are *meant* to do something else in the middle of it, but at least you *can* do something else in the middle of it, and you can do something else while listening to music and you're obviously doing something else while you're in the middle of architecture, and to me that's so significant, in the twenty-first century, because it seems that the twenty-first century, obviously, is a time of no single focus. It kind of teaches you to pay attention to a number of things at the same time, that skimming might be just as important [as] if not more important than reading. . . . Surface might be just as important [as] if not more important than depth. Multi-focus is just as important [as] if not more important than single focus. It seems healthier to me, it seems more like what a city is.

This goes back to the DJ thing, where a DJ is playing records so people can work while music is playing in the background all day, or in a doctor's office.

Yes, yes, yes . . .

Have you ever designed a music club?

No, I'd love to. Well, before the studio became a studio, which was 1988, in '86 I did—that's one of the reasons why the studio formed, was that in the '80s I was obviously doing stuff with people, but they were never credited as collaborators; they were supposedly building stuff for me and I realized, "I'm getting ideas from these people too, so I might as well admit it" [*laughs*]—in 1986 I did a piece in the basement of the Palladium, so it wasn't *exactly* . . . It was a place where people went downstairs to take drugs [*laughs*], the place was filled with needles. I wanted to believe I was doing a surrounding for a music place, but it wasn't really that.

You've said, "My best work has always been connected with the music of [the] moment."

In spite of what I've always thought of as my connection to music, and what I thought of as my dependence on music, I always want to know what time this is. Music's the easiest way to at least have some idea of the time you're in.

Current music?

Yeah.

As a marker?

Yeah. Do I really believe that the music of the time is the anthem of the time? I don't know. But also it's a selective kind of music—when I listen to the supposed music, 'pop music' of the time now, I'm dumbfounded. I don't know when that changed. When you listened to music in the '60s, it really did seem like you were hearing the music of the time. But then it went away.

There's a certain voice of the times, sometimes, at least in underground rock. . . . If you listen to the way Tom Verlaine, David Thomas, Patti Smith, David Byrne were singing, it was a very similar way of singing. And more recently, with Devendra Banhart and CocoRosie, it's all similar to Billie Holiday, with a lot of vibrato, and also this guy Antony [ANOHNI]. But it's interesting that there becomes a trend of a certain singing style, and then that becomes "the voice" of a certain generation of musicians.

But certain things can be outside of time—the Velvet Underground was sort of outside the time it was made, and partially very inside the time.

I wonder if Bob Dylan's stuff was so connected, and almost announced at that time, that it just didn't make any sense [*laughs*], I don't know. Maybe—and this isn't necessarily a bad thing—if you're so connected to the time, it doesn't have any use anymore. The Bob Dylan songs that mean the most to me are the songs that were so ambiguous that I don't have any idea what they were about, like "I'll Keep It With Mine." But in some ways, if you listen carefully, it really is about that time. "How long can you keep looking for what's not lost" [*laughs*]—that's a pretty significant '60s line.

I was curious as to what you thought about Leonard Cohen and Patti Smith, who were poets and then started writing songs.

Yeah. Leonard Cohen I loved; Patti Smith I always . . . disliked. Leonard Cohen says "I" a lot, but the "I" seems to change, there could to be a hundred "I"s; Patti Smith seemed too much like folk music, like someone trying to reveal something, and I just didn't believe it. I used to think that the only kind of music I could listen to was vocal music; now it's the last kind of music I can listen to. The vocalists I loved were Lou Reed, Leonard Cohen. I'm not sure how much I ever loved Bob Dylan. When I saw the Todd Haynes movie

[*I'm Not There*, 2007], which I on the one hand despised but on the other hand would kind of recommend to people, I realized the best thing about this movie is the Bob Dylan music.

I think Mark E. Smith figures in here also; there seems to be a tradition with some of these people where they're using the songs or the singing as a prop for the language. I feel like Mark E. Smith does that, and maybe Leonard Cohen does too.

That's a really good example; with Mark E. Smith the language kind of becomes an instrument. I can probably repeat the words of a few Leonard Cohen songs; I could repeat a phrase or two from Mark E. Smith's songs and I'm not even sure I'd have the phrase right, because Northern British is a very difficult language [*laughs*].

Kate Linker wrote that your installations were props to carry the ideology that was expressed in the audiotapes that went with them. Did you ever think of it in that way?

I'm not sure. The audio was always in the making of those pieces—the audio was always the last thing. Until there was some kind of "setting," I didn't know what the words would be. The text was written, the audio recorded at the very last moment. That doesn't mean that what she's saying was wrong.

I think it's kind of significant that in the installations I did, from '72 to '79, there might have been sixty or seventy installations—only about two or three were video installations, all the others were audio installations. And there really was a reason. I think I was afraid that video was too much of a kind of focal point. As soon as video is in something, a passerby, a viewer is caught up in the video screen. Whereas audio becomes *part* of the space, it's not a point within the space. It seemed really important to me that it be a space you're in the middle of, and not a focal point you're in front of.

You had said that the voice shouldn't carry any more or less weight than any other part of the installation.

That's what I hoped would happen. At the same time, I think some of those things are separable. When I hear the voice part on a CD, I can't say it carries the piece—the installation isn't there anymore, but it kind of has its own life. Whereas if the rest of the installation were there without sound, I don't know how effective it would be.

To go back to what you said about your work being connected to the music of the moment, you had also mentioned being a fan of remixes in the '90s. You had also talked about how you like the idea of renovation, that in architecture nothing is absolutely finalized; did that ring true with the whole remix trend of that time?

It rang especially true. I realized that when most architecture is built, there's a shrug of the shoulders, an assumption that of course it's not going to be useful forever. It has to change—the way people change; it has to change, the way a city changes. It seems to me a much more healthy notion than an artwork that has to be preserved. I think that made sense at some point. It certainly doesn't make sense in eras of reproduction: who cares about an original? But that was something that in the late '60s a lot of people, when work of mine started [appearing] in an art context, started to think about. It was clear that most of the supposedly famous works of art I knew, I knew from reproductions. I didn't know them from the original. So if that's true, how can you validly say that the art resides in these originals? The art resides in a distribution system; I think that was kind of the start of it. But as soon as the distribution system becomes more important than the thing, then change becomes more important than the preservation of something.

I'm saying all this in a very scattered way. . . . When I did both audio and video, I took stuff from music sources as if they were publicly available things—they weren't [*laughs*]. If my stuff hadn't been in a context where nobody paid attention, all the stuff would have been suable.

Although in the early '70s people were not as cognizant of making an issue out of that. If you look at films from back then, they would have songs on the soundtrack that I don't think were licensed.

I'm really drawn to this notion of things being readily available. I admit I didn't see any of those, I wasn't in town a lot of the time, but Marina Abramović just did versions of some of these old performances. She called people and asked if she could do this, and when she called me—I mean, I've known Marina for a while—I thought, "You don't really have to ask. . . ." Because the stuff, it's kind of raw material. But not everybody thinks that way; Chris Burden wouldn't even speak to her. . . .

Everything I've done, if I think hard enough, I can probably think of a source or a number of sources that I've gotten it from. You're always stealing. And probably what makes something happen is, you don't want to totally admit you're stealing, so you try to change it, change it up as much as possible, and in so doing, maybe come on to something new. But I don't know how you come on to something new directly [*laughs*]; you have to start somewhere. There were probably seventy-five movies that I've said, in passing, "This is the best movie ever made," or "this is the biggest influence." . . . I can point out so many influences, the Sex Pistols and the Ramones, or 1962, the first time I read Jean Genet, this was the most important thing in my life—there are a thousand most important things in my life. They kind of goad you on.

Going back to the punk thing, so many of the punk musicians were people who had no background in music, or weren't sitting around studying hard to be musicians . . . and in every phase of your career you found yourself in a field you hadn't trained for—

That's probably one of the reasons why punk so resonated with me. I always felt like I'm a person with a short attention span [*laughs*]; I seem to want to go to some other field. I know the flaws of this position, but I like the idea of coming to a field from other fields because you're kind of like a visitor from another planet. There's a lot of things you don't know because you don't know the language, but at the same time you might notice things that habitants of that field take for granted, so maybe you can stretch something. . . . I know that I could come to architecture from another field, but I know that without working as part of a "we," I couldn't do it. I can only provide one part of it. The studio really is a "we." It really is a group of people playing off each other, in which the individual ideas become part of a whole group of ideas. I don't think in any of the projects we do, you could say, "This is so and so's idea." I find that an incredibly exciting way of thinking. I don't think I could have ever gotten to that alone.

Was Brian Eno someone you were a fan of?

Yes.

Because he strikes me as someone who also—he had no musical training whatsoever—

I didn't know that.

—and when he was doing his solo records he would have his musician friends come in, and it was more of a group project, and he was one of the first to think in terms of ambient sound installations which had an architectural aspect to them, in terms of altering a space through sound . . . and it's all in the same time period as punk, or slightly before it.

Yeah. Strangely, for some reason, the Brian Eno that meant more to me was not *Music for Airports* [PVC, 1978] but the things that came a little before that, *Taking Tiger Mountain (By Strategy)* [Island, 1974], *Here Come the Warm Jets* [Island, 1973]. The other stuff *should* interest me more [*laughs*], that would be the kind of stuff that *now* would interest me more . . . but maybe I wasn't ready for it back then. But *Taking Tiger Mountain* and *Here Come the Warm Jets*, I loved those two records.

*Yeah. But that last vocal record he did [*Another Day on Earth *(Opal, 2005)] was horrible.*

I was just going to say the same thing [*both laugh*]. Interestingly, one or two people in the studio, who are about twenty-five, twenty-six years old, loved that record. But they didn't know the earlier stuff.

I have one friend who really liked the earlier stuff

and he loved that recent record too. We sort of got into an argument about it.

When I first heard it, I wanted to like it so much; the stuff I had heard over the last few years I didn't pay attention to at all. It was really good, but after one listen . . .

I couldn't figure out why he had bothered to make it. When he made Here Come the Warm Jets *and* Taking Tiger Mountain, *it seemed like he still had so many ideas about what a rock record could be; he had the opportunity and he had the desire to make those manifest. And this was like—*

—like he knew it all already, like there was nothing else to find.

In Walk-Over *[1973] and* Turn-On *[1974] you're humming—I was wondering where that came from.*

I really don't know what the source was.

In Turn-On, *you keep humming in between saying, "The time isn't right now, I'll have to wait," so it seems like you're almost humming to fill the time. . . .*

Making a kind of Bernard Herrmann score with just my voice [*laughs*], I'm going to do *Psycho* [1960] and *Vertigo* [1958] [*laughs*], I don't know.

As video was a kind of do-it-yourself format for the moving image, it was the same with its equivalent of movie soundtrack music—instead of having a whole orchestra play it, it was something you also could do yourself. And a lot of your work then was an investigation of self anyway.

Maybe it had to do with the nature of the work, but it never occurred to me to have a cameraperson. With the exception of a long tape I did called *The Red Tapes* [1977], I would turn on the camera, I would stand in front of it. The only editing I did would be to take the beginning off. All the sound stuff I did was with a Pioneer mixer and a TEAC four-track recorder. There were a number of reasons: I didn't have money to have a sound studio, but another person might have been kind of an interference. A lot of that early stuff was a kind of *Notes from the Underground*; nobody else could be let in.

Jutta Koether: On Sonic Youth

Jutta Koether and I met in the late '90s through several mutual friends. As I came to know her better, I found out that she had written for the German rock magazine *Spex*, edited by Diedrich Diederichsen, and that like Diederichsen she was very conversant and actively engaged with both the art world and the underground rock scene. Jutta is well known as a visual artist, but she is also a keyboard player; she had a band called Diadal with fellow painter Rita Ackermann, and another called Electrophilia with the late artist Steven Parrino. Jutta and I have performed together a couple of times, once at Tonic in the early 2000s, and once at Peter Coffin's "Untitled (Greenhouse)" exhibition at Andrew Kreps Gallery in New York in 2002, where we were joined by Tom Verlaine. Jutta and Kim Gordon have also invited me to participate in performances at art spaces, including "Club in the Shadow" in 2003 at Kenny Schacter's gallery Rove (where Tamio Shiraishi and I performed jointly with Electrophilia), and "Dead Already" in 2007 at Reena Spaulings Fine Art. Jutta and Kim are close friends, and these series injected real energy into the surprisingly small nexus of New York's art and music communities. Eventually, Jutta decided to concentrate more on her painting, with great success.

Lee Ranaldo suggested to Roland Groenenboom, the curator of the 2009 exhibition "Sonic Youth Etc.: Sensational Fix," at Malmö Konsthall in Sweden, that Jutta and I have a conversation about the band for the show's catalog. This struck me as a wonderful idea, since despite our personal associations with the band members, she and I had never discussed them very much, in fact possibly not at all. We met up on February 25, 2008, and had this talk.

Maybe we should talk a little bit about artists' taste in rock music, how the art world first became aware of Sonic Youth, and maybe how aware they are of them now. In terms of a band like Talking Heads, at the time that was a band with more of an art world connotation; they had been at RISD, David Byrne was doing different things, and there was the Rauschenberg picture disc. But musically, a rock band that was associated with the art world would not be a hard rock band, usually. The Talking Heads had keyboards; it was always something that was more tempered. Even Laurie Anderson—while that wasn't rock music, it was also something that was looking to make this pop crossover or straddled an art audience and a pop audience. Sonic Youth makes a break with that, but as you see it, how do they fit in with whatever the art world's perception of rock is?

There has been an accumulation of encounters. What you're describing, the notion of the Talking Heads and all that, really relates to an art world of that era, because there is a certain polished-ness, there is a certain product-oriented thing. The aesthetics are really relating to coming out of post-Pop and then going into '80s appropriation art and the aesthetics that come with that. A big perception change has occurred since the '80s: what is perceived as art, and as rock, and as whatever, are almost all now perceived as mediated culture, as well as part of celebrity culture. Taking a position and being able to reflect on it, as well as dealing with the fact that conditions of those reflections keep changing, Sonic Youth keep inserting their reflections and comments into the culture they live in. That is something that has been the steady patch of all their doing, just like their signature guitar-strumming-chords-noise thing. This is the patch from which they take off and return.

You can see that in the Ciccone Youth project,[1] *as a kind of comment on culture at that time, and from these recent collages Thurston [Moore]'s been doing; as a once and future rocker he's been coming at it all along from this '70s-mediated vision of it, from* Rock Scene *and* Creem *magazines. So there's a visual component to that, but also an overall cultural bent.* Creem *especially was reporting on the counterculture as much as on rock music itself, so it's always presenting rock as this particularly energetic force in an overall culture that's emerging. And that's the way Sonic Youth has presented itself as a band, where the music is the primary force but there's all kinds of other cultural influences involved.*

There is a kind of unresolved relation between Sonic Youth and the art world as an economic system. There are incongruities about the content as well (as it has become [a fact] of current art practices that people put music and things together, but for very different reasons). I find this ambiguity, the mixed feelings they cause when planted within an art context, very interesting.

When Kim [Gordon] and Lee [Ranaldo] and Thurston have shown visual artwork in galleries it's been smaller ones, but it still seems to me the work is perceived the same way a recording by a visual artist might be, as opposed to a vanity project of a rock star. Maybe the larger forces in the art world would not perceive it that way, but that's how it's been received by the people who are aware of it.

1 Sonic Youth released a single, an EP, and an album under the moniker Ciccone Youth during the period 1986–89. Ciccone Youth's *The Whitey Album* (Enigma/Blast First, 1989), which began as a playful tribute to Madonna, featured drum machines, rapping, karaoke recordings, industrial renditions of '80s pop songs, and collaborations with Mike Watt of Minutemen and J Mascis of Dinosaur Jr.

Object production by individuals will first be considered part of the larger picture that is SY. But then, within that, each person finds their own way of stepping outside the big picture and to question their very own relation to that world they have created. Thurston's collages are evidence of, and question, the method of productive, obsessive fandom that has influenced the sound of SY. Kim's choices of pictures for sets, and [her] methods of making and placing things, are informed by the same will to conceptualize and simultaneously sensualize a stage with her presence, motions, dress, lights . . . and Lee—

Lee studied with [filmmaker] Ken Jacobs in college, and in a way he's coming back to that interest in experimental film with Text of Light[2] *and Drift.*[3] *There's a film by Ken called* Tom, Tom, the Piper's Son *[1969–71], where he takes an old reel of silent film and then he rephotographs it from different angles. That reminds me of a lot of Lee's loops, taken from records, that he would play in the earlier concerts. On* Bad Moon Rising *[Blast First/Homestead, 1985], where he has "Not Right" by the Stooges and the locked groove from Lou Reed's* Metal Machine Music *[RCA, 1975] in between the songs, where he takes these recognizable things and inserts them in this collage-like way, you could compare that to Rauschenberg also. I've realized, in retrospect, that hearing those on that record was quite similar to my reaction to seeing Rauschenberg's collage [*Tracer, *1963] with Rubens's* Venus at Her Toilet *[ca. 1613–15] in it when I was a kid—that chime of recognition where it was like,*

2 See p. 136.

3 Lee Ranaldo's decades-long collaboration with artist Leah Singer, Drift, pairs the former's poetry and drones with the latter's projected images and films in improvised live performances and gallery installations.

"Oh, he likes Peter Paul Rubens, too" [laughs]. *It's not necessarily putting yourself in the same continuum as that—it's a fanlike gesture. Which is an important gesture to make for bands who are operating at the level that Sonic Youth was at that time. They weren't setting themselves up to be gods; they were still trying to introduce themselves and get beyond some of the categorizations that people were putting them into because they didn't know them well enough.*

That does, somewhat, coincide with a whole new wave of the practice of appropriation within art. And to use those as a structuring element, not in a minimalist way—quoting something and then having it exude meaning—but in a more omnivorous, pop-cultural way. You like it, you absorb it, you point toward it, you make something known, you comment, you move on. That happens at that time very specifically and that kind of propels the whole project forward; it makes it not sit and represent something. Like you said, it's not about being some rock gods, not retelling the story like, "OK, first you were super-underground and then—poof"; it becomes ongoing. A practice for life.

One of the things that is parallel between the art world and the pop world is that trends appear in both sectors. Not necessarily the same thing, but they're both trend-oriented. Do you think that's something that Sonic Youth is very conscious of?

I think so. Then there are trends within trends within trends.

Do you think they made that connection early on? Or more so in recent years?

I think they always have been aware of that. When they started out they were conscious of it, but it wasn't regarded as an asset, necessarily. Also, the late '70s in New York were a really decisive time for conceptualizing art . . . where conceptual art branched out to pop culture again. The arrival of the Pictures generation, for example. Sonic Youth's cover choices definitely have something to do with acknowledging that background.

So I think they were aware of it—it's just I think that the way they think about art isn't connected, necessarily, to an art discourse. They're observers and they're kind of participants, temporarily, via alliances in certain discussions or engagements, and that manifests in these choices.

Almost every record cover has been a forum for either an artist they've been friendly with or someone they liked. Two things to talk about are where that comes from historically—the obvious precedents are Andy Warhol and the Velvets, and Robert Mapplethorpe with Patti Smith and Television, but even the Beatles using Richard Hamilton and Klaus Voormann—and the individual artists themselves and what we know about their relationships to the band.

It's also what gave them a reputation, at least in Europe, as being an "art band," or "art rock," because it is embedded in that kind of historical trajectory—it is a band that is not only defining itself as musicians who are doing music but [has] a self-understanding as a kind of cultural force that has extensions. This is an idea that is already integral to the whole project: it's an artistic thing rather than a music-thing only; it's an art that incorporates different forms of expression, of which music might be the umbrella for everything else. Within the principals of the band there is the wish to be artists who happen to choose music, but who still talk to art and speak within the realm of culture.

I think a lot of that goes back to Dan Graham, who was their friend but also kind of a model for what they were going to do. Kim, in an interview about Dan, was saying that Dan was "an artist who was not satisfied with just making art," and it seems to me that Sonic Youth is a band that wants to do more than just be a band. Whenever they release a record it's not just a collection of songs but [also] a collection of accumulated influences that is shown in the packaging. NYC Ghosts and Flowers *[Geffen, 2000] had the Joe Brainard picture, for example. . . . In addition to whatever the music reflects about what's been going on in their lives since the last record, the choice of images reflects an artist who's come into their orbit in the last few years.*

I thought it made perfect sense for them to get Richard Prince to do the cover for Sonic Nurse *[Geffen, 2004]. It seems like he and Sonic Youth were on a parallel course anyway, in their careers but also in interests: Richard collecting those old paperbacks and using those for the "Nurse" paintings reminded me of the song "I'm Insane," where all the lyrics are taken from the titles to these cheap, lurid paperbacks. And even the way that Richard was using the images from biker porn magazines, these trashy, marginalized sources, reminded me of that video where Kim is doing a karaoke version of "Addicted to Love," but it's this sort of thing that you made for five dollars at Macy's with stock footage. Even their use of very cheap guitars—it was always looking into what's accorded a status of trash in society and looking to use that in an artistic way.*

I found it interesting that it's not just trash for its own sake, and that's also the case with Richard

Prince; it is very consciously picked and used as raw material and then applied. Like a conceptual operator. With empathy but also keeping it away from a personal taste thing. Well, it's not about liking bikers, or having a particular, obscure emotional lyric; it's an appropriation that also makes a very specific cut, reframes the desire. Displaces it. Reframes it. If that wasn't the case, it could have drifted into kitsch or oddball Americana. But that never happened.

*Right. It's not like wearing a T-shirt for biker porn [*laughs*] or whatever—it goes way beyond that.*

I think I would like to point to the ways SY articulate and negotiate some kind of collectivity. One characteristic of SY is [that it's] an open, collective structure. [To] keep it running for such a long time, it's not always easy—but this emphasis on negotiation and conversation that exists in the way they relate to new sounds, new textures, new phenomena, [and also] to other ways of communicating, so it is not always the same. There is a certain band structure that is maintained, and yet different people bring in different influences, and it still remains open to that. It's not just, "Yeah, they're hip to know certain bands in a club," or something. They collaborate, they invite people to come in, they curate, and then that trickles into Sonic Youth as an entity.

Their internal structure resonated with the cross-country networking that existed in the indie rock scene in the '80s, and then also extended to making connections with all kinds of different artists and musicians as they traveled the world. But even when they do things outside the band, in collaborating with people, it's also very—

—Sonic Youth–y [*laughs*].

Yeah, they make the people that they're collaborating with into equals. They're not working with people who are just going to be yes-men, they're looking to them for input. It has to be a mutual thing.

For me, that represents being a very specific type of artist. It's not just an attitude thing, it's a very specific type of practice. Some people sort of make fun of that; they say that's where the Grateful Dead factor is also [*laughs*], that it takes on this viral form, it's a phenomenon for a different world and generation.

*The other similarity with the Dead is, it's a band as a lifestyle signifier. The Dead represents the hippie, psychedelic lifestyle; Sonic Youth represents the post-punk, indie, alternative lifestyle. I knew someone who in the early '90s was starting law school, and said she wore a Sonic Youth T-shirt hoping to find some like-minded people at the law school—got no takers whatsoever [*both laugh*]. But at this point it's one band that people who like that sort of thing can all agree on. Going back to what we've said about it being very much a collective and a band that's stayed in touch with their roots and their audience, there are actually a lot of political reasons for that status.*

Yeah, I think so too. That's the really interesting part, because this feeling of collectivity occurs in America, as I see it, through very temporary phenomena, and usually propelled through drama, the rise and fall, the narrative, the competition, the winner, there's always some kind of dramatic arc. And then collectivity occurs when you mourn together and you celebrate together, and then your use is over and you go somewhere else. It's seeing it as a collectivity that liberates you from the schematics and offers, on first sight, a less glamorous or sexy alternative that involves your own kind of participation and has a completely different time span, and therefore it really represents something else.

Exactly. They outlasted having that arc. Maybe people in the late '80s, when they signed to a major label—indie rock fans felt that was the end and they would turn into something else. Most bands from the indie scene who sign to major labels only last a couple of records and that's the end of it. The fact that they've lasted so long in that world . . . R.E.M. is the only other band I can think of that's done it, in a completely different way. A lot of people starting bands think they can't last, because that's the archetype that's been set up. The other thing is [Sonic Youth] haven't had a top-ten hit, so it hasn't become hinged on that. You don't have people coming to the concerts expecting to hear the big hit, and then having to do that year after year. Maybe "Kool Thing" [on Goo *(DGC, 1990)] was the closest they came to that.*

We should also talk about how they keep constructing and deconstructing the idea, which is inherent in American culture, of the musician or the rock musician as a model or a hero or an iconic figure, because they do play with that, too. I look at Kim in that respect because she also represents a kind of role model for young women and aspiring cultural practitioners in different arenas. I think they are laying out a very interesting, complicated relationship to celebrity, their own celebrity and celebrity culture, that seems to be kept open. Just recently I went to the Marc Jacobs show, where they did the ultimate schlocky thing: show up there and play two songs for a fashion show [*laughs*]. It didn't jell. It represented a difference, a different kind of approach to being in the world. It also still represents, at a certain level, maybe not the way it did before, this other alternative. I wouldn't call it alternative culture, but an outlook. And that was very interesting to see.

*Well, nothing ever seems to be out of bounds for them, and that goes back to the idea of an overall cultural identity rather than a specific thing. For every fashion show they do, they also do Mike Kelley's [*Plato's Cave, Rothko's Chapel, Lincoln's Profile, *1986] performance, or the No Fun Festival, or some other super-underground thing.*

I remember when they chose the Gerhard Richter cover [*Daydream Nation*, Enigma, 1988], I was puzzled—"What? Why are they doing this?" because it represented, at least in German culture, nothing hip or radical, which is what the music of Sonic Youth, and independent music, represented . . . or my projection on them.

So it was almost the opposite; it was like, reactionary to me. For a moment. It raised questions. It also enlightened me, so very literally, [regarding] both their interest *in* trend and a strategic independence from it—the obvious choice would have been a "cool" cover by some underground artist—in making these choices where you could have a very melancholic, almost classicist Gerhard Richter painting [on one cover] and a Mike Kelley stuffed animal on another.

It would be a problem for most bands because they establish rules and inevitably they want to move past those initial rules, and their audience may not be willing to follow them. Sonic Youth strikes an interesting balance: being in the record business in the long term, which means they have to be cognizant of the way the wind is blowing at any given time, and at the same time being fairly consistent in terms of how their records go. It's not an option for them to make their try at whatever the musical trend of the moment is, because they don't have the facility to do that. But they can modify their image, somewhat, to account for that. Looking at the '90s: when they did Dirty *[DGC, 1992], they were referencing the grunge phenomenon; by the end of the decade, they were somewhat referencing DJ culture, working with DJ Olive or DJ Spooky.*

It's maintaining a degree of independence that is not totally outside. It's the same way the music functions; they maintain that special kind of status that is within a larger history of independent rock music, art-rock music, and then it leads them to a place, and yet it's not in the center—there's something evasive about it, it always sort of shifts.

Their roots go back to No Wave, and because No Wave was a scene where so many of the participants were picking up their instruments for the first time; that was one kind of impetus, especially for people who were in art school at the time, as Kim was—or maybe she was just out of art school. There were a lot of people who found that music scene more exciting than the gallery scene. There's also a whole tradition of artists' noisemaking as an extension of their practice, which goes back to Duchamp but also to Jean Dubuffet and Destroy All Monsters, who were pursuing it in isolation. In No Wave there was actually a center for it, a hothouse for it, in the New York club scene at the time. And some of the participants were artists, like Robert Longo or James Nares. Though it's significant that No New York *[Antilles, 1978] came out of that festival at Artists Space, a gallery space, not a club, which then became sort of a model for the Noise Festival that Thurston organized at White Columns. And Neutral, the first label that Sonic Youth was on, was run by Glenn Branca and White Columns' Josh Baer, so it was really sort of a gallery label, not unlike the Chatham Square label, which was run by composer Philip Glass and gallerist Klaus Kertess—both of whom, incidentally, were on White Columns' board of advisers at this time.*

But earlier songs like "Shaking Hell," which was inspired by Dan [Graham]'s Rock My Religion *video [1983–84], and "Brave Men Run (In My Family)," whose title comes from an Ed Ruscha painting—those references would have been lost on the rock audience they were playing to, and were probably lost on the art audiences of the time.*

Of course.

Besides the tradition of artists' noisemaking, there's a whole tradition of artists' writings—artists writing about their work—that doesn't really exist in rock. You have people like Pete Townshend or Brian Eno, where an interview with them is going to be a little more like that, and Townshend reviewed the Who's Meaty, Beaty, Big and Bouncy *album [Track/Polydor, 1971] in* Rolling Stone, *but by and large rock stars are supposed to be preliterate, and Sonic Youth is very postliterate. If you go back to their tour diaries of the late '80s that got published in* Forced Exposure *and the* Village Voice, *Thurston's* Killer *fanzine, all the poetry that Lee and Thurston have done, and Kim writing about Tony Oursler and Branca in* Artforum . . . *they're all writers, so there's a certain amount of reflection already going on.*

This might lead also to understanding who they

are, artistically. Thurston comes from a literary background, and the person who made him want to do things was Patti Smith—somebody who defines being in rock music as a poet, somebody who articulates emotions through words, through all means possible at that moment, a somewhat romantic model. Then you have Kim's approach, much more schooled through conceptual art. John Knight was one of her teachers. But she also was listening to Joni Mitchell and Led Zeppelin. A certain reflective detachment can be found in her lyrics as well as in her critical writing.

Yeah. You could almost say that Patti Smith being published in Creem *in the early '70s is much like Kim writing for* Artforum *in the early '80s.*

My own fantasy of Sonic Youth: when I first heard them I located them always as some sort of modern—or my generational version of—beatniks, freethinkers, something like that. People who would do something arty, or like poets, where you do what you do because you want to do that, and you don't take into account that it might not lead anywhere. With all the inbuilt, inevitable inadequacies—that curse of eternal DIY dissatisfactions, always aware of its own histories. No redemption, really. The pictures are large tapestries never able to be finished, always fragments, open patches, labor that cannot really be [justly compensated], ever. I like that they are out there creating multiple traces.

They contributed things to those issues of [Glenn Branca and Barbara Ess's] Just Another Asshole*—one issue is a book of photographs, one is a record, one is a book of short stories, and so on. They were part of that whole scene with Glenn, and the fact that they fit in with that group, where they're working with different artists* *in different media, from issue to issue, says a lot about that, considering the conversation between poetry and jazz in the beatnik era—*

—and film.

And film, where it's all kind of interrelated. No Wave became a scene like that too, where the musicians were acting in films, and making films. There was a lot of cross-pollination going on, and I think that must have been part of the appeal to Kim, Thurston, and Lee, as much as the music was. Lee, of course, is a real devotee of Kerouac, and I also think he's always looked at rock touring as a kind of extension of the lure of the open road in Kerouac's writing and in Beat-generation lore.

For a band that was often typified as quintessentially New York, they do celebrate America in that Allen Ginsberg/Robert Frank lineage, rather than some Americana or "roots music" way. I think the fact that each member of the group comes from a different geographical area in the US—Kim from California, Thurston from the South and then Connecticut, Lee from Long Island, Steve from Michigan—has something to do with that, and it partially explains their popularity. Each member has a connection with at least three of the main regions of the country and brings that to the collective, and in turn that also widens the range of things about the group the audience can relate to, as opposed to a band where the members all grew up together in the same town. It's also given the music a bicoastal feel, once you get past the surface, which is so urban New York. Not only the influence of Joni Mitchell on Kim and Lee, and the Dead on Lee, but the song topics—"Death Valley '69," "PCH," and "Expressway to Your Skull," all "take place" in California. And the labels they were signed to after Bad Moon Rising*—SST, Enigma, and Geffen—were* *all based in LA. The number of both LA and New York artists they've used for the record covers sort of speaks to this, too.*

And SY have been playing with unresolved elements in American culture all along: longing for, talking about, tapping into feelings of being somebody, being a conceptual art hero, a real underdog, a myth, a rocker, a sensitive composer, a rebel. This is, of course, a completely strange undertaking that never can be resolved or ended—Todd Haynes should make a movie on Sonic Youth! In the style of *I'm Not There* [2007]! SY is like a big montage in motion.

ANOHNI

In the fall of 2008, the *Wire* approached me about doing a cover feature on ANOHNI in conjunction with the release of *The Crying Light* (Secretly Canadian, 2009), the third album from her band Antony and the Johnsons. I knew her from having booked the group at Tonic in 2003–2004, and quite liked “Another World,” the single that preceded *The Crying Light*. Lou Reed had also discussed ANOHNI a bit when I interviewed him about *The Raven* (Sire/Reprise, 2003) in 2002.[1] I attended an Antony and the Johnsons show at the legendary Apollo Theater in Harlem a few days before the interview. Unusually, I was not given an advance copy or download of the album; as leaking to the internet was more of a concern back then, I was asked to listen to it in full at ANOHNI’s office space, which turned out to be the studio apartment where she had first lived in New York. Her assistant was present the entire time, making it kind of a listening party for one. A couple of days later, we met up at Kitchenette in TriBeCa for an interview.

1 See pp. 155–171.

Were the songs on The Crying Light *written over the last two years?*

This group of songs was [written] over the last six or seven years . . . the better ones of that group. I'm not really a one-album-a-year kind of person; I'm already on the Kate Bush schedule [*laughs*].

Only with fewer onstage costume changes.

Well, we'll see—who knows? [*Laughs.*]

On the new album, a lot of the songs are concerned with nature, with climate change—is that something you've been thinking about more lately?

I've kind of been obsessed with that since I was a teenager. A lot of the songs are exploring my relationship to the environment, to the world around me. The landscape beyond my inner landscape. Or, how do those two things integrate? I kept thinking about it in terms of gardens. There's a couple of songs that are pretty direct in their address of that subject.

A lot of the songs on I Am a Bird Now *[Secretly Canadian, 2005] addressed the subject of gender, and it seems like there's less of that on the new album.*

Hmm. It's definitely a different body of work—I think of [the songs on *The Crying Light*] as a group, definitely emerging from me at a different point in my life, songs I've written in my thirties, things I think about or care about now. Gender is an issue that's innate in everything I do. As a transgender person, I'm always seeing things through that lens. A lot of the songs deal with addressing the feminine landscape. I've got a big standoff with a lot of male-based spiritual ideas, the whole male construct of heaven as somewhere else, as someplace where things aren't mysterious or don't get born, seems like a male gig. This is quite a pagan record.

Did you ever see the movie God Told Me To *[1976]?*

No.

It's a Larry Cohen movie. He mostly does these schlocky horror films, but in this movie a group of people are going around killing people and then killing themselves, and when someone asks them why, they say, "God told me to." There's a kind of cult leader, who is a hermaphrodite, and turns out to be the God they were talking about; he's the product of a virgin birth by a woman who was abducted by aliens. It's pretty crazy. But then, and this is something that Genesis P-Orridge talked about in an interview, in the Middle Ages there were paintings that depicted Adam and Eve—and God—as hermaphrodites.

Yeah, I would say that's probably pretty practical.

Makes sense, right? But the church has destroyed all these paintings—there's only four or five left.

Everyone thinks religion is such an oasis or retreat from patriarchy. It's the same hogwash. They're all peddling the same thing. . . . I kept thinking about paradise, and how it pertains to our relationship to the natural world today—what will we be left with when there's no nature? What does paradise mean? For me, paradise doesn't mean an empty, white, eternal expanse of aloneness—that's not my idea of heaven. My idea of heaven is probably something unfurling, the way that nature unfurls in its infinite forms, you know? It's creative; that's the fun of being an artist, that we get to dance in the shadow of that.

I noticed the poster for the Peter Semple film Just Visiting This Planet *[1991] in your office; that phrase could be applied to the environment, the idea that the human race is just visiting this planet.*

Well, visiting from where? I think we get born from the earth. This album is like: I was born out of this place, I'm made out of this place, if there's a possibility for paradise, this is it. I'm not dreaming about elsewhere, I'm not visiting. I'm made of this place. But all those religions, they're all bashing away, they all chipped away at things, at the sacredness of this place. And that's how we got in this mess, I think. You can't sell something into slavery unless you've devalued it so that you can no longer recognize it, you know what I mean? Until you've degraded it, or dehumanized it, or detached yourself from its value—and that's what these religions really do. Sorry, I get a little opinionated.

*Can you talk a little bit about Kazuo Ohno, who's on the cover of the EP [*Another World *(Secretly Canadian, 2008)] and the album?*

Yeah, it's funny about the photo on the cover of the EP. I went to school in France when I was fifteen for a summer, and they were putting up posters for a theater troupe near where I was studying, and there was this picture, which is now on the cover of the EP. I didn't know what it was, but I was like, "Please can I have one of those posters?" and I put it up over my bed. I've had it over every bed I've slept in. I got to New York in 1991 and I saw that *Just Visiting This Planet*, and there was suddenly this footage of an old Japanese person doing a dance with rocks, where his fingers were crumbling around the rock, and rocks were falling, and he was kind of crying without water coming from his face. Anyway, I started sobbing so hard, and I didn't know why I was crying, and I went home and that picture was over my bed, and I said, "Shit, that's the same man." I didn't realize it for a couple of days, but then I realized I'd had a picture of that man over my bed since I was a teenager—by this time I was twenty-one.

I got into it more, and researched him. When I finished school I started studying with a dancer who had studied with him—her name was Maureen Fleming. I studied butoh with her for a few months, but I realized it was him I was really interested in. The form is amazing, but it's his impression that strikes me. I'm not really butoh-crazy, I'm Kazuo Ohno–crazy. He's had an interesting history; he converted to Christianity. It's so funny to realize that here we go from the West to the East—everyone goes Buddhist and does yoga—but they're doing the same thing because they're interested in the passions, in the devotional, the saints, the blood, and the ritual in a different way, that had an appeal to someone who'd been raised in a more stoic kind of tradition. He was really my model, especially as someone getting older as an artist. He made his masterworks as a solo dancer between the ages of seventy-five and ninety-five. I always really believed in him; some of his solutions are really inspiring to me—the way he walks through his life. He kind of became catatonic—he doesn't move now—but he's still alive: he's 102. There's this amazing video called *O, Kind God!* [2003] that's a film of him after he's wheelchair-bound and doesn't speak anymore, but he really practiced his form until he couldn't move any longer. He just danced with his hands. I loved that he danced until he couldn't move and then he kept taking the right steps inside himself.

What's so nice about his butoh is that it was so much about returning to the child, the divine child. There were sort of two schools, the Min Tanaka school and the Kazuo school. The Min Tanaka school is really depraved, and really explores insanity and suffering. And Kazuo is sort of the opposite. It's so interesting 'cause they call it "dance of darkness," but he's always seemed to be seeking some kind of a radiance that was redemptive for him personally, and I guess that appealed to me, so, as a singer, I became interested in translating some of his ideas into musical ideas.

Have you met him?

I met him a couple of times. I went to two or three performances in the '90s. I saw him do *Water Lilies* in 1993, and another piece at the Japan Society. I met him both of those times just to shake his hand.

Orchestration is something you seem to have been interested in from the beginning—it's on all of your records. Was that in your mind even when you just had a live ensemble, before you made a record?

I actually recorded the first album [*Antony and the Johnsons* (Durtro, 2000)] before I ever did a concert with a band. I'd just done shows with tapes. I got that band together to record an album. With this album, it's collaborative—some of my own ideas and some of the ideas of people around me—I worked with Maxim Moston, who plays violin and makes some beautiful things, and Nico Muhly added some arrangements. A lot of the songs on this album have three arrangers. We really did them in layers; there's bits of everyone on them.

How did you connect with Nico?

He came to one of my shows. We did a project together where he arranged some of my back catalog for orchestra, for a concert in Europe, and from there we developed that a little bit more and I asked him if he'd be interested in working on some arrangements more collaboratively, on new songs, where we would sit together and find a relationship. We did that with a couple of songs on this record. On "Her Eyes Are Underneath the Ground," there are some more subtle things Nico added that were really beautiful, and on "Everglade," and a couple of the details on the ends of different songs. Doug Wieselman did a lot of horn arrangements and brought another dimension 'cause he has a really free, avant-jazz sensibility that's so refreshing. . . . So, things coming from a lot of different directions.

Was there stuff you listened to growing up that formed your interest in orchestrations?

When I got the Marc and the Mambas album *Torment and Toreros* [Some Bizzare, 1983] when I was thirteen years old, I decided I wanted a string section when I grew up, and it just developed from there. This record has the most diverse input by far. The first album was just my keyboard arrangement ideas transposed into strings. The second album was me, Max Moston, and Julia Kent. And this one, the process was dense—we tried to pull it all back again at the end of the day. We recorded [the first album] in a day, or two days. I didn't even know what it meant to record an album, so I just did it, which was great. When it was time to record the vocals, I'd lost my voice, so that album was what it was—it was really a live performance. The second album was more arduously conceived. I don't know if I'm going to do another album in this manner. I think I must have exhausted the potential—like a Guns N' Roses kind of thing [*laughs*], but I don't think I want to do another really arduous record.

At the Apollo show the other night, you were completely cloaked in darkness onstage at the beginning and the lighting gradually revealed you, but you were still in shadow for a lot of it, which I thought was an interesting way to approach concert lighting—can you talk a bit about your concept for that?

I mean, I could just make something up [*laughs*]. . . . For me the live shows are more and more about finding a way to trick myself into stepping into the present, and inviting the audience to experience the present in a different way—to step out of more pedestrian expectations. Just the simplest gesture changes everything, and makes everyone go, "Oh! I'm alive." When I go to a show, I'm always looking for opportunities to take a deeper breath, to feel in my heart the experience of being alive more fully than I'm allowed to in real life. There's lots of opportunity for magic in live shows, and it gets back to that paradise thing, seeing things freshly, seeing light bouncing off of things—it's so refreshing. Since I was a child, I remember the refuge I took in cutting shapes out of colored paper. It brought me so much joy. So I think that's still probably, in a weird way, what I'm searching for, the possibility for creative dreaming in a clear space. And I think the idea of *The Crying Light* was about casting a circle, a sanctuary where you're safe to emerge, where you're not being traumatized. I can't start to feel until it's safe to come out. That's part of what's interesting to me about those folky kids that came out in the early 2000s. They were exploring, for the first time in a while, an idea of an inner garden: this doesn't have anything to do with the rest of the world . . . and there would be a very high wall—they weren't even dealing with the world outside the wall. I'm interested in the inner garden, but I think the next step is, how does this relate to the greater world? What can we bring forth from that place and introduce to the greater world—can we start to make bridges between them? It seems useful.

Maybe that's what David Tibet liked about your music, or your sensibility—that sounds like something he would talk about liking, or looking for, in other artists.

David Tibet? I don't know if that's what he liked about me. I'm always changing, too. Some guys really like the outfits and the extremity of it—that's not really my tip right now. Sometimes even my record company wants the lights up really bright so they can see how crazy my face looks when I'm singing, you know what I mean? I'm not so fascinated by that. I'm really interested in the space that we share; I'm not so interested in the weird space around me.

You talk about shadows and ghosts on the record—is that related to what you were doing with the lighting at all?

Yeah . . . the lighting was an experiment, too. Marina Abramović suggested it. She said, "Why don't you try a thing where you go from black to white during the show?" and I said, "OK, we'll try it." The lighting kind of squiggled around, but I liked it. I remember seeing Cat Power do a show where she didn't turn on the lights the whole night and I got so mad—I was like, "I can't see your face" [*laughs*].

I saw Tricky about ten years ago and it was the same thing: the lights were out pretty much for the entire show, but every member of the band had one glow-in-the-dark sticker or something on their clothes, and a few times during the concert a light would shine on Tricky's face for ten or fifteen seconds. But I found that to be really dramatic.

I'm interested in the *space*. I want to try to work with the lighting person to be painterly with the space, to show possibilities. . . . It's a work in progress, lights.

Did you like playing at the Apollo?

[*Pauses.*] Yeah, I did. It's kind of an intense place to play. . . .

Because of its history?

Yeah, as a white person going in there doing your number, bringing in that white audience. So much of what I have in my hands—tools I use—comes from Black America. It's all theirs, filtered through a few generations of white pop musicians. With some things from other places—but it can't be denied. The show had a really emotional finale for me, 'cause the security guard came up to me after the show and said, "Let me be the first to welcome you to the legendary Apollo Theater; you are *always* welcome back." I started crying so hard, because the only person who really matters that likes the show is the security guards, 'cause they're the only ones who will tell you the truth. They've got no reason to lie to you. Then I felt much better.

It seemed like everyone working at the Apollo took a tremendous amount of pride in the place.

The staff is, I think, genius. Just the catering staff is so outrageous; the lady who's doing the catering used to be James Brown's backup singer, and she's microwaving veggies for you, talking a mile a minute. It's just . . . magic.

Can you talk about working with Lou Reed and Hal Willner?

Hal bought my CD *I Fell in Love with a Dead Boy* [Durtro, 2001] at Other Music, and brought it in a stack of CDs for Lou to consider [as potential] singers for *The Raven*. Lou said, "Let's try this one." Hal brought me in, warned me, "If he doesn't like you, he may just go to the back room and then you'll be escorted out of the studio" [*laughs*]. Hal was pretty nervous, but it worked out fine. Then we worked on a bunch of songs for that record, and it was through them that I met Doug and all those great horn players. Hal puts together a lot of different kinds of events. Hal's been instrumental in connecting a lot of the dots for me over the years—he's been a great friend and ally. He and Lou kind of took it on to champion me in a really heavy way. I would say that the reason my record got released in Europe was at Lou's insistence, basically. Every label in England passed on *I Am a Bird Now*, every one of them. Lou had just been signed to Sanctuary, and he was barking at them, "You gotta get Antony signed in Europe," and they went to Rough Trade, who'd already passed on it, and said, "Really, give this another listen. You should release this." Sanctuary at that point owned Rough Trade, half-owned it, and Rough Trade said, "OK, we'll release it." And then, you know, it won the Mercury Prize, and every label in England was sitting in that room the day that it was declared the best record of the year [*laughs*].

Every single fucking one of them—and some of them not very politely.

David [Tibet], too, did the same thing. He said, "This is legitimate," at a time when 90 percent of the people outside of my own community wanted to write me off as some kind of drag sensation. And David was like, "Oh, actually it's an artist." So a lot of people would be like—"Oh, OK, it's an artist if David said so."

How did David find out about you?

Through a friend of mine, John Marchant, an English guy who came to the first concert we did at the Kitchen. We did a concert with Billy Basinski, he had curated a night in 1997 called Life on Mars. Billy and I were really old friends and had done a lot of work together in his loft throughout the '90s. That's where I first saw Julia Kent—Billy had shows and he'd have Rasputina, and I saw Julia and thought—"One day! One day that cool person will be in my band." John saw that concert, went back to England, and told David about it. He brought David my CD, which I was just peddling, and David said, "I'll release it." And he sent it to the *Wire*, and the *Wire* reviewed it. Devendra [Banhart] did the same thing. . . . I have the best possible karma in music in terms of the trajectory of people's awareness of me, because I was put forward by other artists, never really by the press, until later. Devendra, when he got signed, he was talking to XL like crazy, going, "Sign Antony, sign Antony." Hal was on Daniel Miller [of Mute Records] like, "Sign Antony," and Daniel Miller was like, "I don't care how many famous people are telling me to sign Antony—I will never sign Antony and the Johnsons." Devendra recontextualized me. By putting me on that folk compilation [*The Golden Apples of the Sun* (Bastet, 2004)] . . . it was crazy. Suddenly, overnight, I'd been totally recontextualized by this new generation of kids, who didn't really have any clue as to where I came from or the fact that I'd been doing a soft-shoe in Manhattan for twelve years already, done a ton of different kinds of work. So I always felt like I was kind of a weird bridge. People want to nail stuff down in order to feel comfortable listening to it. I've been doing very similar work my whole life, and I think my influences are pretty transparent. So on one level it is what it is; it's been mutable enough to fit into different categories, different periods. That's been central to the work. But it's fascinating, and it's what carries it along—it's the wind that carries it along. I'm really interested in older people, I really want old people to listen to my music, that's my goal. Does that seem crazy?

Like eighty-year-olds?

Like sixty-five, sixty-six . . . Moms, I guess [*laughs*]. I guess it's part of my mom-ism religion. I just want to be sure moms have access, that's all I'm saying.

You came to NYC in 1990 after seeing the documentary Mondo New York *[1988], and you've said you turned into a bit of a historian when you got here, trying to find out more about the gay underground performance scene. And when you arrived, a lot of that was disappearing fast. There's a pattern: a lot of people moved here chasing after the CBGB scene, and that had changed by the time they got to town, even in the late '70s.*

Yeah, it's classic. I watched this New York documentary and there were quotes from these people from the late nineteenth century bemoaning the fact that a man could return to the neighborhood of his birth thirty years later, in 1890, and not recognize a single building on the block. The character of the city is that it reinvents itself every ten years—from the ground up. It's not like Rome, which builds on top of itself; this city knocks itself down. It's as if previous iterations didn't exist. It exists maybe in books. People don't even know that they're inhabiting ghosts of people who were here ten years earlier, twenty years earlier, and yet weirdly it transmutes/transfers some of these cultural impulses unknowingly, from one to the other. And you can look back and connect the dots and find out more about what you've done and realize, "Shit, I was practically possessed by someone who had done that ten years earlier." But you made that little change, and that made it of *your* time. Like any old whale passing a song from one generation to the next.

Martin Worman, a writer for the Cockettes, was one of my teachers, as was Ron Argelander, a scholar of experimental underground performance. He was in Jack Smith's production of Ibsen's *Ghosts* before he was replaced by a penguin in a shopping cart [*laughs*]. Ron was the one who let me into the school, NYU. He said, "You should come to New York." I went there for two years, and a couple of the faculty members took me under their wing. Within that community of scholars there was a sense of urgency, because no one knew how it was going to pan out, no one knew how culture ultimately was going to be recollected in ten years, what would be preserved, what wouldn't be preserved. There was really a feeling, in those performance studies departments, kind of like the feeling now with all the amphibians, that for them to survive . . . they can't scramble to get the grain seeds into the fuckin' freezer in Svalbard fast enough. You could probably write a good paper about the disappearance of culture [as a result of] AIDS and the almost apocalyptic disappearance of biodiversity—what happened in New York City and what happened, on a different kind of a scale, to the environment.

The thing I always wonder is, "What filled the void?" There are all those guys—we could make a list of ten key cultural players. What did we get served instead? What became valuable instead of Charles Ludlam, Jack Smith? I always think about what it would be like if all those guys had kept going.

There was that retrospective of Jack Smith at PS1 in 1997, but when he died in 1989 he was leading a very marginal existence. . . . I love his quote, something along the lines of, "It's a funny thing being a legend when you can't pay your rent and the public's never heard of you."

Top to bottom. I was just going down Christopher Street the other day in a taxi, and I passed Hudson Street, and Hudson and Christopher is now called Sylvia Rivera Way. And I remember bumping into Sylvia Rivera in 1998 on the West Side Highway in the middle of winter, and she didn't have a fuckin' sweater. She had cysts all over her face, and I took off my sweater and I gave it to her 'cause she was so fucking cold. And less than ten years later there's a fucking street named after her. Something's wrong with the picture. Why aren't we paying the rent of our greatest cultural revolutionaries? Capitalism is . . . really a trip.

*[*Laughs.*] Was Blacklips Performance Cult coming out of the void that you're talking about, in a way? Or an attempt to fill the void?*

It was just us making a din. I was more hell-bent in those days [*laughs*]. I was really fiery about stuff. I have it written in my college journal, before I moved to New York, "I want to move to downtown New York, start a band of perverts, and we'll do midnight musicals," blah blah blah blah blah. And we did it, that's what we did. We got way more than we bargained for. I didn't even know what crack was when I was writing that down, what crack- and heroin-addicted drag queens really were [*laughs*]. But it was amazing—it was very vigorous and colorful, inspiring. But it was very small, it wasn't even on the map.

It was at the Pyramid Club—

After the Pyramid's heyday—it was the cleanup of the Pyramid. We were still making a distinction between theater and murder. By the very end of that era at Pyramid, a different weekly event at the Pyramid called Trip and Go Naked wasn't even making that distinction too vigorously [*laughs*]. By the end it was getting pretty close there. All the songs on the first album are from the Blacklips period, and "Fistful of Love" is from that period, even pre–that period. I wrote "Fistful of Love" when I was twenty years old, when I was performing at Crow Bar—when Blacklips was still just a cabaret format.

When was the transition between the more theatrical thing and doing songs in a concert framework?

It was kind of like wearing a few different hats. We'd been putting together these stage shows, and my role was always to come out and do a song. It was almost like that's the way I justified singing a song. I probably didn't have the confidence to just do it on its own, but with twenty people doing the can-can behind you [*laughs*], with a character and whatever . . . My role was always to do music in the show. I got to a point after we finished with Blacklips at the Pyramid—we started doing PS 122 and Jackie 60—where my shows were getting more and more fragmented, and more and more like a series of tableaux, less and less narrative. I did a show in 1996 called *Miracle Now* at PS 122, and that was the first time I had Dr. Julia [Yasuda] in one of my shows, and then I tried to start raising money for a millennial piece I wanted to do. I'd written three plays, *Love*, *Womb*, and *Father*, which one day I think I'll make a movie of, but I wanted to combine them into one piece for the millennium. I tried to raise money for it for several years and I got rejected by all these institutions. The Jerome Foundation shit on me, all these institutions shit on me, told me my work wasn't legitimate because of the kind of casting, the people I worked with. I said, "Fuck this, I'm not doing theater anymore, this is a dead end." I decided that my investment in it, ultimately, was the music. So I said, "I'll just do music, and maybe I'll come back to some of this stuff later." I got a NYFA [New York Foundation for the Arts] grant, I used that to make a record, and I never did another play. I'll still probably go back to it later.

Richard Foreman

I loved going to the theater as a kid, and at Vassar my major was officially in drama/film, but halfway through the first semester of my senior year I decided that I hated drama, and simply stopped doing the readings for a required course in ancient theater (I managed to pass by the skin of my teeth). I've seldom gone to the theater since, but Richard Foreman's work caught my attention, and I began attending plays at his Ontological-Hysteric Theater space, housed in St. Mark's Church-in-the-Bowery every year. These works, with their radical soundscapes, dreamlike costumes and set designs, and dialogue composed of poetic non sequiturs, are compelling for anyone invested in avant-garde aesthetics. I also got to know Richard a bit when I helped Jay Sanders organize a benefit for Ontological-Hysteric at Tonic.

I had been aware of Richard's background in the '60s and '70s avant-garde and his associations with Philip Glass, Steve Reich, and Michael Snow; and I also knew of his friendship with John Zorn and their mutual connection to Jack Smith, whose work they had championed. When I heard that Zorn was releasing the DVD *Sophia: The Cliffs/ 35+ Year Retrospective Compilation* (2009) documenting some of Foreman's plays, and had done the score for a new play called *Astronome: A Night at the Opera* (2009), I pitched an article on Richard to the *Wire,* hoping to get across the idea that, if nothing else, a fan of Zorn should be a fan of Foreman (indeed, Zorn's compositional techniques, such as the use of cues on cards to make works like "Cobra" [1984], are very much related to Foreman's own strategies, which include writing down individual lines on separate note cards to construct dialogue for his plays). I went over to Richard's loft in SoHo the first week of February 2009 to discuss his projects. As it turned out, hating theater was one other thing, besides music, that we had in common.

When did you and John Zorn meet, in the '70s?

I don't remember the exact year, but John was friendly with a number of people who were extras—we called them "dwarves"—in some of my early shows when I had my loft theater on lower Broadway at Broome Street. He used to hang around then, and that's when I met him. He did a little tabletop theater as one of his first events there on lower Broadway, fourth floor.

Did you two ever discuss music back then?

Hmmm, who knows, I don't think so. He was just starting. I doubt that we had any serious discussions about music, no.

Did you go to some of the Theatre of Musical Optics performances?

I can't remember. You know in those days, whenever I wasn't in New York doing a show, I would go to Paris. So I wasn't around when he did many of his events, I'm sure. I think the first time I ever saw him perform as a musician was for some dance company.

He did the music for your The Mind King *[1992] in Japan, correct?*

Yes, but I had nothing to do with that. A friend of his, Makigami Koichi, who had started coming to my plays years ago—he even came when I did a play in Singapore—asked to direct a play, and he's done two or three in Japan, but the first one was *The Mind King*, and John did the music for it live—I've seen a video of it.

I wanted to ask about your working and writing

methods. In the past you've said you've done the scenery and the text separately and then brought them together.

The text always came first. I considered myself a writer, I went to Yale as a writer, and the only reason I started directing my plays was that nobody else would do them. I designed my own plays from the beginning. For a while, when I did other people's plays, I had a designer, but I never was that happy working that way.

But I start with a text, and then I start designing a set, making little models, and collecting music at about the same time. I never really wrote, except in the very early years; I just continually was making notations, and then I look through all of that to find key phrases, sentences, tiny little exchanges of dialogue, that I think I can build a play around, looking for things to add, and illuminate it. But at that point, I'm also starting to think of what music I might choose. When I go into rehearsal, even though I start with text, I'm directing a lot of my focus to the music.

In doing this with John, did you follow some of the process where he had all the music well ahead of time?

Oh yeah, we ran into each other on the street maybe five years ago. He said, "Richard, what are you doing?" I said, "I'm doing this opera in California with a composer who I like," who shall remain nameless, and John said, "Oh. Why do you work with such terrible composers all the time?" [*laughs*]. And I said, "Well, John, why don't you write me something?" He said, "Oh, but I can't write for words, I can only write vocalese." I said, "Well, do me an opera in vocalese." "Really?" "OK." And then I would talk to him occasionally over a period of two years, and I would say, "John, where's my opera?" He'd say, "Oh yeah, yeah, I'll do something, I'll do something." . . . And one day he just called me up and said, "Richard guess what? I did it!" [*Laughs.*] "We're doing it at Royal Albert Hall as a concert." So then the record came out, he sent it to me, and I said, "Well, OK we'll do it." Period [*laughs*].

Originally I thought it was just going to be a little introductory ten minutes that I would use with some text of mine, plus some little sections from one of his other pieces, a string quartet piece. It didn't work, so I cut that. He didn't come to too many rehearsals; he came to an early rehearsal and he liked it, and said, "Why don't you interrupt?" I mean, he was encouraging me, like most composers do, to do much more, to interfere much more, and I don't like to do that. I feel I've got the music, I've got to deal with that. But he said, "Why don't you write little interludes between the acts, like you have at the beginning?" I put in a few phrases that were from his description of what he felt was going on in the opera that was on the album, and then one or two phrases that I added, but not much more, because when I do an opera or a musical I think the music's the thing.

You've directed several much more traditional operas. How is your approach to those different from your approach to this collaboration with John?

The collaboration with John is different since there aren't singers. We were originally going to use live musicians, but we had to bump it up a year and they weren't available. In a way, for me it was probably lucky, because then I had complete freedom; everything was on tape. When I'm working in a more classical opera, where the singers are singing, that's not as possible, because I have to worry about them being able to sing. I usually have a lot of extras who are doing all kinds of eccentric things in the background and are swirling around the singers. My tendency is to have the singers sing kind of straight, not doing a lot of gyrations and physical stuff. I want the audience to be able to listen to the music and not be watching events. So that's one of my primary concerns, and thankfully John said that in the finished version he saw he was able to hear many more things in the score than he had heard just listening to the music, which I take as a great compliment.

You have a long history with opera forms—you've done some librettos, and mentioned Gilbert and Sullivan as a very early influence. Is opera as important to you as theater?

No. When I did *Don Giovanni*—I mean, I've done the greatest opera, why should I do any others? [*laughs*]—the big thing for me with *Don Giovanni*, which was done at the Opera de Lille [in France], was I'd get ten ideas from one aria, and we'd do it and it's going good and then go—"Oh my God, she's still got to sing for five more minutes, what do I do now?" In my youth there was a period where I bought a lot of operas, listened to a lot of operas. I'm not a great fan of classic opera; some contemporary opera I find more interesting. But the problem is that I am so obsessed with working out my own program—for whatever it's worth, I'm a creator—so when I am subservient to music, and I can't alter it, or change it, make it shorter or longer, it's a bit of a frustration. But I learn from that; I don't regret having done any of that, but it's not the necessity that my own work is.

Since John used his kind of heavy metal sound, I was wondering how you saw this work in relation to what that you've termed your rock-and-roll plays, like

Penguin Touquet *[1981] and* Miss Universal Happiness *[1985].*

I termed them my rock-and-roll plays? [*Laughs.*]

In writing you did.

Well, again, the difference is that I have to follow the rules that the music articulates, and I can't . . . I mean, probably John would have allowed it, but I don't feel it's right, I don't think he'd like it if I'd taken it that far, if I took a fragment of it and made it a loop, then took another fragment and cut it out—that's what I do when I'm working by myself. I've got to confess, and John knows this, when I first heard the record, my first reaction was, "What the hell am I going to do with this?" I mean, all I hear is this loud noise [*laughs*], for forty-five minutes. But of course as we worked on it I got to understand it more and get into it, and appreciate what was really going on, and I think I can only do that when I'm working on it. So much music, so much contemporary music, even music I'm interested in, 'cause I buy a lot of stuff to listen to, when I hear it the first time I think, "Ugh, why did I get this, this isn't interesting." And then after I've heard it a second or third time I start understanding that I'm in this labyrinth where a lot of things are happening.

Is that where a lot of source material for the music in the other plays comes from now—CDs you buy?

Oh yeah. Used to be, when I was working in Paris, it was the heyday of the pirate radio station, and I would have my radio on all day, and whenever I'd hear some interesting stuff I would record it on cassette tapes and make loops out of it. I haven't done that in years;

sometimes I listen to WFMU, but I've gotten out of the habit, so now it mostly comes from stuff that I buy.

In some of the shows you'd have forty or fifty cassettes, which were all loops.

Oh yeah.

And you used to have a four-speaker sound system?

That was at one point in the early days. It was mostly for the dialogue; I'd have individual words of the dialogue coming from the four corners of the audience, so you're being surrounded by this circular weave of language. I never did anything like that with the music.

In 1988 you collaborated with Philip Glass on The Fall of the House of Usher *[1987], and you presented one of his early concerts and wrote about him and Michael Snow.*

Right. I don't collaborate too much with anybody: my ideal, when I started making theater, was I wanted to make theater like a painter paints paintings; I wanted to have everything funneled through me because I think that is always what's interesting about twentieth-century art. I've known Phil for years, and I just take it, and Phil's a very easy guy to work with, very hands-off. That early concert [in 1974], was, I think, the first concert of Phil and Steve Reich together, in the days when they would play together. Steve is much more, uh, demanding [*laughs*], shall we say, but Phil is very easygoing, so I would just stage it and he'd come in the last week just to see things and pay attention to the music. It was an interesting experience in that I got to do two totally different productions—the one in America [first at the American Repertory Theater in Cambridge, Massachusetts] was totally different from the one we did in Italy, at the Maggio Musicale [Festival] in Florence. The second was—I won't say more abstract, but it was more far out in a way, the first one was sort of beautiful, almost a combination romantic/art deco set, and the second one was in this big pink room, with many mirrors on the wall—it was just a wilder production, which Phil said, for that reason, he liked better.

Sophia=(Wisdom) Part 3: The Cliffs *[1972] is from the period where you've said you felt like you were aligned with Glass and Reich.*

Yes, originally we all felt together, all the minimalist-oriented artists, even though I shortly began to realize I wasn't so minimalist. I was basically still a romantic baroque artist, but minimalism was very important to me when I was a young man.

You can see ideas of augmentation, with people being added to the sets.

Yes.

*I was also thinking about a couple of times where you lean on the buzzer, and that made me think of La Monte [Young] [*laughs*].*

Oh absolutely, La Monte was another big influence on me, when I first heard him I thought it was the greatest thing I ever heard.

Did his heavy amplification have any effect on your decision to use microphones on the actors?

No, the decision to use microphones was mostly because I've always hated the sound of the official projected voice of the theater, and I like the sound of somebody talking more intimately.

There was something online for Wake Up Mr. Sleepy! Your Unconscious Mind Is Dead! *[2007] where one of the cast members asked you, "What type of music does your life reflect?" and you answered, "Stockhausen" [*laughs*]. Can you elaborate on that?*

For many years I was interested in all kinds of music, mainly so I could steal little loops from them. It could be anything from classical opera to jazz to whatever. In the early days I used to use a lot of '30s jazz slowed down; it seemed very lugubrious and strange. I've heard [Karlheinz] Stockhausen since I was very young also, but never really related to it that much. I don't remember why, but maybe six or eight years ago, maybe when I first started buying the operas, *Licht* [1977–2003], they really impressed me, and I may be one of the few people in the world who does my walking exercise every morning listening to *Licht* straight through [*laughs*]. I find it the most incredible contemporary music that I know of. There are other post-Stockhausen people that I'm kind of interested in. . . . It varies. I will get fascinated with a composer or a writer for anywhere from two days, where I'll think they're the greatest in the world, to a couple of months, through Stockhausen, Cage, and a few others, for a number of years.

Your plays have always reminded me of Morton Feldman. The way one would follow the plays, I feel, is similar to the way one would follow his scores.

You know, I didn't really appreciate Feldman, again, until a couple of years ago, and now I appreciate him a great deal; I also appreciate his writing a great deal. It was never a conscious influence, but certainly I can see the links, and I have great respect and appreciation for him. But I'm not a Feldman expert in the way that I'm sort of a Stockhausen expert.

Can you think of the composers you've used in the plays besides the collaborations?

Often, especially in the days in France when I used to take music from the radio, I wouldn't have any recollection of who they were. First of all, they'd be announced after they'd played twelve items, and they'd be talking French, and even though the names were recognizable my French wasn't that good. But I used to slow things down—I used to use Eddie Lang and Joe Venuti, the Blue Steele Orchestra, a very esoteric group—there was one cut that I used again and again and again, slowed down. I didn't use too much contemporary minimalist music, because it was too close, maybe, to what I was doing. . . . I would use such tiny fragments that you couldn't tell what they were from, and I always forgot, but it was certainly an eclectic mix. For one show I used a theme from Messiaen's *St. Francis* [*of Assisi*, 1983], and I usually tended to use music that was sort of low in register, had a certain melancholy, that would hit you in the solar plexus. That's one of the reasons I slowed it down.

I remember recognizing something in one of your plays as being Éliane Radigue.

She's somebody, again, that I only discovered a couple of years ago, but I just love her stuff, and as a matter of fact, I use *Trilogie de la Morte* [1985–93]—I'm making films now, and I've used films in my plays; we've been to nine countries, and what I do now is I ask for a boom box, and to get everybody in the proper mood I play Éliane Radigue until the time that I indicate to stop because somebody's going to say a line—so that's playing in the background, to get everybody sort of lifted off the ground. And it's amazing to me how some of the people hate it, saying, "Oh can't you turn off that horrible noise" [*laughs*]. But I love it.

Nowadays I just play Éliane Radigue in the apartment. In the old days I used to play two or three of my loops going at the same time [at home].

And you did that in some of the plays, also.

Yes, I like hearing the different rhythms fighting each other and everything always changing, a little like what Steve did in his early pieces, *It's Gonna Rain* [1965] or something, but that was the background music to my life, back then.

You've said that some of the use of music in '60s avant-garde films, particularly by Ron Rice, influenced you, and some of them use '30s songs. Jack Smith used—

Jack, Ron, I think maybe Ron uses Bartók, or something like that. The thing is, I hate the way music is used in almost every contemporary film; I think it just washes out, stops you from seeing. And what I've always tried to do with the music in my plays, especially lately—I am not interested in music that will take people deeper into what's happening. In the very early days, somebody saw one of my plays and said to me, "Oh Richard, I don't understand, you start this nice music and we all start going with it, and then you stop it, it's like you slap us in the face." And even back then I'd say, "Yeah, I want you to wake up, I want you not to get sucked in to where the music might take you." And more and more these days I use just fragments, and I'm influenced not only by Stockhausen but by this composer I like very much, Beat Furrer. I don't know if you know him, a Swiss-born composer who does what a lot of people do now, which is very slight noise with occasional interruptions of sound. What I like to do with the music these days is to suggest to people, just for a moment, that there could be music here—and it could take you in this direction—but of course, you want to stop that, before you *relax* into that direction. So it's a continual suggestion of the *possibility* of music.

Right, although on the DVD in the commentary you say you're using tools of the theater to make music.

Yes, yes—it's certainly a cliché to say so, but I think that I work in terms of an almost musical kind of form, rather than a theatrical form, because I've always . . . hated theater [*laughs*], for a *long* time. I don't like what the theater does, I don't like seeing theater, I just fell into the trap of making it, but I'm doing something else, I think.

What about your collaborations with Stanley Silverman, which are so different from those with other composers?

It's been a long time since we worked together, but I respected Stanley's music and liked it. It's very different from what I do in the theater, and I looked upon that as a challenge, simply because that wasn't the direction in which my aesthetic was taking me. But seeing whether I could use Stanley's very accessible, very sweet music, in a form that was more austere, mysterious, fragmentary, was, for me, an interesting problem. And Stanley, bless his heart, even though his music was very different from the thrust of my theater, was very open to, and appreciative of, what I was doing.

[Bertolt Brecht's] The Threepenny Opera *[1928] was also at the other end of the spectrum.*

I was enamored of Brecht for about thirty years, I'm not anymore. But when I heard the record of *Threepenny* I must have been fourteen years old. The original German record was what I first heard, and I thought, "This is another world, this is amazing, what is this?" So I got to do *Threepenny*, and a lot of my downtown friends thought I sort of sold out on the production [*laughs*], but of course I never liked it as much as [Brecht and Kurt Weill's 1930 *The Rise and Fall of the City of*] *Mahagonny*, which I suggested to Joe Papp after I'd done *Threepenny* and he said, "Well, it's not as good as *Threepenny*."

Many years later, after I'd done *Don Giovanni*, the same opera house in Lille asked me what I wanted to do; I said, "I want to do *Mahagonny*." They said, "OK." They set it up, and at that point Kate [Manheim, Foreman's wife] got very sick, and I said, "Sorry, I can't do it." They said, "OK, we'll wait for you." Four years later they called up and said, "Richard, how's Kate? You want to do *Mahagonny*?" I said, "Yeah." Everything was all set, I designed the set, all the singers were signed, I was signed, then there was some political turmoil in Lille: they cut off the funds for the opera house, so two months before I was supposed to go over and do it, it was canceled. All of the singers and I got paid our full salary, but we never did this production. It was all there, raring to go. Of all those people working in that kind of theater, I have the most respect for Kurt Weill.

You talked about going to see Martha Graham and how the music seemed to be really hitting the dancers.

Yeah, yeah, I thought that her dancing style, as opposed to other dancers that I'd seen, seemed to be her being attacked by the music, and her body responding to that attack.

Was that something you thought about in Astronome*, also?*

No, not consciously, no. My main focus was to provide some kind of staging—obviously it stops sometimes, and freezes, and you just listen to the music—but the rest of the time I do a staging that's a little bit off the beat of the music, so you're really conscious of what the music is doing, rather than using the music to support a particular stage action.

Glenn Branca

In a 1983 article for *DownBeat*, "The Electric Miles," Greg Tate noted parenthetically that guitarist Pete Cosey had told him he had "'thirty-two systems for tuning the instrument,' meaning Glenn Branca can sit down and Robert Fripp has got a lot of scales to go." This was the first time I had heard of Branca, and I would later see his name mentioned in articles about Sonic Youth and elsewhere. As someone who was interested in working within both the rock and experimental music worlds in New York, I noted Thurston Moore and Lee Ranaldo's simultaneous activity in both Sonic Youth and Branca's early massed-guitar ensembles, and its precedent in John Cale's dual membership in the Velvet Underground and La Monte Young's Theatre of Eternal Music (or the Dream Syndicate, as he and Tony Conrad referred to it). In 1985, I finally bought *The Ascension* (99 Records, 1981) and *Symphony No. 3 (Gloria)* (Neutral Records, 1983), two albums of Branca's music, and they became landmarks for me as an aspiring guitarist who was navigating the terrains of underground rock and different forms of twentieth-century composition. In the early '90s, I was playing in the indie band Love Child and with Rudolph Grey's electric free jazz trio the Blue Humans; Rudolph was a good friend of Glenn's, but I never met Glenn until he came to see Text of Light in the early 2000s.

Music promoter Adam Shore proposed that I do a public talk with Glenn as part of the Red Bull Music Academy Festival in May 2016. This is an edited transcript of that talk, which took place at the Red Bull Studios New York on Eighteenth Street. At the outset I told the audience, by way of introduction, that "for my money Glenn is the one person that I can think of who has made really convincing rock music and really convincing classical music, without coming off as a pretender in either one," and I stand by that. Glenn was extremely hoarse throughout the talk, apologizing that he was “practically yelling” despite the choked whisper coming out of his mouth. When he and his wife, Reg Bloor, arrived at Red Bull, he said he had lost his voice on the way over. Two years later, when I learned that he had died of throat cancer, I realized that he must have been ill then, although he didn’t admit it.

Early on, you were much more involved in theater, correct?

Yes, when I was very, very young. I started acting when I was eleven. I wanted to go to an acting school in New York, after I got out of high school, and my dad said, "No way, you've got to go to a school that gives a liberal arts degree." So I went to Emerson [College in Boston], which, at that time, was just about the best acting school that gave a liberal arts degree. I was very lucky—it was a great school, and I got to do a lot of acting. In fact, I did so much acting that I flunked out in my first year, but they let me come back a year later; that was very nice of them.

[Laughs.]

But I didn't give a shit about any of the other courses; all I wanted to do was act. I had a teacher who was my first real mentor, a guy named Dr. Tom Haas, and he was really brilliant. I had never seen anything like him before in my life. He was a true artist. He was a director, so I immediately changed my major to directing. I must have read hundreds and hundreds of plays, trying to find something that I wanted to direct. I mean, I directed a number of plays, but once I got out of school, I couldn't find anything I wanted to direct, because I would take these plays and do the wrong thing with them. I would make them into my own types of ideas. Which you're not supposed to do as a director; if anyone knows anything about theater, you go with the playwright and what the playwright wants. That didn't interest me, so I started writing my own plays.

But I was also a music lover—I was a record collector, I had everything, I listened to absolutely everything. The only kind of music that I didn't listen to was country and western. Nowadays, there's some of that old country and western that I think is really cool, but at the time, I hated the shit, especially because in Harrisburg [Pennsylvania], which is where I grew up, that's about all you could hear on the radio. I listened to music incessantly, although I never had *any* intention, whatso*ever*, of being a musician, although I could play the guitar.

And you had a cover band, in Harrisburg—

That's right, you've done your research. [*AL and audience laugh.*]

—which was arguably the first band to ever cover "In-A-Gadda-Da-Vida" by Iron Butterfly.

No, we covered the "Iron Butterfly Theme." They did a show in Lancaster, PA. Not "Lan-cast-er," "*Lan*caster" [*laughs*], in a gym, with the Jefferson Airplane. Our lead guitarist was actually able to memorize the piece just from hearing it. They also played "In-A-Gadda-Da-Vida," which knocked us out, and we did actually go backstage—well, there was no actual backstage, they were just standing around after the show, you know. I'm actually a very shy guy, I've always been—but we went up to them and said, "What was that song, 'In a Gobba Dagobba'?" And he actually told us, "We were so drunk at one rehearsal . . . we had written the song as 'In the Garden of Eden,' but we were so drunk that we sang 'In-A-Gadda-Da-Vida.'" That's one of my favorite stories [*audience laughs*], it goes way back to the '60s. We got the inside story on that fucking song. I mean, did anyone know that that song was actually called "In the Garden of Eden"? No, nobody even fuckin' knows that.

Until now.

Did you have anything else you wanted to ask me or are we done? [*AL and audience laugh.*]

Well, to follow up on the theater thing, I was curious as to how much that informed a lot of the work you do in music. Being a playwright who also directs their plays, and you're a composer who also conducts his own music and in some cases is also a performer in his own music, too.

OK. We're all the way back, into the distant past; most of you weren't even born. I was writing plays, but I was *obsessed* with music at the same time. And I wanted to start my own theater company. I met a guy in Boston—this was after I had gotten back from London and actually had one of my plays produced. It was kind of a Tom Stoppard/Richard Foreman thing. It was very funny; I think that play is still so funny today—I would produce it today but I don't get around to those things. But the point is, when I started the Bastard Theater in Boston I was collaborating with a friend of mine who also was obsessed with music: classical music, jazz music, rock music, everything—jazz fusion, that's what was going on at the time, in the early-to-mid- '70s. So we incorporated music into the productions. The plays were not conventional by any stretch of the imagination; there were no characters, there was no plot. In New York it probably would have been called performance art, but it really wasn't, because there were many, many theatrical elements. I was more interested in what would be called the mise-en-scène, everything *but* the actors and the plot. I loved lighting and sets and movement, every other aspect combined with music. So we both started writing music, and had the actors who were not musicians play instruments, and that's when I developed the idea of structured improvisation, from my point of view. I didn't know that such a thing even existed, at the time; but we had to do it, because these people weren't musicians. So in the mid-'70s I was kind of doing a John Zorn thing . . . ask me another question.

[Laughs.] *OK—although both of you are fans of Richard Foreman—it's interesting that two guys who are inspired by Richard Foreman can go off from that in such totally different directions.*

Yeah, I had never even heard of Richard Foreman when I wrote my first play. But as it turned out it was *very* similar. I had read about him, in the same way that I had read about Patti Smith and the whole punk scene. I was a *gigantic* fan of the Boston rock scene. There were *great* bands, but there was *no* audience. It was a college town; they went to see what was advertised in the papers. They didn't go to the clubs. And there were great—I guess you would call them proto-punk bands. I moved to New York in '76; I came here to do experimental theater, because this was the home of experimental theater. This is where you *had* to come. But I was a gigantic punk fan. I loved Patti Smith; I would even dress up like her sometimes [*audience laughs*]. No, really, with the white shirt and the black tie . . . I mean, I loved her, I must have listened to that album [*Horses* (Arista, 1975)] as loud as you could turn it up. And the Ramones, yeah, they were OK, but—

Had you seen the Modern Lovers in Boston?

No, but I had seen Jonathan Richman at a party playing songs on an acoustic guitar. I'd also seen him on the Cambridge Commons, this was during the hippie days, all the bands had hair down to here. Richman comes out, I don't know *how* he got this gig by himself, without a band, with his head totally shaved, playing the most obnoxious crap I've *ever* heard in my life. I mean, that guy had balls bigger than coconuts [*audience laughs*], I mean, really. But when the first Modern Lovers record finally came out, I thought it was a masterpiece, which of course everyone else does too . . . unless you're under fifty [*audience laughs*].

I saw an interview with you where you said that you had wanted to do a kind of "hallucinatory theater," where people would see things and not completely believe what they were seeing, and it struck me that a lot of the acoustic phenomena in your music contains the same idea, that that might have taken over from the original idea that you had in terms of theater.

Yeah, there's no question about that.

Do you think that Theoretical Girls or the Static were in some way a transition between doing the music in Bastard Theater and the symphonies?

No, it was not a transition—it was a bizarre thing. I had met this guy, Jeff Lohn, who was a genius, who was brilliant. He was doing visual art, he was a trained pianist, he would play for me in his loft. He would play this bizarre combination of Beethoven and the blues. I would just sit there—my mind was *blown*, this guy was such a fucking genius, and he was really funny. Because he'd be playing, and I'd be sitting there, and he would keep looking around at me, with this shit-eating grin on his face like, "Have you *ever* heard anything like this before?" No, I hadn't.

But the fact is, we were going to do *theater*. He

had a loft in SoHo; we were painting it black, we were getting it ready to do theater, and one day I decided I was going to start a rock band. Out of the blue—I just couldn't hold it back. And I started putting up posters, you know, looking for musicians to start a band. I didn't even have a guitar, other than this acoustic nylon-string guitar, but I was just going to do it. That's the way I've *always* done things, I just decide I'm going to do something and figure out a way of doing it. But Jeff saw one of the posters; he said, "Why didn't you ask me if I want to be in this band?" I said, "I know you *hate* rock music"—I didn't think he'd want to do it. Jeff says, "Of course I want to do it."

And this is the story: he had a friend named Dan Graham, one of the most brilliant and important artists of the twentieth century. A conceptual artist who went back to the '60s, but he loved rock music, especially punk. And when he found out Jeff and I were going to start a band, he said, "Well, I've got a gig at Franklin Furnace in three weeks, and if you're going to do a band, you can play on the bill with my performance art piece." So in three weeks, we somehow got ahold of all of the instruments that we needed, we wrote *all* of the songs from scratch—I didn't actually have any songs written—and we borrowed a drummer from another band. And the show was a *smash*. After that, we were invited to play everywhere, because Dan was so highly respected. The audience at Franklin Furnace were all really heavy-duty people, people who would become very, very famous in the '80s, although they were still young kids at the time. They loved us, *loved* us.

We had no choice but to keep doing it. What we said to each other was, "Yeah, we'll do this band for a while, and then we'll go back and do the theater." The problem was, the audience just got bigger and bigger and bigger, and there was a point at which we realized,

"We're on a stage, we're in front of an audience, *this* is our theater." That's what Theoretical Girls was—a band that only lasted for about eight months.

And after that was the Static, which Dan Graham had a lot to do with, too, in terms of getting you over to Europe.

Yeah.

And you were on one show with Einstürzende Neubauten, which was their first gig anywhere?

Yeah, you've really done your research. Neubauten . . . they were terrible [*audience laughs*]. We played at SO36 in Berlin—which is still there. This is not the kind of shit that happens in Manhattan [*audience laughs*]. We don't give a shit about our history in Manhattan. Paris was smart, they had their grand epoch and they retained a semblance of it, that's why it's the most popular tourist city in the world. We're just tearing it all down here . . . I mean, fuck it [*audience laughs*]. But the cool thing about Neubauten was they had a metal drum kit—the whole drum kit was made out of metal. That was the coolest thing I'd ever seen, because I was into instrument building at that time, and long before, with the Bastard Theater. They just couldn't play their instruments; it took them a year or so to figure out how to play. It doesn't take long, really [*audience laughs*]. I mean, *come on*.

After the Static you did "Instrumental for Six Guitars" [1979], which was the beginning of the multiple-guitar lineups.

No, you're *completely* wrong about that [*audience*

laughs]. There was a point at which I was doing the Static, Theoretical Girls, *and* the guitar instrumentals all at the same time. I would get invited to do gigs; I'd have ideas about things I wanted to do with the guitar that were outside of the realm of a traditional rock band, so I was kind of doing it all. But you're right—"Instrumental for Six Guitars" was the first one.

I'm going to skip ahead a little here, because people will know of Lesson No. 1 *[99 Records, 1980], and then* The Ascension, *which was with a four-guitar band,* Symphony No. 1 *[99 Records, 1980] and* Indeterminate Activity of Resultant Masses *[Atavistic, 2006], which was with ten guitars. . . . One of the things I found listening back to* Symphony No. 1 *was there were horns, which I don't think you used again until* Symphony No. 15 *[2010]. I was curious about how you got the idea to use horns on* Symphony No. 1 *and why you didn't use them again, because you weren't satisfied with them, or—*

I don't fucking remember [*audience laughs*], to be brutally honest.

*Fair enough [*laughs*]. It's also interesting to see how fast-moving your growth was at this point; you go from the* Ascension *band, which is four guitars, and by the second symphony you're already starting to build the adapted harpsichords and the mallet guitars, and* Symphony No. 3 *is moving even more in that direction; you're starting to compose around the harmonic series, and this is all within a couple of years—it's less than five years. It's sort of mind-boggling when you look back at it. Can you remember that period—did it feel like you were really on a roll, and things were coming one right after the other?*

I never imagined I would live this long [*audience laughs*]. You have no idea how hard I broke my ass doing all that stuff. I had all of these instruments built for *Symphony No. 3* at the Brooklyn Academy of Music, but I had gotten a commission from Vienna to write a new piece that they wanted two and a half months after that. And even the critics and the reviewers refused to believe that I wrote an entirely new symphony just two and a half months after the premiere of *Symphony No. 3*; they had the stinking audacity to say that I was just performing the same piece and calling it *Symphony No. 4*, which was utterly untrue. And will be proven when I finally get the recordings that were made of that piece on a CD or an MP3, or whatever. There were very few good recordings of it, but we did about twenty shows in fifteen cities all over Europe; it was never performed in New York. But it was an entirely different piece.

And basically, that's the way my life went, from there on—just one after the other after the other. And I was crazy enough to want to write for the orchestra. I had to learn staff notation; I wasn't a musician. I had never been trained, I had never gone to music school, but I deeply wanted to write for the orchestra because my music has always been about complexity and about different voices. With guitars, you have one single timbre, that's it; with the orchestra you have this tremendous variety of timbres. And I was still thinking of it the way I thought about theater, the way I would have thought about writing novels if that's what I had decided to do, or being a choreographer. I liked large groups playing or performing in complex situations. I can't even say that I regret deciding to write for the orchestra, because most people in New York thought that I had disappeared off the face of the earth. I was writing one orchestral piece after the other; I was getting tons of commissions. I was doing film soundtracks—well, I did *one* film soundtrack, for Peter Greenaway, who is not the sweetest guy in the world, as it turns out [*audience laughs*].

At the same time, you've been keeping your ensemble going and been writing guitar symphonies still, even while you've been doing the orchestral things—I think I saw you say somewhere that your career doesn't have periods, you do everything at the same time. You can't say, "This was when he was doing the guitars"—it's always gone back and forth.

I was just going to say that. In those days, everybody—musicians, visual artists, you name it—had *periods*. And I constantly had to deal with interviewers saying, "Well now you've moved on to a different period." And I constantly had to say, "No, I'm just doing it all. I'm doing whatever I feel like doing, or whatever I'm commissioned to do, at any given time." I haven't quit doing that stuff. I mean, the truth is, I haven't even quit doing theater; I've written a couple of pieces for chamber ensembles who both act and play their instruments at the same time. I still like to write plays, I've got part of a novel . . . but I have to go where the money is. I've got no choice, I've got to pay the rent. I live in fuckin' Manhattan, man—in fact, I just live down the street from here.

Something else I wanted to ask about was the Neutral record label, which you ran in the '80s.

Oh yes.

Which doesn't get discussed that much anymore, although—

Sonic. Youth.

[Laughs.] *Right, the first release on Neutral was the first Sonic Youth record, and an early Swans record, but also an album by Eric Bogosian, which is a really cool record, and the first Michael Gordon record, from Bang on a Can.*

I'm very proud of that one.

And there was a crazy box set by the artist Jack Goldstein of six ten-inch records called Planets *[1986]; it was sound effects from a sound library?*

The Jack Goldstein was not a Neutral record—he produced it himself, he made the package himself, and we distributed it. He went to the Lincoln Center Library, where you could buy—this is classic '80s neo-conceptualism—you could buy the copyright to pre-written music, pretty much garbage-y stuff that was used on television shows, and the stuff on his records was that kind of junk. He just bought the copyrights really cheap and released these *horrible* records. But the package was gorgeous, and Jack Goldstein was a tremendous artist—one of the major artists of that period. So it was fun to release that thing. I think I had an extra one left in my library and I sold it on eBay for a ton.

Yeah, it's quite a valuable record now. And before the label folded you were supposed to release a record by Phill Niblock and one by Charlemagne Palestine, do you remember that?

You remember that? [*AL and audience laugh.*] Jesus Christ . . . We actually paid to do the recording for the Charlemagne Palestine record and for the performance of it. And we had to fucking rent a goddamn Bösendorfer [piano] for it. But then we didn't have the money to release it. We were broke; all of the indie distributors were going out of business, and they were not paying their bills. We were owed something like twelve or fifteen thousand dollars in records that had been sold at the time; and in those days, that would have been more than enough to keep us going.

Phill Niblock produced his own record; he wouldn't have it any other way. Phill had never released a record and didn't want to, because his work was so much about the live sound. If you've ever heard Phill's stuff at his studio, he had a quadraphonic system and it was all very much about the harmonics that developed from the drone. He didn't feel this could be reproduced on a record. But I convinced him; I was determined. I mean, I knew what records could do for someone's career, and Phill deserved to be heard.

Part of our problem was that we had released Sonic Youth, Rat at Rat R, Swans, these really great New York bands, but I wanted to go in a New Music direction, and the distributors just were not interested in the stuff. I mean, it didn't sell. That's why I say that I'm proud that we got the Michael Gordon record out, because Michael is such a fine composer, right to this day. It's ironic that he's the one who hasn't won a Pulitzer Prize—his two buddies including his wife have won it [*laughs*], and as much as I like their music, Michael is my guy. He, in my mind, is right up there with Steve Reich and Phil Glass; he's a truly brilliant composer. As I said, I'm proud that I got to release his first record.

And the label you have now, Systems Neutralizers, that's what you released the Ascension *sequel [2010] on, yeah?*

Yeah. Well, it's kind of bad timing. People don't buy CDs anymore; *I* don't even buy CDs anymore. So I'm releasing—this is going to sound really funny—my new recordings with my old label, Atavistic, the label that I released many of my older records with, and [the label owner, Kurt Kellison, is] very happy to have me back. *Symphony No. 13*, by the way, is coming out on May 6, and it is *not* to be missed. It's a killer.

That's the one for one hundred guitars?

That's the first one for one hundred guitars. We got very lucky. We got a radio station recording and they really did a fantastic job on it. So it sounds as good as a studio recording. I'm really interested to see what people think of it, because I was trying to replicate—[*off-mic, to Reg Bloor*] What was I trying to replicate?

*[*Laughs.*] You mean the live sound?*

I was trying to replicate an orchestral sound with guitars. And I think if [Anton] Bruckner had been alive today he'd get off on it. [*Applause.*]

*Maybe so [*laughs*].*

Is that enough? What time is it?

*[*Laughs.*] I think we're OK, I've got a couple more things I want to ask you about that I don't think people have talked to you about so much. One was a collaboration you did with David Bowie and Tony Oursler, a gallery installation from 2001.*

It's not a very interesting story. Tony was doing video stuff for David, and then he asked David if he would come in and do this session on a piece that Tony was doing for the World's Fair in Germany. Tony had this gigantic idea about the piece from voices and images coming from all over the room, and Tony's text—he wrote the text—was brilliant. I think that's the reason David did it. Reg and I were at the session—my wife, the one lit up over there, that's my beautiful Reg—and David was *incredible*. This guy was a much, much better actor than anything anyone's seen from his videos or from the films he's done. I knew about acting; I wasn't just an actor when I was young, I was a *good* actor [*audience laughs*]. This guy *killed*. He could take this stuff and just turn it into something beautiful, incredible, intense, monstrous, gorgeous.

He, by the way, was something to meet; I've never met anyone like him before. He knew how to be a *star*; I've never met someone who knew how to present himself as a star. This was clearly very important to him, and when he walked into the studio—I'm looking at Reg because she was there too—he did like a ten-minute stand-up comedy routine, with impressions, the whole thing. We were so blown away. You realize all the music had already been recorded, so he was just dubbing over it, but when he came in . . . I should tell you one more thing about Bowie, since that is going to be of interest to *everyone*. First time I met Bowie, with Tony—I only ever met David twice, and he was just a great guy both times—but he had just put up his company on Wall Street; he went public and made fifty million dollars in one day. He was so excited, you wouldn't have believed it. I'm a book collector, and he was a book collector too, so we started talking about that, and he had told me that he had just bought a book that cost fifty thousand dollars. Wow. I don't know what that book was; I'm sorry I don't know what it was [*audience laughs*]. Fifty fucking thousand dollars, what was it, the Gutenberg Bible or something? And he was so excited about it. He even gave me a book that he had just finished reading, I don't even remember the name of it, but the funny thing was—and he was married to Iman at the time—it stank of whore perfume [*AL and audience laugh*]. I mean, for like, months. You can't tell me your wife wears perfume like this [*audience laughs*]. I didn't say anything to him about it. It wasn't the kind of book that I was interested in.

It wasn't cyberpunk?

I was *big* into cyberpunk. When I was involved with the harmonic series in the mid-'80s, I got into mathematics because I was trying to figure just what the hell this thing the harmonic series is, and I came across a book called *Infinity and the Mind* [1982], which was a brilliant book by a writer named Rudy Rucker. And it turned out this guy had written some science-fiction books, and I'm thinking this brilliant mathematician, who's talking about stuff that's *really* interesting to me, is also a science-fiction writer? I had never been into science fiction, even when I was a kid, except for Jules Verne. So I picked up his books and they were great, they were really funny, they were crazy, they used wicked language, they had stoners in them. So I started looking around for more books by him, and that's when I found out that he was one of the founding members of the cyberpunk movement. So I started reading everybody's books, and that's when I came across *Neuromancer* [1983] by William Gibson, and a lot of other books. So yeah, I got heavily, heavily into that scene at the time, and having a collector mentality, I kind of put together a list of all of the cyberpunk books, of which there weren't many, that were written from the early '80s through the early '90s. After that, cyberpunk had become just part of science fiction, and there were a lot of crappy cyberpunk TV shows.

The other thing I didn't know about before was a piece you did called In Perpetuity *[2002], which is for thirty guitars but it was played by all MTV employees? [*audience laughs.*] This is true.*

Yeah. I got good money for that [*audience laughs*].

I'll bet!

It took me a year to *squeeze* the money out of them. They were the cheapest bastards I have ever worked with [*audience laughs*]. But there were so many lawyers and accountants and secretaries who played the guitar and wanted to play my music. They had to pay me. I'm not cheap, by the way—I may be broke, but I ain't cheap.

How long a piece was it, like fifteen minutes?

Reg, how long was the piece?

Reg Bloor
Twenty minutes.

There's a video of it; they didn't do a bad job. It was not written in staff notation. Nowadays, everything's in staff notation because I want it to be exact. So everybody who's in this Red Bull piece is busting their fucking asses. [Arad] Evans, you're in it, right? Now, Evans is a member of my ensemble, but he's also going to be playing in the Red Bull piece. And you can imagine the difficulty these sons of bitches are having. Well, I mean they're great musicians, good rock musicians, but they're not used to reading staff notation. Believe me, I'm not putting them down, I respect them, all of them, they are doing their work and we've been working with them online now for weeks. And it's a lot of work, but I think they're going to get it, and if they do get it, it's going to sound *fantastic*. It's going to be beautiful.

Do you want to talk about the pieces you're going to play in this concert? It's Symphonies 8 *[1992],* 10 *[1997], and* 12 *[2000].*

Well, the *8* and *10* have already been released on record, so I don't know. Red Bull has told me that they want to record the *12* and maybe even release it; that hasn't been released yet, and that would be interesting. It's in a *fantastic* room, the [Manhattan] Masonic Temple, it's all marble, it's *really* resonant. And for this particular music, it's perfect. People always used to have me playing in churches, because the music would just resound, and it would sound like orchestras, choirs, brass ensembles, all at the same time. And in a room like this, they might get that sound. You know, that would be cool; I'd *love* to hear that sound again. It's been many years; they just don't let you play loud anymore.

Audience member

That was the Brooklyn Anchorage piece—that piece was loud.

That was a mistake. That piece was *not* supposed to be that loud. I'm not going to get into the reasons why, but it had nothing to do with me. It was the people at the Anchorage, [who] cranked it. But everybody loved it, they went nuts. But I can't play that loud anymore; if I play that loud in France I'd be arrested. Were you there for that one gig?

Audience member

Yeah.

No, it's hilarious—what's going on right now, especially in Europe, is electronica is basically what's happening as far as New Music is concerned. Now of course it's also happening in discos, but I'm talking about serious New Music. So every fucking club has subwoofers under the stage, even when we played at the Kitchen a couple of months ago. They had subwoofers underneath the audience. I can't use subwoofers; the bass drowns everything else out. All you get is drums. It's high-range sounds that pin the meter. So they can get away with cranking these subwoofers so they shake the fucking building. It's not my kind of sound; it's not what I'm into. I did electronica in the mid-'70s when I was in Boston, and I'm going to be releasing those tapes. I think they sound really cool, and if they want to play them through subwoofers that's fine with me. But that's not the kind of music I do. I write music, not sound. I'm interested in music. I'm interested in structure. I'm interested in complexity, not just shaking people's bodies. Which is cool, but I'm not into it, and I will *never* do it.

*All right [*laughs*]. I think we're good, right?*

[*Drops mic; audience laughs, applauds.*] All right, let's get the fuck out of here, man.

Rhys Chatham

I'd been a fan of Rhys Chatham since the mid-'80s, when I discovered his ferocious, multiple-guitar No Wave piece "Drastic Classicism" on *Antarctica: New Music From Antarctica, Vol. 1*, (Antarctica, 1982), an obscure compilation album, and his *Die Donnergötter* was a big record for me on its release by Dossier in 1987; I immediately connected its *Guitar Trio* (1977) with the loud guitar drone of Sonic Youth and the overtone music of La Monte Young and Arnold Dreyblatt. His mentions, in the liner notes, of Charlemagne Palestine, Maryanne Amacher, and Éliane Radigue being his early influences, alongside Tony Conrad, with whom I was already familiar, made me determined to investigate their music, as I was then trying to listen to the work of every minimalist composer who had ever lived. I was overjoyed when he asked me to be in a performance of *Guitar Trio* at ISSUE Project Room in 2006. Afterward, I told him that playing the piece—where each note of an E minor chord is introduced one by one and then the chord is played for an indeterminate amount of time—reminded me of watching Michael Snow's *Wavelength* [1967], in that once the structure of the work was revealed early on you could just enjoy watching it unfold; he said that was the greatest compliment he could imagine getting.

Rhys and I had another commonality: we had both worked in booking for New Music venues in New York—he was at the Kitchen in the '70s, and in fact had been their first music director, while I shared programming duties at Tonic with Melissa Caruso-Scott from early 2000 until the space closed in April 2007. I thought this would make for a good contribution to *BOMB* magazine, where artists interview each other, so I met up with Rhys at the office of artist Robert Longo in the summer of 2008, a few days after a major outdoor performance of "A Crimson Grail," his work for two hundred guitars, had been rained out. Rhys seemed unfazed, both during the rain and during our interview, where he smiled beatifically, just as he had the first time I encountered him at a rehearsal in La Monte Young's loft circa 1989.

The first thing I want to talk about is something that we both have in common: producing concerts in venues. You were the music director at the Kitchen two separate times, right?

Yup.

And I was doing the same thing at Tonic from 2000 until 2007. It's also interesting that a couple people you worked with, like Arthur Russell and John King, also—

—ended up being music directors there and programming there.

I wanted to talk to you a little about your experience of doing that, and compare our experiences in terms of the musical climate at the time—but also, being a composer, where you want to draw the line in terms of your identity.

Yeah, I know just what you mean. There were two very different periods when I was at the Kitchen—two very different situations. The first time I was there was between 1971 and '73. The Kitchen had just been founded by Woody and Steina Vasulka, who were video artists. I met them both in 1970. I was working with a choreographer named Daniel Nagrin. Every Saturday he would have improvisatory sessions involving his dance company, and I would play conga and flute. He'd invite different musicians. One weekend Woody and Steina came down and we got along very well, and they were *very* interested in electronic music. Woody had a Putney synthesizer and he was very interested in the Buchla synthesizer that I was working with in Morton Subotnick's studio at New York University, where I was going at the time. So I took the two of them down to the studio, we made friends, and they left me with a video recorder and said, "Why don't you put some electronic music on the film?" I couldn't *believe* they were leaving me with their video recorder—it was so trusting of them. So that's how we got to know each other. And then they started this place called the Kitchen. Originally it was a place for video artists to show their work, but they were very interested in music and wanted a music program there, so they asked me if I would organize a concert series there.

The scene back then was very much divided into uptown music and downtown music, uptown music being music in a postserialist vein—academic music, you could say, coming out of Elliott Carter, Charles Wuorinen, Milton Babbitt, composers like that. When people like Philip Glass and Steve Reich would try to play uptown it wasn't very easy. I believe Steve played *Four Organs* [1970] in a contemporary music program that [Pierre] Boulez was organizing and it wasn't well received at all. The music just wasn't liked, because of its tonal implications, because it was accessible, and for all kinds of reasons. So we needed a place to present this kind of music, coming more out of the Cage side of things, the Fluxus side of things. I was just a kid going to NYU, and I had no idea that there was such a need for a place to present this kind of music downtown. Initially, I just asked my friends to play—different people from NYU, like Laurie Spiegel and Serge Tcherepnin. I don't think Charlemagne [Palestine] played there until later, 'cause he had gone out to CalArts with Morton [Subotnick]. Tony Conrad was playing; we had Frederic Rzewski there, Tom Johnson, Maryanne Amacher, La Monte Young even. La Monte Young needed to pay his rent that month—

[Laughs.]

—and he wanted to sell his records. So he did a concert there where he played the record. A lot of people came and he sold a lot of records.

He just played the record?

He just played the record—that was the concert. He actually took the needle from the record player and put it on the record. So that was the feeling at the Kitchen between 1971 and '73. I became a very popular person.

[Laughs.]

No one knew who Rhys Chatham was in 1971, but then all of a sudden they knew who he was as music director of the Kitchen. I didn't have any problem balancing the programming and compositional activities I was doing, because at that time nothing was at stake. We had no funding, or very little funding, for the music program, so we gave the composers or the people who played there 100 percent of the door. I think it cost one dollar to get in. But still, it was a showcase for people's work. We had a nice grand piano, we had a PA system, and before you knew it, we were in the Sunday *Times*—the program really took off. We were doing things there every week. Whenever someone wanted to do something that was coming out of the right aesthetic, I didn't have to say no to anyone, and because of that I was very much loved in the downtown music scene as a programmer.

The situation, getting back to your question, from 1977 through 1980 was quite different, because the scene was different. In 1977, when I came back to the Kitchen, things had changed quite a bit. I had left in 1973 because I was tired. None of us made any money off this—we were doing it completely out of love and to make something happen. Of course, to present our own work but also to present the work of all our friends. But after you produce concert after concert for two years, and you're working for free and filling out grant applications, you get tired. And I won't say that Woody, Steina, and I were fed up—we were just tired and we needed to move on. So we gave the Kitchen to a person who worked at the Paula Cooper Gallery, an art administrator named Robert Sterns, and the music program went to Jim Burton. Robert was great because he took the Kitchen from being a completely underground institution to the next step up, a bit more professional, where we could pay all the artists. A composer would get a fee anywhere between $250, $500, $1,000, which back then was really, really good. All to say, we started getting funding, and the people who were programming started to get paid. The first music director was Jim Burton, then after that we had Arthur Russell, who was the programmer there, and was the first person to put a rock act in the Kitchen with the Talking Heads. I think he put Jonathan Richman in there also. I should say, just out of a point of interest, 1975 was an interesting time on the downtown music scene. Prior to that, most of the music at the Kitchen was coming out of Fluxus and John Cage. But then you had this whole crew of people come out from the West Coast—Arthur Russell, Peter Gordon, Jill Kroesen—and they were doing something *really* strange. Peter and Jill studied with Robert Ashley; they were doing music that was quote-unquote crazy, but at the same time they were doing rock pieces.

Right, songs.

Yeah, songs, or rock-influenced instrumental pieces. After I left the Kitchen I became a harpsichord tuner to make money during school. But then the digital tuner was invented in 1973 and it put me out of business, so I became a bartender at a bar called Sobossek's, which was by Phebe's and CBGB on the Bowery. I was roommates with Arthur and I programmed him at Sobossek's every week, and that's where he developed his songs. Arthur was this quote-unquote composer who went to Manhattan School of Music but was writing songs, or, with his piece *Instrumentals* [1974], using IIm7-V7-I7 progressions, in a way that we hadn't heard before. I thought that all this was completely perverse. I wasn't sure what I thought of it at all. I was a hard-core minimalist who had studied with La Monte Young and played in Tony Conrad's group. Eventually I played flute in Peter's orchestra, the Love of Life Orchestra, and, happily, I got won over.

I had never been to a rock concert in my entire life, and Peter took me to a show. He said, "Rhys, have you ever been to CBGB?" I said, "No." And he said, "Well, there's this good group playing tonight, you should really come and hear it." So I went; it was the Ramones. They had just put their album out, and I was completely blown away. I had never seen anything like it. And I thought, you know, "I might be playing one chord, and these guys are a lot more complex than what I'm doing—they're playing three chords." But I felt a relationship with what they were doing. The next day I asked my friend Scott Johnson if I could borrow his extra Telecaster. And after a month of *extremely* sore fingers I learned how to play barre chords, and that's how I got into playing guitar.

So by the time I became music director of the Kitchen in '77, the scene had changed completely. We had had an explosion of punk rock in New York. You had Patti Smith, Television, Richard Hell, and Talking Heads all playing at CBGB at that time. I can't begin to describe how exciting it was. Everyone in the art community, down in SoHo and in Tribeca, was taking note. At first, we were all going to CBGB and checking it out, and pretty soon, within a year, half the audience at CBGB was from the art world and the other half were in the bands. It was really, really great. What I wanted to do at the Kitchen was continue the tradition of programming music coming out of a classical tradition, coming out of Fluxus, coming out of Cage, but at the same time program the composers that were making rock-influenced pieces, like Laurie Anderson, Peter Gordon, Scott Johnson, people like that, along with people coming out of a rock context who were really trying to bend the parameters of rock. Like [Robert] Fripp with Frippertronics came down there to play. We had DNA there, not that they really needed a place to play, but just to show the relationship between this music, and that there was really no hierarchy—I mean, that this was composition also. Because back then you had this notion of music that came out of a classical tradition being at the top of a hierarchical pyramid, with jazz somewhere *underneath*. [*Speaks sarcastically:*] "I mean, all they're doing is *improvising*." And rock was barely considered music in the classical community. There was very much a feeling of breaking down these barriers, [all] of us being secret agents infiltrating another scene.

Even when Fripp played in the Kitchen there was a sense of transgression, or when Oliver Lake would play, coming out of the jazz community. This first happened with the music director before me, Garrett List—he really started this. Arthur very quietly had snuck in Jonathan Richman and David Byrne, but it was Garrett who really—if you don't mind, just to back up to this for a bit, Frederic Rzewski had come to New York in the early '70s with a group called Musica Elettronica Viva, which was an improvisatory orchestra of music coming out of a classical tradition, only to discover,

"Hey, you know, there were guys doing this a long time before us—people coming out of a jazz tradition, African American art music—and maybe we should be working with them." So Frederic started working with Anthony Braxton and with Karl Berger's Creative Music Studio. Garrett wanted to reflect that, and so he'd have Don Cherry playing at the Kitchen, the Art Ensemble of Chicago, Leo Smith. This caused quite a bit of tension in the downtown art community, 'cause they said, "Hey, these guys already have a place to play. They can play at Studio Rivbea, there's already a jazz loft scene in the East Village. We don't have that many places to play—you shouldn't be programming stuff like this here." But Garrett put his foot down. He wanted to make a point of where the improvisatory influences were coming from. So when I came to the Kitchen, I wanted to do the same thing, except with rock.

All this really sets the stage for where Tonic came into the picture, ten years ago. I mean, obviously by the time that happened the Knitting Factory had been going for ten years. It started off trying to strike a balance between experimental music and free jazz and rock, like underground rock, or indie rock, and had sort of drifted away from that. And then in the '90s there was also a place called the Cooler, which was doing sort of the same thing—

—with a focus on electronica. Because that was big back then.

Yeah, that was big. But they were also doing a Monday night series, and that would always be free admission, and that's when they had probably the more interesting—

People like Ben Neill.

*Yeah, but also there would also be experimental rock stuff, and so on and so forth. They would do some of that on the weekends, too. But it was a different feeling than Tonic. Tonic really had the feeling of the late '90s. I think part of it was even the internet boom, and this sort of wide-open feeling that anything was possible. Maybe because so many people had become their own entrepreneurs, starting their own websites and stuff like that, there was a real feeling of self-empowerment, and that was something that kind of came across at Tonic. When [John] Zorn found out about it, he booked a month of shows there. He convinced them to do this with rotating curators—a different musician would book the club for the full month every month, which is what he does now at the Stone. That lasted for a couple of years at Tonic, and it just became hard to support financially, because Tonic was not a nonprofit, and that was sort of the interesting thing about it: it was a venue that was supposed to turn a profit [*laughs*] but operated like a nonprofit venue in terms of the programming.*

Zorn didn't own that club?

No.

Our perception of Tonic in Europe, or at least for me when I started hearing about it, was a place like the Kitchen, where there was interesting music that couldn't happen in other places, or wouldn't be likely to happen, and it would get exposure and really represented the music of now.

It was actually a common perception that Zorn owned the club, or that it was his club somehow, and in fact, when I took over booking it, it took a lot of convincing on my part to get more rock-based music in there, because a lot of times booking agents thought that it was way off the usual beaten path of clubs to play in New York.

When did you start curating there?

I started in 2000.

And did you have a certain vision for the kind of music you wanted to put in there?

There was already a template in place there—what was interesting was that Sunday night was considered songwriter night, and then the rest of the week was given over to whoever was curating that month, usually experimental music. I thought that Friday and Saturday night we should probably have someone in there who was going to be more of a draw. When I got there, I wasn't sure how much that would be a factor—booking people that would keep the club going financially. It turned out that it actually was something that they were concerned with, but they still kept the rotating curator system in place for another couple of years.

Who is "they"?

It was a couple, John and Melissa Scott.

So it really sounds like a parallel to what the Kitchen was trying to do in the '70s in relation to this dichotomy between uptown and downtown music. People needed a place to play. During a certain period the Knitting Factory was providing that, but then it got bigger and bigger and bigger, so Tonic provided an outlet for more experimental music.

I think there was more of a sense of competition, though. It was actually a little more free-market than what you're describing, because the Cooler and the Knitting Factory still existed when Tonic was started. There was a little more trying to do it better, or different in some way, than those places.

And also, don't forget that the more places we can have, the better.

Yeah, of course.

Because it means that musicians can play more. How did you come to work there?

I performed there with Will Oldham, who goes under the name Bonnie "Prince" Billy, and I think the way I met John and Melissa was playing a show with Will—it was a Halloween show. I talked to them about programming the Sunday night series, doing a month, and getting different people—and again, it was my friends—to play, but it was like Thurston Moore and Dredd Foole.

You had very nice friends.

Yeah! Then I also proposed doing film series there with Will, and both these series did pretty well. And I knew the guy who was sort of helping Melissa book the club, Chris Corsano. I heard that Chris was leaving the job and I basically proposed myself to replace him. They were receptive to the idea. That's when I took over.

Getting to the second half of the original question, it was great because I did meet a lot of people through working there, and then ultimately played with some of them. I was always a little conscious that people might only associate me with being "the guy at Tonic." I mean, I had ten years' worth of recordings and live concerts in New York under my belt before I ever started working for Tonic, so a number of people already were familiar with me from that. During the time I was still working there, people would interview me—I would never really bring up the subject of being the booking agent there.

It's difficult being a programmer and being a composer/performer at the same time. I'd be having breakfast right by the Kitchen and people would come in and say, "Why didn't you give me a gig this year at the Kitchen?" They'd ruin my breakfast.

Jill Kroesen even wrote a song about it with me, 'cause she was with me one time when it happened. When I was at the Kitchen for the first two years it wasn't a problem, because I didn't have to say no to anyone. But when I came back, there was a limited number of spaces available—we could only do two or three concerts per month. Eventually I solved things by saying, "OK, if you play at the Kitchen one year, the next year, you aren't playing there so we can give everyone a chance." But as more and more people knew about it, more and more people all over the world wanted to perform there—man, I was never in so much trouble in all my life. And it's true one's name gets associated with it. If I did an interview as a composer with John Rockwell or someone like that, I would be, like you, very careful not to make mention of the venue where I worked, but of course, in the review they would always say, "Rhys Chatham, music director of the Kitchen, couldn't stand straight at his gig last night at Max's Kansas City." [*AL laughs.*]

We did a wonderful, wonderful performance of *Guitar Trio*, and I had had a little bit too much to drink that night, perhaps, but in the review, John

Rockwell wrote: "Not everyone was at his or her best. Mr. Chatham, for instance, who is music director of the Kitchen, seemed to be having considerable trouble just maintaining a vertical position." It was really funny, I thought. Mind you, the executive director of the Kitchen didn't think it was funny. But I'm sure you've had things like that happen too. These were issues that came up, but we learn how to deal with them. What's your experience been? You seem to be continuing to play.

Sort of like you were saying, I was paid to work there, but I wasn't making a whole lot of money. The whole time I really had to be doing concerts, recording records, writing, and so on.

Yeah, like everyone else.

When Tonic was closing, people asked me what I was planning to do. I said, "I'll just be working twenty hours a day instead of twenty-four hours a day," 'cause I used to work at Tonic five days a week, four hours a day, just in the afternoons. The thing that's the real loss is just having a kind of home base in terms of a place to play, because I had also kept my amp there as the house amp, and it made things very easy. If someone was coming to town, I could easily set up a gig for them. If it was someone I was already friendly with and playing with, then we could do a gig there. This actually would happen at the Cooler quite a lot, too. Things would tend to happen a lot more spontaneously. You could do things almost at the last minute. Sometimes, especially at the Cooler, someone would be hanging out backstage, and the next thing you knew they were up onstage doing some sort of improvisation. I don't think you really have that as much now with places like ISSUE Project Room, which is still great, but they're booked much more in advance, I think, than we would tend to book at Tonic. I mean, there were certain weeks at Tonic where I had to get the ad in at the end of the day on Monday and I still didn't know who was playing that Friday.

It's great when you have that. We didn't have that kind of spontaneity at the Kitchen—we booked things a year in advance.

Yeah, a lot of it was very much seat-of-your-pants. Things would get canceled and then you would have to scramble to find something else.

The days that I spent at the Kitchen were absolutely marvelous. I mean, there were all kinds of pressures, as you said, being a producer—but having contact with people, being able to play with them, seeing all that work, was just marvelous. But, I have to say, after I finished doing it, I was very happy to get back more into my own work. I'm sure you've had the same experience.

To some extent, I feel the same way. The day I got the news that Tonic was closing up shop was the same day I got the galleys for my book Sound Art: Beyond Music, Between Categories *[2007]. I got home and I was like, "Well, I'm out of a job, but I just wrote this three-hundred-page art book." So that almost took the place of it. Now, instead of people saying, "How's Tonic going?" they say, "How's your book doing?"*

How does that feel?

Well, it's good to have both experiences. I think something that drew both of us to take on these positions was, basically, standing up as a member of the downtown music community—

That's what it was for me. It was something that fell into my lap. But the other thing I have to say, and I think it might be true of you, too, is that I was a real fan of this work. I *loved* Philip Glass and Steve Reich, and had heard the entire development of [Glass's] *Music in Twelve Parts* [1971–74] and the original performance of [Reich's] *Drumming* [1970–71]. So I was quite pleased to be putting these people on, and then when the people who performed at the Kitchen started to be my own age, I began playing in their bands. I met Tony Conrad by offering him a gig at the Kitchen, and he said, "Oh, by the way, I need a player." That's how I joined his band. I made a lot of good contacts while I was there.

Yeah. I mean that's how I got to play really with Arto [Lindsay]—there were a couple of gigs I did at Tonic with Arto and Ikue Mori. It was not quite DNA, but we improvised things, and that would likely not have happened if I hadn't been in the position I was in. I wanted to talk to you a bit about No Wave, since I know you're in a couple of these recent histories that have come out [such as No Wave *by Marc Masters (2007) and* No Wave: Post-Punk. Underground. New York 1976–1980 *by Byron Coley and Thurston Moore (2008)]. I was wondering what your whole take on that scene was at the time, because that's not something I think you really go into in any of those books. What did you make of DNA and Teenage Jesus, and did you really see the bands you were playing in as fitting in with those groups?*

I think I saw the second gig that Teenage Jesus and the Jerks did, when James Chance was still in the band. And either the first or second gig that Arto did with DNA, when Robin [Crutchfield] was still in the band. What was interesting and what was amazing to me about the No Wave bands is that they were incorporating elements that we normally associate with a classical tradition. In the Contortions, James Nares was playing tone clusters—OK, tone clusters, we think of Henry Cowell. Or Lydia [Lunch] playing this completely out-of-tune guitar, and Arto in DNA incorporating all these elements of noise in a way that wasn't intellectual. These No Wave groups weren't making a big deal of it, but they were putting all kinds of things in the sound palette of rock that we didn't normally associate with rock, and yet it was still rock. That was what was amazing to me—that we had this intersection of formal concerns from people coming out of a rock tradition, people coming out of a jazz tradition, and people coming out of a classical music tradition. Somehow, for that brief period, they intersected so that even though our backgrounds were radically different, we found ourselves playing in the same spaces, talking to each other, and it not being a foreign language. I was, like, a hard-core minimalist, and yet there I was playing *Guitar Trio* in the same space as Arto Lindsay with DNA, and it felt completely right.

Did you have any relationship to rock music before the Ramones concert?

My father's a harpsichordist, and so we had early music in the house, and of course I knew who the Rolling Stones were and the Beatles, but as I was growing up I was a flute player. I wanted to play drums, but I grew up in New York City in a small apartment, so my parents said, "Rhys, drums are great, but there is *a much* larger repertory on flute." And I was so stupid, I listened to them. I became a flutist and became a fan of contemporary music. I was out buying John Cage records when I was fifteen, the way another kid might be buying some arcane rock record. And so I didn't know anything about rock until I was twenty-five, and as I said, I went to that first concert that Peter Gordon took me to. I was deeply influenced by La Monte, Steve, and Philip, and I needed to find my own voice. So I said to myself: "OK, Philip can use jazz instrumentation in his work, saxophones and things like that; Steve can use African music coming out of Ghana in his. Maybe this thing with rock would work for me."

I wanted to see if I could use rock instrumentation with the minimalism thing I was doing. Except this whole issue came up after I started trying to do that—it was called "posing." Because, already back then, there was talk about people coming from the art community into the rock community and doing this bullshit stuff, so I decided I wasn't ready to make a composition, initially. I joined someone else's group—it was a group called Arsenal with this guy named Charlie [Nash] in it. I was just the guitarist and spent a year doing that. It was only until I had experience playing on the rock scene that I decided to make a piece in the genre of rock. And another reason this is important, Alan, is 'cause in coming out of a classical context, you could do whatever you wanted. I mean, we had pieces coming out of Fluxus, La Monte Young's pieces to feed a piano a bale of hay, let a butterfly out of a jar. I mean, if you can call that music, then of course I could go into a place like the Kitchen and play a rock-influenced piece, and it would be accepted in that community. But what I really wanted to do was see if I could take this music and play it at CBGB, and Max's, and be accepted there, 'cause back then, even if the audience liked you they would throw beer bottles at you, with the beer still in the bottles—and that's if they *liked* you, so you can imagine what they would think if they didn't like you. The first time we performed *Guitar Trio* at Max's, I was nervous. I wasn't even calling myself a rock musician then, 'cause I had too much respect for the form. I said, "It's a representation," like Robert

Longo was doing representations of images. I was doing a representation of a rock band, although I was using rock musicians and rock instrumentation. So we played it at Max's and people came back to the soundboard and said, "Where are you hiding the singers?"

Oh, 'cause they were hearing the overtones.

Yeah, they were hearing the overtones. So it worked out at Max's, and then I knew I was OK.

That's actually an interesting difference between what you and Glenn Branca were doing at that time, and what later people like Bang on a Can were doing, who did not really try to put this into a rock milieu per se. A lot of their stuff has very explicit references to rock, or they're sort of adapting some kind of rock song or album into a classical piece, but it's not really aimed at the rock scene itself.

Yeah. I went directly into the rock scene. And at the time I was thinking of myself as like a secret agent working in a rock context. But these days, I am more like the spy that came out of the cold, because I've played more in rock clubs at this point in my life than I have in a classical context.

You were talking about hard-core minimalism, and at a certain point people began to suspect that this could be appealing to a rock audience, but I don't think any of those composers had rock bands, or any history of being influenced by rock music. I remember talking to Arnold Dreyblatt about it and he didn't seem to have any. I don't think Charlemagne did either.

Charlemagne listened to rock, but he didn't play rock.

There were other rock bands who had kind of an avant-garde classical influence. Were you aware of the Velvet Underground or even "Baba O'Riley," the Who song that name-checks Terry Riley?

As a teenager I'd heard and liked the Velvet Underground, but it wasn't until later that I understood how close John Cale was to this whole tradition. John Cale played with La Monte in the Theatre of Eternal Music; I was a member of that group, but that was later. Tony, of course, when I played in his band, played me some of those early tapes, and all I can say is, from what I hear from Tony Conrad and Henry Flynt, John Cale was wailing away on low E-strings for hours and hours ten years before I was.

Did you know about Tony playing with Faust and—

I was really jealous of that, and a little bit pissed off, because—and you can quote me on that—

*[*Laughs.*]*

—because we had developed a music as a trio, with Tony, Laurie Spiegel, and myself, and played out. Then Tony went on tour and a record of that music came and we were so sad, because—

Oh, that's true, because the first side of the Outside

the Dream Syndicate *album [Caroline, 1973] does sound like* Ten Years Alive on the Infinite Plain.[1]

Exactly. But I got over being jealous really, really quickly. Because I liked what they were doing so much, and I still listen to the album with great pleasure.

I wanted to talk also about composition and improvisation and notation and non-notation, 'cause I know you've said that from '71 to '81 you did non-notated music.

Mm-hmm.

And you did notate afterward, and I know you've worked in situations that are improvised—

—completely improvisatory, yeah.

And even within some of your compositions I think there's room for improv—

Guitar Trio, for example.

Exactly. I also played in the 77 Boa Drum performance that the Boredoms organized a year ago. And it immediately reminded me of playing in Guitar Trio, *because even though everyone's sort of playing the same thing, you can really put your personal stamp on whatever it is that you're doing. And there's a whole kind of support system of people, everyone kind of working together but at the same time, doing their own sort of take*

1 A Conrad piece developed and performed with Chatham and Spiegel at the Kitchen in 1972.

on it, not copying what the next person is doing, but sort of—

—counterpointing it.

Exactly. I know you've studied with La Monte, who has quite a lot of improvisation within composed pieces. Can you talk a little bit about where you see composition and improvisation at this point?

I trained initially as a classical flutist and keyboard player, and I studied composition, first with Morton Subotnick, who made me do a lot of counterpoint. But then I started playing saxophone at twenty 'cause I got sick of flute—it wasn't loud enough. The reason I really picked flute was so I could sit with all the girls in the orchestra section, and that worked out fine, but by the time you're nineteen you want something a little louder. The fingering between flute and the saxophone is very similar, so I started studying with this guy Keshavan Maslak, who's a horn player in the jazz tradition, and free jazz was at its height back then, so I started going to all of his concerts at Studio Rivbea—was deeply influenced by it. But then Patti Smith and the Ramones came on the scene, so I got rid of my saxophone and took up a guitar, and jazz went out the window until 1983, when I wrote a piece called *For Brass*—George Lewis was the one who did the contracting and got these incredible players including Olu Dara. And I thought, "Wow, trumpet seems like a really cool instrument. I'm losing my hearing playing guitar, so maybe I do some woodshedding and start playing trumpet." So that's what I did. First I studied with a classical player, but then I said, "Why should I do that?" I've already studied that kind of tradition and I can't really improvise over standard chord changes, so this would be a good time, while nobody's looking, to learn how to do that, so I learned how to play trumpet and I learned everything that a jazz musician is supposed to know, like how to play the blues at any tempo in any scale, all my majors, all my minors, playing over 2-5-1 progressions in any tempo and everything like that. But I never played standard jazz. When the electronica came out, I kept all my rock-and-roll modules and put my trumpet through distortion devices.

To answer your question directly and succinctly, in the piece *For Brass* we had an incredible drummer on that, Anton Fier, and I asked him to play a 120-bar solo. First I asked him to play a forty-eight-bar solo. He said, "Cool," I said, "No. Wait. Change that. 120." He said, "Oh no!" But he came up with something that sounded a little bit like marching band music, with his use of the toms, and I thought that sounded really tough. So later, for a piece that we did at Lincoln Center, at Alice Tully Hall, I asked Anton and a drummer named James Lo to improvise that kind of music in the context of a brass piece I'd written, and it sounded kinda wimpy. It didn't sound good at all. So I realized that there's some music that you can only get through improvisation—that's the only way you can get there—and there's another kind of music, the only way you can get there is notation.

With a piece like *Guitar Trio*, if I had written those things out with specific notes for everyone to play, it would sound stiff, it would sound terrible. If, in the context of *For Brass*, I wrote out all the solos, it wouldn't sound good—but with other music, if you're writing like Phil Glass or someone like that, you could improvise it but it wouldn't sound the same.

Both kinds of music have really strict formal and compositional concerns that have to be thought about, whether it's improvised or whether it's written out, but they're to be used for different purposes, and it's good to know how to do both.

That sort of leads into the idea of composer as performer. You were saying that you were a real fan of Phil Glass and Steve Reich.

And Terry Riley.

Were those your models in terms of thinking of yourself as a kind of a composer/performer?

My first model was Charlemagne Palestine because I knew him since I was sixteen years old. He was twenty-three or something like that. He was a friend of my father's, and I thought, "He's crazy, but great." Philip lived in the same building as me, on East Sixth Street. So he became like an uncle figure, and I just wanted to be like those guys, like Steve, like Philip, La Monte, Charlemagne, and Terry.

Terry was a big, big inspiration, because he's such a good musician, playing all by himself and just going on all night with those organ pieces. That's how I got away from postserialism. Before, I was a serialist composer wanting to be just like Pierre Boulez or Charles Wuorinen, and there was this series at a place called the Electric Circus in the East Village on Saint Mark's Place in the late '60s. Thais Latham was the programmer. I had read a book called *An Anthology* [1963] edited by La Monte and Jackson Mac Low, and I saw this score that looked a little bit like [John Cage's 1965] *Variations V* that Terry Riley had written. I thought, "Wow, noise, this is going to be great." So I went to the concert and there was this weird, long-haired, redheaded guy playing circus organ. The music was tonal, and tonal was not hip back then, if you were a young composer, so I asked for my money back.

[Laughs.]

And they wouldn't give it to me, so I said, "OK." It was five dollars, which was a lot of money, so I went and listened to it. By the time I got out, it changed my life. That's when I became a minimalist.

I was actually just looking at a film of a performance of Variations VII *[1966/1972] the other night that the E.A.T. organized—Billy Klüver and Robert Rauschenberg and all that stuff. David Tudor was performing in it, David Behrman, and I think three other people. They're all kind of puttering around in their shirts and ties and short cropped hair, but the music is noise, like you would hear now at the No Fun festival, or anything that is more geared to kids coming out of listening to rock. What occurred to me was, if this piece had been performed by guys with long hair and paisley shirts, or something like that, there might have been even more of a kind of crossover between the rock audience and the avant-garde classical world at the time. The crossover might have happened ten years earlier than it did, in the mid-to-late '70s. Even for myself, growing up, I think when I would see pictures of Terry Riley in a book about avant-garde music, they were not quite as attractive to me as photos of Jimi Hendrix or somebody like that, and Terry is one example of somebody who was a little more palatable to a counterculture kind of audience, maybe because the music was tonal, too.*

It was more tonal. People perhaps weren't ready for noise back then.

Right. Although, when the Beatles did "Revolution 9," or Frank Zappa was doing things that—

Or *Metal Machine Music* [Lou Reed; RCA, 1975].

Yeah, right. Which is later, but even in the late '60s, there was a certain amount of appropriation of that within the rock world.

And Musica Elettronica Viva did quite well in Europe, and they were more palatable in terms of their look. I'll just come out and say it: they looked like hippies.

*[*Laughs.*] Right.*

I'd never thought of that as a factor—you might be right.

Until the spate of releases on Table of the Elements in 2006, you hadn't really released that many records. There was Die Donnergötter *and* Factor X *[Moers Music, 1983]. What was your attitude toward commercial recordings of your work?*

In the '80s I wasn't really interested in it. I was primarily interested in live performance. And then I realized that this wasn't a very good attitude, because if you don't put out recordings, you don't tour as much. So I got more interested in recordings later.

In the '70s, even when you were playing in the bands, was there any idea of doing a single or whatever?

Oh, in the '70s I think what happened is that I came out of this contemporary music mentality that it was very, very difficult for us to sell records, and why even bother? The only record label that would have been open to me at the time was Lovely Music, which was expensive in that it was self-financed, and it wasn't until I got more and more firmly into rock that I realized,

"Oh, you know, there are people who'd be happy to put this out and even give me an advance." I think it wasn't until I was thirty-two that I realized that.

Did you feel that a recording wouldn't do justice to what you were doing? Because that's something that La Monte and Maryanne [Amacher] were very resistant to—they felt that the recording wouldn't really capture everything that was going on in the music. And I think that's something that Branca's also said—people often say that recordings don't really capture the sound of his concerts.

No. Glenn and I have discussed this. He complains all the time with his hundred-electric-guitar piece that it doesn't sound like what it is in performance, and he said, "By the way, neither does yours."

*[*Laughs.*]*

And he's right. I realized after the recording of *Die Donnergötter*, which I'm very happy with—it's not the same as experiencing it at ABC No Rio, or in a club with a really great PA system. It's the difference between live music and recorded music. In the '70s, I wasn't worried about recording, 'cause I didn't think I could get the sound I wanted. Maryanne was always saying to me, "Maybe when digital comes out, we'll be able to get the sound we like." So I just never concerned myself with that issue. But after *Die Donnergötter* I realized that it was possible to at least get a representation of the sound, and then if people wanted to hear it live, they could hear it live.

It's almost like the performance is happening

without you being there, and I think that's what a lot of people are kind of reluctant to let go of.

Yeah, it's really nerve-racking at the mix. Then it doesn't sound the way that you want it to sound, and then it gets released. *A Crimson Grail* [Table of Elements, 2006]—the recording, I can barely listen to it because I know what the real sound is. But I'm glad it's out.

The thing you sort of have to get your head around is that there's so few people that have the same perspective on it. To someone who's just listening to it on their stereo, it may sound fine.

In a way of summing up, you've gone through so many phases in terms of composition: Tom Johnson talks about you doing very soft electronic music originally in the early '70s, and then you moved on to the loud guitar stuff, and then the pieces for horns, the martial drumming, and then back to guitar—and then the stuff in the '90s with electronica. What do you see as the through line between all these different phases of writing?

I like a lot of different kinds of music and I've always considered it really important not to get stuck in one particular kind. If there's a line that goes through it, I'd say it's my background as a minimalist. And funnily enough, studying with Pandit Pran Nath, I think, has deeply influenced my voice on trumpet and also my voice as a composer. You can always hear that modal thing going on, whether I'm playing trumpet, or whether I'm in a group like Essentialist.

In the early days, I'd just take one sound and just keep it going basically, like in the piece *Two Gongs* [1971]. After that, my concern was primarily with harmony, with vertical things, as in *Guitar Trio*. But then, with trumpet I was forced to approach melody, and that was a really difficult thing for me, because before I was primarily doing it with chords, so that was a ten-year exploration, and my other big influence on that was Don Cherry. My trumpet music's completely coming out of Don Cherry meets Pandit Pran Nath. And in fact Don Cherry did meet Pandit Pran Nath. Don was part of that La Monte Young scene. He and La Monte were close because—

Oh right, 'cause La Monte was playing with Billy Higgins and all those people in California—even before they played with Ornette [Coleman], I think, or slightly before, or roughly around the same time. Had you ever talked to Jon Hassell about Pran Nath?

In the early '70s, Jon and I hung out a lot together and we played in the Theatre of Eternal Music together, and you can believe when I was first playing trumpet that I listened very carefully to what Don Cherry was playing and very carefully to what Jon Hassell was playing. When *Neon* [Ntone, 1997] came out, of course I sent a copy right away to Jon—and I was so happy: he said, "Oh, very good, Rhys." He was like a mentor figure.

In a way, to even go back to the beginning of this talk, in terms of curating the Kitchen, there seems to be a common denominator of trying to break down barriers between different genres of music. Even if you're working in areas that emphasize chords or melody, there's an idea of not thinking about the category as much as the essential components that these genres may share in terms of the basic musical ingredients.

Don't you think there's more and more of that happening now? If we were trying to tear the walls down between the various communities coming out of rock, jazz, and music from a classical tradition, there's more of a sense of building up the walls again in the sense of defining what the formal concerns are in each. But there's more of a freedom to borrow from each other than there might have been before.

Phill Niblock

I first visited Phill Niblock's Chinatown loft in December 1993; I had gone to see Éliane Radigue as part of the Experimental Intermedia concert series Niblock hosted there. I introduced myself to Phill, mentioning the "Minimalism Update" article he was in that I had co-authored for *Option* a couple of years earlier.[1] Later, when Jim O'Rourke recommended to Phill that I join in a performance of his 1996 EBow guitar piece "Guitar Too, for Four," I got to know Phill a bit better, and I eventually played on the "massed" version of it Jim released on his Moikai label in 2002. I began attending the remarkably convivial gigs at Phill's loft more regularly. Every December 21, Phill hosts a winter solstice concert where he plays six hours of his drone music and films—it is one of the most powerful experiences of music and visuals that one can have, and I feel fortunate to have been able to experience it year after year, for two decades.

In 2010, Yvan Etienne asked me to write an essay about Phill as a filmmaker for the book he was editing for Les Presses du Reel, published with two DVDs as *Phill Niblock: Working Title* in 2013. This was a great subject to discuss with Phill, as it's an aspect of his output that has received virtually no critical notice or discussion. Despite my background in film studies and distribution, I had never really talked to him about filmmaking in any detail. Before making the trip to Chinatown on January 12, I dutifully watched his six early short films and his series *The Movement of People Working* (*MOPW*), made on and off between 1973 and 1992. *MOPW* was shot internationally and is composed, in the main, of footage of people laboring outdoors; it always accompanies presentations of Phill's music.

1 See p. 61.

How codependent do you find sound and image to be? Since 1973 most of the performances of your music have been with your films, so I'm wondering how integral you feel the films are to making the music public, and if that was part of the reason you were so resistant to putting out recordings, at least until the CD era?

It was actually sort of the reverse—the thing about recordings had nothing to do with that, it had to do with the fact that having the music played on somebody's home music system, quietly, was against the music. It wasn't the music. But I realized that by not having a record, I simply was missing a huge opportunity to be heard, to be known, and to get more gigs to play live. So, I then decided to do a record—but I was never satisfied with the sound of the LPs. When people talk about how much better vinyl sounds, I wonder if I missed something.

To go back to the other thing, I began to do music because I was working with people at Judson Dance Theater, and it sort of slated me to do live intermedia performance. I had had not-such-great feelings about collaborating with music people—I did a collaboration with Max Neuhaus and it was complete shit, I thought [*laughs*]. I very early knew what I wanted, so then it was the question of making it. I was interested in this idea of composed drones, but primarily to use microtonal intervals to produce harmonic interactions. Drones, because I was more interested in how it sounded over a period of time instead of in short bursts, like tuning a piano or something like that. Because I was doing this intermedia performance stuff, which always had live dance and multiple images, I simply couldn't tour. I would get a couple of gigs out of town, but I could only do one gig a year; it was very frustrating. But I was still interested in doing film, so I was interested to have something that was performance material while giving up the live dance. I was working with nature footage, primarily, during that early period, and I had sort of reached the end of that; for *Ten Hundred Inch Radii* [an installation work from 1972] I thought I had really done the stuff. [Incidentally] I just transferred to digital the one film I finished out of that material, *T H I R*. And I was really tired of the artificiality of dance, even given Merce Cunningham [*laughs*], so I was very interested to find something where there was movement, where I could use movement, follow movement—where there was movement in the frames, without having dance. This idea of people working, where the movement is very natural and something that they do in a repeated fashion, as unselfconsciously as possible, even with the camera trained on them, was ideal. I thought I would probably do it for three years and move on to something else, but in fact, it was such a good idea that I continued for twenty years [*laughs*]. And I started again in November [2009] [*laughs*].

We'll get to The Movement of People Working. *I wanted to go more chronologically. Your grandfather did music for silent films?*

He played percussion, which included xylophone—when I was a kid there was a xylophone in his garage. And he worked a lot with another musician who played organ and piano, a family friend.

And the first time you heard Duke Ellington was in a movie theater?

The concert in 1948. Every city had big movie theaters, and Anderson [Indiana] was big enough to have two quite large theaters where there could be stage shows—they must have been built during the teens or something like that. There was an organ—there must have been a couple thousand seats or something, with balconies, and a fairly good-size stage.

It's interesting that there are these early associations of music and film together, although Ellington obviously didn't incorporate film. What sort of relationship did you have to movies?

When I was ten, twelve, fifteen, I went to the movies a lot, and of course on the weekends there were serials for kids, for ten cents. I would go see movies all the time. Saturday, it was all day long, and I would go to different theaters. There was one relatively near to my house, which was next door to the school, which was also next door to the factory where my father worked, which was half a block from the factory where my grandfather worked, all of which was the same—Delco Remy, part of General Motors. And then there were theaters uptown; I'd take the bus up.

Did you continue going to the movies as an adult?

When I was in college, we were more looking at art films—at Indiana University, in Bloomington, there was a place that showed art films, not too avant-garde [*laughs*]. They were narrative films—I don't even remember seeing documentaries other than newsreel type. I don't remember much about it at all. It was at the same time I was reading a lot of mysteries and Westerns, and at some point I became really aware of [Dashiell] Hammett as a writer. When I was in school I thought about being a writer; even in high school I thought about it. The only problem was I couldn't write for shit [*laughs*]—it's not a natural ability for me. I do great emails, but anything over that . . .

When did you become aware of experimental film, was that in New York?

I came to New York in '58, right after the army, and right after school—I graduated Indiana University and walked immediately into the army, for two years, and two weeks after that I was driving up Fifth Avenue. And it stuck; I didn't leave New York. I was interested in art, and particularly in music, because I went to a lot of jazz clubs, but I also went to a lot of concerts. And it was possible to go to a lot of concerts, not the highest-rank ones, for free—there was a guy who had booked a lot of people, and he made it where you could get a pass to go to any of the concerts he booked for free [*laughs*]. So I went to a lot of stuff, in the classical scene as well as jazz. Then there were some mixed series of contemporary music, particularly the Max Pollikoff series at the 92nd Street Y. It was in '61 that I went to a concert, and it was [Morton] Feldman playing *Durations* [1960–61]. But there were many concerts at that time, mostly classical composers, fairly academic guys, and Pollikoff didn't distinguish that much. He wasn't that interested in the avant-garde, or what we would consider to be the avant-garde now. But he wasn't unaware of it.

I didn't find a good job for a while. Finally, I started working for a guy whose primary thing was to make corporate audiovisual rooms, so he would design a room with 16-mm projection and slides. He was interested to develop the school market. I had a car, so I started going to visit schools in Westchester and Long Island, trying to sell audiovisual equipment to them, which was a doomed operation, because he had a lot of franchises, but they were not franchises for the areas where I was trying to sell—[the schools] had exclusives to other people. So when I made a couple of sales they actually had problems, had to buy from another dealer and sell [our equipment] either at a loss or no profit. We thought we should get a camera to shoot product shots for presentations, since we would be selling to schools, and the audiovisual place had a company that sold them. So I bought a Topcon single-lens camera as I left that company to join Programmed Teaching Aids as the vice president and the only paid employee [*laughs*], until they ran out of money in a year or so. The guy I was working for was really a super guy, one of the great father figures of all time. As I began to take more and more photographs, he came up one day, in his station wagon, and he gave me a complete darkroom. He was an amateur photographer, and he wasn't doing it at all, so he brought up the enlarger, trays, everything, so I started to print, and I began really to work after that.

That's the long way around of saying: I was then living with a woman who was much older than me, and she wasn't in the artistic area at all, but after this company I was working for a book publisher, in a new department about teaching machines and program instruction, advanced learning techniques. There was a woman working for the medical department who I started going with; she was married to an artist. They were living on the Nassau/Suffolk border [on Long Island]; he was teaching up there and she was commuting in [to the city]. We started an affair and I left the other woman. [The new woman] got an apartment in the city and we moved in together for a long time. She was a playwright and she was working with the Open Theater, but she was also very interested in the arts. I did a lot of photographs of the Open Theater; she opened up this idea of going to see different stuff. I was always going to a lot of galleries anyways, looking at visual art, and it was that period when [Leo] Castelli was probably the best gallery around. I would see classic stuff—[Mark] Rothko, Barnett Newman, early Jasper Johns. So I was enough around the arts scene that it was all beginning to coalesce, and I was seeing a lot of independent films. And when I began to work particularly with Elaine Summers in 1965, and to do films, I soon moved on to mostly working by myself, the way I worked in photography. I saw a lot of experimental films in that period, two or three years, and actually pretty much decided that that was *not* what I was interested to do. I'm really a photographic maven. I really want to see an image and want the stuff to be clear and crisp, so the idea of using 16-mm film was to make a really good photographic image, and that's *exactly* what the nature things, especially, were. But *The Movement of People Working* was very much about having a graphic, real, photographic image.

That sort of answered my question about Morning *[1966–69], which is how you got involved with the Open Theater.* Morning *was cowritten with Jean-Claude Van Itallie and stars Joe Chaikin. The Open Theater is known for nonverbal improvisation, and the film has a soundtrack, which is nonsynchronous but verbal.*

Yeah. I think that the film really has nothing to do with the Open Theater, that it has nothing to do with Jean-Claude Van Itallie. He and I talked about the original idea; he was going to write something but never did, so the stuff was written mostly by Lee Worley, and then one section was written by Michael Corner, who is Philip Corner's twin brother.

Wow.

[*Laughs.*] Weird coincidences.

Did you know him through Phil Corner?

I knew him through the Open Theater. His wife was very involved with people in the Open Theater, and so it was a big social thing. I would go to dinners with people from the Open Theater and Michael would show up. He was living in Holland—he's always lived in Holland. His wife was Dutch.

What's interesting about that film, in retrospect, is it actually is about the movement of people working—you see the guy going to work, and then you see the massage, and getting groceries and preparing food.

I never really thought about it—that's interesting.

Then The Magic Sun *[1966] was through Martin Bough, someone you were doing photography with, who knew Sun Ra.*

Martin Bough was a very close friend, and we were photographing—I shot the *Money Jungle* [United Artists Jazz, 1962] session [with Duke Ellington, Charles Mingus, and Max Roach] and met the guy who was the art director, who came to the shoot. The photographs that are on the album are his, Frank Gauna. He said, "Come on, bring me some photographs." I did, and so he hired me to photograph for Solid State, which was a sublabel of United Artists, which I did for about a year. I thought it would be really fun to do that with Martin, and we were just fantastic together. We were like Mutt and Jeff—we made a really great comedy act, and everybody loved us. We were both very interested in music and we knew recording, so we were never near a microphone. We were extremely cool in the studio.

Then it was a couple of years later, and he knew Sun Ra. Sonny [Blount, Sun Ra] asked us if we wanted to film, and I had this idea of something I could shoot in twenty minutes and it would be a finished film. Didn't work out, of course [*laughs*]. But it was a lot of experimentation with that film, working with different lab processes, different film stocks. It took two years to evolve to where it ended up, and two-thirds of the film was shot in the last session and is in pretty much chronological order. I think I cut out about 20 percent of the shots, and that was it—it totally was there.

Was it shot during a rehearsal, or a concert?

It was shot in Sun Ra's apartment, on Second Avenue and Second Street. They had a New York apartment as well as one in Philadelphia. People were just sitting around, somebody was playing records, so I would just have somebody sit down and I would shoot. I just had one 100-watt light bulb, and I took aluminum foil and crumpled it, so that the bulb was surrounded by tin foil. Basically I'm shooting at the light bulb, and everything is silhouetted. You see these big fingertips—

Yeah, it's a lot of extreme close-ups.

I was working with a Bolex at the time, and I had an old 135-mm lens and extension tubes. So I had the extension tubes from the C-mount adapter to this lens, and the lens was slow anyway, and when stopped down a bit, it was quite slower. But it gave me a lot of distance between the musician and the light. It was sharp enough to be good for that stuff. I was using this *very* high-contrast film, processed in a high-contrast bath. It's black—we were trying for a density of form in the black areas, and it was really there, and yet it just blocked the light from the projector. When you projected it you didn't see any light other than the white highlights—it was really black. Because it was very high contrast, so you saw a lot of white and very little gray. I took the first part of the film, which was shot on reversal film, and then printed it on negative so it's reversed—you see the reversed image.

There's a lot of extreme close-ups in these early short films, which maybe relates to the amplification you used in the sound pieces, to bring out the overtones. Also Sur Una *and* Sur Dos *[from* MOPW*] feature close-ups of hands.*

The idea in those first two [*MOPW*] films was to do hands [*laughs*]. I shot one of them in the summer of '73 in Mexico, the second in January of '74 in Peru. I think the Peru stuff was really superb. I'm very happy to have that on the Extreme DVD.[2] I think that side of the Extreme DVD works really great. And the prints were Kodachrome prints—they look just fantastic, they don't fade. The prints were from '74.

The Magic Sun *was projected behind dancers and other musicians?*

When I was shooting and developing it, Sonny and the band were playing at Slugs' a lot, on Third Street. And I would go there with a 16-mm projector and project onto the bandstand. Finally, after it was finished, he had a Carnegie Hall concert, and we projected it on the back of the Carnegie Hall stage, thirty-five feet wide. It's only seventeen minutes, so it was only that much of a concert, but it was great to do.

2 An edition of *The Movement of People Working* released in 2003 by Extreme Records.

Had you seen Tony Conrad's The Flicker *[1966] when you made* The Magic Sun*?*

As far as I know I had, but I don't have any memory of it. It would be likely that I would have seen it, but it didn't have any particular effect that I know of.

Or Michael Snow's New York Eye and Ear Control *[1964], which doesn't show Albert Ayler and his group performing, but there's some shots of them.*

I don't remember anything about that at all, so I would assume that I might have seen it, but . . . I saw a fair amount of [Stan] Brakhage stuff. The person who was much more of an influence was Elaine Summers, because she did something with relatively high-contrast black and white, with a dancer rolling slowly and making a kind of moving landscape. She was wearing a black leotard against a white wall. And it's possible I shot it, I don't remember.

*The Max Neuhaus [dedicated] film [*Max, *1967]—the soundtrack is four different versions of [Karlheinz] Stockhausen's* Zyklus *[1959] overlaid—*

Yeah. You read the credits, huh? [*Laughs.*]

And then the Max-Feed *[1966], which was a box that [Neuhaus] made?*

I have a Max-Feed! It's probably worth something.

Yeah, I would think so.

Yeah, yeah, yeah, I should get it off the shelf, it's full of dust. . . .

So was that Max's idea?

Yeah, totally his idea.

So it's just coincidental that there's all the superimposition in the film, and then the idea was to do these superimpositions on the soundtrack.

I don't actually know whether [Neuhaus] had the idea of superimposition independently, or—

It could just be a Cage-influenced thing also, where Cage was superimposing different scores on top of each other.

I don't know where he slowed the tapes of *Zyklus* down, but when we did the mix we went to the New York Institute of Technology, a studio of James Tenney. It was my first meeting with Tenney, who I didn't even know was a composer. He was just a guy running this studio.

*The film of Ann Danoff [*Annie, *1968] that also had a sound collage that you made—what were the elements of that?*

That was the first sound collage piece. I know that some of the stuff was made in Florida in a very funky zoo, so all the bird sounds are from that. There weren't that many recordings—it wasn't like I had twenty of them superimposed. It was more like two or three or four. I don't remember what the rest of it is; I'd have to listen to it again myself, and I have no idea where any of that material is. Theoretically, I should have the elements, but I haven't seen anything of that.

What made you want to use that as the sound component for the film?

Very interesting question; I don't have an answer. It was before I began to make music, and I don't remember exactly when that movie was finished either, because those films were started as early as '66, and they were all completed by '70, or '69. But I don't know exactly when any of them was done. I assume that I made a mix by playing several tape recorders together or dumping from one tape recorder to another, which is the way I was working in the '60s. That's how I built the stuff up. And I have no idea what they were recorded on. I was recording some with a half-track Uher, which I borrowed from an architect who was on the sixth floor of the building I had been living in since 1968—he was the son-in-law of Walter Gropius [*laughs*]. And I had a Revox in '69. My first grant was from a guy—his father had this shop on Madison Avenue, a needlepoint crafts shop, and he became interested and he gave me five hundred bucks and I bought a Revox, my first real high-quality tape recorder. So I was borrowing the Uher for days at a time, 'cause [the architect] wasn't using it, and I would just dub stuff back and forth. I had a couple of quarter-inch machines.

Somewhere you said that every dancer back then wanted to have a movie to project behind them. Was this film another case of that?

It was very much in vogue then, especially with people working in Judson: they wanted to have a film. I was the filmmaker who was around, so I did a bunch of things with people who weren't particularly well known, like Tina Kroll, at which I technically failed. I underexposed some film. But I shot the first film of Yvonne

Rainer, and I shot some stuff with Meredith Monk that was used for performances. Mostly when I did documentation, people hated it—but when I worked on a special project for a piece, then it was really fun. I shot a documentary of Lucinda Childs, and she had just been ill, and she wasn't really dancing, and she was heavy, for her—she's normally extremely skinny, and she was virtually zaftig [*laughs*]. I got them to do it nude—so Sally Gross was in it, and Joe Schlichter, who was married to Trisha Brown, and it was shot in Schlichter and Trisha's loft, which was in 80 Wooster Street, the first George Maciunas building. Anthology Film Archives was in the basement. [Childs] hated it. She took the print back—she didn't realize that I had the negative. I've never done anything with it, but I have the negative.

Dogtrack *[1969], to me, bears the least resemblance to—*

[*Laughs.*] Anything!

It's a found text—

Right, it's a found text that's very much more like *Morning* in its text orientation. My simple idea was that I was interested to make a film where you were never seeing what you heard on the soundtrack, and you would forget what you had actually seen. You would remember it as if you had seen it, and the text was perfect—it was so graphic, and still I see those images myself. It was Barbara Niblock[3] who was reading it, and she was a trained actress, but we had to do it twenty times to get it so that it was so flat. It was *really* hard to do. For one thing, it was supposed to be an interview by someone,

3 Phill Niblock's then wife, also credited as Barbara Porte.

and it's not—it's written—and you can't say it, so that there are some parts of it where you simply cannot parse the text. It's totally fictional; it's disguised porn. I found the book because there was a rabbi on the fifth floor who had a bookbinding outfit, and it was one of the books that he had bound [*laughs*].

There's a lot of time-lapse photography in Dogtrack, *which also is used in the Raoul Middleman film [*Raoul *(1968–69)].*

And at the very end of the film there's this abstract stuff, which is very Brakhage-like.

What's interesting about that is, in the beginning of the film, the footage that's shot in the city is very high-speed, because of the time-lapse, and then the shots in the country are in real time. And then that last section in the country is shot with much faster camera movement.

I assume that I was shooting out the window of a car, and what figures in that, I think, is the graveyard that James Dean is buried in, in Fairmount, Indiana. We were on the way to visit friends—relatives, actually—in Fairmount, who had a farm, and we stopped at the cemetery.

Which, in a roundabout way, leads me to something I was going to bring up, which is that you were a motorcycle rider during all this time. Thinking about the high-speed motion in these films, but also about the sound collage in Annie *as repetitive sound, and of course most of your music is drones, and the sound of a motorcycle is kind of a drone, a mechanical sound: I feel like that might have fed into your consciousness, or subconscious.*

You were riding around on a motorcycle, and there was all this landscape going by at a fast speed.

There's a famous statement [from me], where I was riding before I was making music, in the '66–'68 period, on the Blue Ridge Parkway, and I was going up a hill behind a truck—it had to be south, because trucks don't drive on the Blue Ridge going north—and the [motorcycle's] throttle was wide open, so the beating [sonic frequencies] of the truck engine laboring and the motorcycle . . . I'm not sure how much real effect that had, but it made a really great story.

And of course the motorcycle is in the Raoul Middleman film, where he's painting you standing next to the motorcycle.

Also, there's a shot in *Dogtrack*—it's four frames within the one frame of the film. We projected in 16 mm, so it projects all four frames, and it came upside down for the second film, so the film shots are right side up, but one of them is going backward. If you look at it you can try and figure out which one is going backward [*laughs*]. And it was on a motorcycle—Barbara was riding on the back, holding a camera closer to the ground.

The soundtrack to the Raoul film is the two of you just talking?

It was just a conversation. We went to galleries; we went to see works of another friend, Colin Greenly, who made this big room that's all glass, a very beautiful, crystal thing. You hear Raoul knocking on the glass.

In the movie he's painting on a window at first, and then later painting on a mirror.

And that mirror was the first shot—it was a time-lapse, and I have a feeling that was shot with the Beaulieu, the camera I was using at the time, at two frames per second. It could be that it was shot with a Bolex, because I made several time-lapse motor mechanisms for the Bolex, where you change both the frame rate and the exposure, so you change the shutter speed. And that mirror was here when I moved in; there was an incredible amount of stuff left over in my loft from 1968—it was an exhibit display house that had the whole floor. When I came to see the loft, there was a pile of leftover garbage and wood coming out of the archway from the other side of the building.

The recording was made with the idea that it would be the soundtrack to the Raoul film—where did that idea come from?

It needed a soundtrack, and I thought we would make a real drone, which it pretty much is—there's very little that you need to understand. There's one or two parts in the restaurant, where there's a kid whose parents sent him there because they're out working, so the waiter takes care of the kid [*laughs*]. You hear the waiter say to the kid, "You did a really great job" [*laughs*]. We went to the Frick [Museum], so part of that is recorded at the Frick, looking at Rembrandts and shit like that. Then we went to two galleries. And then, the first scene, where he's painting on the glass with the sunrise, I wanted it to be silent—but I knew that you can't start a film silent, because people will try turning it up and then when there is sound it will be too loud. So I actually recorded the first part of the track, and it's very loud—it's too loud if you have the sound set at the normal level, and I didn't tell them to reduce the volume when they were mastering the films. And that huge mirror was sitting right here behind this door, where the record shelf is, and somehow [my son] Jasper went through the door and the mirror fell. I was gone, and when I came back he was terrified that I was going to strangle him, and I was so incredibly relieved that he didn't get hurt. So the picture's gone, too. And the huge painting—there's one that's really enormous where you see the mirror, and you see him working—Raoul destroyed, he didn't like it. He destroyed a lot of stuff.

Where did the idea come from to shoot The Movement of People Working *in foreign countries?*

The idea [was] to shoot movement of people working, and I didn't think I would find it here. The one shot in New York State in 1975 is a case in point, because the people don't really move that much, they use their machines. There's these very lyrical scenes of people sitting on a tractor, driving around, but that's not so interesting.

How much research is involved in deciding where to shoot?

Virtually nothing, and there were a couple that were complete failures because we didn't find that out in advance. We went to Norway to shoot along the coast, to shoot fishing people, where nothing's happening. It was summertime—it's completely a winter thing. If I had gone straight north to Hammerfest I probably would have found some activity, but I started in the south, in Trondheim. I only got to Tromsö, and nothing was happening in the fishing industry.

You were shooting in the summertime because you wanted to use natural light, or because of your schedule?

Yes, I was very interested in shooting in natural light. I didn't always shoot in the summertime, as a matter of fact. Because I was teaching, I had January off, so I shot in South Africa that month, in the mountains, and I almost got caught in a snowstorm flying over. And I shot in Portugal in the winter; it was very cold, it was only supposed to go to forty degrees but there was no heat anywhere. In '92 Stella [Varveris] wanted to go to visit relatives in Greece, and she didn't want me to shoot. I said, "Well, OK." And I never shot again, that was it. Because that was about the same time that my hip started to go to hell. I just never got back to it, until last November.

Other than the one sequence, which is shot in a sewing shop in Hungary, almost everything on the Extreme DVD is from outdoors. And the outdoors provides—besides watching the movement of the people, there's also the movement of nature in the background, which creates visual interest in a lot of the films. If you watch it with the music, there are a lot of unintentional synchronicities between things going on in nature and those going on in the overtones.

You actually remembered that shot, wow.

All the Movement of People Working *stuff was shot on 16 mm—was there ever any thought of shooting it on video?*

Yes, these two projects—in 1989 I shot in Japan and then the film labs stopped, and to go to another film lab was way out of my budget.

But in the '70s you never thought about doing it on a Sony Portapak?

Shit no, I hated it. Video really looked like crap to me. I'm a photographer.

There wasn't really much video projection back then, either.

Not that you could really get access to, that anybody would have—they would have monitors. But by '90 the Hi8 was looking quite good, and VHS was OK, but not great. But Hi8 was extremely fragile—it's really a problem because there's a lot of dropout. The tapes fall apart.

Are these MOPW *films edited in-camera?*

Virtually. I either discarded a shot, which didn't happen that often, or I trimmed the ends. If something happened at the end of a shot I would trim off whatever I didn't like, but mostly I would just trim off the flash frames, 'cause I was using an Arriflex and it stops anywhere. It would stop with the shutter open, so there would be five frames blanked out.

There's never an attempt to edit the sound piece to the film.

There's absolutely no relationship. It's never the same.[4] I can't imagine that the same piece of music would be playing with the same image, because even if I used the same music they wouldn't be in sync. And there was mostly more than one film showing.

4 The music and films are created separately and matched at random, so that the exact combinations of sound and image are never repeated.

When you were filming, did you just shoot as long as you felt like shooting and then . . .

Yeah, either something having to do with what I thought about it, or something to do with what they were doing. If they stopped doing [an action] I would stop. It was my theory that ten seconds is the max amount of time where you get the feeling of editing for time, so that if all the shots are over ten seconds long, it doesn't make so much difference whether they're thirty seconds or two minutes. And of course, one hundred feet of film is two minutes and forty-five seconds. The nature stuff—I fairly often got maybe two shots per reel.

Are the combinations of pieces of music with films indeterminate, or have you gone back and found certain combinations that you would return to as a favorite?

Totally indeterminate—nothing that had to do with the combination. In the last year I transferred three pieces of film from 16 mm to HD, and it just looks incredible compared to previous transfers. So I've been tending to play those. I've been playing the Extreme DVD for years, because it was the best-looking stuff I had on DVD. The other stuff I had transferred in '86, mostly to U-matic videotape on a Moviola/Videola, which was not great—you could see the image, but it was not fantastic. So this stuff is really great, and in September I transferred another five hours of material, so I have eleven and a half hours of newly transferred film, and that is nearly all of it.

There's no beginning, middle, or end to the films.

Yeah, the real idea was against resolution—so the music doesn't resolve, but also the films don't resolve.

There's no climax, there's no development, there's no building, there's just the phenomena. The music has more development.

How well do you know the MOPW *films? They've been shown so many times over the years—when you look at them again, do you remember what comes next, or is it still kind of surprising?*

Sometimes yes, sometimes no—there's so much footage that I don't always remember. Sometimes I'm looking at films and thinking, "Are we near the end?" Especially *Romania* [1991], because I never finished cutting that, and it's never been a video before. I only showed the one reel a few times on December 21 [for one of the annual six-hour-long winter solstice concerts]. And what happened was, last year I said, "Let's look at this," and then they put on the reel, which was uncut by mistake, because it wasn't marked well enough. I probably hadn't seen that in twenty years.

Did you ever encounter any resistance from the people working? Did people ever say they didn't want you to film?

Extremely seldom. I once got stopped by a Chinese overseer as I was leaving a shoot, not while I was filming. We were on the path leaving some fields and the guy was quite testy that we were there, "exploiting" their workers. I don't know where this guy got this statement—it's totally not true.

Did you explain precisely what you were shooting the footage for?

Mostly I couldn't. I pretty much always traveled

with someone who spoke the language, although sometimes, particularly in China, the dialect is completely different than Standard Chinese—most people will understand Standard Chinese because they have TV.

I went to this one village, and every house had electricity and a color TV set, so they were watching people wearing normal Western clothes and talking in Standard Chinese all the time. I would walk by houses, and there would be a TV set in the corner. Sometimes not too small either. I wandered off by myself and I went to this place in the center of the village. There was a big hole in the sidewalk, and there were these big gouges on the side—it was the well, and the gouges were where the ropes being put down had worn away the rock over a century or so. It was very hard stone. It was weird. That was the water supply. I looked up, and there was a big row of toilets, completely open, and a woman sitting on the toilet, looking at me. She was really shocked, and I was really shocked [*laughs*]. The man who controls the toilets is the rich man in town, because the fertilizer is shit, human shit, so they store that stuff. In fact, in *China 88* [1988] you see this murky stuff in the bottom of a boat and this guy's digging around it, and it's shit—shit and water.

Because it's not a documentary, or a feature film . . .

These people would have some idea what a documentary was. But whether you could explain to them, in the language they understand, that it's not a documentary . . . Because they don't have any context other than what they see on TV. I couldn't describe what I was doing well enough, so we made a sort of gesture, if need be, but most of the time, if not 90 percent of the time, I would simply set up and start filming. It's really seldom that anyone looks at me. It's really amazing, people just turn, just don't look. And I do something in the way that I set up the camera which makes me a worker and sort of defuses that, I think. I mean, I'm this weird-looking guy with a beard and all that shit, but still, I concentrate while I'm setting up, putting the tripod up, putting the camera on the tripod, putting in batteries, very concentrated, and I deliberately do that, so when I step behind the camera and turn it toward them, it's more of the process of my working, and I think that that must have had something to do with it. Either that, or I exude some sort of aura that makes me invisible.

The other interesting difference between MOPW *and the six short films was that the short films were made in cooperation with people who would have seen the finished product, and* MOPW *was made with people's cooperation, but they were never going to see the film in its final context—and part of what makes it effective, I think, is the fact that not only are the music and films separate, but that the subjects of the films are oblivious to the music's existence entirely.*

That might be about it for this interview.

You really got much more concise and specific statements out of me than anybody ever did.

Rudy Wurlitzer

I first encountered Monte Hellman's *Two-Lane Blacktop* (1971), scripted by novelist and screenwriter Rudy Wurlitzer, when it was shown in a campus screening series at Vassar. I had heard that it featured musicians James Taylor and Dennis Wilson in acting roles, and that it had a cult following as a kind of Beckettian existential drama with dialogue mostly limited to car talk. I love off-beat cinema, but I wasn't totally won over by *Two-Lane*, and I missed the ending because I had to leave to do my radio show. The next day, I asked a friend how it had ended and he described the closing device where the film stock appeared to burn up in the projector. That made me want to see the whole thing, and on second viewing I fully connected with it. I've seen it many times since, and I often thought about it while I was on tour, especially in the '90s; in a way I consider it to be kind of an indie-rock road movie, with drag races instead of shows. In fact, it's the only film I can think of that has inspired an indie-rock tribute album: *You Can Never Go Fast Enough* (Plain Recordings, 2003), to which Will Oldham and I contributed the track "Don't Cry, Driver."

Over the years, I sought out all the other films Wurlitzer scripted and the experimental literature he's written. In 2011, when Drag City published an audio book of Will reading Wurlitzer's 1984 novel *Slow Fade*, they asked me to participate in a release event at Anthology Film Archives in New York, where I met Rudy for the first time. Shortly after that, the label asked if I would want to interview him for the *Believer*. I jumped at the chance, and that June I took the train upstate to speak with him at the house he shares with his wife, photographer Lynn Davis. The *Believer* sat on the piece for two years and cut it drastically; the version here presents the conversation in full.

You've compared writing to music, in terms of the way you've done your books; The Drop Edge of Yonder *[2008] you said had a sonata form, and in an interview, you said, "Everything I write, there's always one complete draft and I write it just for the sound . . . the sensual feel of language . . . the rhythm of it."*

Yeah, at first I try to get underneath the language and hear a subject, sort of in a musical way, in terms of how large a sound it is, what the rhythms of a subject are. And then in the actual composition of a piece, I always try to arrive at a place where I've left the conceptual mind behind and I am going toward the unknown. In that way, I'm rescued by the *sound* of language, which a lot of times will deliver me to the subject in an intuitive way. So the actual rhythm of language is really important to me, 'cause a lot of times it'll dictate something more objective.

One of the things that I've tried to evolve in writing, not always successfully, especially in prose and books, is to break through a conceptual paradigm, [to avoid programming] in a traditional way, with a beginning, middle, and end. Maybe that's a relief from having to write screenplays—books became much more free-form, in a sense, like old-time jazz. It's like that old [Charles] Mingus saying: "Take it easy, but take it." I was really influenced in the early days by that kind of music, which also broke out of the more classical thing that I was raised in. It's always the frontier of my mind that I'm reaching for. So sometimes that takes place in a more concrete way, in terms of the actual Western frontier, but it isn't really the West that I'm so obsessed by. It's really about leaving my own traditions, and leaving my own set of descriptions, and the traditions that I was raised in, in a very academically orthodox way. I was initially raised in a very formal music tradition, to be a violinist. My family was generations of music people. But I needed to push past that grid and become more open-ended and spontaneous. I've been around music all my life, but it's transferred into the actual sound and rhythm of language as a deliverance. Does that make sense?

Mm-hmm. I found this short piece that you wrote about Philip Glass for the "Anti-Illusion: Procedures/Materials" show at the Whitney Museum [of American Art] back in 1969.

I don't remember that. [*Laughs.*]

You said in an interview later that you were really writing about your own work, especially Nog *[1969], in that piece. You described how a "refusal to remember what has or has not happened before, hold the attention, becomes the continuity itself, the focus" and "duration becomes a catalyst toward contemplating the present"; "the drama can be one of transcendence" and "notes refer only to themselves."*

I was better spoken in those days than I am now [*laughs*]. But yeah, Phil is probably my oldest friend, and in the '60s, when he was writing *Music with Changing Parts* [Chatham Square, 1971] and his early work, we were both in New York, and I was very much involved with what he was going through musically, which resonated with what I was going through in terms of *Nog*, the first book I wrote. I just finished a libretto for him, and I've done one before; it's fun working with him after all these years. When I write a libretto with him in mind, I know the music so well that it's sort of fun to do. It's rare that you have a collaboration that really works that way.

You did that piece online where you talked about songs you were listening to while writing Drop Edge.

They came out of a time, that nineteenth-century music hall thing. . . . When I write, a lot of times I'll hear songs, or I'll be drawn to finding out what songs are relevant to a scene, and sort of ease my way into incorporating a musical interlude that adds a different chord to the whole thing. It just comes spontaneously.

There are some fun song choices on the soundtrack of Two-Lane Blacktop, *like the Doors's "Moonlight Drive" and [Jerry Lee Lewis's] "Hit the Road Jack." [*RW laughs.*] And there is usually someone singing in your screenplays: Laurie Bird sings "(I Can't Get No) Satisfaction" and Warren Oates sings along with [Chuck Berry's] "Maybellene" in* Two-Lane, *and Billy sings something in the published screenplay of* Pat Garrett and Billy the Kid *[1973].*

The whole dynamic between [Bob] Dylan and [Kris] Kristofferson [in *Pat Garrett*] was really interesting. And then what Bob brought to the score afterward, with these street musicians in Mexico City, was quite amazing. I really liked that score. Also, with *Walker* [1987], Alex Cox's film we did in Nicaragua, music was very much a part of that; Joe Strummer brought a sense of the local music and its episodic rhythms.

Having Joe do that soundtrack reinforced the feeling that Walker *was a tribute of sorts to* Pat Garrett.

That's really interesting that you would say that, because he [Cox] is a big fan of that film; when we first met each other—at a film festival in Rotterdam, I can't remember why I was there [*laughs*]—that was the big common ground that we had, [Sam] Peckinpah stories, you know. So he thought I would be a good person to write *Walker* because of that. Also, the sense of period, and the sense of outrageousness that Peckinpah brought to bear . . .

[William] Walker is almost a Peckinpah-esque figure.

He is, and as we went on, he became more and more of a Peckinpah figure, as happened with Peckinpah [*laughs*].

What Joe wrote is completely instrumental, so you never hear his voice. He's in the film very briefly—you just spot him a couple of times—whereas with Dylan, it's a bit strange that he's acting in the film and then you also hear his voice on the soundtrack, kind of commenting on it as if he were an outside observer.

Yeah, it was really interesting how he came into that film. He came to see me, I think I told you. He thought that he had a direct connection to Billy the Kid [*laughs*], that he *was* Billy the Kid. . . . I called the producer, and the producer said, "Yeah, great, write him a part." So I wrote him the part on the back of an envelope or whatever on the way down to Mexico. He became integrated into the film in a very offhand, spontaneous way, so his voice was not arranged. . . . That's why I wrote that scene of him reading the cans, because that was another secret, ironic play on him singing, that whole sense of language. He added a lot to that film.

Where he's reading the cans, that's also similar to a couple of things in your novels: In Nog, *someone is listing mountains—*

Yeah, I think if I ever do a memoir, it will just be a series of laundry lists [*laughs*].

There was a piece you did that was a list of everything in your apartment.

Yeah, that's right. I didn't know anyone read that [*laughs*].

In the Two-Lane Blacktop *DVD commentary, you talked about how the language in* Two-Lane *is so "one-note," which is interesting because there's this pervasive motor drone of the car engine, which the Mechanic is listening to, and at one point, the Driver is talking to the Girl about listening to the cicadas, a sound which is a kind of drone—there's a literal drone element and then this drone of language.*

That's another thing about the sense of music—initially, when I was doing research for the film, I'd hang out with these car guys in the Valley, outside of LA, and the whole language was car language. It was like a whole different note for me. So when I would introduce that into the script, it was like a piece of music. And then the monosyllabic language of the principals—James Taylor, Dennis Wilson, and Laurie Bird, who were not actors—had one *tone* to it. Introducing really evolved, developed, theatrical actors, like Warren Oates and Harry Dean Stanton, brought a different chord, a kind of manic, over-the-top chord that made the nonactors seem even more innocent than they were. Merge that with the sound of the engine . . . It was very musical for me. I never quite thought about it like that, but that's actually the way it happened. Because I inherited a script that Monte [Hellman] wanted totally rewritten, and the only thing I could keep was the idea of the Driver, the Mechanic and the Girl, and a drive across the country. Other than that, it was a completely new script for me. So that's how I got into it—musically—'cause I didn't know a car from a cow [*laughs*]. To play that off the other rhythms became an intuitive way to go on this episodic, existential journey to nowhere.

Even within the music world, there's all these different sets of lingo—a classical musician will talk about music in a completely different way than a jazz musician would, or a rock musician.

That's really true.

Because of your experience with the violin, I was wondering about the scene of the kid playing the out-of-tune violin in the sitting room in Walker.

That was an old memory-echo of being in these rooms as a kid and having to play for various luminaries who would come over and hang out with my father, like Fritz Kreisler or Jascha Heifetz. They'd say, "Oh, break out the fiddle, play. . . ." I was always terrified to do that [*laughs*] and seized with awkwardness. I had to survive those moments. Usually I'd run away [*laughs*].

You said that you worked on an oil tanker and that experience informed your early stories.

I did when I was seventeen. "The Boiler Room" [1966] was about that. Again, I really wanted to break out of my formal upbringing, so I got a job on an oil tanker through a distant relative who worked for an oil shipping company. I got a job as a wiper in the engine room. I was seventeen, you know—I could barely tie my shoelaces. This oil tanker went from Philadelphia to Venezuela to Spanish Morocco to Kuwait, so it was a long voyage. It was a frontier for me. The tanker was under the Liberian flag; most of the crew was Black. I was the youngest, and the white guy. They introduced me to all kinds of exotic terrifying adventures at these various ports of call [*laughs*], which I learned in very primal experiences of a, well, male-female kind of thing [*laughs*]. That was a big journey for me; it was difficult, but it was life-changing.

When I went to Columbia [University] after that, it was a very different experience. I just felt trapped there, in the academic world. On a spring vacation during my sophomore year, a friend and I went to Cuba. As soon as we arrived in Havana, it was the end of the whole uprising. Castro's troops came into the city, completely took it over. A lot of the soldiers, and a lot of girls, were my age, and we had an amazing time. I became involved with an older woman over there and didn't go back to school for a while. When I got back to Columbia, I was *out*. So I joined the army for a couple of years and had the usual kind of terrible experiences, and then when I came back, I finished up at Columbia and then went to Paris and then Spain. Then back to New York. That's when I started to write *Nog*.

You did some sports writing around this time, too.

Yeah, for the *Saturday Evening Post*, I went on the road with the Golden State Warriors, which was great. I got to talk to all these great players. That was fun.

You also reviewed Frederick Exley's novel A Fan's Notes *[1968], which is all about sports. Were you more interested in sports back then?*

Yeah, if I could have, I would have been a

professional ball player, but I wasn't good enough [*laughs*]. I was always a sports freak. I was a big fan. Who knows, I could have become a sports writer . . . but I was too strange and weird.

That's interesting, because again on the DVD commentary, you said that Two-Lane *is a film where no one wins and no one loses; it's an existential version of sport, a competition that's never-ending, and even along the way, the players become confused as to whether they're still* in *competition.*

Yeah, that's true, that's absolutely true. I would get involved in these competitive linear situations, and then, out of my innate perversity, try to pull the rug out from underneath, and be in the present. Not get trapped in results. I've always been aware of the tyranny of having to be attached to results, so that's what *Two-Lane* is about. When I did films with Robert Frank, it was all about being in the moment, being in the present, not having any idea of an ending. We did several short films together, *Keep Busy* [1975] and *Energy and How to Get It* [1981], and then a feature, *Candy Mountain* [1988], where I wrote the script. That presented certain problems, because all of a sudden, we were in this feature film that involved money and time, and those were the last things that Robert wanted to have to deal with [*laughs*]. That's why jazz is so great, because it's in the process, in the moment, surrendering to the moment, without any kind of conceptual program about where you're going to end up. That carried over for me. And also feeling deeply trapped in what became the corporate LA films. I was always naive; I thought it was still possible to be collaborative and have a situation that would not be so sublimated to a corporate grid. But it got worse and worse, and I drifted off to Europe . . . always in the hope, but never getting there [*laughs*].

Was the story "The Octopus" [1966], in the Paris Review, *a precursor to* Nog?

That was the first chapter of *Nog*, yeah.

You've cited [Samuel] Beckett as a big influence at this time, but was Buddhism an influence at this point? Had you gotten into that yet?

In a sense. I've always been aware of the idea of self-cherishing, which is a dharmic expression about the self, and I've always been aware, in my half-assed way, about the fallibility and illusions of self, which plays a lot in my books, I think. So I was attracted to the basic tenets of Buddhism before I ever encountered it. Even before that, I meditated in various groups in New York—not in a very evolved way, just something drew me to that. I went to India around the time of *Two-Lane*; I wrote a script that took place in India and I thought I better go over there [*laughs*] and see what it's about. I went with a friend of mine, a producer, and we were both very naive and didn't know what was happening either in films or in India or anywhere else. I had various adventures there and got exposed a little bit to the dharma, to Buddhism. On another trip, I spent a lot of time in Nepal and met a Tibetan lama who became a teacher of mine. And then I became more seriously involved and helped start a dharma center in New York, went back and forth between Nepal, the States, and India. Then it became more internalized, the actual practice, but I consider myself an amateur. I've been involved for maybe forty years with Buddhism, and had the privilege of being around some very evolved people, and I've maybe learned a little that trickled down, just from their great compassion and grace, you know. But at best, I'm a poor pilgrim [*laughs*].

The feeling of emptying out that's in a lot of your late-'60s, early-'70s work—

To say it in an academic way, the first shock of being exposed by someone who manifested what he was saying empowered the basic tenet of the nonduality of form and emptiness. That blew me away. And I've been involved with figuring that out, with living with that, ever since—dissolving the separation that exists, that we all have, between one another. That's why music is so important, because it dissolves the separation for those moments. I've always had the need to try to at least point toward an integration of what I was involved with as a writer, a filmmaker, whatever, and study the basic tenets of not just dharma, but spiritual views, Sufis, or whatever—it didn't matter to me where it came from, as long as it was authentic and played the same sounds, you know?

The sense of time, or timelessness, in Nog, Flats *[1970], and maybe* Two-Lane *to some extent—was that related to drugs?* Nog *has been described as a psychedelic novel, but it doesn't seem psychedelic to me. . . .*

I did, like everyone else in those days, make a few rounds with LSD and mushrooms, and certainly had more than a few tokes of grass, but I was not really a druggie. It was recreational. I never got into anything harder than that. I wasn't involved with drugs at all when I was writing *Nog*; I was just mostly on the road, in various isolated places. In New York as well, but I went out to LA, where I didn't know anyone. I didn't turn anything down [*laughs*], but I wasn't obsessively looking for it either. I wouldn't think that was drug-related. Probably there are those tendrils of fabric in the upholstery, but not self-consciously, no.

A lot of your work is about the road, and the end of the road, and then questioning whether there is—

Whether there is a road—

Whether there is a road or whether there is an end to the road.

Again, it's the myth of the frontier, the road leading to the end of the road, which leads to an open space you've never encountered before. I wrote in the early days a little essay on this old Western writer Louis L'Amour ["Riding Through," published in *For Now*, 1970], and what fascinated me and still continues to fascinate me about Louis L'Amour is that he's a real old Western genre hack, you know, but the first two or three pages of a Louis L'Amour book are about just riding into open space. You don't know where the rider is going; there's no particular destination. It's really about its own rhythm, its own process. That's what I loved about Louis L'Amour. And when the plot kicks in, that's where I stopped. I was always trying to get back to that early sense of being in the moment.

You've talked about how, in the old West, it didn't matter if you went north, south, or west—it was all uncharted territory.

Yeah, that's a good way to say it: What I was trying to find was uncharted territory. And so initially, to a primitive guy, it seemed like you could go out West, take the car and drive. In those days, I would deliberately go east and then south and then north, to try to completely confuse myself. Because I had no real destination. But then the destination leaked in, and as time went on, I was always going for a reason, you know—for a gig, for a girl, for whatever [*laughs*].

There's a similar progression in your work: In Glen and Randa *[1971], they set sail into the ocean. They're on the beach and they can't get any farther on land. And in* Two-Lane, *at the end, the Driver is just hustling another drag race and nobody is sure of their next destination. But in* Pat Garrett and Billy the Kid, *Pat is actively looking for Billy, and in* Slow Fade, *Walker is looking for Clementine in India.*

I was thinking about that—I hadn't read *Slow Fade* since it came out. I picked it up, and I didn't remember a lot of it; I was so struck by how much of it is influenced by writing films, and I was trying to break that, create different voices to go back and forth from the prose to the screenplay in a circular way. I try to break that sense of inevitability toward a destination.

Was it also trying to reconcile the two experiences of writing novels and screenplays?

Oh yeah, that's really what it was about.

Nog *was written in motels, and there were so many motels in* Two-Lane—

Well, the reason Monte hired me to do *Two-Lane Blacktop* was that he read *Nog* and he thought that I could break the traditional form of a rote race movie, which is a beginning and end and all the rest of it, and

I guess he was right. *Two-Lane* came right after *Nog*; and because of *Nog*, *Two-Lane* happened. And because of *Two-Lane*, *Pat Garrett* happened.

Had you seen [Hellman's] The Shooting *[1966]?*

Yeah. So I knew where Monte was coming from, pretty much. But in those days, everything was personal and open-ended and independent. It was Roger Corman country. We all felt a little bit like privileged outlaws. And I knew the woman who wrote *The Shooting*, Carole Eastman; she was a good friend.

Actually, when you were describing your experience of running off to the oil tanker, it made me think of Five Easy Pieces *[1970], also written by Carole Eastman [under the pseudonym Adrien Joyce], in which Jack Nicholson's character does the same thing, and comes from a musical family, like you.*

Yeah. *Five Easy Pieces* resonated with me because of the whole music thing in it; I used to talk to her about that. It was a totally different time. We all knew each other—Nicholson and [the film's director Bob] Rafelson, and the BBS [production] company.

Was Two-Lane *before* Flats*?*

Flats was earlier than that. I was living with a girl in Cambridge, Massachusetts; I wrote *Flats* in her attic. I forgot about that. That happened before *Two-Lane*.

In Flats, *the characters' names are all taken from cities; I know from touring the US that after you've been on the road for a few weeks, all these cities start to look the same, so that resonated with me as a way to signify the interchangeability, or mutability, of the different characters.*

Yeah, especially in, for want of a better expression, a postapocalyptic avenue, place has a different resonance.

Even GTO [in Two-Lane*]—his home is his car, so calling him GTO is related to the naming of the characters in* Flats. *One of the things about* Two-Lane *is that each character represents a different degree of freedom. The girl is the freest of all; at the end of the movie, she drops her bags and just takes off on a motorcycle. She doesn't seem attached to possessions at all.*

She didn't have an identity, whereas the others' identities were involved with motors and cars and speed.

The Driver and the Mechanic, their identities are wound up in this car that they customize themselves, whereas GTO's identity is more caught up in the factory-made machine, and everything is kind of factory-made with him: He hasn't put his own stamp on anything, he just changes depending on which way the wind is blowing. He keeps picking up people to ride with him to lay his rap on; the Girl is also moving from vehicle to vehicle, but with her it's about changing companions, and maybe not as a sexual thing—

It didn't feel like that to me.

It didn't feel like that to me either—it's more about not wanting the same thing every single day, changing that up as much as possible. In the screenplay, but not in the film, there's a line where GTO says, "Everything is going too fast and not fast enough," which shows how imbalanced he feels, and maybe goes back to the Buddhism thing in terms of needing an internal balance.

To have a center of stillness, the essence of the middle way.

Which the Driver and the Mechanic seem to have, with the car, until the Girl shows up and throws it off, at least for the Driver.

Yeah, well, you know, passions intrude [*laughs*]. And once again, you're making a fool of yourself, getting into some big trouble. That's inevitable. At least it is for me. It was funny seeing those films again at Anthology Film Archives. First of all, it was interesting to see how dated films are compared to books, compared to, say, *Slow Fade*, which is twenty-five years old but actually seems more relevant now than it did then. During the screening of *Glen and Randa*, this friend of mine, an old Zen student, was sitting behind me, and he said in this loud voice, "I hate that film!" [*Laughs.*] It was shocking—he thought it was very . . . nihilistic, that's what bothered him about it. I think aspects were, but it was the mid-to-late '60s and there was more of a hippie, solipsistic thing. I found it so interesting to think about in those days. I was just trying to write that thing with this friend of mine, Lorenzo Mans, and to figure out how to write scripts. It was kind of fun. But I didn't have any idealistic, nihilist point of view, you know? [*Laughs.*]

Nihilism has been talked about in relation to Two-Lane Blacktop *also; it shows a sort of nihilistic underside to the late '60s that then becomes more articulated in the punk scene. In watching it again, I was struck by how the 1955 Chevy is so stripped down but so souped up at the same time; it's really like the Ramones! This band that was musically stripped down but also revved up with big amps and all that. And 1955 is the birth of rock and roll, and punk rock was to some extent trying to go back to early rock and roll.*

That's interesting, that's a good way to think about it. But I didn't feel *Two-Lane* was overtly nihilistic.

No, it's a couple of steps removed from that. They're not on the road because they think, "It doesn't matter anyway. . . ."

They're on the road for its own sake.

You mention the phenomenology of Western space in the published Pat Garrett *screenplay, and in the late '60s, phenomenology was being discussed in the art world in terms of conceptualism and Minimalism. You knew Richard Serra, and you did that piece on Philip Glass for the catalog of the "Anti-Illusion" show at the Whitney, which was an important exhibition of that era. Were there other of those artists you were involved with?*

In the early days, I was involved with Claes Oldenberg. I did a filmed Happening with him up at my family's place in upstate New York. It was called *Birth of the Flag I, II*, 1965. It was kind of like *Two-Lane*, now that I think about it; it was just the process itself without any result, just filming whatever happened, with this relatively spontaneous collection of wacked-out characters from New York.

Like Keep Busy *[1975].*

Yeah. And I was in a few other Happenings with him, so I was very aware of that, [Robert] Rauschenberg and Jasper Johns as well, and was influenced a lot by Phil [Glass]'s music, and John Coltrane's. New York was a very vibrant place for me in those days; music and the art world were really interesting. I was always very aware of what was happening.

Did you know Walter De Maria at all?

A little bit, yeah.

He made this one film, in 1969, called Hard Core.

Yeah.

You know this film?

Yeah, a little bit.

It's him and Michael Heizer, dressed up like cowboys, in this empty desert space. He does these 360-degree pans for thirty minutes. And Land art in general was much about wide-open space.

Right. That fits right in with that time. [Robert] Smithson was another guy that I liked a lot. Donald Judd . . . Yeah, that was a formative, open-ended time.

Compared to Flats *or* Nog, Quake *[1972] and* Slow Fade *were more specific, and more developed in narrative. Do you think you would have gone in that direction as a novelist if you hadn't been writing screenplays?*

I don't think so. *Nog* broke a lot of rules. The first review of anything I ever wrote was in the *New York Times*. The first sentence was, "'Wurlitzer' means music to millions, but obviously literature to none" [*laughs*].

I've come to cherish that [*laughs*]. It did touch a few sore spots with the critical establishment.

The only other experimental writer I can think of who wrote screenplays was Don Carpenter, who did the screenplay for Payday *[1973].*

Right. I didn't know him.

I couldn't think of anybody else.

Not many. Certainly *Quake* and *Slow Fade* were influenced by my experiences in LA, in the film business. I remember writing *Quake*, completely damaged, in my hideout in Canada. It was a catharsis, though I didn't think of it as that at the time. And *Slow Fade* was too, but further along, fifteen years later. And *The Drop Edge of Yonder* was also the result of various screenplays.

That was a screenplay that you turned into a novel. I was really taken aback at how different Slow Fade *was from* Nog *and* Flats, *in that it deals with family.*

It really is. It comes from a different place, from films. That narrative, those interlocking stories, the sense of going toward some resolution. It's an old-fashioned book, relatively [*laughs*].

The trip you took to India for that script, did that inspire some of the scenes in India in Slow Fade*?*

I'd taken several trips to India by that time—four trips, maybe even more. I had written a script that I was going to direct in India, and it never got on because I went over there with this producer who was a friend and the production manager from Universal, who had hardly been out of California. We went to Benares and went into this place where you could get these drinks, and they were laced with all kinds of opiate drugs. We didn't know that at the time; we drank these things down, and my friend and I felt fine—we went down to the burning ghats on the river, and it was terrifying and moving and empowering, and all the rest of it. But the poor production manager flipped out and we had to take him back to the hotel and call a doctor because he was having heart palpitations, and the next day he left and flew back to LA. So by the time we got back there, three or four weeks later, we no longer had a parking space at Universal [*laughs*]. We were forever banned from any discussions of India.

That probably accounts for the section in Slow Fade *where they slip something into the young couple's drinks.*

On the train? That was a different time [*laughs*]. India, in those days . . . there's lots of those little stories embedded in the fabric of India.

In Walker, *there's all these anachronisms*—Time *and* Newsweek, *and the helicopters at the end. And in your introduction to the* Pat Garrett *published screenplay, you wrote, "Billy became an anachronism that could not be tolerated." Can you talk a little about the idea of anachronism?*

In terms of *Walker*, Alex ran with that idea. I was nervous about it, because it deliberately broke the whole period. So I thought it would cause a lot of trouble, and it did. But since then, these days, I think it makes great sense [*laughs*], so I'm happy about it, you know. When we opened it at Lincoln Center, people were really freaked by it. I was there with Joe Strummer and he said, "Oh man, we're deeply fucked, we've got to get out of here" [*laughs*].

The way that language is used in the movie I think gives permission to the anachronisms. Walker is speaking in a nineteenth-century style, but everyone else is using late-twentieth-century vernacular—one woman says, "Clearly, this is no ordinary asshole."

[*Laughs.*] Yeah, we took a lot of liberties. It was really laying down the gauntlet. It upset liberals more than anything else, because they were very attached to what they perceived to be the integrity of the poor, about Nicaragua.

Unfortunately, the United States hasn't really learned its lesson; we keep making the same mistakes over and over again.

No, exactly [*laughs*]. Which is the whole point of using the idea of an anachronism in a historical way—things repeat themselves. If you don't much understand what you're doing, you're doomed to repeat yourself. It's an ancient truth, all the way back to Aristotle.

Had you seen Cox's Repo Man *[1984]?*

Yeah, I had met him in LA. We became friends. We shared a lot of stuff together. He was interested in doing a Western of mine that got passed around to various directors. So actually, in terms of my experiences with directors, he was enormous fun to work with, because he has a great sense of equality; he's not into the hierarchies of the situation. He's really unusual that way, because most films, people have different layers, and levels, of sublimation, but he's wide open. The people working with him are really part of the process. It was a real collaboration. Whereas usually, it's a terrifying meeting with three or four people that you've never seen before giving you their votes [*laughs*].

I've heard that you suggested Sam Shepard to act in [Terrence Malick's 1978] Days of Heaven*?*

Yeah, I did. I was a friend of Terry's and I knew Sam, and I thought he would be really good, even though he never really acted, you know. Terry was wide open.

Was it true that you had met Sam in relation to Bob Dylan's [1975–76] Rolling Thunder Revue?

I knew him then, but I think I knew him before. He had a place with his then wife in Nova Scotia; I'd seen him up there, and in New York, around. . . . He's been a great witness and a great friend. He's an old warrior; he's got a lot of arrows in his quiver.

Sam's Rolling Thunder Logbook *[1977], his journal from the tour, is partly dedicated to you.*

It is?

It says, "To Rudy Wurlitzer—who helped me through the first hump of this thing." Dylan had Sam on that tour because he was going to make a film, which became Renaldo and Clara *[1978]—*

And that's something that Lynn worked on; she knew Dylan quite well in those days, and she was around in LA when they were editing *Renaldo and Clara*.

Sam talks about the film in his journal of the tour.

He says that Dylan tells him he wants it to be like Shoot the Piano Player *[1960] or* Children of Paradise *[1945]. And I know that you and Dylan started working on a script on the set of* Pat Garrett *that was supposed to be like* Shoot the Piano Player.

Yeah, in Mexico—just to pass the time. Bob was really bored out of his mind 'cause you have to wait such a long time before being called, especially because Bob didn't have such a big part. So he'd come to wherever my little scribbly shack was and it was like, "All right, let's do something." "What about *Shoot the Piano Player*?" I think if we had continued to work on it, it would have turned into *Shoot the Director* [*laughs*]. It never got finished, we just started.

No one ever mentions it, but I'm sure that Renaldo and Clara *is informed by [Robert Frank's]* Me and My Brother *[1968]; Sam wrote a couple of scenes in* Me and My Brother, *and there's two guys playing Julius [Orlovsky] and somebody playing Robert Frank. And in* Renaldo and Clara, *Bob is playing Renaldo and Ronnie Hawkins is playing Bob. And Allen Ginsberg is in both films.*

Yeah, that's interesting. Sam and I knew each other in those days too, through Robert.

I've also heard that Sam was offered the role of the Driver in Two-Lane Blacktop, *and he turned it down because his wife was pregnant.*

Yeah, that's right, I forgot about that.

Was that through you, or through Monte?

I think it was Monte—maybe it was through me, I can't remember. Wow. That would have been a different film. You know so much more about all this than I do [*laughs*].

*Well, I didn't have to live through it! [*Laughs.*] Twenty years from now, when people start asking me about early-'90s indie rock, it's going to be the same thing.*

George W. S. Trow mentions Two-Lane Blacktop, *as well as you being a friend, in his book* My Pilgrim's Progress: Media Studies, 1950–1998 *[1999]. I wanted to ask you about him.*

I was involved in his last days, before he went to Naples and lost it completely. That was a very intense time for George. We ran into him in Texas; we were driving cross-country, and we could see that he had become really, truly lost. He came from Alaska and drove to Texas, trying to find his myths of origins, so to speak. And he ended up in Newfoundland; we helped him come to Cape Breton. This friend of his, Rory Nugent, a really good writer, is writing a book that George will be part of, about the profound implications and meaning of rescuing and being rescued. George was a big fan of *Two-Lane*.

In that book, he articulates, to an almost painful degree, the way in which the world that he was very carefully taught to prepare for had disappeared by the time he was of age to inherit it, the mid to late '60s and after.

He was totally attached to those sets of descriptions, and those hierarchies and social venues and all the rest of it, in New York and the *New Yorker*—certain types of imagined privileges. And when that fell apart for him—you know, he wrote that thing "Within The Context of No Context" [1980], that's his story as well—but he could never regroup after that. He went on the road, to rescue himself, but finally, in turn, he had to be rescued from that journey.

I've found it curious that in the early '70s, he was writing for National Lampoon *on the one hand and the* New Yorker *on the other, and that also suggests that he was somehow caught between two worlds.*

He was. And then he became much more attached to the *New Yorker*, as having more substance. And then the editor changed, and that was the end, for George. But it also wasn't about that either, you know—that was just a flag. . . . Tragic, sad story. I never became attached to those worlds. Luckily.

When we think about the late '60s and how rapidly things changed in the culture, even in a period of five years, 1964 to 1969—

But *nothing* has changed as fast as the last three to five years now, don't you think?

In terms of?

In terms of the whole internet phenomena, the whole sense of what art is, and literature, and streaming, music and films, the whole media, and the whole corporate takeover.

The speed at which information travels now—

It's just amazing. And the addiction to it. There's a very good article in the last *New York Review of Books* about the internet, and how that mind-speak is being taken over on many different levels—quite alarming. There's various books about it.

Even watching the new Malick film, Tree of Life *[2011]—it's a very audacious film in some ways, and one of the things I admire about it is it's composed almost entirely of unnecessary shots [*laughs*].*

That's what I hear.

In the past, something like Chantal Akerman's Jeanne Dielman *[1975] took a more meditative approach to what she called "the images between the images," daily life things that ordinarily wouldn't be shown in a film, with very long takes. But Terry's movie is all really fast cutting and the camera's constantly in movement. It looks more like a fashion commercial. So, barring the obvious differences between a studio film and an independent feature, it's disconcerting that now even something that's trying to capture "real life" is presented with a nanosecond attention span in mind.*

Yeah, the attention span and the whole act of concentration is totally finished.

Can you talk about the change in bohemian New York over the years?

It's completely different now. The conversation among all the different venues—music, art, film, Oldenberg and Rauschenberg and Johns and various other people, [William S.] Burroughs and all different kinds of poetry, the whole literary thing—was much more open, and it was all mixed. Very, very interesting conversation, in general. *Pull My Daisy* [1959], that kind of conversation between Ginsberg and Robert Frank, that just doesn't happen any more, that I'm aware of, anyway. It's much more isolated, and very defended. The whole thing about not having any money was not so terrifying in those days. You knew you could somehow survive. I had an apartment on East Tenth Street for forty bucks a month—it was fine, you know [*laughs*]. You could get jobs as a bartender or something . . .

That's why a lot of people are moving up to Hudson; they are young and finding it hard to be in the mix of New York, and not only to find work but to deal with the money situation, which is so extreme. But also, the one-to-one personal encounters that really form someone in their twenties don't happen as much, that kind of spontaneity and intercourse of floating relations.

Some of it is because people are spread among the outer boroughs and not so concentrated downtown.

That's true, too. Brooklyn was not an "it" place in those days . . .

*It was someplace that people escaped from [*laughs*], not escaped to.*

It's a very different city now.

I went to see a Trisha Brown dance performance on the High Line, Roof Piece [1971], *that originally took place back in the early '70s. For a long time, I've had a photo of the original performance on the wall at home, so I'm used to seeing the dancers on the rooftops in SoHo. That seems like an expression of that community, and that neighborhood back then. Putting it on the High Line, it becomes part of the tourist trade; people are just walking by. It's a totally different thing.*

It's not as empowering; it doesn't have the energy, it doesn't have any chi—it's all distracted.

And yet, people are still very interested in things that happened back then.

There's a certain nostalgia for that time, which is why my first three books are being reissued. There's a kind of counter-nostalgia thing; the communication was a bit different. Communication was so *present* that you could do things like mine which would sort of pull the rug out from under communication. That was another way to go, but there was a communication about *that*. But now, all that is lost.

Kelly Reichardt

I first heard of Kelly Reichardt, in the early 1990s, as being Bob Lawton's friend who was into movies; Bob was the booking agent for Yo La Tengo and Sonic Youth, and my roommate in Hoboken worked in his office. I saw Kelly's first movie, *River of Grass* (1994), when it came out and I loved it; it was the first independent film made by someone I personally knew that I felt was very strong. We became friends over the years, as part of a small circle of people who were close to both Sonic Youth and Yo La Tengo (back in the '90s, the fans and social worlds of those bands were largely mutually exclusive). We also worked at the same film distribution company for a time. Kelly went on to make a number of critically acclaimed films, all of which I have been enormously moved by, both as a moviegoer and a friend. While compiling these interviews, I found that the collection was lacking a conversation about being involved, professionally and socially, with both movies and indie rock. Kelly was the natural pick for a discussion about that shared experience, which was a dominant aspect of my life in the '90s.

I know you were in Boston prior to moving to New York, but what I don't really know is the origin story of how you met the people in the Boston music scene—the band Christmas, for one—who would eventually connect you to similar people in New York.

Being from Florida, I had seen bands playing other people's music, but I hadn't really gone out and seen people playing their own music, which sounds like something someone in their seventies would say—not someone as young as me, Alan. [*Laughs.*] In Florida, it was just people I knew, like my sister's boyfriends who were in bad bands, or whatever.

Mostly it was cover bands—that was my experience too, in New Jersey.

Oh really?

Nobody played their own songs; everyone in high school was in a cover band.

In Boston, there were all these bands around playing at the Rat, and Joe Harvard and Greg Kendall did a talk show, of sorts, on Monday nights, and different people would come and they'd be interviewed and maybe do something they were afraid to do in public. Just going to the Rat and T. T. the Bear's Place and the Middle East. I saw a lot of bands, all of a sudden. I ended up being roommates with Michael Cudahy [of Christmas]; Dan Castelli, who was the bass player in Christmas; Nick [Cudahy], who was sometimes the bass player in Christmas; and Steve Michener [bass player of Big Dipper]. A house of people who never washed a dish—somehow, I ended up moving in with them. And Liz Cox [drummer of Christmas] was a block away, in the house she grew up in.

I went to art school, randomly—first I went to MassArt, taking night classes, to get [access to] a camera. Then I met someone, Hubbard Moore, and I followed him to the Museum School of Fine Arts. At the Museum School, I ended up doing music videos for some local bands, kind of the beginning of MTV—they would play anything then. When I was living with Michael Cudahy, a lot of bands that came through town stayed at our house. Ira [Kaplan] and Georgia [Hubley] and temporary Yo La bassist Wolf Knapp stayed one weekend. We had a fun time hanging out, so they invited me to New Jersey to come to their wedding.

You knew Bob Lawton, who was Yo La's booking agent for a long time, from Boston, too.

Bob moved to New York, and he said to me, "You wanna be a nobody and stay in Boston or are you gonna come to New York and . . ." Whatever. I came to New York and I started working at the Labor Board [Lawton's first booking agency]. I worked there on and off through many variations, in between PA-ing on films I worked on for Bob. [Filmmaker] Phil Morrison and I kind of leapfrogged each other in that job, because Phil would sometimes be working for [Robert] DeNiro . . . so there was a kind of film/music thing with Phil and I working in both of those worlds, but for a long time, the music and film worlds seemed completely separate to me. I remember when those crowds started hanging out together—maybe it was around when Mary Harron did *I Shot Andy Warhol* [1996]. I guess it was Sonic Youth who cruised into the film world first. I remember, at that Mary Harron release party, Kim Gordon and all those guys being there, and I was like, "Oh wow, all the music people are at the film party."

Which was in the late '90s, right?

Yeah. I'm sure if you go back—I mean, [director Jonathan] Demme was doing stuff with the Talking Heads, and there are other examples you could think of: [Jim] Jarmusch—

Yeah, Jim, although Jim was in a band [the Del-Byzanteens].

Right. But in our world . . . and I was asking Phil Morrison about it to see if he felt this was true too, because David Doernberg, who became, eventually, a production designer, was always at rock shows . . . there started to be a mix of things.

Yeah, I knew that Phil and Dave had feet in both worlds, and there were other people working in film production who I knew and used to see a lot at shows at Maxwell's [in Hoboken, New Jersey]: editors like Joe Klotz and Andy Hafitz, the director Jeff Feuerzeig, and the assistant director Jeff Lazar. But also, working at [film distributor] Kino International during all those years in the '90s—it was like living in two completely different worlds: the film nuts and the music nuts. A couple of people at Kino were interested in rock music, not really indie rock per se, but they were older guys: Gary, the general manager, who had seen Bruce Springsteen in Boston in the early '70s, maybe even the same show that Jon Landau saw, where he said he had seen the future of rock and roll and it was Springsteen; and Laurence, who I was mainly working with in the beginning and was gone, I think, by the time you started working there.

He was at Kino a couple of days a week doing video sales and then he was working at Golden Disc, a record store on Bleecker Street, the other days. And he had tour-managed Defunkt, because he was friends with their manager. But those guys weren't really going out to clubs. Come to think of it, though, in my early days there I got Gary to call in passes for me at Film Forum, and when I picked up the tickets, someone had written "Love Child" on the back of one and "Forced Exposure" on the back of the other. So someone in the ticket booth there was an indie rock fan, but I've never known who it was.

Ah hilarious! And of course, Ira and Georgia were such cinephiles, and Georgia's in that Springsteen video they shot at Maxwell's.[1] But there wasn't a lot of crossover in the beginning, as you know, and then there was.

I made *River of Grass* and naively, on two levels, filled it with music. We were cutting that film on three-quarter-inch video, without any time code, in [actor] Larry Fessenden's apartment on East Second Street. I just pulled from my records, putting music in there, which was naive in that it's a bad idea; it just doesn't help the film in any way. I think it's distracting. But also, it's hugely expensive—*River of Grass* played in Sundance in 1994 and got good reviews, but no distributor would touch it because of the music.

When you're young, you think the most fun part of making a film is to get to combine music and images, but I find it to be one of the most trying parts of filmmaking. Part of that is probably because music is somewhat mysterious to me: I have no concept at all of how music is written, and conceiving it [for the film] before it exists is not something I can do. I've been in a lot of mixes

1 Bruce Springsteen's "Glory Days" music video was directed by John Sayles, who also directed a teenage Will Oldham, pre-Palace/Bonnie "Prince" Billy, in *Matewan* (1987).

with Todd [Haynes] and he can be so specific about what he wants—even before it exists, he can conceptualize music. I can give examples and sort of get people in the zone, but can't really tell if it's working or not until it's cut into the movie. So I started with using records, and then I spent a year and a half raising money so that I could afford to switch out the music. Ira and Georgia, just being friends, swapped out some of the music for me, and helped me redo cues that were already in the film.

Then the obvious thing, a decade later, was to have Yo La Tengo do the music for *Old Joy* [2006], and for that I went to their practice space in Hoboken. We would play scenes that were already cut, and they would play to them on a monitor, or they would give me cassette tapes of things. If I was just listening to the music without the picture, I would be like, "This is *great*, fantastic," and then I'd edit it into the film and it wouldn't work: Once it was with the image, it might be too romantic, or it would take the tension away from the scene. But those guys would just be forking over all this music to me, for no money, I'm sure, and I'd be going, "No, no, no." [*Laughs.*] And at one point, Ira was like, "This is the music, period" [*laughs*].

Was Smokey [Hormel] also playing with them, when you went to see them in the rehearsal space, or did he come in later?

I wasn't there on the days they worked with Smokey. I love the music in *Old Joy*, but I also think that I used too much of it. Having emotional attachment to the music was still getting me into some of the traps I had from having emotional attachments to my records.

Between *River of Grass* and *Old Joy*, I should say, I did some shorts, and Ira did music for those. And that was just me and him, in the rehearsal space. It was Ira playing guitar with some feedback, but more sounds than actual music. Yo La Tengo also did music for *Ode* [1999], along with Will Oldham, separately. The music in *Ode* is better than the movie. The idea of that film is like, it's an after-school special, and I was trying to get over my fear of sentiment, because I felt like *River of Grass* was so removed, in a way. So it was perfectly fine to have Georgia's lovely voice over Super 8, sunset-y scenes. They did a beautiful cover of Sun Ra's "Dreaming." Will released the stuff he did.[2]

And I remember that Will's involvement came about because he and I showed River of Grass *at Tonic when we curated a film series there in 1999, as a double bill with* 92 in the Shade *[1975].*

Oh, that's right. *92 in the Shade*, that's the Florida Keys I grew up in, and that film felt so specifically right on the money. We went to dinner for Chinese food one night with Will, and filmmaker Dianne Bellino—maybe it was the night of that screening—and we talked about Miami. Those guys were talking about moving to Miami, at that point. And I think she did move there, and Will ended up not going. I just remember that all we talked about was Miami that night. Yeah, and then we went over to Tonic, which was a very special place, because then I started holding my SVA [School of Visual Arts] classes at Tonic during the day.

You did? That must have been before I worked there.

2 Will Oldham, *Ode Music* (Drag City, 2000).

No, I think you might have been there, because I knew the owners through you.

I already knew them before I started booking there; I might have just introduced you at some point.

Oh, OK. There was nothing happening there during the day, and at SVA, we could never talk about sound in my class because there was a huge air conditioner duct blowing in my room. So we started holding the classes at Tonic and we would just screen stuff there, and the art school kids would be smoking their cigarettes in the bar, during class. [*Laughs.*] Tonic was a nice way of seeing bands and movies.

Yeah, they had a film series there when they first started, and that's why I pitched the idea of Will and I doing a series of screenings, because they showed movies every Monday night. And Maxwell's used to show movies too.

That I don't remember, although that would have been out of my neighborhood. But I did go to see movies at Tonic. And yeah, that's how I met Will, through your thing programming movies at Tonic. That's how I ended up asking him to do music for *Ode*, and then that's how he ended up in *Old Joy*, eventually.

And it's funny because my whole friendship with Will goes back to this party I went to at the house he was sharing with [Pavement band member] Bob Nastanovich and [Slint band member] Britt Walford in Louisville, when I was on tour with Love Child. We were both in the kitchen and he asked me if I had a job outside of music, and I said I worked for a film distribution company, Kino, and he was super interested in that. We had an hour-long conversation about how film distribution functioned and what it entailed.

I took over your job there in the mailroom at Kino. When I was teaching at SVA, I was also working at Kino; those two things overlapped. Of course, Kino ended up distributing *Old Joy*; I wasn't working there anymore, but I had an attachment to all those people.

We had two meetings with distributors on the same day: We went over to IFC and we were in this windowed office where you could see the city outside. They brought the whole team in. There were chocolate-covered strawberries and cappuccinos; it was so deluxe. They really rolled out the red carpet. And then we walked up to Kino in midtown and the meeting was in that windowless paneled conference room. It was summer, and it was one hundred degrees in that room, and Don [Krim, head of Kino] gave out Dixie cups of water [*laughs*], and that was the meeting. We came out of the meeting and I was like, "Well, we gotta go with Kino" [*laughs*], and everyone was like, "What?!" Just because I knew everyone there, it felt impossible not to go with Kino.

I remember going to the party after the premiere of Old Joy *and Ira and Georgia and all of the people I used to work with at Kino were in the same room, and they had never crossed paths before. What I was saying about being in two different worlds—suddenly those two worlds were colliding. Not in a bad way at all, but that really was kind of a mind-blower for me.*

There's not that much music in Wendy and Lucy *[2008]; maybe Smokey [Hormel] did some music for it?*

He did the music in the grocery-store scene. The idea in *Wendy and Lucy* was to use the trains, the sounds of the trains, as if they were the score. Not that anyone would know, but that's what I did. I already had a girl and her dog and I didn't want things to get overly romanticized or anything like that. I was putting a rigor to it by not letting myself have music in the film. So there isn't actually a score in *Wendy and Lucy*. The little thing that Wendy's humming in the beginning is something Will wrote for Michelle [Williams].

Then in Meek's Cutoff *[2010], there's a score, but no songs at all.*

That's when I started working with Jeff Grace, and everything was made with things that would have been available at the time [in 1845]. He did things like put rocks under guitar strings and make sounds more than anything. Jeff used a lot of wind instruments in *Meek's*. That was the first time I started getting sounds early in the editing process, and Jeff lived close by, so I spent a lot of time going over there—I'd cut all week, and then at the end of the week, I'd go to his place with what was new and rework the score. That was a different experience. I was learning to edit with the music as I went. Usually, I would have all the other sounds and then, later in the process, I'd start working with music, but all the times I worked with Jeff Grace, on *Night Moves* [2013], too, we started working with musical sounds much earlier. In *Meek's*, I had some weird sounds of an echoing wind over a giant playa, and that was sort of our jumping-off point. In *Night Moves*, it was a weird hollow sound at the dam; everything bounced off the water. Again, I was trying to avoid "music" and just use—

—diegetic location sound?

As a place to begin, so you end up somewhere in between score and sound.

In Night Moves, *you used some bands, like Bear in Heaven and A Place to Bury Strangers. Was that [music supervisor] Lyle [Hysen]'s doing?*[3]

Lyle helped me find music for things characters would be listening to, like on a car radio, or if they went to a sporting-goods store—things of that nature. I think there was some music for a film that's in the film. Actually, Larry Fessenden was the person who made that eco-environmentalist film-within-a-film, and I think he did the music for it. And I should say that Larry's the person who taught me how to edit, and he was the first person who got me thinking about sound; he liked to sit in a room and just listen to sound from films and talk about it. And Lyle has sort of been connected in all of these films, because he'll just start sending me stuff early on.

Certain Women *[2016] has hardly any music in it.*

Smokey Hormel did some beautiful music for the end credits. There's a small piece by Jeff Grace in there. If I cut without music, I get used to the sounds I have, and then somehow, putting music in . . . even though that was the intention, and Jeff kept sending me stuff, nothing felt right; everything seemed to make things too easy. I was out West and he was in New York, and it was a lot harder doing the music remotely than it was just being able to be in a room and hammer it out together. I

3 Hysen was the drummer of Das Damen and producer of the second Love Child album. He invited Licht to join him in a latter-day lineup of the '60s band Love with Arthur Lee.

had this conversation a lot with Todd Haynes during the making of the movie, and Todd would say, "Why does it have to have such rigor? Music could do nice things here or there." But I don't know—for some reason, it felt like a cheat or something.

The one bit of score I ended up using, I put it in, I took it out, I put it in, I took it out—it's over the part where Lily Gladstone drives off the road in her truck. I was like, "Should I just allow myself this one movie moment?" Sometimes I felt strongly that, "Yes, I should," and some days I was like, "No, I shouldn't." But then the day came when I had to mix the film and I had to decide, and on that day, I left it in. But it could have gone either way.

There were so many different beautiful wind sounds where we shot, whether it was bouncing off buildings or in more open space. In fact, I've come to find out that Livingston [Montana] is the windiest place in America. It's like a wind trap; trucks stop at the edge of it and don't go through for days because they can't drive through the wind. And it'll snow and be beautiful, and you'll get two shots, and then the wind will have blown all the snow away before you get to your next shot. We shot at this gas station a lot, and when the wind would go through the bottom of the trucks, it sounded like people singing. So I just started working with those sounds, which would sometimes be hard to record because there would also be some other sound happening; if you're trying to get a bunch of guys to turn off their giant trucks so that you can get the singsong sound of the wind, it just takes one guy to not cooperate and the whole thing is shot. But we tried to at least find samples that we could re-create in the mix. That became the basis of the sound more than some kind of score.

This is reminding me of two different movies.

One is, do you know the James Benning movie One Way Boogie Woogie *[1977]?*

No.

It's made up of sixty one-minute shots of different locations in Milwaukee, and all you hear is whatever sounds are there in the environment while he's shooting. And then, twenty-seven years later, he went back to all of the same sites, but he kept the original sounds from 1977. He revised the film and called it One Way Boogie Woogie / 27 Years Later, *appending the new footage to the original film but retaining the old sounds, so you're watching the first sixty shots and then the revisited ones as if it were a double-bill. It's amazing; for some shots in the new footage, you really remember the sound, but of course the image is different because things are not necessarily still there after thirty years, although in some cases, they are. And sometimes you remember the image but not the sound, or neither.*

The other thing I was thinking of was Two-Lane Blacktop *[1971]; there's very little non-diegetic music in that film, but there's one montage with some music over it, and I remember how superfluous the music seemed. It's the only part of the movie where the characters are kind of yukking it up, just for two minutes out of a one-hundred-minute movie, which, for the most part, eschews those feel-good movie things.*

Yeah, the engine of the Chevy gets introduced early on, and you're following the sound of that engine constantly.

*I actually talked about that with [*Two-Lane *screenwriter] Rudy Wurlitzer.*[4]

4 See p. 485.

Oh, really?

Yeah, and he said the dialogue between James Taylor and Dennis Wilson, the Driver and the Mechanic, is also a kind of drone, because the way they're talking is so non-conversational; you zone out listening to it, because it's all car-freak jargon.

They're always talking over the engine. [*Laughs.*]

*Yeah exactly, it's like a raga. [*Laughs.*]*

But even when there's a shot and there's no car in it, you find yourself listening for it.

We haven't talked about First Cow *[2019] yet.*

I had so many different thoughts about what the music should be, and I hired these musical historians to help me find stuff. I was trying all kinds of things to bring historic music into it—music from Indigenous people, or music that came over from Europe. The possibilities seemed so many, and everything felt really wrong—too exacting, or it suddenly felt like, "Oh, where's Peter Coyote's voice for this?" [*Laughs.*] And then Stephen Malkmus suggested I try William Tyler. And I knew William's music in Lambchop and Silver Jews, but not his solo stuff. I was editing in New York and William came for a long weekend. He came to the editing room with a dulcimer and all his guitars and I just played him scenes and he played to them, and he'd go home and I'd try editing at night with those things, and then he'd come back. It was pretty clear that it would work, pretty early on. So we sort of did that for three days, and as the cut changed a little bit, we worked on refining it, remotely.

William's a bit of a cinephile, from what I can tell—I've only gotten to know him somewhat recently, but I think he's a guy who would have known something like the Peter Fonda Western The Hired Hand *[1971], and Bruce Langhorne's music score for that, as a point of reference.*

I had put some of those cues from *The Hired Hand* in the film, just to try, in the process of trying everything, and yeah, he was really familiar with that soundtrack record. But it was nice to get away from the period as far as sound went, to have the dulcimer but not have it be so spot-on.

And to go back to the social element in choosing musicians for your films, the fact that William records for Merge, which is Superchunk's label, and that [Superchunk drummer] Jon Wurster was in Ode, *plus there's a Bob Lawton connection [since he was Superchunk's booking agent], and Ira and Georgia are friends with William—when I heard he was doing the music for* First Cow, *it seemed to me like you'd circled back to that.*

It's a tiny, tiny world.

You say it's a small world, but I would counter that, even in indie filmmaking, it's usually not that small a world in terms of what music people choose to include. Your feeling that putting your record collection in a movie is a mistake does not appear to be shared by a lot of directors, who do exactly that and keep doing it over and over again. There's no social component whatsoever in how they select the music. In your case, the soundtracks also reflect a community that exists for you outside of the temporary community of the people working on the film itself.

I guess the main thing I want to get across is that Smokey, and Yo La Tengo, and William, and Will Oldham—people have been very generous to me with sharing their music for the films. It's very fortunate for me.

I think it's something they would want to be involved in, either because of their friendship with you or because, in general, musicians like the idea of making music for a film. And some of them have had some pretty rocky dealings along the way with music supervisors who shall remain nameless, so I think what you can offer is a way of working that's probably more palatable to them, too.

The one other person I wanted to ask about is Richard Hell—I remember you being friends with him but I couldn't remember how you knew him.

[Hell's unfinished/unreleased film] *The Theresa Stern Story* was one of the first films I worked on in New York. I was doing art-department stuff, and Richard asked me to help with the art stuff on there, and he took me all around New York: He took me to Chinatown, he took me to [Blondie guitarist] Chris Stein's house, he showed me all of his favorite things. And I thought, "Oh, this is what living in New York is going to be like," having everything pointed out to you. [*Laughs.*] Of course, nothing like that ever really happened again, but it was really fun.

How did Richard know you?

I believe I met Richard through the writer Mike

DeCapite. And Richard is a movie hound; I run into him and his wife when I'm in New York all the time. They see a lot of stuff. He would always write me about my movies after he saw them. Richard would write a pretty thorough thing about what he liked or didn't like about the movie. That was kind of cool; I appreciated it, whichever way it went, to have someone write in detail why it worked for them or didn't.

Well, Richard's spiked hairstyle in the '70s came from The 400 Blows *[1959]; the kid's hair was one of the things he modeled it on. Back then, Richard also worked at a film bookstore, Cinemabilia, for Terry Ork, and Terry Ork managed Television and was friends with [director] Nicholas Ray; he brought Nick Ray down to see Television. And the term "New Wave" is appropriated from the French New Wave. Some critics were making the point that these bands were mining '60s garage rock—which was the first thing to be labeled "punk," at the time—the same way that [Jean-Luc] Godard and [François] Truffaut were paying homage to American B movies. The* Rolling Stone *review of the first Ramones record involved Paul Nelson taking the entry on Samuel Fuller from Andrew Sarris's book* The American Cinema *[1968] and putting "The Ramones" in everywhere it said "Samuel Fuller." [*Laughs.*]

Whoa.

So that's another thread here; even though most musicians that we encounter are not cineastes, in the kind of scene we're talking about, there is *one root of it where people were inspired by movie culture and can relate independent filmmaking to the indie rock scene.*

That's interesting, yeah. Well, it makes perfect

sense, of course. I'll have to look up that Paul Nelson review because I used to rent movies at the Evergreen video store where he used to work [in the 1990s–2000s]. My friend and I would go in separately, and we would always be asking each other, "Did you talk to the Thin Man?" We called him "the Thin Man," which ultimately is kind of sad. Paul just had great recommendations and on some days you could get into a good conversation with him, and sometimes he didn't talk at all. Somehow, he knew I'd made *River of Grass*, and one time I went in there and he talked to me about the film. I was like, "Oh, cool, who is this person?" [*Laughs.*] I didn't know who Paul Nelson was; Ira probably told me who he was.

Alessandra Novaga

One day I noticed an announcement for the upcoming release of *I Should Have Been a Gardener* (Die Schachtel, 2020), an album inspired by Derek Jarman's Prospect Cottage, a small home the filmmaker maintained on the southeast coast of England, which I had visited in 2018 and found enchanting. The record was by an experimental guitarist I was unfamiliar with, Alessandra Novaga, and was on a label I mainly associated with some beautifully done archival releases, Die Schachtel. I made a note of it, and as the release approached, I serendipitously received an offer for a review copy and a proposal for a possible interview. My copy arrived, and it was clear that the whole package—that is, the music but also the twelve-by-twelve-inch booklet, the great cover photo of Jarman outside the cottage in Dungeness, Kent, and Novaga's liner notes—was essential to what Novaga was expressing about her experience of the cottage. I did some research and it turned out her previous record, *Fassbinder Wunderkammer* (Setola di Maiale, 2017) had also been film-related—a tribute to Fassbinder and his go-to film music composer, Peer Raben. I was intrigued, and followed my intuition that an interview with Alessandra would illuminate her new record, and my own experiences with music and film, more than a record review ever could. We did the interview in a series of emails in September 2020, and the conversation grew well beyond the few questions I had prepared—much like a musical improvisation might grow beyond the standard "conversation starter" motifs that every improviser has at their disposal in performance. *BOMB* had agreed to my proposal to interview Alessandra, but ran a considerably truncated version of our exchange; I'm pleased that we are able to share a fuller transcript here.

Have you been to the cottage or is the record just based on photos and Jarman's memoir? If you have visited, how did it compare with the way you envisioned it after reading about it? And how did being there specifically impact the music? Was the music all made after the visit, or before?

I think it all started with *Modern Nature*, the diary that Derek Jarman kept between 1989 and 1990. I read it because of my great interest in gardens and gardening literature. I was very impressed and influenced by this book—a real discovery of a man and artist. From there, I started to look for images, videos, or any testimony of the garden that Jarman created around Prospect Cottage. After one year of research on his life and work, I composed "I Should Have Been a Gardener," the title track of the album. In the diaries he says that while he was gardening, he listened to John Adams's *The Wound-Dresser* [1988–89], which moved him very much. It is a piece for baritone and orchestra with lyrics by Walt Whitman.

I started listening to it obsessively and fell in love with it, so I made my version for solo guitar. At that point, I went to Dungeness to see, with my own eyes, the cottage and the garden. It was one of the most meaningful and touching experiences of my life. I could feel his presence there as if he was next to me. It seems like being on the moon, at the world's edge. On one side a gray sea and an expanse of pebbles; then the road and a succession of fishermen's cottages without fences; a little farther, a majestic gray nuclear power plant, which he compared to the Emerald City with its glittering lights. I walked around the cottage at all hours. I listened to the two pieces I recorded in the form of notes, sitting on the shingle in the back of the house, to see if there was empathy with the place. I recorded my steps on those shingles, and you can hear them in the piece that opens the album, "April 21."

Some pieces were born before I visited the cottage, some after, strongly influenced by the experience. During the working process, I was surrounded by photographs, almost all by Howard Sooley—a great photographer and Derek's close friend. I was fortunate to be able to use these photographs for the album's graphic design. I had printed a photo of Derek walking in front of the house and hung it over the chair I play on. My favorite one. I still didn't know Howard personally. That photo became the cover of the record!

I also visited the cottage and found it to be a moving experience. But I was only there during the day—it would be interesting to see that area at night. And I was there in the summer; in the winter it can be a very harsh environment, from some of his descriptions in Modern Nature.

More specifically, in what way do you think your experience with the cottage shaped the music? In other words, how are these pieces different from other music you've done that had nothing to do with Jarman, or landscape? People sometimes make music to evoke specific places, and I often wonder how that really translates.

I don't think the experience with the cottage shaped the music, but I think it came from a long and deep investigation into the man and artist that Jarman was. My purpose was to make a portrait of him. This is my fourth solo album, and the four albums are very different from each other. I am very slow when I work on a project; I have no productivity anxiety. I decide to record only after a long work, a long reflection, and only after having thought that it is really worthwhile to capture the result, at least for me. This album, in particular, took almost two years to take shape, and to tell the truth, the most interesting and exciting part has been researching Jarman, an extremely complex and multifaceted man. He was first of all an artist, then a film director, an activist for gay rights, one of the first who came out as HIV-positive, when nobody would dare to. He said, "I did it for myself . . . because my whole life had been a struggle to make my life open and acceptable. . . . I did it for my own self-respect." This is one of the highest and most inspiring thoughts. He was brave. He talked about his unspeakable suffering, with [his last feature film] *Blue* [1993], for example, without ever being pathetic or trying to inspire pity. Life, illness, joy, love, sex, art, and death are all put on the same level. They are all exposed. I find this wonderful and for me it is a great source of inspiration; it helps me to live better. And then he was a gardener—wonderful, imaginative, original. He moves me a lot. His diaries were written in the knowledge that they would be published. When *Modern Nature* came out he was still alive. But of course I'm also there, in the music I wrote. *I Should Have Been a Gardener* is a sentence in which I too identify myself completely. Vivaldi's *Stabat Mater* [ca. 1727], which I evoke in "April 21," in the recording of my footsteps around the cottage, is one of the musical works I love the most. Well, maybe that's the only piece of the album where Prospect Cottage is present, even if only trivially, because it is the garden itself that plays, through my footsteps. And while I play it I am there, and I try to evoke Jarman walking through his plants and his sculptures.

For me he is beauty, yearning, and the *Stabat Mater* is the thing that most resembles this feeling. But I confess that I don't really love to explain my music, because I think that whoever listens to it should have the opportunity to make out their own personal journey.

Music is its own language and its own reality, which does make it difficult to explain—that's partially why I tend to question how reasonable it is to pursue a musical rendering of a place or a person. But ultimately it's a reflection of inspiration, as you said. To go back to your previous project, Fassbinder Wunderkammer, *you made arrangements of themes from some of the soundtracks to films by Rainer Werner Fassbinder, who used the same composer, Peer Raben, on nearly every film. That was a much more direct way of working with a musical aspect of an extra-musical influence. I have to confess that while I've seen numerous Fassbinder films, I don't recollect the scores so well; I mostly recall his use of pop songs, which are quite memorable—the Walker Brothers' "In My Room" in* The Bitter Tears of Petra von Kant *[1972]; Suicide's "Frankie Teardrop" in* In a Year of 13 Moons *[1978]; Fleetwood Mac's "Albatross" in* World on a Wire *[1973]. I was wondering if you'd always taken notice of the music in his films, or if that was something that you began to appreciate more over time?*

I always loved Fassbinder's films. The first one I watched was *Veronika Voss* [1982], when I was seventeen years old. I think that if you like a film you like every part of it, including the music, but actually the first time I took notice of Peer Raben's soundtracks separately from the films was in 2000, when in a record shop in Berlin I found a record with some of them on it. Two years later, the Milan-based Teatro dell'Elfo organized a Fassbinder tribute festival, inviting a lot of actresses and actors who played in his films, and they included Peer Raben. I remember an extraordinary concert of Ingrid Caven, who sang a lot of Raben's songs. I have always loved the particular synergy that happens to some director-composer couples such as [Federico] Fellini/[Nino] Rota, [David] Lynch/[Angelo] Badalamenti. The music composed by Peer Raben adheres so closely to the atmospheres of Fassbinder's cinema that I always think of the two men as a single person.

It's true that part of what can make a great film is when all the elements are intertwined and equally compelling, including the music and/or the sound design. But sometimes music that I really like in the context of a film doesn't work for me so well on a soundtrack album. I'm particularly thinking of Ennio Morricone's score for Leone's Duck, You Sucker!, *also known as* A Fistful of Dynamite *[1972], which I loved when I saw the film in the theater and then found disappointing when I bought the soundtrack. Which is surprising, because Morricone's music tends to work better than most once it's separated from the film it was composed for. Do you have a relationship to soundtrack albums in general? And have you yourself ever composed music for a film, or done live accompaniment to a film?*

I agree with you when you say that sometimes listening to soundtracks separately from the film is disappointing. I think, for example, that David Lynch's movies would be completely different without Badalamenti's music, but I have no need to listen to those soundtracks only as music. On the contrary, I think of films like Alain Resnais's *Hiroshima, Mon Amour* [1959] with music by [Georges] Delerue and [Giovanni] Fusco; or *Muriel, or The Time of Return* [1963] with music by Hans Werner Henze; or *Un homme et une femme* [A Man and a Woman, 1966] with music by Francis Lai; or Tarkovsky's *Stalker* [1979] with music by Eduard Artemiev; and Louis Malle's *Ascenseur pour l'échafaud* [Elevator to the Gallows, 1958] with its Miles Davis soundtrack; all Fassbinder's cinema with music by Peer Raben. In my personal experience, all this music can exist even without the movies probably because it evokes films that I loved very much; I don't know exactly. This is complex because maybe we shouldn't consider films and soundtracks separately in some cases, but we should ask ourselves why we love a film, and it is too much now, in this interview I mean. But I would love to mention a new discovery for me, a Soviet soundtrack composer of Armenian descent, Mikael Tariverdiev. I definitely love his music and I listen to it a lot, and even if I haven't seen any of those Russian movies that this music was written for, I dream images and black-and-white situations.

I've never composed music for cinema, but I used to compose, and sometimes to perform onstage, for the theater. I only do it when there is a great understanding with the project and with the director. I really like working for the theater; for me it is very different from my musical projects because I feel that my music, in a show, has a task to fulfill, which I don't think when I play alone. It becomes part of the dramaturgy and the directorial idea, and this fascinates me very much.

Yes, actually the soundtrack to Tarkovsky's Solaris *[1972] is one I loved in the movie, not only Artemiev's electronic score but the Bach organ piece he uses as a theme, and when the album soundtrack was belatedly released I loved listening to it also, not just as a reminder of the film, which is my favorite of his, but as a standalone album of music. And Miles's soundtrack for the Malle film I like even better as an album than I do in the context of the film.*

I also love very much the Bach piece used by Tarkovsky in *Solaris*. I believe that in his films something very rare happens—difficult to explain. It is as if he further illuminates artists who are already very great.

For example, if "now," I mean after having seen *Solaris*, I listen to Bach's Chorale Prelude in F Minor [*Ich ruf zu dir, Herr Jesu Christ*, ca. 1732], I am immediately pervaded by the sacredness of *Solaris*, while if I think for example of all of Bach's music used by Bergman (which I love very much) in almost all his films, the association is completely different; in Bergman the use of music is perhaps more functional. Tarkovsky does the same thing in *The Mirror* [1974], when the child leafs through a book with reproductions of Leonardo da Vinci for a long time, and those reproductions—and Leonardo himself, although already immense on his own—are further ennobled because they are in Tarkovsky's hands.

Tarkovsky made Solaris *as an "answer" to Kubrick's* 2001: A Space Odyssey *[1968], and when you compare the use of the Bach chorale and the Artemiev electronic score to the "Blue Danube" waltz [by Johann Strauss II, 1866] and the [György] Ligeti pieces in* 2001, *the differences between the two films become even more striking. But also Bach, Leonardo, and the Bruegel painting of the hunters that figures in* Solaris *are examples of a certain longing for Western European culture on Tarkovsky's part, while also calling attention to these works' indomitability over space and time, and the power of art to endure. Which in turn is an allegory and aspiration in Tarkovsky's navigation of life as an artist in the Soviet Union. For Bergman, Bach's work would have a much different significance in terms of the society and culture he was raised and living in, and often in the societies and cultures depicted in his films.*

It's interesting that you composed music for theater, because theater is very much a live experience and film screenings are mediated ones—so the making of a film reminds me of the making of an album, and for theater you have rehearsals that go into a live performance. Did you find the experience of working on music for theater similar to the experience of preparing for concerts?

Yes, the two experiences are very close to each other, especially when I perform onstage with the actors. For me the rehearsals are very important because I used to compose onstage while we were working together; I never compose for theater at home alone. I need to be there in the action, with the right lights, and I do the same even when I have to record the music, because I won't be onstage. In this case, I play with the actors, recording everything on my loop station. At the end, everybody makes silence, and the sound engineer records all I recorded on my loop. It works very well.

The fact that you compose for the theater within the space itself, with the actors, is fascinating to me as a kind of conflation of film composition, where you have to leave room for dialogue and sound design, and free improvisation, where solo practice and group activity are very distinct. When you say that you even record live with the actors when you know the score will not be performed live, it reminds me of Neil Young's approach to scoring Jarmusch's film Dead Man *[1995], where he played live to the film, single takes only, all improvised.*

A friend, the late David Berman, once told me that he gave movies "a B-minus" as a genre, because he said you couldn't trace a film to a single author, unlike books, and maybe, to a certain degree, music. I suppose that could apply to narrative film, but certainly not to experimental filmmakers like Stan Brakhage and others. It strikes me that your Jarman record is in some ways a collaboration with the cottage, since the inspiration of it is so essential to the work, and even the album packaging, with the booklet of photos, seems quite integral to what you're trying to communicate. So I guess my question is:

One, how much of your work would you say is collaborative, in this rather expanded concept of collaboration, and two, to what extent do you consider yourself the sole author of a composition?

I find this question extremely interesting, and extremely complex! Again, we are dealing with topics that philosophically speaking are really huge, so I'll try to be very concise. Berman faces an important issue, the authorial one, but I don't know if I agree with his idea that maybe is a little trenchant. It is true that a film needs an incredible amount of people, and the same thing can be said of theater, but if we are talking about great authors, such as Tarkovsky, Fassbinder, Jarman, Fellini, [Éric] Rohmer, Peter Brook, Richard Foreman, etc., etc., we cannot deny that they are the generating center, they choose the collaborators, the set designers, the musicians, the screenwriters, the costume designers, the actors. It is true that directors like Stan Brakhage or Jonas Mekas are practically self-sufficient but, I speak above all for Mekas, whom I know best, as he is one of my favorite artists of all time—he has filmed the lives of dozens of people, known or less known, it does not matter—he used music by others sometimes, and the inspiration could be his family, it could be the return to Lithuania from his mother he hasn't seen for decades, or Ginsberg's deathbed; that too is a collaboration, in my opinion, but each of his works is imbued with his vision. The "vision" is the key concept to define an author, in my opinion. If I'm not mistaken, Stan Brakhage filmed a birth [in *Window Water Baby Moving*, 1959]; I would say that there is collaboration, too.

If you think about painters, they don't need anyone, and writers, too, apparently; but even a painter alone in his studio certainly resorts to an imaginary, to philosophical ideas, if not precisely to models or landscapes. What about literature? Think of the role of editors who sometimes rewrite books and are not even mentioned except, in some rare cases, in the final thanks. I read a story by Carver both in the original and in the edited version—two different things, two different authors! In my works, which are all in my name only, I know very well that I am indebted to a multitude of people, books, films, other musicians, and I could also tell you about enlightening conversations with friends. You are right in saying that my latest record is the result of the work of many people to whom all my gratitude goes. First of all, it goes to Derek Jarman, who is the source of everything, to his diaries, to his garden, to his thoughts; then there is the music that I have revisited: *The Wound-Dresser* by John Adams, "It's a Sin" by Pet Shop Boys, and the *Stabat Mater* by Vivaldi. This rewriting of existing music is a topic that interests me very much. If I think about the work I did on the Adams piece, I can tell you that the original is for orchestra and baritone; imagine what limits I would have had with the guitar if I had wanted to transcribe it. What I have tried to do is to return the impressions that this song has left on me. The voice of the baritone, the theme in short, there is only in a short stretch—I have transformed some areas of the orchestra in the main theme: the balances, the timbres, the proportions are distorted; I don't think anyone would recognize it, but when I listen to it, the starting point is very recognizable to me. Without putting myself on the same level as Francis Bacon, of course, think about what he did with Velázquez's [c. 1650] Pope Innocent X [*Study After Velázquez's Portrait of Pope Innocent X*, 1953]. Then there are the beautiful photos, full of enormous meaning for me, by Howard Sooley, and last but not least, the graphic concept by Bruno Stucchi, one of the two producers at Die Schachtel. I could add that there are those who helped me choose the photos, who listened to all the pieces and gave me advice that I followed; there are those who recorded [the album] and those who made the master, and who knows who else escapes me now. The fact remains that I think I am the author of this record precisely because I appropriated, in the true sense of the word, all this, and made it mine. It is my personal vision of a man and the world he created as I perceive it. And the need and desire to realize this record was mine, and the inspiration and research, too. And the idea. All the people I have listed are obviously mentioned in the credits of the album and I know that without them it would not exist, so for Berman even a work like this would have been considered "a B-minus"? Probably yes, but the record wouldn't exist if I didn't want it.

I'm glad I asked! Thank you for this detailed reply. I also fundamentally disagreed with David, although when the screenplay is written by someone other than the director, the question of authorship becomes a little more difficult (which was Pauline Kael's whole argument against Orson Welles and Citizen Kane *[1941], though I find that problematic as well). This is tangential, but I always felt David's comment says more about his own ambivalence about attaching his writing to a rock-band format, perhaps, than about cinema.*

I also wanted to ask about graphic scores, since another one of your previous albums, La Chambre des Jeux Sonores *[Setola di Maiale, 2014], was comprised of your interpretations of five different graphic scores. In general I find graphic scores intriguing, at least visually, but I have no real interest in interpreting one. I'd rather just improvise. An exception would be Christian Marclay's [video score]* Screen Play *[2005], which I have performed several times and enjoy working with, maybe because the cues are visual and you're not meant to translate the images into sound. So what happens is a lot of aleatory combinations of sound and image, which I find vastly appealing. For a long time Lee Ranaldo and I had a project called Text of Light, where we improvised music alongside a screening of different experimental films, mostly by Brakhage but by others too, which didn't have a soundtrack to begin with. We weren't trying to score the films—it was more of a mixed-media experiment to see what would happen simultaneously; we wouldn't watch the films while we were playing, or even beforehand. So I'd like to hear your thoughts on graphic scores: what you like about them and how they relate, or not, to the visual stimuli we've talked about from Fassbinder films or Derek Jarman's garden—and I realize those are about much more than simple visuals.*

La Chambre des Jeux Sonores is my first solo album with the electric guitar. After thirty years spent exclusively playing classical guitar, and therefore interpreting works in exact notation, I looked out into another territory. You know well that the term *graphic scores* includes a multitude of types; we have those in which there are only images, photos, visual suggestions, in short, or those in which we have instructions, therefore more textual than graphic, and then others that are less [able to be] cataloged. My need, at that moment, was to get out of the concept of "exact notation" and explore other ways of relating with composers, so I asked five of them to write me pieces for electric guitar, a completely new instrument for me. I had learned to play it, if we can say so, for the great desire to interpret Fausto Romitelli's "Trash TV Trance" [2002], the most important piece in the electric guitar's repertoire, in my opinion. My requests were basically two, that they weren't in exact notation—no staves—and that there were indications about the sounds, the timbres, which was something [for which] I was still groping about in the dark. Being five composers of completely different backgrounds, I had five completely different pieces. The most graphic of all is "Untitled, January," by Francesco Gagliardi, who in fact is not a musician but has a theatrical and philosophical background, and who is a performance composer. The score is a photo of a foggy landscape taken from a train; the only indication is: "One drone, any drones, any durations." After several experiments, the idea of how to do it came to me while crossing a street in New York City a few days before performing it for the first time. For me this was enlightening. At last I came out of the slavery of the instrument, of instrumental practice. The idea was born on the street and not on the chair! Francesco, who first put me in contact with a form of thought that at the time was very far from me, then put me in touch with an environment based essentially in New York, which had a strong impact on me—I speak of Travis Just and Kara Feely [of the New York collective Object Collection] and G. Douglas Barrett, mainly. With them I organized some performance concerts of graphic/textual scores in Italy, where not much happens in this area. Travis Just, on the other hand, is a musician, and he wrote several pieces for me; on the album there is one very interesting one, "International Hash Ring," basically built on time sections—I have to use a stopwatch, in each one I have to perform written actions and to use certain effects. Also very interesting is that one by Paula Matthusen, who is one of the most interesting American composers of recent years. I then performed, with [composer and guitarist] Elliott Sharp, his *Foliage* [2012], a piece based entirely on images projected on one screen during the performance. But I haven't been involved with this kind of composition for many years, and like you, I definitely prefer to improvise. Obviously I do not reject this album and these collaborations, indeed I am very grateful to all the composers mentioned, but I think for me that represented a moment of transition necessary to be able to go with my legs; it helped me to understand what I could do alone. As for a possible relationship with my last two works, I don't think there is any. Both are based on very different assumptions both practically and conceptually.

I like the idea of graphic scores as a transition for a classical player who is used to standard notation and is trying to break free from that lineup. I came to improvisation through rock, and obviously rock guitar notation is mostly chord charts, so my sight reading was never very good and I never thought it would help me make the music that I wanted to do. Although I refer to myself as a musician, I actually reject many of the things a professional musician should do, such as playing other people's music from a score. I mentioned the exception of playing Christian Marclay's Screen Play, *and a few years ago I even participated in a version of Terry Riley's* In C *[1964], but I hated doing it—it was like when you're with a large group of people and everyone's trying to decide where to go to dinner or have a drink, and it's just an endless discussion and it takes forty-five minutes to make a move.*

As far as I'm concerned, the desire to move away from written notation does not mean that I disavow my background. When you can study classical music at a high level, and luckily for me I did, studying scores written by others can mean many important things. Glenn Gould often talked about re-composition when referring to his interpretations, and indeed Gould's Mozart is not the Mozart we usually listen to. Arturo Benedetti Michelangeli, who obviously knew a vast piano repertoire, always played the same pieces; imagine how much he was able to dig them! Through the profound study of the scores of the great authors, you find a world—the history, the phenomenology of music; you then find the sound, the gesture, you find a dialogue with people who died centuries before, as if you were a medium—you find beauty that is difficult to find elsewhere; your vision of the piece and yourself, when you're lucky. The masters I have chosen have been able to show me all this. The one who followed me in the last part of my training, Oscar Ghiglia, is one of the greatest artists of the 1900s, and perhaps, he is the most significant student of [guitarist] Andrés Segovia, and I learned a lot from him besides music—a guitar lesson was not less significant than going with him to the Kunstmuseum in Basel, where I studied and lived, to look at the paintings. There is another incredible guitarist that I point out to you, Paul Galbraith, with whom I had the fortune to do some lessons, who is a pure visionary; his *Chaconne* by Bach [ca. 1717–23] is beyond any violin version I have ever heard. But at a certain point, I realized that my voice, in that context, did not add anything new, and luckily this did not create any imbalance or trauma. On the contrary it is as if I had had the opportunity to live a second life, and I think that this is a huge fortune. And anyway, not a day goes by without playing Bach.

Yes, you can learn a lot by studying a score, and Glenn Gould is a good example of someone who knows all the rules and then made extraordinary interpretations of some very familiar scores. When I was a teenager studying guitar, I used to transcribe solos, and transcribing John Coltrane's saxophone solos was fascinating—to see how his mind was working. But even when I was listening almost exclusively to classical music, before the age of ten, which is when I started listening to rock and playing guitar, I never had any inclination to learn an instrument that would be in an orchestra, or piano, or anything that

*I could play it on. And I think a part of that was a resistance to having to read notation, strangely enough—also, I didn't want to practice [*laughs*]. Whereas with rock music somehow I thought the guitar was my ticket into not just the music, but the whole environment. The real reason I picked up the instrument was the painting of Paul McCartney and Wings in the gatefold sleeve of the* Wings Over America *[Capitol, 1976] triple album, where they're onstage in the middle of a light show. I think I wanted to be in the light show more than I wanted to be a musician, that a guitar was just the means to that end [*laughs*]—and my name is* "Licht" *after all! But this goes back to a relationship between music and visuals, which has been very significant to me.*

We know that there has always been a sonic accompaniment to the film, even in the silent era, whether it's records or a live keyboard player, or even a barker reading titles aloud, but sometimes people have been reluctant to assign pictures to music, especially music videos. Yet I think people also feel a visual lack with records. Jarman's record, as I said earlier, seems particularly in need of its cover and booklet, and there are many other records where my relationship with them—and indeed what I feel is their total communication—is subordinated to the combination of the packaging and the music on the disc itself. And I will almost always prefer watching someone play music rather than just listening to a recording. So how do you feel about a need in music for images?

There are also directors who don't like putting music in their films at all; think about Éric Rohmer. How real and concrete is the atmosphere you breathe in films that never have music but only the sounds of reality they tell. If I remember correctly, the absence of the soundtracks was also a point of the Dogme 95 manifesto, but that has less charm for me because I feel very distant from the "currents" and "manifestos." It is not a topic that you solve with little thought, however. Think about how all this, the records and their visual aspect, are Jurassic topics if you think about how music is enjoyed by people of twenty-five to thirty years and under, who only download MP3s. Covers, booklets, are archaeology but for a niche of enthusiasts. As for my record and its graphics, I agree with you that the photos of Howard Sooley and the graphic work of Bruno Stucchi are incredibly organic with the musical content, but I think, and I hope, that the music would have the same impact even without the images.

The images are an extension, incredibly natural here, but when I sent the master to Howard, who did not yet know that I would ask him for the photos, he told me things that deeply moved me; he gave me the blessing I needed. It gave me the feeling that I had come very close to the source of inspiration, Derek Jarman, and only after his reaction did I have the courage to ask him for the photos. Furthermore, several critics have reviewed the album without having it physically, due to Covid-related postal delays, but only listening to the files. By answering the last part of your question, I also love live concerts, especially solo concerts, but I have some records that I couldn't do without. Attending a concert and listening to a record, for me, puts you in two completely different conditions where you find different important things.

I'm not so much pointing out a need for music in film, but for sound as opposed to silence—even if it's just dialogue and ambient sound. That no one has ever been comfortable in a completely silent film screening. Recently I saw a discussion between a couple of composers, and one was saying they usually prefer listening to music on records at home because of the vagaries of acoustics in concert halls. But I really feel that you have to experience music both on record and in concert. I have to buy John Coltrane albums because he died before I was born, and I also try to catch current people live more than I'm motivated to buy their records because usually it's better live. But of course there are exceptions to that, and finding out what those are is part of the passion of following music.

I did want to ask one other question, since you have only come to electric guitar recently: How do you see the differences between electric and acoustic instruments? I started on a nylon-string guitar; even though I never played classical style, I was always oriented toward electric music. But in the last few years I've begun playing acoustic, too, and even recorded an album of solo acoustic pieces, Currents *[Vin Du Select Qualitite, 2015]. At least for me, acoustic versus electric is a little like riding a bike versus driving a car—acoustic is more physically demanding, while electric is more technologically advanced and power-oriented.*

I like the comparison with the bike and car. It's funny because you and I have the opposite experience, if we can say so. It is absolutely true that an acoustic instrument, in my case I would say classical, is much more demanding than an electric instrument. When I started playing the electric guitar ten years ago, my impressions were multiple: on the one hand, the relief of finally playing an instrument that everyone could hear, which filled the entire room where I was playing; on the other, a sense of frustration that I could not find and realize all the inflections and nuances, and the directions of sound, which I manage naturally on nylon strings. Over time I realized that nothing changes between electric and acoustic in that sense—that I could learn to manage the direction of the sound that at first seemed to escape me, as if I could not be in control. Of course, the sense of liberation and pure joy when I started improvising, using distortions, managing feedbacks, was incredible! What I find very different, even today, is the management of the sound. I find it very tiring to resist a long time with such a loud sound. You can turn down the volume, but even with not-loud volumes, after a while I feel physically tired; listening tires me, while I can stay up to three hours without getting up from the chair with a classical guitar. When I was studying, sitting with it was practically the only thing I did, and it was normal to spend eight hours a day with the guitar in hand. But today I feel infinitely richer than I did then.

Adris Hoyos

In the heyday of grunge in the early '90s, a number of underground bands better fit the genre's image of itself—as an anti-fashionable, messy music—than did its aboveground title bearers who simply churned out updated '70s hard rock sprinkled with lessons learned from '80s college radio charts. Royal Trux, the Dead C, and especially Harry Pussy come to mind; indeed, the cover of the last's untitled first seven-inch [ESYNC, 1993] sported a Xerox detail from the December 1992 "grunge issue" of *Vogue,* cleverly emphasizing the chasm between the co-opting of youth counterculture and the noise quotient of Harry Pussy's music itself, which was highly resistant to subcultural commodification. Emerging from the unlikely environs of Miami (never fertile ground for rock music after the Allman Brothers and Lynyrd Skynyrd), the band consisted of guitarist Bill Orcutt and drummer Adris Hoyos (the pair were married at the time), with occasional second guitarists coming and going over the years. They specialized in neo–No Wave and thrash tantrums. I was a fan and a Siltbreeze labelmate; I first met them in 1994 when we were all performing at the Siltbreeze Festival at the Khyber Pass Pub in Philadelphia. They were shy but I struck up a conversation and found them to be just as cool as they came across on their records. Live they were electrifying; Adris in particular was like a dervish behind the drums, and her vocals were as hair-raising as those of any performer you could name working in rock or in any avant-garde.

In the music industry of the late '90s, parallel to grunge, there was a wave of new women in rock and singing-songwriting that culminated in the Lilith Fair festivals. The underground participated, too, and in New York there was a fanzine called *chickfactor* that documented the proliferation of women in indie rock through interviews—at least half a dozen in every issue.

Editor Gail O'Hara used to organize release shows for each new edition, and was also hosting other theme-based club nights, which I duly enjoyed and occasionally played. She was also the music editor at *Time Out New York* for a while, and was generally a force in the city's music community at the time. While *chickfactor* leaned more toward the pop end of indie, Gail wanted to include as many kinds of voices as possible, so when I suggested interviewing Adris Hoyos, Gail readily accepted. We conducted the interview by mail in fall 1995, making this the oldest text in this book, and my queries are very much in line with the template questions that Gail and other contributors might use. As such, it is the only interview here that directly adopts a publication's house style, and the only one where I am using what you might call a "fanzine voice." Nevertheless, I think it shows how singular of a figure Adris was, and remains, in the already multifarious worlds of indie rock and noise.

What is Miami like? Is there a "scene"? Do you guys just cruise around all the time? Is it seedy? Collegiate?

Certain parts of Miami are like Havana would've been like if Castro hadn't taken over. I like it here because I feel comfortable living around people like me, who speak the same language I do and who have the same customs I do. There isn't much happening in the music scene. Mostly bands playing pop music. I'm not involved in any scene. My life isn't that exciting.

When did you start playing drums? Do you play any other instruments and do you plan on singing more?

Bill and I started playing music together, just for fun. I had never played drums before, but I really enjoyed doing it, so we formed Harry Pussy. I had played drums only a couple of times before we recorded our first single. When we started playing in front of audiences, I would usually sing and play guitar for a couple of songs. I'm getting back into that; I've started writing "songs," but I still see myself primarily as a drummer.

What is your "day job"? Would you do Harry Pussy full-time if you had a chance? Would you be bummed or happy if the band became hugely popular?

I can't imagine anything I'd rather be doing than touring. I love being on the road and performing. I wouldn't be "bummed" if HP became popular. Personally, I'm a quiet person. I don't have quite a lot of friends; I like spending time by myself. As far as the band, I'm still trying to adjust to the fact that not everyone hates the music. In Miami, people who watch us play are there to insult us and the rest just walk out. People who come up to me after the show usually have something nasty to say. In the beginning, a lot of people had the attitude that HP wasn't a real band because there was a girl playing drums with guys playing guitar. But I enjoyed that. This attitude gave us license to do anything we wanted and it justified us being aggressive and unpleasant to the audience. And I haven't been able to lose those feelings even when I play outside of Miami, maybe because I enjoy feeling angry onstage. Even now, when someone comes up to me after I play, my first instinct is to say something nasty before they can insult me—and I'm trying to learn not to do that, because when I play out of Miami, some people do tell me they like my drumming or they come up to me just to talk.

Have you bonded with people in other bands? Other couples in bands?

I'm a shy person, but it's usually easier for me to talk to other drummers. I'm grateful that drummers in the bands I've toured with have been really supportive as far as helping me out with problems or giving me advice. I usually have so much anxiety over the condition of my drums when I'm on tour that, to an extent, I was emotionally dependent on other drummers.

OK, here's one straight from the Kim Deal Spin *interview: When you were growing up, were there any female rockers that you admired?*

No, there weren't any.

How did your tours with Sebadoh and the Dead C go?

Both tours went really well. One of the main reasons I like touring is that I get to see really good bands.

Sebadoh and the Dead C are two of my favorite bands, so that was great. And they were both really friendly to us. I also like touring because I've never traveled much. I like going to different cities and finding out if my preconceptions are true or not. Some of the clubs I've been in are amazing, like the Pussycat Tavern in New Orleans, which has circus acts go on before the bands. I like doing shows every night; I love performing and having to do something different every night.

What kind of music were you into in high school? Were you goth? New Wave? Metal? Hardcore? Southern rock?

When I was young I listened to pop and Hispanic music, especially salsa. For a long time, I felt that rock music was for white Americans and it had nothing to do with me. My high school was something like 90 percent Hispanic; I didn't know anyone who was into rock music. When I was a senior in high school, a friend of mine started listening to the Doors, and I got into that for a while, but even then I didn't listen to other classic rock. It wasn't until I was in college that I got into buying records and listening to different types of music.

What's the biggest mistake Harry Pussy has ever made?

I can honestly say HP has never made any mistakes; it's not like HP has any goal to accomplish or purpose to achieve. HP has allowed us to experiment with different ideas about music and performance.

Milford Graves

Milford Graves is a true rara avis. A pioneer of what came to be called free jazz drumming, he made only a few records, which are collector's items, and after the early '70s he has rarely performed live. "Cross-disciplinary" barely seems adequate to describe him as an artist and thinker: far more than a musician, Graves was a professor at Bennington College for nearly thirty years, a master of martial arts, an herbalist, and an acupuncturist, and he has also studied the human heart extensively, applying his findings to his music and more recently, visual art.

Milford Graves Full Mantis (2018), Jake Meginsky's documentary on Graves, who had been his teacher, is a poetic, evocative, pitch-perfect portrait of the man, and the *Wire* prevailed upon me to do a feature on Graves on the occasion of its release. It was the first piece I had written for them in a number of years. Remarkably, there had never been a previous article about Graves in the magazine's nearly forty-year history, and Meginsky insisted on (and got) a cover story for his film's subject. In January 2018, I trekked out to Jamaica, Queens, and arrived at Graves's house—a marvel, its exterior covered in beautiful mosaic tiles handmade and installed by Milford himself. I was quickly ushered downstairs by his wife, Lois, and found Milford standing among several large computer monitors, percussion instruments of all stripes, jars of herbal extracts, books, and bric-a-brac. The interview lasted three hours, and as it ended I handed Milford a copy of the live CD of a trio of Michael Snow, Aki Onda, and me; as a teenager, Aki had photographed a late-'80s tour of Milford and Min Tanaka in Japan, and I figured Milford might have known Michael through Roswell Rudd in the '60s (Snow also did the cover art for Paul Bley's 1965 *Barrage* album for ESP that Milford plays on). Milford lit up, happy to be reminded of Michael, and then we had another two-hour conversation, off the record.

Of all the interviews I've done, the experience of spending time with Milford in his very personally cultivated home environment made me feel like the records of his that I own and cherish, and the concerts I've seen him give over the last thirty years, really only scratched the surface of the totality of who he is as a person. You can't fit his worldview, his breadth of knowledge, onto a twelve-inch record or a CD booklet. At a concert you're only seeing him behind a drum set for an hour; as amazing as it might be, it's just the tip of the iceberg. When I got home I realized that, in a way, the interview with Milford brought me full circle to when I had met with Maryanne Amacher for the same magazine exactly twenty years before, virtually to the day. (As it turned out, both issues ran these features as ALAN LICHT MEETS . . . and they are the only two occasions where my byline has been on a *Wire* cover.) Both were older avant-garde artists (born in 1941, Graves is three years Amacher's junior) who had been around since the '60s; both were working in relative obscurity; and even more so than Milford's, I recognized that Maryanne's work was highly resistant to being effectively recorded—it could only come off properly in the most carefully staged and calibrated live situations. While their work has been ill-served by the usual channels of distribution and promotion, Milford and Maryanne are musicians I stand in awe of, and it was enormously rewarding to make personal contact with them and to share whatever insights into their art I have been able to glean.

One thing I took away from the film Milford Graves Full Mantis *was that you're trying to get to the source of something, or the root of it. You were saying how you looked to the praying mantis because you felt that it was the source of some of the motion in the martial arts, and to the heartbeat, also, as a source of rhythm. Was the* Dialogue of the Drums *[IPS, 1974] duo album with drummer Andrew Cyrille a way to get to the source of jazz drumming?*

Yes and no. If I had to use any recording as an example of getting to the source, it would be the one that I did on ESP—and it said "Milford Graves Percussion Ensemble," so you would think that it was an ensemble and not a duo. I think that was [label head] Bernard Stollman who came up with "ensemble," 'cause I didn't say nothing about an ensemble. I tried different drummers, and Sonny Morgan was the only one who was able to pass the test, so to speak, because of his background in West African drumming and some of the Caribbean drumming.

I'm particular about doing any kind of group work with another drummer, or drummers. As I'm getting older, I said to myself, "I've got to make a statement, make it clear." Jazz drumming was a deviation from the source—it was an interruption, in a way, of African culture, or African mind. Being brought out of Africa through slavery, they got interrupted when they got to the States; they got altered and disguised, where people felt they had to make all kinds of adjustments to fit into this new society. People don't want to speak the truth because they feel as though, "If I speak the truth about how I feel, maybe I won't get no more work," or anything like that. But I feel it's the right time, now, that the truth came out about jazz. Guys would be in the so-called neighborhood, in the community, playing, and they thought they had to make adjustments, particularly to get into Manhattan School of Music or Juilliard—African Americans trying to get into Juilliard was not that easy back when I was coming up. But that was the thing, to learn to read and write music. And I'm saying, "You're doing that not 'cause you really feel it, you're just trying to make that adjustment to improve your economics." The true story of jazz is that it developed here in America, not Africa. It adapted here, but it still had that thing that came out of Africa.

So, I said, "If I play with another drummer, how would I do this and not be emotionally affected by the fact that the concept of drumming, as an accommodation, is a way of expressing yourself?" The drums, relative to what the other instruments are playing in the jazz band—which was something that Max Roach did a lot, try to play melodic lines on the drums. But the way he played, it wasn't really manipulating the membrane, in a sense, to get the full expression. It was limited—limited like a keyboard. I'll act like this guy [Graves's collaborator] is trying to play jazz, and I'm trying to show some kind of connective situation. The rhythmic system that you're playing is not African in the sense that it has an ethnic relationship—most of those rhythms that you're playing, they're so cardiac-related, they're human rhythms, they got nothing to do with you being African, nothing like that. But you're coming to the Western world, which got so academic and intellectual, and you try to play a number game, and you've got to write the rhythms as a graph, like A. M. Jones did when he was doing all that research on Ghanaian music—it was amazing what those guys did. They used to have a machine where a master drummer would tap on a metal plate; then they would try to graphically figure out what was going on, and then they said, "Oh, there's no bar lines—where's the bar line?" So they had these imaginary bar lines—why are you trying to make it into something that it's not? It's not a bar line, where you have a symmetry going on. It's so biological—it belongs to all of us. Alan, it belongs to all of us! You don't own it because you're African—maybe it developed there, but don't tell me you have a monopoly on this. That's the amazing thing about working and dealing with heart rhythms. It just blew me away when I got the knowledge to use the technology.

In the movie you talk about how there's an unequal amount of time between heartbeats, and that immediately made me think of that as being analogous to the idea of equal temperament versus just intonation. What you're talking about is the same thing, but with rhythm.

Right, right. I'm just trying to get back to how we vibrate as humans. As musicians, we're supposed to be just like a chef is when they cook—you're supposed to meet the demands of the body's physiological system.

Do you think that part of what Western society imposed on it is the idea of mathematics—that's why you have notation, and why people are trying to adapt to a strict metronomic—

Exactly. It's control, controlling people. People want to empower themselves to get control and say, "OK, we need some new faces up here, so we're going to get rid of you and get somebody else in here. And here's the plan—you've got to follow this plan."

How far back does your interest in the heart go? Was it an outgrowth of playing drums, or was it something you always had a parallel interest in?

I don't remember the actual age, but I was young. There was always this connection between, metaphorically speaking, the drum and the heart. People say, "Where does the drum come from? Where does music come from?" They say it's the heart, and they're just repeating what they heard, 'cause most people probably never heard a heartbeat in their life. I was talking about this a lot, and when I started teaching at Bennington College in 1973, I said, "I'm going to make this part of my course content." I thought I had to get intellectual—teaching college? Wow, that's another thing. They're going to get some smart young kids in there, and I've got to be on top of it. In 1975, one of my former students who had graduated a year or two before that sent me an article from a journal called *Circulations*. They were talking about diagnosing the heart in a different kind of way. It was saying that you have to listen to the *pitch* of the beats, not counting the number of cycles that you have per minute. They were talking about the opening and closing of the valves, the harmonics that are taking place in the heart muscle. I called one of the authors of it—they were brothers, one of them was an MD, the other was an electrical engineer. I called the MD, and he said, "Oh no, you don't want to talk to me, you want to talk to my brother, 'cause he knows all about this." We had a two- or three-hour conversation on the phone, and he was telling me he was trying to convince these doctors that they had to listen to the actual pitch, and it would give them more information than just making sure that your heart is contracting and relaxing.

That led me to—I used to go to Barnes and Noble, and I'd seen this recording of heart sounds by Dr. George David Geckeler. I brought that record home and I put it on, and I immediately started calling my friends up. I said, "I have a recording of real clinical heartbeats that was made for doctors, and there are so many different kinds of heart rhythms—all these arrhythmias are very similar to what we're doing with ritual drumming." This is amazing. This way, I don't have to worry about someone coming from a very closed culture, from Africa, or Cuba, or whatever else, and waiting around forever for them to show you the next pattern. I bought an electronic stethoscope and I had my reel-to-reel recorder here. Everybody who would come to my house—all the musicians—I said, "Come on, let's go, I'm going to record your heart." I'd say to musicians, "What's the frequency, what's the note on there, man?" We'd be sitting around trying to figure this out, and people would say, "I don't know, I don't know what that one is—it's in between this note and that note." That led me into getting some really sophisticated computer equipment.

That's interesting, because then the subdivisions that you're doing are a lot like the subdivisions that you hear drummers using in so-called free jazz.

Right, that's what it is. The free jazz guys, we were really cardiac! We were really on the cellular level—you guys had been on the muscle, you guys were playing motor music. That's surface stuff. It's valid—it's a concept—but I said, "I want to get deep down inside and make sure we're in sync with how the body really vibrates."

I was going to bring up Derek Bailey, who always said that improvisation was the most basic form of music-making. I know you played with Derek and Min Tanaka in 1982, and in the film they show a picture of you and Aquirax Aida, the promoter in Japan who brought you over there on an earlier trip where you recorded Meditation Among Us *[Kitty, 1977]. He brought Derek over also.*

I went there in '77 first. Three weeks or a month, maybe—but it was like I was there for years. The great thing was that it wasn't a jazz promoter that brought me there, because if it was a jazz promoter I would have been in Osaka, Tokyo—I would have been in a more commercial, hip set. But they made sure that I traveled north, south, east, and west. I said, "That's great—I'm in with the people, the culture." I remember when I first arrived there, Aida was very apologetic and said, "The Japanese people won't show their emotion; they may really love you or like you, but they won't show their emotion." I said, "Aida, do they have ears? Can they hear?" He said, "Yeah, yeah"—he didn't know what I was talking about. I said, "OK, no problem." And then, in the end, he looked at me and said, "You have too much influence on Japanese people," because some of the things I did, they got very emotional [*laughs*]. I said, "This is bigger than me, I'm just following orders."

I played different types of cultural music. Before I was even thinking about being academic about the music, I was always a musician who played by ear—you feel, and you learn how to play that way. The idea was, you have to turn the people on. If you didn't turn the people on, I don't care what kind of piece of paper you have from a conservatory—if the people didn't feel it . . . they don't want to intellectualize on it. That's the way I came up. From Brazil to Trinidad to Jamaica to Haiti to Puerto Rico, I heard all of that stuff, and it could be from [the early days] playing Afro-Cuban to some of the voodoo stuff to calypso—you name it. From all those cultures, I found that what really turned the people on was the rhythms. So I said, "This is interesting": suppose you take a samba and you mix it with this kind of thing from this culture, that culture, I think you're going to come up with something that's much more powerful than staying in that one little closed set.

For example, I had a partner—his name was Ray McKinley. We were doing ballroom dancing music in local dance halls in this area here on the weekend. It was like a funk-blues—we played a little Latin, all that stuff. I was playing more congas, hand drums, and timbales. One time we had two different engagements on the same night. We split the band: I played in the city, and he played out here. I finished early, so I came to the ballroom. I was going to party and dance with everybody—I'm about nineteen years old at this point. He said to play with the band—he had a fifteen-piece band. He was doing calypso—it was that kind of crowd, a Caribbean crowd. He said, "The people don't want to get up and dance," and I'm listening, and I said, "OK, I'll do something." I just grabbed a cowbell, and I played this cowbell rhythm, and it was amazing—people were jumping from the tables! A cowbell over a whole fifteen-piece band! So it's not Milford Graves so much—it's that they're missing that one little ingredient. We know that sometimes from cooking, somebody says, "I don't know, it don't taste too good." You say, "Well, try this spice in there." That's it, that's what was missing. Ralph MacDonald made a recording at that time—it was a hit—and there was a cowbell on there. They really amplified it. *Dit-dit-be-didi-DUM, dit-dit-be-didi-DUM*. If you're playing Caribbean music you have to have that one in there—if you have everything else going and you miss that one, then you're going to see the difference. As soon as you hear that, then people start twisting them hips and moving them shoulders.

I don't play in a symmetrical way—if you play it too metronomic, then it doesn't work, there's no life to it. It's too still, man. The first thing you look at before you touch a body when they're on the ground, if somebody falls out, you look to see if you can see the chest moving. Somebody says, "They're not moving!" Somebody says,

"They dead, that's why they're not moving." Well, that's the same thing when you're playing all these metronomic rhythms. The so-called bar lines shouldn't be stagnant; they should be flowing back and forth, so you're going to have a time differential between the two. And that's how the heart works. I tell everybody: you don't need no digital machine to tell you the time value—all you've got to do is feel your wrist pulse and start counting, and you're going to find yourself at times counting a little faster and a little slower. You're not going to have a steady beat. If you have a steady beat, that's dangerous. *Extremely* dangerous. They know that now. They didn't know that years ago. Any hospital you go to now—if they do EKGs, they have to measure the heart rate variability. When they chart out the time values, it should be a wave; the more it begins to be a flat line, you're in *trouble*, man!

Have you noticed changes in your own heartbeat, both as you age but also depending on your activity? Before or after playing music, or martial arts, or—

Oh, yeah. I went through the Kundalini yoga training where I was manipulating my heart rate—not my pulse rate—a lot of people get that mixed up. You want to know the rate of the heart; a lot of times the wrist doesn't pick up the smaller movements that the heart's doing, so a lot of times you may not be getting the true pulse rate. I learned how to breathe in a certain way, so that it's in sync with my heart rate. I went beyond the ratio between heart rate and respiratory rate. I take long breaths—they may want to call it yoga breathing. I kind of do that according to the situation. When I'm playing . . . I will create certain kinds of tonal changes—not so much the pulse changes, it's the tones that I want. My thing will change during the course of playing, and then after, I don't need to do that. I'll come back to more relaxed breathing. I used to set up very dynamic, endurance sparring sessions, and I could take on five, six, eight guys, back-to-back. They'd be breathing hard, and they'd say, "You're not breathing hard." I said, "I know how to take long inhalations—I can hold that breath and then I can exhale for a long period of time." A lot of people practice yoga breathing, and the worst kind of breathing that they can do, they try to count in a way that's very symmetrical. "I'm going to breathe for four counts," "I'm going to hold for eight"—we don't breathe like that! That's the worst thing you can do.

You do a lot of vocalizing in your solo playing—how does that enter into the breath control? Is there a difference between if you're just playing the drums and if you're trying to vocalize and play the drums at the same time?

Yeah, two or three years ago I did something at the Vision Festival, and the next day these people were telling me that they were there with this guy from Africa, and the guy got very upset. He said, "What language is he speaking? It sounds African but I don't understand what he's saying." One guy said, "But you liked it, didn't you?" He was upset because he wanted to tell these guys what I was saying.

Years ago I started to be part of a group of guys here who wanted to learn how to speak the Yoruba language. I said, "I don't think I'm going to spend a lot of time trying to speak Yoruba per se, but the language I *like*"—the tonal shifting they were doing . . . and when I was in Nigeria in 1977 I heard some old people speaking. I said, "When you hear Nigerian people speaking it, they don't sound the same." There's one time I was in New York, Chinatown, and I was in this store, and I heard these voices coming from the back. I thought it was a little quartet singing. I said, "They're speaking!" They were like the older folks in Nigeria. They're really singing—they're making those pitch changes. And the way the Yorubas do it, for me, has a little more dynamics than the Chinese language. Because they're taking that language, and they're playing it on the *drum*. You got a low pitch, and then you're gliding between that low and that higher pitch. To get those sounds you have to go deep down in your gut, talk about the diaphragm and the navel area, the so-called Chinese *dantian* point or the Japanese *hara* point, and getting down into that lower energy center, and then if you're going to come all the way up through the lungs and up into the nasal area and start saying sounds that's the *m*'s and the *n*'s, I'll take some of the Yoruba thing, then I'll take some of the Bantu language. . . . I'm not thinking of language per se, I'm thinking of the international phonetics, 'cause I studied all that stuff. I see how natives speak, all their consonants, their vowels. I'm saying, anatomically, what areas are they utilizing? If they're in the nasal area, I say, "What is the neuromuscular relationship to singing something that's nasal, that's dealing with your lips or the tip of your tongue?" I try to think not of the actual meaning of the words but how that is manipulating my whole nervous system, the whole cranial system—and when I finish it feels good! They say, "What were you saying?" I say, "Well, what did you feel?" "Well, I liked it, but I don't understand what you're saying." I said, "That's good enough." I look for what order the vowels, consonants, or syllables, or nonsense syllables are in—same way in tabla. *Dun-ga-ginda-geta-gita-geta-geh*—I changed some things around.

I remember in 1965 when I started studying tabla, I found a teacher from India. I'm twenty-three at the time, this guy was sixty-four—he was [Ahmed]

Abdul-Malik's teacher, who taught oud and all those string instruments, and his name was Dr. Wasantha Singh. He was very adamant that whatever you played, you must be able to vocalize it. You can't just go through the mechanical movements.

They're still like that in teaching raga now. I went to India a few years ago, and I was talking to somebody about it, and he said with sitar the teacher will make you play a ten-minute solo and then you have to sing it back to them.

That's it. Your vocal system is not just in the throat area; it's your whole body, so you've got to make that come all through your limbs. I had a hard time in the beginning, I'm saying "da," and he was saying, "da-ach, no, da-ach." I was saying, "What's that, how do you do that?" One day, the lesson was over, and he happened to be going to Brooklyn, so we rode the train together. I'm not taking no tabla lesson now; I'm relaxed. After he got off the train, I said, "Now I know what to do." I listened to the way he spoke English. Now I got it. I go home, pick the tabla up and go, "Da din-din-da." It's not about counting numbers—you've got to go deeper inside. Because I'm just an improviser. I love the improvisational aspect—I don't want to know what I want to do before time. I want to surprise myself, surprise the audience, and not be all calculated. So, to come back and sing the same thing, I said no—I will sing you something based off the next kind of mood changes. That's the only problem: I don't like the traditional things people do, even in ragas. It has its value, but I don't want to be stagnant like that. That's great, maybe, when you're in your own little community—you don't leave, you don't go no place. But once you start traveling and you start meeting people, they speak different languages, they eat different—you're not going to be as stagnant.

You talk about a "global garden" in the movie, and people who stay within their own area . . .

Somebody says, "Oh, I like this area [in Queens], seems kind of multicultural." I say, "Yeah, it's cool, but it's not cool—because people will stay to their own." Nobody wants to talk to each other. But not me. What happens with me, I'm the oddball guy, because Hispanics may come and see the house, some people from Asia may come, and they'll look at the house, and it reminds them of something back home. They'll look at me with a little smile. I get people from the Hindu temple—they'll come through here, because all my bamboo I got growing back here, and because of all their ceremonies they want my bamboo, and we'll have a little discussion about certain things. They'll say, "Oh, your house looks like in South India—where are you from?" I'll say, "I'm right from here, right here in South Jamaica." I've traveled around a lot, and I got inspired; that turned me on. The way I grow my plants, they're all mixed up. They're like the neighbors—I got Jamaicans here, I got Chinese here, Puerto Ricans over here, the whole nine yards. They come from all over.

This is like what you were talking about in terms of getting things from different kinds of languages, and the different kinds of rhythms from different cultures. Looking at your discography, when you were recording with Montego Joe and Miriam Makeba, that's the same time that you were doing all the free jazz ESP records—Paul Bley and the New York Art Quartet. Where was the transition for you between playing Latin jazz and the avant-garde stuff? Was it a very slow transition? How much of an overlap was there?

See, first of all, I never planned to do that—that was an accident. A good accident [*laughs*]. I wasn't planning on playing no jazz. I remember my uncle—he was like a blues-country guy, but he understood playing jazz. I must have been seventeen. He came over to my house and I had my timbales set up, and he said, "You got any brushes here to play these drums with?" And I went down and brought him a whisk broom. "I'm not talking about no whisk broom, I'm talking about drum brushes you play drums with." [*Laughs.*] That shows you how much I was thinking about playing jazz with brushes.

I was playing in a Latin jazz band with Don Alias and this guy Vladimir, from Russia, and Dick Meza, who was Mexican, an alto saxophone player. I got this gig because I had met Don so many months before that when he came into New York. Don was living in Rhode Island, but he was frequently in Boston, so he called me up and said they had a gig, and would I like to come and play for the summer up in Boston in this club? One night we were in the club, and there were not too many people there. The Mexican guy, he wanted to play jazz, and I'm on timbales. I said, "Jazz? I'm not gonna play no jazz, man, I'm gonna play some Latin." See, the reason Latin was turning me on was that a lot of times we'd get together, we'd have five or six drummers, and when I heard the jazz drummers I said, "I don't know man, there ain't enough rhythm stuff going on." I heard all these different rhythms happening, 'cause I was exposed to them. He said, "Well, you got the cymbal there, act like you're a jazz drummer." So I just nonchalantly played. I mean, I heard the rhythm. I played my little *dank-danky-dang*, my old ride cymbal rhythm—I was playing that. But Dick was *amazed*. He turned around to the guys and said, "Do you see what he's doing with his left hand, man?" I wasn't even thinking about what I was doing with my left hand—I just know I'm supposed to be responding to him. And then I had a chance to buy a set of trap drums, because I had met Hal Galper, who had some drums and was going to sell them. I brought them back to my house and I just started playing. I was hitting them skins. I wasn't thinking about no jazz or nobody.

I had met Giuseppi Logan up there in Boston. Giuseppi was coming to my loft, and a few other guys were coming there, playing, and I said, "This is pretty neat." Then I started getting all these different compliments, just drumming—wasn't no particular style. It didn't feel like no rules or regulations, 'cause with Giuseppi nobody was telling me, "Hey man, could you give me some time?" They just accepted what I was doing. When I left there in September to come back to New York, I persuaded Giuseppi to come, and Giuseppi had met Roswell Rudd and John Tchicai, and they invited him to a rehearsal that included Don Moore and J. C. Moses. So we went over to this rehearsal, and Giuseppi asked them if I could sit in. I sat in and just played. They had taped the rehearsal, and J. C. Moses left after that. They listened to the tape, and Roswell and John said, "That's the kind of drumming we want." That was the New York Art Quartet. J. C. lost his job, and J. C. didn't want to speak to me after that. He couldn't take me no longer. I just came right into it.

Next thing I knew, I was the new kid on the block, so to speak. "You've got to go hear this guy Milford Graves." Alan, I was just doing what I thought you're supposed to be doing—I wasn't thinking about no Kenny Clarke, Max [Roach], Philly [Joe Jones], none of them guys' playing. All I knew was, "I see some skins in front of me and play them skins, man." I'm trying to sound like the four or five guys, drums that I'm used to hearing. And then I start reading that I'm this avant-garde drummer and Amiri Baraka starts writing about me. All these guys, Nat Hentoff—I said, "I guess I'm doing something." And then I got compliments from Max, Roy [Haynes], Philly. These guys were showing up to some of the gigs I was playing. Because the word was around: you've got to go check Milford Graves out. They were talking about this guy, man, who don't sit back there with no restricted time—"It's like he's soloing through the whole doggone tune! He's liberated, man!" I said, "I know why Max and those guys like me, 'cause those guys are saying, 'That's what I want to do, too. I'm tired of being just some little time-keeper.'"

It came quick, man. And at the same time, when I did the thing with Montego Joe, I had known Montego Joe since 1961, 'cause I was playing with this dancer named Mike Quashie who was called the Limbo King—he was out of Trinidad. I did a big show and that's when I met Montego Joe, those guys who recorded the *Drums of Passion* [Columbia, 1960] with [Babatunde] Olatunji. Mike Quashie had been on this big program up at the 92nd Street Y. I was the little kid. "Look at that little kid, the way he can handle them sticks on the drums." So after that, Montego Joe and I became close, because I could do a lot of the difficult stick techniques that the older guys couldn't do. I always had that—to this day, you could put me in a Latin band, I can come back and—I haven't lost it, man. I can play as free as I want, or I can hold a pattern for hours if you want me to hold it.

It was a *very* quick transition. It wasn't like I was saying, "I'm going to go out and do this and do that." It was just being spotted. Paul Bley, Albert Ayler: all those guys started calling me—"I'd like for you to play in the band."

Chick Corea was someone you were playing with during the Latin period.

Chick Corea. We were all eighteen, nineteen years old. I met Chick Corea through Bill Fitch. Bill Fitch had told me, "There's this piano player that's coming down from Boston that can play better Latin than the piano player I had in the band up here." When I heard Chick I said, "Wow, that guy knows how to play all those Latin *montunos*, man."

One of the other reasons why I made the transition, and this is important, is that unless you were Hispanic, getting a job with a Latin band playing congas and timbales was extremely difficult. You didn't see that. I think that still holds today. The one thing I say about jazz, I tell people jazz is the most integrated music out of all the musics. All different kinds of people play jazz, man. I always tell—I call them my Latin brothers—"Y'all got to wake up, man. There's a lot of non-Latin guys can play them skins, if you all want to change what you're doing." I refused to change my name. Guys used to come up to me, and they'd start speaking Spanish. When I was up in Boston, one night we had a big night, and there were a lot of Cubans there who got out of Cuba on them little rafts. *Packed*, man. We took a break, and Dick Meza's over at this table with this guy talking Spanish. He calls me over and says, "I'm trying to tell this guy you're not from Cuba." I said, "No, no, I'm not from Cuba, no, no." And the guy was hitting the table. Dick was laughing—he says, "The guy don't believe you." He thought that I was some guy who escaped from Cuba like him, and didn't want nobody to know that I was a refugee or escaped out of there. The guy said, "Only Cubans can play like that."

I knew a Hispanic guy, a dancer, from the Palladium—he would always talk English. He came up to me, and I didn't expect to see him up in Boston, and he didn't even speak English. He starts speaking Spanish. This guy must have thought I was Spanish, and I'm not supposed to speak English now, 'cause it was a whole big Latin set. I knew another guy who falsified his information and changed his name. I said, "I'm not going to do that." I'm always thinking about what's going to happen when people find out that you're not that. I'm going to be who I am. And then, when I was switching over to the traps, people would say, "You should play *jazz*, man—you know how to handle them trap drums." So I said, "You know what?"—and this was really the deciding move—"This way, at least I'm going to get a chance to perform with people."

Since you weren't coming from jazz, I was curious about the New York Art Quartet recording of Charlie Parker's "Mohawk"—how did that version come about? Was it something John and Roswell wanted to do?

That was probably either John or Ros. I was just there. We play the tune, man, whatever they thought was appropriate. What was great was, those bands I was playing in, nobody was telling me what to do. Tchicai said something on the liner notes on that box set that Ben Young had put out—when I came on the scene everybody had to rethink polyrhythms. If I had to listen to what some people are saying today and what people told me, musicians—I wasn't even thinking about this, but musicians who I respect, they have learned a lot from me. I think what they're talking about is, I gave them another kind of rhythm template to play off of, and I see most of the drummers, either they still try to play Roy or Kenny, Philly or Max—those same old kind of licks. I tell people, "With me you're going to have four basic choices: you're going to listen to my upper limbs or my lower limbs." William Parker always likes to be by my hi-hat. Some people don't hear everything I'm doing, 'cause if you listen to my right hand you might not hear all the rest of the stuff going on; if you listen to the left you may not know what the bass drum is going on. It takes some time to hear me—some people, they have to come ten, twelve times. There is a review on Amazon—and I always tell William about this—different reviews of the two of us playing together. They get him mixed up with me. They be hearing my drum tones, and they think it's him on bass doing it.

When I was playing for dancers, and I was doing a lot of African-oriented drumming, you're supposed to be stimulating the dancer—you yourself have to know how to dance if you're the drummer. That's the tradition. I took that whole concept of stimulating a person to be a little more creative than what [was happening in] so-called jazz. I heard somebody playing, and I said, "Wow, they're on that one little, narrow path, and there's some other stuff they can add in there—why do they keep doing the same old stuff?" People play "All the Things You Are"—the drummer will play a little brushes. I said, "That is so dry, man."

You said you wanted drums to be in the foreground, not in the background; so I wanted to ask about your ideas about solo versus group playing, and how your relationship to playing with other people might have changed as you started doing more solo performing.

I never thought about just going out and doing a solo—people were *asking* me to do solo. Some people said straight out: "You know what? I would rather hear you do a solo than play with other people." I start thinking about it and said, "OK, maybe I'm just trying to make this situation happen"—but that's not really how

I want to limit myself. I found it was a limitation there for the musicians I would be playing with, and if they just do that one thing, they're not going to hear something else. Some people, when I'm playing with them, I'm trying to get them to be stimulated. I reduce things, sometimes, to make it happen. Because I'll do something, and I'll say, "There's no response here, there's no interplay here." And they're not hearing it, they're not seeing it—they're just doing their licks that they practiced for the last months and months and months. It has nothing to do with actual *playing*, man. It's just like if you go to play basketball, and you have somebody that is a great individual player, and they're dribbling all over the court—they take some ridiculous shot, and one of the other players is right underneath the rim! The guy didn't even see the guy underneath the rim. He's by himself—you should have passed the ball to him. . . . I'm trying to listen to everybody, and if I hear a person playing something, I will try to complement them, or I'll get in between and I'll start angling myself all around them, to try and inspire them, and that's how we interplay with each other. So when some players told me I've taken them places that they haven't been before—embouchure changes—they give me high respect. Then they say, "You're the *man*." I know why they're saying that; they played with all these people, and none of them did what I did.

The different disciplines that I deal with cause me to be able to take my thought processes in all these different areas, and it don't have to be dealing with acupuncture, or herbs, or whatever else. It takes deep focus. When I was working as a laboratory technician for a veterinarian, I was doing bacteriological work, doing antibiotic sensitivity testing. If I'm trying to find different kinds of electrolytes in the blood, and the machinery I was using would require gas in there, I could have blown myself up in the lab. I had to focus on all that. All of that enabled me to develop my mindset; I'm taking my drumming just as serious. When I'm coming down to stroke that drum and another person's on that stage, and you get that *bah* and I go *bah-boom* a little tag on it . . . it's causing me to react, man. What am I going to do with that, how am I going to manipulate that, how am I going to breathe?

Does this apply to solo playing also?

Right. When I come to the concert, I'm not going to have security guards in my dressing room, and I'm sitting there waiting to go on, and I come to the side entrance, and when I come to the stage, I start performing . . . I take a quick look at the audience. If I see an audience out there and they're tight, I say, "We got a problem here—we've got to loosen them up." And then when I want to get that so-called grand sound, the total sound of all the voices, you got thirty people in the room and they're all talking—you don't know what the hell is going on. It's amazing. I don't think people realize that. I listen to all that and I say, "What is the grand, fundamental sound that's coming from underneath all of that?" I put it all together. I want the fundamental, I don't want the harmonics. That group over there, that's just the harmonics—I want the fundamental. I come out on that stage, man, and that first sound I hit, I want to make sure that it contains the basic fundamental frequency that's going on. In the solo I will try to create something off what I feel from the environment, not be coming out with some predetermined thing. That's the problem I have with trying to write a piece of music. It may not have nothing to do with what's happening. People going to a restaurant—"OK, I'll be a vegetarian. When I'm traveling, I don't want nothing on the menu.

I'll say, 'Do you have this, do you have that, can you do this, can you do that?' I'll have my set menu," and then you get upset—no, you've got to work with people. If you come in there with some composition, it may have *nothing* to do with that kind of vibe that's in the audience there. That's what I do: I just groove off the solo and I build and I build and I build, and then when you're building like that, if you know the fundamental then you can know how you can build—it's like the whole concept of that Lydian scale that George Russell popularized.[1]

The question I always ask musicians is, "Why does the minor scale give you more of a melancholic feeling than a major?"

You talk about that in the movie—the tear ducts.

The tear ducts, yeah, so anatomically you can stimulate that. I can understand why the old blues was doing that. . . . You didn't have no medicine, it could have been just a natural survival instinct of human beings. I can't imagine people being under those harsh conditions. If you get your adrenaline flowing, you got to cool out. I grew up all around it; my grandparents, especially my grandfather, he'd be out there in that yard with spoons, the washbasin, the one-by-four with one string, and all that Geechee sound, that just cools you out, man, makes you smile. If you set that up with people, that's the interplay, the so-called yin-yang. In the solo, I'm thinking about all that stuff. How much do you do without exhausting somebody?

In the so-called free jazz, I said, "These guys don't know how to play, man." They get up there, and they be screaming. I say, "You're screaming too long—you have an

1 See George Russell, *The Lydian Chromatic Concept of Tonal Organization*, (New York, Concept Publishing Co., 1953).

audience, you can't take the audience on that kind of trip. You get there, and then you've got to calm them down. You've got to know the point. That's being a musician-healer. So when I do solo, that's what I'm thinking about. What you see in a lot of old traditions, you see a musician-healer.

Somebody I wanted to bring up was Lowell Davidson, who was a biochemist as well as a musician, and you played on the one record he made, for ESP.

That guy, he was a real academically smart guy. He was part of the Harvard Eighteen, and he realized that he was just part of a supposedly experimental thing that was going on at Harvard. I don't know what was experimental about that—it was about eighteen African Americans they allowed in during this time. Lowell was part of that, and I didn't know that. One of my friends in high school, who was one of the smart guys, he was valedictorian, a Regents scholar—he can't be no experiment. The experiment is getting some dude that's supposed to be from the ghetto that's barely passing courses, and you take him and see if Harvard can take him from being a D student to an A student. This ain't no experiment with the guys you had—y'all playing it safe. Lowell was the high school East Coast quarter-mile champion. So he was an athletic guy. I really enjoyed being around him. He took me to his lab, and he was working with this guy Dr. [John Tileston] Edsall, in Jamaica Plains—I said, "This guy's legitimate." One time [Lowell] brought a tape over to my house, and it was him playing drums. I said, "Don't try to play like me, man." He said, "I'm good!" I said, "You sound doggone good, man!" He had this high respect for me.

When you're out there and you're doing something that's different, and it's odd, and the only reference is maybe to yourself saying, "I like what I'm doing," at the same time you can have those times when you doubt what you're doing, and you need some people that you know—the so-called heavyweights that you respect—to come over and tell you that you're on a *high* level. One time I was hanging out with Lowell and he had to go to work, so he left me in the house. He gave me some books on biochemistry and said, "I will be back in so many hours—you're going to read this book and we will talk about it later." I was like, "Yes, Lowell." I was just so humbled by this guy [*laughs*]. He was no joke, he was a real smart guy. But sometimes smartness wipes you out, man. He was a test tube on himself. People said he shouldn't have died like that, in the streets, but that's what happened.

On Meditation Among Us *you're playing piano—that's the only recording of you playing piano.*

I got my own little private [recordings] here. I got one on trumpet, too. I was in Kyoto a year and a half ago, to do a duo with Toshi Tsuchitori, and Toshi sent me an email saying, "People are requesting that you play piano, too." I said, "Toshi, I don't want to play the keyboard—I don't want to hear that sound. We're doing a drum duo together." We got to the gig and people are asking, "Will he play piano, will he play piano?" One guy came up, he was so disappointed. After we finished, Toshi said, "You know why they wanted you to play piano?" Aida's last book he wrote, he put in there that I was a better piano player than Cecil Taylor and Don Pullen. [*AL laughs.*] I said, "Oh, that's what this is all about?"

Based on that track "Response" from Meditation Among Us.

Based on that recording, 'cause they were right in the studio, man. I don't know about playing better than Cecil Taylor—Cecil does what he does. But I know what they were talking about. I'm bringing something else to that table. I'm bringing tabla things, a different kind of rhythm—that's what they heard, man. There's a lot of stuff you can be doing on that keyboard. I hear some other things going on. But that don't make you a *better* player.

Like, my kitchen is an international kitchen—I got spices and herbs from all over the place. So sometimes I have gatherings here and I make my soup, my favorite peanut butter soup, and everyone says, "What do you have in there?" I got the *world* in there, Alan. I fix that stuff up. I may use some Native American stuff, some Moroccan stuff, some Indian stuff, some Japanese stuff, the whole nine yards—I put that in, they don't realize. Living here in the States, you can go into all these neighborhoods and buy the stuff. So that's what I'm hearing, when I break those [piano] keys down. I can feel another thing. And then my martial arts training: I got all those limb movements, so it gives a different kind of sound, man.

I wanted to ask about a couple of recent things you recorded with Sam Amidon—how did that come about? He's more of a singer-songwriter.

Shahzad [Ismaily]. They were fans of mine; they worked it out. I didn't know Sam, Shahzad told me he's a nice guy, blah blah blah. I said, "You know what? I could sit back here and say, 'Well, I'm Milford Graves, man, who is this guy Sam, I don't know who this guy is.'" But I said, "You know what? I want to work with some of these young people. What the heck." It's a little different. He's doing all that folk. I said, "This is great!"

If I can play some loose style to this guy doing this folk, that's pretty neat, huh? A whole kind of different situation, man.

There was paper that had to do with stem cells . . .

With Carlo Ventura in Bologna [Italy]—he's a microbiologist, cardiologist. That's an ongoing project that hopefully will be kind of finalized with some of the new research they're doing by the end of this year. That's another kind of work—basically I just supply them with a series of frequencies. A very short melody—just under four seconds—that I was able to extract from this person's heart sound who was going through a crisis, that I thought was at the particular point that the body was trying to respond in a very positive way. So the doctors started working, converting that sound into a vibrational component in the medium that stem cells were growing in, and the cells took to them and they started differentiating. That was enough to give the doctors a general idea of growing them down on a deeper level, to use sound to stimulate the body, or use a mechanical motion to stimulate the body to deal with the regeneration of damaged tissue, instead of injecting stem cells into the body—to get the body to create its own stem cells. They said, "Probably the way you play, you're stimulating the stem cells anyway." I said, "I *feel* that."

Was this something they contacted you about?

Yeah, this guy sent me an email about four years ago and identified himself. He read the *New York Times* article that was done on me. I went over there in 2016 and did this program called "Cell Melodies," went over to their laboratories.

There's something happening. I'm working with

a guy right now who's actually recording patients—he sends me the sound files of all kinds of different heart patterns, and I can take them apart. He's a homeopathic acupuncturist, got a practice out of Brooklyn. He's seeing all of this stuff, all kinds of problems, more than before, way more than before. I'm seeing people with wave forms from all other stuff. New things are starting to develop for me right now. Which is great. I had thought, "Maybe I'll cool out, take some vacations," but it's hard, man. Seems like my mind is just getting more creative and innovative than it's ever been.

You have a sculpture, Beyond Polymath *[2017]; how did it come about? It's a kinetic sculpture?*

The curator Jenny Jaskey came here and checked everything out, and she asked, "Could you do something that would demonstrate the way you think and what you do?" I had no plans at all. Then she looked at the skeleton, and said, "Wow." I said, "I'll put something together," and that's how it came about. I just started hooking things up; instead of writing it out and doing diagrams, I said, "Why don't I do a piece of sculpture, do something a little different?" It's like laboratory science with a sculpture—it's truly an art-science piece. I'm working on my second piece now. People are asking me to do some more stuff.

Had you been in touch recently with Roswell Rudd?[2]

He was almost a guy like Lowell Davidson, a different kind of guy. I think those guys that I met, like them

2 American trombonist Roswell Rudd played with Graves in the New York Art Quartet in 1964–65; he passed away on December 21, 2017, three weeks before this interview was conducted.

and Amiri Baraka, who I met when he was LeRoi Jones and he was studying at the New School and Columbia and he was the new guy out here—I used to go to his house a bunch 'cause I enjoyed his conversation and his whole character at that time, coming from the housing projects. . . . I had some nice friends, but I didn't have an intellectual group of friends like these guys. Roswell was a smart guy, too. He was always a smooth and cool man. He was always smiling, even when he was angry—you'd never know he was angry. I was thinking the other day, he was just a great kind of guy you'd want to have as a friend. The last we musically functioned together was when I got that Lifetime Achievement Award from the Vision Festival. We briefly talked on the phone, not that much. I remember Roswell making a statement on that stage—he looked over at me and said, "Thank you, I've learned a lot from you." I said, "Wow." And then you get a report—somebody called me up and said Roswell died. So here's another proof that you ain't going to be around forever, man. Whatever you have to do, you do it—don't mess around and don't hesitate.

You taught at Bennington for close to forty years—

Thirty-nine years.

In our conversation you've been saying that you didn't really come from academia. What was the Bennington experience like, having not come from an academic background—or how did it change over the years?

I remember Valerie Wilmer doing something in one of those newspapers in England—she named me as a cultural Black nationalist or something, going up there to Bennington and teaching white kids. I don't know where that was coming from, man. But it did cause a spark on both ends. I got feedback from certain people in the African American community wanting to know why I was going up to Bennington teaching these white kids. There was a little bit of suspicion. I went up there about a year before that, because Bill Dixon was there at that time—they were having a Black music festival. We drove up there and I remember going into the town of Bennington and saying, "This little town looks like one of those towns in movies I saw as a kid where aliens would come in a spaceship and land." It felt *weird*—something's strange about this little town. And then we get on to campus for this Black music festival, and I'm saying, "Where are all the Black students? I don't see no Black students." That was my first experience. We did the concert—everyone was cool and nice.

That was 1972, and all through the '60s I'm in Bedford-Stuyvesant, I'm in Harlem, the Black Nationalist movement's going on, the civil rights movement's going on, everybody wants voting rights, it was a whole thing. This was a whole Black–white damn environment, so you were very conscious of the Black–white situation going on—the rebellions, race riots, whatever you want to call them. So for me to head up to Bennington, that was different, man. And then when Bill went on sabbatical, he asked me to teach there. He told me they decided to form a Black Music department with a small budget. I said, "I don't know if I want to go and teach"—and this wasn't about an ethnic situation, this was about teaching *college*, man. I was already teaching, but I was in the community here teaching—it was a certain style we teach. Go to college, that's another kind of academic setting. I don't know if I'm ready for that kind of stuff. At that time I had five kids, and Bill just said one thing: "Graves, you will get a steady paycheck." I said, "A steady paycheck . . . Bill, I think I'll try it!"

Let me tell you something, Alan—the students were laughing at me when I first came up there. I had a shopping bag full of papers, I had notes on top of notes. . . . I said, "OK, we're going to start the lesson by blah blah blah." The students are looking at me—this is Bennington, they're so damn loose, and I'm trying to be this strict academician. I had to keep a dictionary, a pocket dictionary, because these white kids were talking some English language—they weren't talking no ghetto language. I had to say, "What the hell does this word mean?" [*Laughs.*] And they didn't know what the hell I was talking about! One day I said, "They went up against their wig, man." "Oh, they had a wig on?" "Oh no, we're just talking about their head!" [*Laughs.*] I was exciting to those kids. I was loose with them and talked stuff, African stuff, Asian stuff, and I think they liked that. I got to know the kids. I became very popular—all the kids wanted to take my class. And I'm learning a lot from these kids, too—we're both teaching each other. Then I start realizing, this is what the damn problem is—everybody is so separate from each other, and we're told all this dumb stuff about each other, that we never get together and get down, hash this out, and we all come out with something. We improve our relationships.

So that was a great move I made. 'Cause it made me organize myself. Some of the kids would come up to me and say, "Wow, I didn't realize how racist I was. Not that anyone would speak of Black people, it's just that my viewpoints were totally wrong." That's the example I'm going to have to show, that you got to learn how to deal with people. I told all those people who said I shouldn't be up there, "I'm glad I made that move." 'Cause I haven't lost any identity. I didn't go up there and try to be somebody I'm not—I said, "I'm going to bring my experience into this classroom, as a human person, to show these kids you don't want to walk that kind of path." And I helped a lot of those students out, 'cause I would straighten them out. Guys who would come up there having problems with different drugs on the campus, I'd call them in and try to talk a little street talk with them, saying, "That's some dumbass stuff you're doing—it don't pay off, my man." For them, hearing it from a guy they think may be coming from the streets, I was better for talking to those kids than those counselors up there, with their PhDs, who never had one ounce of experience in their damn life about doing any damn stuff.

That was a hell of an experience. I met tons of people up there. It's very rare that you will see teachers stay in contact with their students after twenty, thirty, forty years. People say, "I owe it to you. You was an example." One guy, a scientist, tells me, "It's because of you, man. You have highly influenced me—one thing I got from you is you can be anything you want to be if you put your mind to it."

There was a drummer over here the other day. He hadn't seen me in a little while, but he saw me down there at the New School last month, and we were just talking about the concept of playing. I said, "I can play these five parts now and not the four parts because my one hand, I can hold two sticks here." He said, "Oh yeah, vibes players do that." I said, "No no no, but they're playing the same damn thing, they're just playing intervals. I've got the independent thing going on here—one rhythm going on here, one rhythm going on here." He looks at me and jumps right out of the chair—he says, "I'm going to test you, man! Here's the sticks—let me see that." And he was just amazed. Most people wouldn't say nothing to me about that. Wouldn't it be easier if you say, "Man, would you show me how to do that?" Instead of you going home trying to get two sticks and say, "That's difficult what that guy's doing." I've heard it from some guys who are honest. He was trying to figure out—"How did you get that, man? Was it your martial arts, your training?" He was trying everything in the world. I told him very simply, "It was determination, man." I worked my *butt* off to separate this stuff. It was something I wanted to do, not to show you some dexterity, something I can do—there's a reason why I wanted to do that. Sometimes I'll do it on a gig: I'll play a little bebop, do all the licks that any of them cats can do in tradition with this here hand, but this hand is free jazzing over here. Look—why are the bebop dudes fighting free jazz guys, man? I'll be playing bebop here from the conservatory, and then free jazz over here. I'm showing you that it is possible for us as individuals to get together and act like my right hand and act like my left hand.

Another reason I did it is because of the recording I did, *Pieces of Time* [Soul Note, 1984], there's a track on there where I'm taking a chorus—we each had a chorus—and somebody asked me, "Were you taking your chorus solo and playing *dang-danky-dang* at the same time?" No, I said, "That was Kenny Clarke playing *dang-danky-dang*." And the reason that happened was that the chorus was taking sixteen measures, and Kenny Clarke was trying to count it four-four-four-four. And after four measures Kenny was looking for that downbeat to come. I wasn't giving him no clear-cut downbeat. And Kenny was supposed to come in right after me. And Andrew [Cyrille] said, "Kenny, you're supposed to come in," and Kenny said, "I can't hear his one." And so I kept doing it, and Kenny said, "I just don't hear the one." He says, "I know what to do," and starts playing [swing]: *ch, ch-ch ch, ch-ch ch, ch-ch ch*. He's playing that, but I'm playing all my off stuff, and *BAM*, Kenny was able to get it. It can be done. It don't come overnight—you got to work.

I tell drummers—I said this yesterday—"Y'all shouldn't be disliking me and hating me. I'm trying to get us to play all liberated, to be respected in the band, man. So if I'm the guy starting it, you may get upset, but you guys got to go back and woodshed a little bit now—you got that little thing you want to do." I get more younger guys here, but some of the guys that are established, they got their rep, they'll come through. But they ain't about to try to do this—they say, "Man, what you're doing is kind of difficult, it's too hard." It's not about the physical thing, they just can't think that way. They cannot leave that snare drum with the snares on, taking regular solos with the same old licks—they cannot leave that, they've been doing it too long. Well, it's never too late! It's never too late to make a change! But if you got your rep, man, they ain't about to go out there and say, "I'm playing like Milford Graves now." You ain't going to play like Milford Graves—maybe the liberated concept, but you're going to do it the way you do it. All I'm saying is, take the instrument and stop being pushed to the back and disrespected because they're saying "You're not a musician, you're a drummer." That's my mission. I'm the one that's making the sacrifice, getting less gigs—lots of guys don't want to call me. They say. "He's doing too much stuff, playing too much stuff—you got to play something basic so we can groove! He's making me *work*, man." I'm aware of all of that. But I get younger people coming through that are more inspired, and this is going to improve the music—it's gonna improve the music, man.

Alan Licht

Common Tones

Selected interviews
with artists and musicians

1995–2020

Editors: Ciarán Finlayson and Lawrence Kumpf

Additional editors: Joe Bucciero, Mira Dayal, Dana Kopel, and Hiji Nam

Copy editors: Claire Lehmann and Polly Watson

Design: Alec Mapes-Frances

Blank Forms Editions is produced with support from Robert Rauschenberg Foundation, The Andy Warhol Foundation for the Visual Arts, and Agnes Gund.

Additional support for *Common Tones* was generously provided by Gladstone Gallery.

Blank Forms would like to thank Anthony Elms, J. Hoberman, Andrew Lampert, Morgan Levine, Jake Meginsky, Christina Radner, Camila Santos, Amy Via, and John Zorn for their research assistance.

Additional thanks to Laurie Anderson, Maria Acconci, Reg Bloor, and Liz Lamere.

Portions of some of these interviews and writings appeared in *ArtReview*, *Believer*, *BOMB*, *chickfactor*, *Christian Marclay*, *Purple*, *Sight & Sound*, *Sonic Youth etc.: Sensational Fix*, the *Wire*, and *Working Title*.

Blank Forms
468 Grand Ave, Unit 3D
Brooklyn, NY 11238
blankforms.org

ISBN 978-1-953691-01-9
(softcover edition)

ISBN 978-1-953691-06-4
(hardback edition)

Printed by Ofset Yapımevi
in Istanbul

First edition